Aspects of Police Work

Aspects of Police Work

EGON BITTNER

NORTHEASTERN UNIVERSITY PRESS
Boston

Northeastern University Press

Library of Congress Cataloging-in-Publication Data
Bittner, Egon, 1921–
    Aspects of police work / by Egon Bittner.
        p.   cm.
    ISBN 1-55553-069-9
    1. Police—United States.   I. Title.
HV8138.B47   1990
363.2′0973—dc20   89-28827
                                    CIP

Designed by Patricia Dunbar

This book was composed in Baskerville by Coghill Composition
Company in Richmond, Virginia. It was printed and bound by
Edwards Brothers, Inc., in Ann Arbor, Michigan. The paper is
Glatfelter, an acid-free sheet.

Manufactured in the United States of America
94   93   92   91   90   5   4   3   2   1

For my steadfast companions,
Jean, Tom, and Debora,
who made this work possible and necessary.

Contents

Acknowledgments

TWENTY-FIVE YEARS AGO the chief of San Francisco's finest entrusted me to the guidance of patrolman Ray Hanson who was the first of many humane, judicious, and skilled police officers I came to meet over the years. They taught me all I know about policing. Later I had the opportunity to work with many enlightened members of the police brass in connection with my Fellowship at the Police Foundation and my membership on the Commission on Accreditation for Law Enforcement Agencies, and gained much from it.

The encouragement and the critique of my fellow researchers always mattered greatly. I am especially grateful to Sheldon Messinger for his friendship and collaboration. My colleague and former student, Susan Silbey, is responsible for getting me to put this volume together; her friendly interest in my work has always been very important. I know that I bear the responsibility for the shortcomings of my work, but I don't think that lets all those I mentioned above, named and unnamed, entirely off the hook.

We gratefully acknowledge the following:

Ciba Foundation, for permission to reprint "The Concept of Mental Abnormality in the Administration of Justice Outside the Courtroom," from *Ciba Foundation Symposium on the Mentally Abnormal Offender*. Copyright © 1968 by Ciba Foundation.

The Free Press, for permission to reprint "Urban Police," from *Encyclopedia of Crime and Justice* 3, Sanford Kadish, ed. Copyright © 1983 by The Free Press, a Division of Macmillan, Inc.

The International Association of Chiefs of Police, Inc., for permission to reprint "Police Research and Police Work," from *Police Yearbook.* Copyright © 1973 by The International Association of Chiefs of Police, Inc.

The International City Management Association, for permission to reprint "Emerging Police Issues," from *Local Government Police Management,* 2d ed. Copyright © 1982 by The International City Management Association.

The Johns Hopkins University Press, for permission to reprint "The Rise and Fall of the Thin Blue Line," a review of R. M. Fogelson's *Big City Police,* from *Reviews in American History* 6, no. 3, (September 1978).

The MIT Press, for permission to reprint "Legality and Workmanship," from *Control in the Police Organization.* Copyright © 1983 by The MIT Press.

The Society for the Study of Social Problems, for permission to reprint "Police Discretion in Emergency Apprehension of Mentally Ill Persons," from *Social Problems* 14, no. 3. Copyright © 1967 by the Society for the Study of Social Problems.

The University of Chicago Press, for permission to reprint "Policing Juveniles: The Social Context of Common Practice," from *Pursuing Justice for the Child.* Copyright © 1976 by The University of Chicago Press.

John Wiley & Sons, Inc., for permission to reprint "The Impact of Police–Community Relations on the Police System," from *Community Relations and the Administration of Justice.* Copyright © 1979 by John Wiley & Sons, Inc.

Aspects of Police Work

Introduction

THE WRITINGS COLLECTED in this volume reflect twenty-five years of study of the police in the United States. During the first five years this involved intensive empirical research, mainly of an ethnographic nature. In the remaining time I maintained uninterrupted contact with the police through a variety of activities and ties, including collaboration in several research projects, participation in countless workshops and conferences, consultantships to police agencies, engagement in some of the endeavors of the Police Foundation, and membership on the Commission on Accreditation for Law Enforcement Agencies during the first nine years of its existence. As a result of all this I came to be known as something of an external expert on police work. I value this recognition greatly, but I must also acknowledge that during the past two decades the study of the police has not been my sole, and at times even my main, scholarly interest. This circumstance is not always readily evident in what I wrote, nor did I insist on making it known; it did not seem to matter at the time. But now, when putting together a postscript to these efforts, I remember a conversation of many years ago with Professor Herman Goldstein in which he distinguished between the work of scholars who were fully committed to the study of the police and those who also pursued other scholarly projects. Speaking for myself, being of the second kind never meant that the study of the police was less important or less serious than other work. It only meant that I could afford to be more selective in what I chose to attend to, and that I could draw inferences from my observations and propose conclusions that did not take full account of considerations of local and timely constraints of feasibility. In other words, I felt free to theorize without regard for practicality. I realize, of course, that saying this is a convoluted excuse for the weakness of my work, but I hope it is also the basis of some of its strength, such as it is.

In this introduction I try to restate some of the things I learned about the police. I have chosen for discussion those parts of the lesson that help me understand the significance of changes in policing that are just getting started now. I do not try to discuss, or even mention, all the ongoing reform efforts. Instead, I will concentrate on those innovations that in my judgment have the potential to produce a fundamental transformation of the institution. This transformation will allow the police to meet its inherited responsibilities at a higher level of technical adequacy than prevails now; and it will extend institutional interests and procedures into areas that are sensibly related to those responsibilities but have heretofore been viewed as beyond the scope of police competence. The innovations I speak of are all located in the routine practices of line personnel; that is, they concern police work in the most literal sense of the term. Of course, some changes will also have to take place in the operations of the departmental headquarters to reconcile them with changes taking place in the activities of the line personnel. Since I do not intend to discuss problems of police management here, I want to mention that I view the work of the Commission on Accreditation for Law Enforcement Agencies as critically important in creating favorable conditions in the administrative machinery of departments for the projected changes in the police work on the streets.

Genuinely fruitful study of the police requires an appreciation of the specific nature and direction of change the institution has been undergoing over the course of its existence. While it might be interesting to go back to 1829 to trace the development of what we have today, it is quite enough to start with the reforms initiated in the period between the two world wars. August Volmer is commonly mentioned as the initiator of what came to be known as the "professionalization" of the police, although it is not at all clear that he intended it to move in the direction it did. The term "profession," as used in this context, was obviously not intended in the sense in which the term is used by students of occupations—that is, referring to an occupation requiring postgraduate education, based on complex theoretical knowledge, requiring a high level of technical skills, and involving a substantial degree of practitioner autonomy. Instead, it was intended to indicate the resolute rejection of earlier patterns of policing that were controlled by urban machine politics, which reformers condemned as corrupt and inefficient; they saw independence from the political spoils system as the basic condition for all other change. After this was achieved, at least by and large, in collaboration with more general reform movements in urban politics in the two decades on both sides of the mid-century, the reformers turned their attention to transforming policing into a goal oriented, rationally streamlined operation.

O. J. Wilson, who, relying on modern managerial wisdom and technique, developed the theory and engaged in the practice of modern police management, deserves credit for being the model of a leader in the field. Without going into detail, Wilson and several other reform chiefs of his generation intended to make real what was always purported to be the case—namely, that the police was a politically neutral governmental function devoted to criminal law enforcement and crime prevention and concerned with some other conditions that, albeit not formally criminal, required similar coercive control. This function was entrusted to a corps of operatives working under a strict, quasi-military regime of internal supervision. Though not made explicit, it was quite well understood that the crime control activities assigned to the police were directed to what might be called residual crime. A large variety of other law enforcement agencies divided the tasks of dealing with crime taking place in banks, offices, boardrooms, government agencies, and so forth, which is almost entirely nonviolent and demands sophistication on the part of both the perpetrator and law enforcement. The preponderant majority of what is left for the police is what is sometimes referred to as "street crime." The salience of so-called street crime, which frequently involves acts of violence, in the perceived police mandate dictated the definition of the person suitable to wage the struggle against it. The strengths sought in recruits were the "manly virtues" of honesty, loyalty, aggressiveness, and visceral courage. It was also understood that police recruits should be able and willing to follow uncritically all received commands and regulations. Of course, they had to be literate enough to read instructions and to write short reports. But it was taken for granted that police work was not for people whose intellectual aspirations reached far beyond this level. Thus, the recruiters and the recruited knew that police work was a relatively low-grade occupation, often chosen as an alternative to semiskilled labor by people who would be content with an occupation that was thought to consist of, to a large extent, doing what one is told. This disciplinary aspect of police work was balanced by the nobility of the service, the opportunity to contribute to the betterment of life, and last but not least, the promise of adventure.

One can speculate that Wilson and his like-minded colleagues among the chiefs of the police might have succeeded in creating the kind of institution they had in mind if they had invented it from scratch. Two technical developments worked in their favor, and they tried to make the best possible use of them. The automobile offered the possibility of rapid mobility and pervasive coverage and the radio created continuous communication. Taken together, the two devices afforded the administration a wholly unprecedented degree of control over the activities of the line staff, or so it seemed from a planning perspective. Unfortunately, as virtually everybody recognizes, the great advantage the automobile and the radio created in opening and increasing the density of communicative contacts between management at the headquarters and the troops in the field was balanced by the decline in opportunities for contact, familiarity, and formation of trust between police officers and the citizenry. Of course, one can argue that the latter effect would not have been a significant disadvantage if the reformers had had complete freedom in defining and structuring the nature and scope of the police function and in limiting the activities of officers accordingly. The professional law enforcement agent envisioned in the professionalization of the police was not necessarily seriously impaired in carrying out his or her mandate by losing contact with the people in the community he or she policed—no more, in any case, than were postal inspectors, FBI agents, or any other law enforcement officials.

Of course, the reformers did not invent the police from scratch; instead, they inherited an ongoing institution, an institution that responded to firmly established, customary social demands and needs that could not be left unanswered, even while the propriety of responding to these demands was questioned and disparaged as not being "real police work." Citizens availed themselves of the well-entrenched recourse of "calling the cops," and they typically expected, and received, the kind of response James Q. Wilson associated with "watchman"-type policing of the sort the reformers did not favor.

The professionalization of the police succeeded in the administrative streamlining of departments, overcame police dependence on political pressure, and came a long way in eliminating the systemic corruption associated with it. But apart from the effects of the automobile and radio, its effects on the work of the line personnel was minimal at best. Apart from personnel allocation and job assignments, the work of police officers was not closely regulated or supervised. This was especially the case for those activities that were not connected with criminal complaints and that make up the preponderant majority of the tasks performed by the preponderant majority of officers.

It is difficult to exaggerate the incongruity of this situation. The official definition of the police mandate is that of a law enforcement agency. Its demands for the resources and for support are justified by responsibilities connected to dealing with crimes and other violations of law. The internal organization and division of labor within departments reflect categories of crime control. The public record of its accomplishments and failures is expressed in crime statistics. Recognition for meritorious performance is given for feats of valor and ingenuity in crime fighting. But the day-to-day work of most officers has very little to do with all of this. These officers are engaged in what is now commonly referred to as peacekeeping and order maintenance, activities in which arrests are extremely rare.

Those arrests that do occur are for the most part peacekeeping expedients rather than measures of law enforcement of the sort employed against thieves, rapists, or perpetrators of other major crimes. For the rich variety of services of every kind, involving all sorts of emergencies, abatements of nuisances, dispute settlements, and an almost infinite range of repairs on the flow of life in modern society, the police neither receives nor claims credit. Nor is there any recognition of the fact that many of these human and social problems are quite complex, serious, and important, and that dealing with them requires skill, prudence, judgment, and knowledge. In fact, recruitment and training are conducted with virtually a total disregard for these job requirements.

The official, authoritative version of policing as law enforcement controls the public perception of the institution's mandate, even while the public "calls the cops" for all kinds of problems that have nothing to do with this mandate. The majority of police administrators are honestly and strongly committed to the official mandate. Even those police officers whose work contains few opportunities for invoking the law insist on defining their mandate as professional law enforcement, a task from which they are, alas, all too often diverted. One could argue, of course, that the professionalization of the police is not yet complete, and that an administrative ordering of the presently uncoordinated form of peacekeeping is still pending. But this view disregards the inherent incompatibility between the reform ideology formulated half a century ago and peacekeeping work done by the line personnel. In fact, it seems more likely that the two stand in a paradoxically functional relationship to each other. The official version of the mandate, the identified elements of organizational structure, the reported record of accomplishments, the strategic and tactical planning, and the public image building reduce the tasks of peacekeeping and order maintenance to the status of an adventitiously inherited burden that, as things are now, cannot be entirely disavowed but will be borne, insofar as it must be borne, by indirection. That is, one way to preserve and cultivate the ideal of professional law enforcement is to leave peacekeeping and order maintenance to the unplanned and uncoordinated ingenuity and personal resourcefulness of the line personnel, who are free to be as resolute or irresolute as they are capable of being so long as they do nothing to embarrass the department they represent. Thus, the clamor expressed in "calling the cops" will be met minimally, while avoiding entanglements and commitments for which there is no room in the concept of professional law enforcement.

The concept of professional law enforcement continues to dominate American police practices in the 1980s. But the decade also contains the onset of a movement to form new approaches to police work. The intellectual origins of the most recent reform efforts can be traced to the disclosures about the real content of police work in studies that began to appear in the now legendary 1960s, the earliest of which was Michael Banton's *The Policeman in the Community* (1964). The title of the book contains the odd juxtaposition of an almost archaic-sounding identification of the police officer as a policeman with the then not yet fully appreciated real context and referent target of his (to retain the gender identity) work, namely, the community. One of the earliest conceptual clarifications of the reform movement of the 1980s appeared in an immensely influential article by Herman Goldstein referring to it as "problem-oriented policing" (*Crime & Delinquency,* April 1979, 236–58). In the ensuing years, the designation "community-oriented policing" has been used increasingly to identify the reform efforts.

It is clearly too early to make definitive pronouncements about community-oriented policing, but one can fruitfully discuss the conditions and considerations that give it energy and direction. While it made some sense to imagine the reformers of fifty years ago as engaged in reinventing the police, the reformers of the 1980s accept the entire range of existing police practices as constituting the institution's mandate, and they attempt to reorganize these practices into an effective communal service. The proposed approach does not challenge the primacy of criminal law enforcement in the police mandate; however, it does raise to a position of equal importance those formerly neglected services subsumed under the heading of peacekeeping. Indeed, most of the reform efforts concern those services, thereby compensating for past neglect.

The proposed changes derive some of their cogency and urgency from a consideration of what they will replace, especially in the area of present peacekeeping practices. Since peacekeeping is presently the orphan left to fend for itself, it is impossible to summarize its features to take into account the full range of its variety. Much of it deals with relatively trivial concerns and is done in a manner of casual improvisation. In most of such situations officers do whatever they want to do, including nothing; absent any serious untoward consequences no one will be concerned with their action or inaction. But many cases to which the police are summoned involve critically serious social and human problems. Because these encounters are "all in a day's work," it would be surprising if police officers did not develop some routines for dealing with them—routines based on certain underlying ideas, assumptions, and aims. Of course, there are likely to be many differences among officers. Notwithstanding these differences, it does seem to be the case that there has developed spontaneously a basic occupational outlook that directs and patterns the activities of police officers engaged in peacekeeping. In outlining my perception of this pattern, I must emphasize once more that this is the conclusion of an outsider—one based on a great deal, but nevertheless a limited amount, of direct observation of ordinary practice. The formulation I propose does not take into account the ever-present and all-important situational modifiers that come into play in each actual case, which responsibly acting officers cannot afford to disregard in practice. In this sense, the formulation involves an idealization of the average officer's approach to police work, especially in peacekeeping cases.

Officers are clearly aware that they are perceived as, and actually are, the tangible "or else" of society. By "or else" I mean of course the potential recourse to coercive means—including physical force—to achieve whatever end is intended. The relative likelihood of actual recourse to force varies quite considerably from assignment to assignment while remaining generally small. It is virtually zero for some officers; for others it rises to the level of a relatively unlikely, but still distinct, possibility to which one must be permanently alert. Thus, being a police officer means being authorized and required to act coercively when coercion is required, as determined by the officer's evaluation of local and timely conditions. Acting as society's "or else" is what citizens expect when they "call the cops." The noisy neighbor, the uncooperative tenant, the abusive spouse, the assaultive customer, the unruly youth, the unmanageable patient, and so forth are all the sort of challenges citizens hand over to the police with the expectation that the officer may, can, and will force the recalcitrant into compliance "then and there." There is of course a vast difference between the officer who knows that he or she may have to act coercively, all else failing, and the officer who is impulsively violent; but both know that a person who cannot imagine ever using force had better not seek employment in the police.

The tasks associated with being society's "or else" cause officers to rely on three distinct ways of doing police work, which are combined in actual practice, albeit in varying proportions. One approach involves negotiating techniques employed as a means of persuasion to secure compliance. The second consists of using preemptively coercive means, such as intimidation and threats, to obtain compliance. The third relies on physical prowess. No officer in the field completely avoids bargaining or intimidation, and none can afford to disregard entirely reliance on physical force. There are considerable differences among officers in the skill in, and the preference for, one or the other approach. Accordingly, there are large differences in the speed and likelihood with which officers move from the least to the most coercive method of control.

Second only to the sense of being society's "or else" is the belief in the inherently impermanent effects of police interventions in adventitiously episodic disorders. All dispute resolutions, all nuisance abatements, and all emergency rescues are viewed as merely temporary. The point here is not so much that there are no permanent solutions to many of the problems, but rather that the mission of the police is limited to imposing provisional solutions to uncontexted emergencies. Inquiries and interests in causes and circumstances that give rise to problems, and efforts to address such factors are deemed to be beyond the scope of police competence and proper police business. The only long-range effect officers seek to foster and to protect is the general attitude of "respect for authority." The alleged decline of respect for authority, especially among to-day's youth, comes up in almost all conversations with police officers. While the complaint has broader implications, the immediate reference is the perceived unwillingness of increasing numbers of people to submit spontaneously to police control in situations officers seek to control. The poignancy of this complaint is properly understood in connection with a basic condition of police work, namely its isolation. Under ordinary circumstances and in most assignments, but especially in the uniformed patrol, police officers work alone or in pairs, among strangers. The very same people who expect to know their children's teacher, their clergyman, their physician, their mail carrier, and most other persons who respond to their needs, do not expect to know the police officers who work in their neighborhoods. Moreover, police officers are sent to their assignments with the understanding that they are on their own. Thus, occupational competence, recognized among officers, manifests itself prominently in the capacity to "take care of oneself." That is, the highest regard of both peers and superiors goes to those independently resourceful officers whose manner indicates clearly that they brook no nonsense, who do not retreat in the face of opposition, who finish what they start without entering into entanglements or causing repercussions, and who accomplish all this without relying on assistance in all but the most extreme circumstances. The ideal of unintimidated self-sufficiency can be approximated in various ways, including officers who rely minimally and maximally on coercive means, all of whom are, however, united in their sense of being points on a beleaguered "thin blue line."

The occupational posture indicated in this brief sketch ought to be seen as an adaptive adjustment between demand-determined routine occupational practices and the organizational ideology of professional law enforcement. By adjustment I mean a state of affairs that accommodates a disfavored but unavoidable practice—that is, informal peacekeeping—while preventing it from functioning at a level of adequacy commensurate with the problems it addresses. I believe that the movement toward community-oriented policing of the 1980s must be seen as an effort to emancipate policing from the constraints of this adjustment. Just as the "professionalization" of the police half a century ago liberated the institution from the control of urban machine politics, community-oriented policing liberates it from the dogmatics of "professional law enforcement." This involves, above all else, a movement away from the haphazard concatenation of fragmentary and purely reactive intervention and a movement toward a methodical analysis of the problems that require police control and the rational planning of an effective response. Viewed from the perspective of an outsider, one can see three targets of concern and one long-range implication that has not been fully addressed thus far.

The first decisive aspect of community policing involves a shift of concern from dealing with isolated incidents involving individual persons to paying attention to the conditions that affect the likelihood of such incidents and, beyond that, the quality of life of the community as a whole. It is not altogether clear just how far the police may and must go in such inquiries and interventions and what sorts of problems are in its province. But even before these questions are fully formulated, addressed, and answered, there are some nonproblematic situations that can be easily absorbed into the scope of policing without going into great depths of political philosophy. For example, while acts of vandalism should be handled in inherited ways, by tracking down culprits for appropriate treatment, it has been persuasively argued that vandalized neighborhoods invite further acts of vandalism. A broken window that is not repaired will soon be surrounded by other broken windows. Thus, police interest in vandalism is seen as including an interest in the rehabilitation of deteriorated neighborhoods with the reasonable expectation that well-kept surroundings are inhospitable to activities and incidents that cause people to "call the cops." One can readily multiply the ways in which physical settings affect order and disorder in a community and, accordingly, the ways in which they affect police service. Another example of transcending the limit of incident handling is the concern for the fear of crime. At the individual level the fear of crime is a realistic and appropriate response to the threat of crime. Persons who avoid exposing themselves to victimization do reduce its likelihood. But at the level of the community as a whole, pervasive fear of crime has precisely the opposite effect. When the people become intimidated by the threat of crime to the point of withdrawing into private spaces, they actually embolden predators. Obviously, changing community morale in this respect is not a simple matter. It requires measures designed to reduce the estrangement between the police and the community, that is, the creation of a police consisting of easily accessible and recognizable officers whose presence in their patrol areas is seen and felt.

Perhaps it should be said that the community orientation of police work does not involve matters that could never have crossed the mind of a police officer in the past. Its true significance consists of elevating what was previously, at best, an occasional and optional interest on the part of some officers to the forefront of every officer's occupational responsibility. It thus enlarges the scope of police responsibilities from keeping a lid on things to reducing the pressures that cause the eruption of disorder and deviance, at least where those pressures can be readily identified and feasibly addressed in cooperation with the community. It is almost too obvious to need elaboration that in matters like the rehabilitation of decaying neighborhoods and in the raising of community morale, the police can be effective only in closely coordinated work with people and other institutions in the community. In fact, it is not too farfetched to think that in some situations the police function consists of mobilizing and directing the defense of the community with the community's own resources.

While community orientation breaks down the barriers between the police and the outside world, the second critical aspect of the reform requires the creation of collegial relations among officers. This involves the displacement of the present command structure, which, in any case, functions only as an internal disciplinary mechanism and has no functional significance for the way in which police work is done by members of the line personnel who are expected to know what to do and be able to take care of themselves in their respective individual assignments. The need for a more cooperative policing was recognized two decades ago in the idea of "team policing," which, however, was never fully institutionalized and usually took the form of temporary and experimental projects. The abandonment of the pretense that everyone is doing what he or she is told and the institution of genuine consultative and cooperative relations, responsible planning, and shared responsibility for an assigned area of concern are truly daunting tasks; it may well be the case that the restructuring of relations among police officers may be more difficult than the restructuring of relations between officers and the citizenry. It will involve the reorientation of some ingrained and often tacitly assumed norms of interaction among officers, it will create ambiguities about the extent and the nature of reciprocal rights and obligations, and it will produce uncertainties about the career opportunities of individual officers. Police officers were always moved by a strong sense of defensive solidarity that caused them to close ranks under attack. Relations of collegiality replace this largely mechanical solidarity that counterposes "us" against "them" with the functional solidarity of collaborative interdependence.

The third aspect of the reform calls for the creation of a genuine problem-solving service. This is, by a wide margin, the most ambitious aspiration of the reform, the details of which are contained in Goldstein's earlier-mentioned essay. It involves the relentlessly comprehensive investigation of all problems the police officers deal with to achieve a more realistic understanding of their nature, the study of the adequacy of present responses to the problems, the exploration and evaluation of response alternatives, and an appropriate restructuring of resource allocation.

There are two reasons why problem-oriented policing may be the most difficult to achieve. First, it will probably not be immediately apparent to all concerned why a problem like purse-snatching requires study and planning beyond what is already known about it. In fact, it might seem offensive to some to have to look at it as a behavioral pattern, conditioned by circumstances and having a special dynamic, if only because the effort to understand might get us too close to forgiving.

The project of instituting effective control competes with the impulse to condemn. Second, the effort involved in problem-oriented policing requires interests, inclinations, and aptitudes that are not well represented in police personnel at this time. It is not 'that such persons are wholly absent. Their number is actually larger than existing recruitment and training patterns lead us to expect. But in the long run, problem-oriented policing will not be able to rely on an adequate supply of appropriately motivated and endowed people among recruits whose intellectual horizon is limited by a high school diploma and who have chosen police work as an alternative to some other low-level occupation. Nor will it be sufficient to raise the entry-level requirements to having a baccalaureate. If the reforms envisioned by the reformers of the 1980s are to become a practical reality it is necessary—however farfetched it may seem under present conditions—to look forward to the time when entry into police work will be open only to candidates who have completed a postgraduate course of professional education, as is presently the case for teachers, accountants, physicians, social workers, librarians, and so forth, to be followed by a period of on-the-job training. The idea that the principles and procedures employed today in recruitment and training will produce people inclined toward self-directed information gathering and analysis, capable of inventive planning, and motivated to work for long-range solutions seems absurd; and farfetched is better than absurd.

The need for the radical revision of current selection and training structures is not appreciated by those who ask if the requirement of higher education can be justified by the contribution it makes to producing effective police officers. The honest answer is that spending four years studying anthropology, comparative literature, calculus, Latin, and similar subjects is about as related to competence in policing as it is related to competence in dentistry, finance, or social work. Yet no one questions that these and similar occupations ought to be staffed by educated people. At one time, and in the not-too-distant past, one did not need to have a baccalaureate to be a physician, lawyer, or accountant in the United States. But today, it is commonly accepted that to be any of them—or to be a hospital administrator, a librarian, or a teacher—one must have both an undergraduate and a postgraduate education. The requirement is enforced increasingly even when it cannot be shown clearly that it actually equips graduates with all the skills required in the practice of their professions. But education, including postgraduate education, is not really intended to produce skilled practitioners in any profession. Instead, it functions in part as a selection mechanism, but more importantly as the intellectual and moral preparation for people engaged in morally and intellectually demanding occupations. It is hard to see that these demands are not as great in the case of the officer engaged in problem-oriented policing as they are in other human service professions.

In sum, the reforms of the 1980s aim at a radical transformation of the basic meaning of policing. The institutions will still remain the "or else" of society; dealing with the segment of the penal law it now deals with will still be a premier responsibility, as will be the task of peacekeeping. But the "else" in the "or else" will not be the quick-fix, Band-Aid remedy of today. Instead, it will be an answer based on the results of rational inquiry and methodically planned remedial intervention. Admittedly, it is difficult to imagine this kind of police. But all students of the police know that it is not impossible, for they encountered, even as early as twenty-five years ago, officers whose outlook, probity, perception, and skill caused them to practice a version of community-oriented, problem-solving policing, even under severely adverse circumstances. With institutional encouragement, the number of such officers could be significantly increased. But in order for this kind of work to become the standard form of police work, it seems necessary to redefine it from a relatively low-grade occupation to a profession in the full sense of the term. That is, it must become an occupation open to people whose aspirations are strong enough to endure a protracted educational experience, followed by an appropriate internship training period. It always seemed paradoxical that police officers, recruited from among candidates who would qualify only for menial jobs in the private sector, were required to deal with problems that would tax the knowledge, skill, and ingenuity of highly educated human service professionals. But now, when these assignments are openly acknowledged and actually extended, it seems almost too much to have to say that we must begin to recruit police personnel in ways that are commensurate with the work we expect from them.

NOTE

In the essays written in what now seems the distant past, the words "policeman" and "patrolman" and the pronouns associated with them are used where today I would have employed gender-neutral expressions. My insensitivity could be explained, if not excused, by the fact that in the years I conducted my fieldwork I had encountered not even a single woman patrol officer and only one woman detective.

1 | Urban Police

CITIES AND OTHER URBAN AREAS in the United States are policed by a variety of federal, state, and local law enforcement agencies. The municipal police departments are part of this complex (Ostrom and Parks 1978). They are organs of local government—although this was not always the case—and their character and orientation tend to reflect local determinants more than is the case for other law enforcement agencies. Whereas these other agencies are empowered by specific mandates, the mandate of the municipal police is open-ended, comprehensive, and ill defined. There appears to be no limit to what people expect of the police, but the majority of departments are ill equipped to meet many of these expectations.

Urban police departments vary enormously in size (although most are quite small), in the resources at their command, and in the kinds and quality of service they perform. Some of these differences can be traced to legal authorization, but most originate in the differences in past development and present circumstances. Accordingly, municipal policing in the United States is much less the product of carefully considered options than of the vagaries of history (Fogelson 1979).

Viewed from the perspective of the public, the municipal police department is the most easily accessible organ of government and the most conspicuous presence of the state's power for both good and bad. It is one of the conditions of the availability of the police that interactions between citizens and officers are permeated by unease and often by mutual distrust.

If one conceives of policing as an activity carried out by specially empowered and skilled agents within formally organized departmental settings, then it is noteworthy that a large number of these agents are not engaged in policing. For example, all of the administrative work of police departments is done by police officers. Police officers perform an unusual amount of auxiliary work not involving the constituent empowerments and skills of policing: they function within police departments as accountants, computer programmers, stock clerks, dispatchers, radio technicians, and auto mechanics. The justification is that these tasks are apt to be met more efficiently and more reliably by persons who can make use of knowledge and aptitudes acquired in actual policing. For example, radio dispatchers are thought to be better judges of whether it is necessary to send a patrol officer in response to a citizen's complaint if they have been patrol officers themselves. The justification obviously fits some assignments better than others, and probably does not fit some at all.

It would seem likely that the police avoid employing civilians more from a desire to maintain tight internal cohesion and control rather than from considerations of effectiveness. The uniformity of personnel within police departments strengthens internal solidarity, fortifies reciprocal dependence and trust, and fosters a system within which old cronies take care of one another by providing anything from small favors to outright sinecures. This work environment clearly differs from that of other civil service sectors and most other occupations.

Policing proper can be divided into three overlapping but distinct domains: namely, criminal law enforcement, regulatory control, and peacekeeping. The division, reflected in the administrative organization of all but the smallest of departments, is not clear-cut, and it is a common practice to change the definition of a task, thereby shifting it from one sphere into another.

Criminal law enforcement.   Criminal law enforcement is generally recognized as the core of the police mandate and the principal justification for the existence of the police establishment. Indeed, for most police officers, fighting crime alone is "real police work," even though in actual practice only a small part of all police activities involves crime control. Moreover, the police have not developed the technical competence in crime fighting that would make them successful in clearing but a small fraction of all the crimes they are informed about (Greenwood, Chaiken, and Petersilia 1977).

The symbolism of the police officer as a crime fighter is significant in two ways. The very existence of the police betokens society's opposition to crime and is an expression of society's commitment to combat crime. One might say that we draw from the sight of a police officer the same assurance which people in the past drew from public executions—that evil-doers may expect their just deserts. The police constitute visual proof that crime does not go unopposed (Manning 1977).

Aside from their symbolic significance for crime control, the police make an important practical contribution to criminal law enforcement: they launch the process that keeps prosecutors, judges, probation officers, and correctional personnel busy. Moreover, prosecutors ordinarily depend on the police to collect and make ready for trial the evidence and testimony needed to convict.

With regard to the distinction proposed by Herbert Packer between the due process model and the crime control model of the criminal process, the police prefer the second. They do not perceive the legal norms regulating procedure and protecting the rights of defendants as the terms on which crime is to be dealt with, but rather as impediments to efficient crime control and as expressions of excessive solicitude for the rights of defendants (Skolnick 1966).

Although the role of the police in the administration of criminal justice is clearly ministerial, they in fact exercise discretion whether or not to invoke the law. The perception of probable cause required for arrest is occasionally incontrovertible, but often enough it is ambiguous and calls for evaluation and judgment. However, the police do not limit themselves to deciding such matters. Officers at times fail to invoke the law in cases in which no reasonable doubt is possible, and their failure actually exculpates persons who have transgressed against the law. The police are, in fact, expected and encouraged to disregard offenses when recognizing them officially would cause them more harm than good, according to tacit but well-understood principles of judgment. For example, even when the law allows no exception, officers will permit gambling to take place in a church basement, and it is understood that lawmakers take such instances into account when they frame exceptionless norms (LaFave 1965). If the game fell into the hands of organized crime the same officers would presumably learn of this and would know how to act in that case.

The involvement of the police in criminal law enforcement is generally set into motion by complaints from citizens (Reiss 1971). This is true in virtually all instances of serious crimes identified by the Federal Bureau of Investigation as "index crimes." The extent and nature of police involvement ranges from simply posting a record of the case as reported in departmental files, to extensive investigation and efforts to capture suspects. Officers seek to clear a crime by an arrest when there is a substantial probability of speedy success. This criterion varies according to the seriousness of the crime: a higher degree of initial certainty is required in cases of purse-snatching than for crimes deemed more serious.

Some forms of crime control are initiated by the police themselves—for example, the control of prostitution, gambling, and drug trading. Large departments also mount undercover operations to stem violent street crime and trade in stolen property.

Police operations are characteristically directed against the "common crimes" and exclude "white-collar crimes," connected with the conduct of business, the practice of the professions, or deportment in a public office, although there exists no formal basis for such exclusion. It is not unheard of for the municipal police to become involved in the investigation and prosecution of these crimes, but as a general rule, such matters as bribery, tax evasion, embezzlement, fraud, malfeasance in office, and professional malpractice are left to other law enforcement agencies. By their concern for crimes poor people specialize in and their neglect of crimes committed exclusively by well-to-do-individuals, the police give the appearance of acting in a class-biased manner that, owing to the distribution of wealth in the United States, is also apt to include elements of racial bias.

Regulatory control. The regulatory control exercised by municipal police departments involves traffic control and the supervision of certain licensed activities. These comprise a grab bag of responsibilites that vary greatly from jurisdiction to jurisdiction. In some cities the police issue permits to carry firearms, in others they administer the franchising of taxicabs, and in still others they hand out vendor's licenses and supervise registration requirements in hotel registers.

Traffic control is a serious and burdensome task that entails the enforcement of traffic laws and ordinances, including such routine matters as directing heavy traffic, assisting at automobile accidents, towing away illegally parked cars, and controlling pedestrian traffic at street crossings. The only contact many citizens are likely to have with a police officer is as motorists, and departments make an effort to structure these encounters so that the citizens affected by them will not have an unfavorable impression of the police. This effort has not been blessed with much success, however.

The police also administer permits for, and supervise, such events as fairs, parades, and demonstrations. During the 1960s municipal police departments proved quite inadequate in the handling of street demonstrations: their responce was generally chaotic and marred by the use of excessive violence. Since many of these demonstrations were identified with the struggle for social justice, for civil liberties for minorities, and against the war in Vietnam, the police response seemed to indicate that the police were aligned on the side of political and social oppression (Platt 1971).

Peacekeeping. The largest share of the manpower resources of the police is allocated to peacekeeping. Although there is little doubt that the police are uniquely expected to, and competent to, engage in peacekeeping, there exists no norm spelling out explicitly the terms of this authorization. Hence, its legitimacy must be inferred from its being carried out in the open, under the eyes of those authorities who have the power to prohibit it (Bittner 1980).

In criminal law enforcement, officers set into motion a process that is taken over by others, but in peacekeeping they attempt permanent or provisional solutions to problems requiring police attention alone. It is quite possible for a given problem, such as an act of violence, to set in motion either the criminal process or the peacekeeping process (Black 1980). The choice of which course of action is followed is significantly influenced by departmental policy (Wilson 1968).

The heart of peacekeeping involves the handling of critical emergencies and disasters of every kind. In these situations officers are often directly involved in rescue operations, but their more specific task is to prevent chaos, violence, and panic; to maintain order; and to deal with any impediments to rescue and remedial efforts. In doing so they require people to act, or to forbear from acting, in certain ways—by command or, when necessary, by using force.

On a smaller scale, but similar in kind, is police involvement in crises undergone by individual persons. Officers are frequently called upon to deal with those who are suicidal or mentally ill, who are lost or seriously disoriented, who have suffered serious injury or are seriously ill, or who are in need of assistance for some other reason. In many such cases, the help provided by the police could be provided by any competent person. The police are called on mainly because it is known that they are always available and will respond to people in need. Above all, the police are called because they are generally perceived as "officially" empowered to compel compliance.

The most dangerous and frequent instances of peacekeeping are associated with violent or potentially violent disputes between individuals or small groups. The persons in conflict are often members of the same family or are closely acquainted. Other calls for police assistance involve quarrels between neighbors over real or imagined wrongs; complaints about youths whose conduct is said to be offensive, disruptive, or destructive; and disputes between landlords and tenants or between merchants and customers—in fact, any imaginable situation in which people are at odds. It is usually not difficult to find probable cause for charging one or several of the involved persons with assault, battery, larceny, trespass, breach of the peace, or some other crime. But the law is not invoked on the basis of probable cause alone, even in cases of apparent felonies. Instead, the warrant for, or against, invoking the law, where conditions for invoking it are present, is found in the overall social diagnosis officers make of the situation.

Style and organization of policing. Of the three domains of policing, peacekeeping expresses the occupational posture of the police best, the symbolic priority of law enforcement notwithstanding. Police officers appear to be most in their element when dealing with emergencies, with danger, and with conflict. In this work, concrete situational factors play a more decisive role in the choice of action than do formulated rules of procedure. Moreover, in peacekeeping the individual officer's skill, experience, judgment, and intuition are critical, often overshadowing the impact of official policy and regulation.

The organizational setting of police work—the police department—is not in full accord with the individualist activity of peacekeeping. The typical police department is a hybrid of the military and the bureaucratic models, and in all matters connected with internal administration of assignments, command structure, career advancement, and paperwork, police officers are bound by detailed regulation and stringent discipline. However, the formal order that regulates the relation between the officer and the institution is not the order that regulates the work of policing which officers do outside the station house. Internally, the police departments seek to maintain a high level of discipline, but externally they maintain virtually no control and supervision over the work of policing, and there are virtually no practical norms and standards of procedure (Goldstein 1977).

Most policing is done by officers who are literally on their own, working singly or in pairs. Although linked to a dispatcher by radio, they are typically told only where to go, not what to do. The presumption is that, except for certain rare emergencies, officers should be able to handle routine peacekeeping and law enforcement jobs. Ordinarily their practices are not subject to review. Although some formal training is offered, officers learn how to do police work first by working with a more seasoned partner, and then on their own. Some become expert and judicious practitioners; others learn little or nothing at all. Those who are fully competent practitioners do not expect collegial relations with their peers, but they do expect, and receive, strong and unqualified support in situations of physical danger or when under attack from outsiders. That is, within the institution, officers go to great lengths to stay out of one another's way, but in the outside world they maintain a remarkably unified front.

In their encounters with citizens, police officers seek to establish a position of dominance as soon as possible and to maintain it. This is achieved with various degrees of subtlety, and seasoned officers can be identified by the ease with which they assert control. Officers who are less certain of their craft often assert their power by means of aggression and insult, thus reducing their effectiveness and sometimes creating new and more serious problems than the ones originally encountered. It has been established that much police activity, especially in peacekeeping situations, includes recriminations against citizens who have not been appropriately deferential (Chevigny 1969). The aggressive approach is far more common in encounters with persons low on the economic scale and those belonging to racial minorities.

Three points must be made in connection with the frequent instances of police aggressiveness, especially in encounters with the "symbolic assailant," the young black male (Skolnick 1966). First, many such encounters are instances of a long history of reciprocal fear and loathing. Second, since most peacekeeping or petty law enforcement encounters between the police and citizens are relatively insignificant and outside the realm of departmental control, departments have found it impossible or inexpedient to enforce more circumspect conduct by officers. Third, police officers assume that they must always prevail, must not be deterred by resistance, and must not retreat in the face of opposition. Thus, some officers believe that by overwhelming those with whom they deal at the outset, they nip in the bud any potential resistance or opposition.

The police mandate. It is true that police officers can be dissuaded from carrying out their intentions, that they sometimes retreat in the face of opposition, and that they occasionally desist for other reasons from completing what they started. But the very existence of the police is predicated on the assumption that there are crises that must be addressed coercively in the place, and at the time, of their occurrence. Accordingly, the police officers' occupational responsibility is directed to dealing with all situations in which force may have to be used; and their occupational skill consists in being able to avoid using force except where it is utterly unavoidable.

It is, of course, quite difficult to decide whether a situation is of such nature as to constitute proper police business. Threats of serious injury, loss, or disorder are the normal criteria for peacekeeping duties. For criminal law enforcement the proposed formulation of the police mandate explains the concentration on common crimes, as distinct from white-collar crimes. It is commonly assumed that burglars, robbers, and muggers have nothing to lose in evading prosecution illegally. Accordingly, they have to be caught in situations in which force may have to be used. On the other hand, it is assumed that physicians, bankers, and congressmen accused of crimes connected with their work will present themselves for trial in response to a mailed summons; thus, police officers do not regard dealing with them to be their business.

It is difficult to imagine a profession in which there is more opportunity and greater temptation for corruption than policing. This is most obvious in criminal law enforcement, where an officer only has to look the other way to earn a bribe. Clearly, certain assignments are more exposed to the risk of corruption than others—for example, those involving drugs, prostitution, or gambling. This type of corruption has been the target of intensive concern inside and outside the police establishment, and as a result, the problem has significantly declined.

Another form of police corruption, more difficult to define

and to indict, is the abuse of power. Although some accusations of such abuse are politically motivated, it is true that many police officers insult, harass, intimidate, and brutalize citizens during the course of policing. When citizens express resentment they often merely provoke further abuse; when they complain to the officers' superiors, their complaints are not given credence. These practices are the more deplorable for being directed primarily against the socially, politically, and economically least resourceful members of society.

Factors contributing to the abuse of police power include the personality makeup of the individual officer and absence of control on the part of the department, but the main cause is professional incompetence. Police work is an extraordinarily complex, difficult, and serious occupation that frequently demands great skill and consummate judgment. Seasoned and responsible officers are always sensitive to the effects their decisions have on vital human interests. They handle with care and decisiveness situations that would cause panic or paralysis in others. However, such situations are often assigned to officers who are ill equipped to handle them. In view of the inferior manner in which police officers are recruited, trained, and supervised, it is not surprising that highly skilled officers are in the minority. This is because police work is unfairly regarded as a low-grade occupation, and those considered suitable for it are judged to be adequate to its simplest tasks rather than to its most difficult ones.

NOTE

This essay previously appeared in *Encyclopedia of Crime and Justice,* vol. 3, ed. Sanford H. Kadish (New York: The Free Press, 1983), 1135–39.

REFERENCES

Bittner, E. *The Functions of the Police in Modern Society: A Review of Background Factors, Current Practices, and Possible Role Models.* Cambridge, Mass.: Oelgeschlager, Gunn & Hain, 1980.

Black, D. J. *The Manners and Customs of the Police.* New York: Academic Press, 1980.

Chevigny, P. *Police Power: Police Abuses in New York City.* New York: Pantheon, 1969.

Fogelson, R. M. *Big-City Police: An Urban Institute Study.* Cambridge, Mass.: Harvard University Press, 1979.

Goldstein, H. *Policing a Free Society.* Cambridge, Mass.: Ballinger, 1977.

Greenwood, P. W., J. M. Chaiken, and J. Petersilia. *The Criminal Investigation Process.* Lexington, Mass.: Heath, 1977.

LaFave, W. R. *Arrest: The Decision to Take a Suspect into Custody.* Ed. Frank J. Remington. Boston: Little, Brown, 1965.

Manning, P. K. *Police Work: The Social Organization of Policing.* Cambridge, Mass.: MIT Press, 1977.

Ostrom, E., and R. B. Parks. *Patterns of Metropolitan Policing.* Cambridge, Mass.: Ballinger, 1978.

Packer, H. L. *The Limits of the Criminal Sanction.* Stanford, Calif.: Stanford University Press, 1968.

Platt, A., ed. *The Politics of Riot Commissions, 1917–1970: A Collection of Official Reports and Critical Essays.* New York: Macmillan, Collier Books, 1971.

Reiss, A. J. *The Police and the Public.* New Haven: Yale University Press, 1971.

Sherman, L. W. *Scandal and Reform: Controlling Police Corruption.* Berkeley: University of California Press, 1978.

Skolnick, J. H. *Justice without Trial: Law Enforcement in Democratic Society.* New York: John Wiley & Sons, 1966.

Wilson, J. Q. *Varieties of Police Behavior: The Management of Law and Order in Eight Communities.* Cambridge, Mass.: Harvard University Press, 1968.

2 | *The Police on Skid Row*

A Study of Peacekeeping

THE PROTOTYPE of modern police organization, the Metropolitan Police of London, was created to replace an antiquated and corrupt system of law enforcement. The early planners were motivated by the mixture of hardheaded business rationality and humane sentiment that characterized liberal British thought of the first half of the nineteenth century.[1] Partly to meet the objections of a parliamentary committee, which was opposed to the establishment of the police in England, and partly because it was in line with their own thinking, the planners sought to produce an instrument that could not readily be used in the play of internal power politics but which would, instead, advance and protect conditions favorable to industry and commerce and to urban civil life in general. These intentions were not very specific and had to be reconciled with the existing structures of governing, administering justice, and keeping the peace. Consequently, the locus and mandate of the police in the modern polity were ill-defined at the outset. On the one hand, the new institution was to be a part of the executive branch of government, organized, funded, and staffed in accordance with standards that were typical for the entire system of the executive. On the other hand, the duties that were given to the police organization brought it under direct control of the judiciary in its day-to-day operation.

The dual patronage of the police by the executive and the judiciary is characteristic for all democratically governed countries. Moreover, it is generally the case, or at least it is deemed desirable, that judges *rather than* executive officials have control over police use and procedure.[2] This preference is based on two considerations. First, in the tenets of the democratic creed, the possibility of direct control of the police by a government in power is repugnant.[3] Even when the specter of the police state in its more ominous forms is not a concern, close ties between those who govern and those who police are viewed as a sign of political corruption.[4] Hence, mayors, governors, and cabinet officers—although the nominal superiors of the police—tend to maintain, or to pretend, a hands-off policy. Second, it is commonly understood that the main function of the police is the control of crime. Since the concept of crime belongs wholly to the law, and its treatment is exhaustively based on considerations of legality, police procedure automatically stands under the same system of review that controls the administration of justice in general.

By nature, judicial control encompasses only those aspects of police activity that are directly related to full-dress legal prosecution of offenders. The judiciary has neither the authority nor the means to direct, supervise, and review those activities of the police that do not result in prosecution. Yet such other activities are unavoidable, frequent, and largely within the realm of public expectations. It might be assumed that in this domain of practice the police are under executive control. This is not the case, however, except in a marginal sense.[5] Not only are police departments generally free to determine what need be done and how, but aside from informal pressures they are given scant direction in these matters. Thus, there appear to exist two relatively independent domains of police activity. In one, their methods are constrained by the prospect of the future disposition of a case in the courts; in the other, they operate under some other consideration and largely with no structured and continuous outside constraint. Following the terminology suggested by Michael Banton, they may be said to function in the first instance as "law officers" and in the second instance as "peace officers."[6] It must be emphasized that the designation "peace officer" is a residual term, with only some vaguely presumptive content. The role, as Banton speaks of it, is supposed to encompass all occupational routines not directly related to making arrests, without, however, specifying what determines the limits of competence and availability of the police in such actions.

Efforts to characterize a large domain of activities of an important public agency have so far yielded only negative definitions. We know that they do not involve arrests; we also know that they do not stand under judicial control, and that they are not, in any important sense, determined by specific executive or legislative mandates. In police textbooks and manuals, these activities receive only casual attention, and the role of the peace officer is typically stated in terms suggesting that his work is governed mainly by the individual officer's personal wisdom, integrity, and altruism.[7] Police departments generally keep no records of procedures that do not involve making arrests. Policemen, when asked, insist that they merely use common sense when acting as peace officers, though they tend to emphasize the elements of experience and practice in discharging the role adequately. All this ambiguity is the more remarkable for the fact that peacekeeping tasks—that is, procedures not involving the formal legal remedy of arrest—were explicitly built into the program of the modern police from the outset.[8] The early executives of the London police saw with great clarity that their organization had a dual function. While it was to be an arm of the administration of justice, in respect of which it developed certain techniques for bringing offenders to trial, it was also expected to function apart from, and at times in lieu of, the employment of full-dress legal procedure. Despite its early origin, despite a great deal of public knowledge about it, despite the fact that it is routinely done by policemen, no one can say with any clarity what it means to do a good job of keeping the peace. To be sure, there is vague consensus that when policemen direct, aid, inform, pacify, warn, discipline, roust, and do whatever else they do without making arrests, they do this with some reference to the circumstances of the occasion and, thus, somehow contribute to the maintenance of the peace and order. Peacekeeping appears to be a solution to an unknown problem arrived at by unknown means.

The following is an attempt to clarify conceptually the mandate and the practice of keeping the peace. The effort will be directed not to the formulation of a comprehensive solution of the problem but to a detailed consideration of some aspects of it. Only in order to place the particular into the overall domain to which it belongs will the structural determinants of keeping the peace in general be discussed. By structural determinants are meant the typical situations that policemen perceive as *demand conditions* for action without arrest. This will be followed by a description of peacekeeping in skid-row districts, with the object of identifying those aspects of it that constitute a *practical skill.*

Since the major object of this chapter is to elucidate peace-keeping practice as a skilled performance, it is necessary to make clear how the use of the term is intended.

Practical skill will be used to refer to those methods of doing certain things, and to the information that underlies the use of the methods, that *practitioners themselves* view as proper and efficient. Skill is, therefore, a stable orientation to work tasks that is relatively independent of the personal feelings and judgments of those who employ it. Whether the exercise of this skilled performance is desirable or not, and whether it is based on correct information or not, are specifically outside the scope of interest of this presentation. The following is deliberately confined to a description of what police patrolmen consider to be the reality of their work circumstances, what they do, and what they feel they must do to do a good job. That the practice is thought to be determined by normative standards of skill minimizes but does not eliminate the factors of personal interest or inclination. Moreover, the distribution of skill varies among practitioners in the very standards they set for themselves. For example, we will show that patrolmen view a measure of rough informality as good practice vis-à-vis skid-row inhabitants. By this standard, patrolmen who are "not rough enough," or who are "too rough," or whose roughness is determined by personal feelings rather than by situational exigencies, are judged to be poor craftsmen.

The description and analysis are based on twelve months of field work with the police departments of two large cities west of the Mississippi. Eleven weeks of this time were spent in skid row and skid-row-like districts. The observations were augmented by approximately one hundred interviews with police officers of all ranks. The formulations that will be proposed were discussed in these interviews. They were recognized by the respondents as elements of standard practice. The respondents' recognition was often accompanied by remarks indicating that they had never thought about things in this way and that they were not aware how standardized police work was.

STRUCTURAL DEMAND CONDITIONS OF PEACEKEEPING

There exist at least five types of relatively distinct circumstances that produce police activities that do not involve invoking the law and that are only in a trivial sense determined by those considerations of legality that determine law enforcement. This does not mean that these activities are illegal but merely that there is no legal directive that informs the acting policeman whether what he does must be done or how it is to be done. In these circumstances, policemen act as all-purpose and terminal remedial agents, and the confronted problem is solved in the field. If these practices stand under any kind of review at all, and typically they do not, it is only through internal police department control.

1. Although the executive branch of government generally refrains from exercising a controlling influence over the direction of police interest, it manages to extract certain performances from it. Two important examples of this are the supervision of certain licensed services and premises and the regulation of traffic.[9] With respect to the first, the police tend to concentrate on what might be called the moral aspects of establishments rather than on questions relating to the technical adequacy of the service. This orientation is based on the assumption that certain types of businesses lend themselves to exploitation for undesirable and illegal purposes. Since this tendency cannot be fully controlled, it is only natural that the police will be inclined to favor licensees who are at least cooperative. This, however, transforms the task from the mere scrutiny of credentials and the passing of judgments, to the creation and maintenance of a network of connections that

conveys influence, pressure, and information. The duty to inspect is the background of this network, but the resulting contacts acquire additional value for solving crimes and maintaining public order. Bartenders, shopkeepers, and hotel clerks become, for patrolmen, a resource that must be continuously serviced by visits and exchanges of favors. While it is apparent that this condition lends itself to corrupt exploitation by individual officers, even the most flawlessly honest policeman must participate in this network of exchanges if he is to function adequately. Thus, engaging in such exchanges becomes an occupational task that demands attention and time.

Regulation of traffic is considerably less complex. More than anything else, traffic control symbolizes the autonomous authority of policemen. Their commands generally are met with unquestioned compliance. Even when they issue citations, which seemingly refer the case to the courts, it is common practice for the accused to view the allegation as a finding against him and to pay the fine. Police officials emphasize that it is more important to be circumspect than legalistic in traffic control. Officers are often reminded that a large segment of the public has no other contacts with the police, and that the field lends itself to public relations work by the line personnel.[10]

2. Policemen often do not arrest persons who have committed minor offenses in circumstances in which the arrest is technically possible. This practice has recently received considerable attention in legal and sociological literature. The studies were motivated by the realization that "police decisions not to invoke the criminal process determine the outer limits of law enforcement."[11] From these researches, it was learned that the police tend to impose more stringent criteria of law enforcement on certain segments of the community than on others.[12] It was also learned that, from the perspective of the administration of justice, the decisions not to make arrests often are based on compelling reasons.[13] It is less well appreciated that policemen often not only refrain from invoking the law formally but also employ alternative sanctions. For example, it is standard practice that violators are warned not to repeat the offense. This often leads to patrolmen's "keeping an eye" on certain persons. Less frequent, though not unusual, is the practice of

direct disciplining of offenders, especially when they are juveniles, which occasionally involves inducing them to repair the damage occasioned by their misconduct.[14]

The power to arrest and the freedom not to arrest can be used in cases that do not involve patent offenses. An officer can say to a person whose behavior he wishes to control, "I'll let you go this time!" without indicating to him that he could not have been arrested in any case. Nor is this always deliberate misrepresentation, for in many cases the law is sufficiently ambiguous to allow alternative interpretations. In short, not to make an arrest is rarely, if ever, merely a decision not to act; it is most often a decision to act alternatively. In the case of minor offenses, to make an arrest often is merely one of several possible proper actions.

3. There exists a public demand for police intervention in matters that contain no criminal and often no legal aspects.[15] For example, it is commonly assumed that officers will be available to arbitrate quarrels, to pacify the unruly, and to help in keeping order. They are supposed also to aid people in trouble, and there is scarcely a human predicament imaginable for which police aid has not been solicited and obtained at one time or another. Most authors writing about the police consider such activities only marginally related to the police mandate. This view fails to reckon with the fact that the availability of these performances is taken for granted and the police assign a substantial amount of their resources to such work. Although this work cannot be subsumed under the concept of legal action, it does involve the exercise of a form of authority that most people associate with the police. In fact, no matter how trivial the occasion, the device of "calling the cops" transforms any problem. It implies that a situation is, or is getting, out of hand. Police responses to public demands are always oriented to this implication, and the risk of proliferation of troubles makes every call a potentially serious matter.[16]

4. Certain mass phenomena of either a regular or a spontaneous nature require direct monitoring. Most important is the controlling of crowds in incipient stages of disorder. The specter of mob violence frequently calls for measures that involve coercion, including the use of physical force. Legal theory

allows, of course, that public officials are empowered to use coercion in situations of imminent danger.[17] Unfortunately, the doctrine is not sufficiently specific to be of much help as a rule of practice. It is based on the assumption of the adventitiousness of danger, and thus does not lend itself readily to elaborations that could direct the routines of early detection and prevention of untoward developments. It is interesting that the objective of preventing riots by informal means posed one of the central organizational problems for the police in England during the era of the Chartists.[18]

5. The police have certain special duties with respect to persons who are viewed as less than fully accountable for their actions. Examples of those eligible for special consideration are those who are under age[19] and those who are mentally ill.[20] Although it is virtually never acknowledged explicitly, those receiving special treatment include people who do not lead "normal" lives and who occupy a pariah status in society. This group includes residents of ethnic ghettos, certain types of bohemians and vagabonds, and persons of known criminal background. The special treatment of children and of sick persons is permissively sanctioned by the law, but the special treatment of others is, in principle, opposed by the leading theme of legality and the tenets of the democratic faith.[21] The important point is not that such persons are arrested more often than others, which is quite true, but that they are perceived by the police as producing a special problem that necessitates continuous attention and the use of special procedures.

The five types of demand conditions do not exclude the possibility of invoking the criminal process. Indeed, arrests do occur quite frequently in all these circumstances. But the concerns generated in these areas cause activities that usually do not terminate in an arrest. When arrests are made, there exist, at least in the ideal, certain criteria by reference to which the arrest can be judged as having been made more or less properly, and there are some persons who, in the natural course of events, actually judge the performance.[22] But for actions not resulting in arrest there are no such criteria and no such judges. How, then, can one speak of such actions as necessary and proper? Since there does not exist any official answer to this query, and since policemen act in the role of peace officers pretty much without external direction or constraint, the question comes down to asking how the policeman himself knows whether he has any business with a person he does not arrest, and if so, what that business might be. Furthermore, if there exists a domain of concerns and activities that is largely independent of the law enforcement mandate, it is reasonable to assume that it will exercise some degree of influence on how and to what ends the law is invoked in cases of arrests.

Skid row presents one excellent opportunity to study these problems. The area contains a heavy concentration of persons who do not live "normal" lives in terms of prevailing standards of middle-class morality. Since the police respond to this situation by intensive patrolling, the structure of peacekeeping should be readily observable. Needless to say, the findings and conclusions will not be necessarily generalizable to other types of demand conditions.

THE PROBLEM OF KEEPING THE PEACE IN SKID ROW

Skid row has always occupied a special place among the various forms of urban life. While other areas are perceived as being different in many ways, skid row is seen as completely different. Though it is located in the heart of civilization, it is viewed as containing aspects of the primordial jungle, calling for missionary activities and offering opportunities for exotic adventure. While each inhabitant individually can be seen as tragically linked to the vicissitudes of "normal" life, allowing others to say "here but for the Grace of God go I," those who live there are believed to have repudiated the entire role-casting scheme of the majority and to live apart from normalcy. Accordingly, the traditional attitude of civic-mindedness toward skid row has been dominated by the desire to contain it and to salvage souls from its clutches.[23] The specific task of containment has been left to the police. That this task pressed upon the police some rather special duties has never come under explicit consideration, either from the government that expects control or from the police departments that implement it.

Instead, the prevailing method of carrying out the task is to assign patrolmen to the area on a fairly permanent basis and to allow them to work out their own ways of running things. External influence is confined largely to the supply of support and facilities, on the one hand, and to occasional expressions of criticism about the overall conditions, on the other. Within the limits of available resources and general expectations, patrolmen are supposed to know what to do and are free to do it.[24]

Patrolmen who are more or less permanently assigned to skid-row districts tend to develop a conception of the nature of their "domain" that is surprisingly uniform. Individual officers differ in many aspects of practice, emphasize different concerns, and maintain different contacts, but they are in fundamental agreement about the structure of skid-row life. This relatively uniform conception includes an implicit formulation of the problem of keeping the peace in skid row.

In the view of experienced patrolmen, life on skid row is fundamentally different from life in other parts of society. To be sure, they say, around its geographic limits the area tends to blend into the surrounding environment, and its population always encompasses some persons who are only transitionally associated with it. Basically, however, skid row is perceived as the natural habitat of people who lack the capacities and commitments to live "normal" lives on a sustained basis. The presence of these people defines the nature of social reality in the area. In general, and especially in casual encounters, the presumption of incompetence and of the disinclination to be "normal" is the leading theme for the interpretation of all actions and relations. Not only do people approach one another in this manner, but presumably they also expect to be approached in this way, and they conduct themselves accordingly.

In practice, the restriction of interactional possibilities that is based on the patrolman's stereotyped conception of skid-row residents is always subject to revision and modification toward particular individuals. Thus, it is entirely possible, and not unusual, for patrolmen to view certain skid-row inhabitants in terms that involve non-skid-row aspects of normality. Instances of such approaches and relationships invariably involve personal acquaintance and the knowledge of a good deal of individually qualifying information. Such instances are seen, despite their relative frequency, as exceptions to the rule. The awareness of the possibility of breakdown, frustration, and betrayal is ever-present, basic wariness is never wholly dissipated, and undaunted trust can never be fully reconciled with presence on skid row.

What patrolmen view as normal on skid row—and what they also think is taken for granted as "life as usual" by the inhabitants—is not easily summarized. It seems to focus on the idea that the dominant consideration governing all enterprise and association is directed to the occasion of the moment. Nothing is thought of as having a background that might have led up to the present in terms of some compelling moral or practical necessity. There are some exceptions to this rule, of course: the police themselves, and those who run certain establishments, are perceived as engaged in important and necessary activities. But in order to carry them out they, too, must be geared to the overall atmosphere of fortuitousness. In this atmosphere, the range of control that persons have over one another is exceedingly narrow. Good faith, even where it is valued, is seen merely as a personal matter. Its violations are the victim's own hard luck, rather than demonstrable violations of property. There is only a private sense of irony at having been victimized. The overall air is not so much one of active distrust as it is one of irrelevance of trust; as patrolmen often emphasize, the situation does not necessarily cause all relations to be predatory, but the possibility of exploitation is not checked by the expectation that it will not happen.

Just as the past is seen by the policeman as having only the most attenuated relevance to the present, so the future implications of present situations are said to be generally devoid of prospective coherence. No venture, especially no joint venture, can be said to have a strongly predictable future in line with its initial objectives. It is a matter of adventitious circumstance whether or not matters go as anticipated. That which is not within the grasp of momentary control is outside of practical social reality.

Though patrolmen see the temporal framework of the occasion of the moment mainly as a lack of trustworthiness, they also recognize that it involves more than merely the personal motives of individuals. In addition to the fact that everybody *feels* that things matter only at the moment, irresponsibility takes an *objectified* form on skid row. The places the residents occupy, the social relations they entertain, and the activities that engage them are not meaningfully connected over time. Thus, for example, address, occupation, marital status, and so forth matter much less on skid row than in any other part of society. The fact that present whereabouts, activities, and affiliations imply neither continuity nor direction means that life on skid row lacks a socially structured background of accountability. Of course, everybody's life contains some sequential incongruities, but in the life of a skid-row inhabitant every moment is an accident. That a man has no "address" in the future that could be in some way inferred from where he is and what he does makes him a person of *radically reduced visibility*. If he disappears from sight and one wishes to locate him, it is virtually impossible to systematize the search. All one can know with relative certainty is that he will be somewhere on some skid row and the only thing one can do is to trace the factual contiguities of his whereabouts.

It is commonly known that the police are expert in finding people and that they have developed an exquisite technology involving special facilities and procedures of sleuthing. It is less well appreciated that all this technology builds upon those socially structured features of everyday life that render persons findable in the first place.

Under ordinary conditions, the query as to where a person is can be addressed, from the outset, to a restricted realm of possibilities that can be further narrowed by looking into certain places and asking certain persons. The map of whereabouts that normally competent persons use whenever they wish to locate someone is constituted by the basic facts of membership in society. Insofar as membership consists of status incumbencies, each of which has an adumbrated future that substantially reduces unpredictability, it is itself a guarantee of the order within which it is quite difficult to get lost. Membership is thus visible not only now but also as its own projection into the future. It is in terms of this prospective availability that the skid-row inhabitant is a person of reduced visibility. His membership is viewed as extraordinary because its extension into the future is *not* reduced to a restricted realm of possibilities. Neither his subjective dispositions, nor his circumstances, indicate that he is oriented to any particular long-range interests. But, as he may claim every contingent opportunity, his claims are always seen as based on slight merit or right, at least to the extent that interfering with them does not constitute a substantial denial of his freedom.

This, then, constitutes the problem of keeping the peace on skid row. Considerations of momentary expediency are seen as having unqualified priority as maxims of conduct; consequently, the controlling influences of the pursuit of sustained interests are presumed to be absent.

THE PRACTICES OF KEEPING THE PEACE IN SKID ROW

From the perspective of society as a whole, skid-row inhabitants appear troublesome in a variety of ways. The uncommitted life attributed to them is perceived as inherently offensive; its very existence arouses indignation and contempt. More important, however, is the feeling that persons who have repudiated the entire role-status casting system of society, persons whose lives forever collapse into a succession of random moments, are seen as constituting a practical risk. As they have nothing to forsake, nothing is thought safe from them.[25]

The skid-row patrolman's concept of his mandate includes an awareness of this presumed risk. He is constantly attuned to the possibility of violence, and he is convinced that things to which the inhabitants have free access are as good as lost. But his concern is directed toward the continuous condition of peril *in the area* rather than *for society in general.* While he is obviously conscious of the presence of many persons who have committed crimes outside of skid row and will arrest them when they come to his attention, this is a peripheral part of his routine activities. In general, the skid-row patrolman and his superiors take for granted that his main business is to keep the peace and enforce the laws *on skid row*, and that he is involved only incidentally in protecting society at large. Thus, his task is formulated basically as the protection of putative predators from one another. The maintenance of peace and safety is difficult because everyday life on skid row is viewed as an open field for reciprocal exploitation. As the lives of the inhabitants lack the prospective coherence associated with status incumbency, the realization of self-interest does not produce order. Hence, mechanisms that control risk must work primarily from without.

External containment, to be effective, must be oriented to the realities of existence. Thus, the skid-row patrolman employs an approach that he views as appropriate to the *ad hoc* nature of skid-row life. The following are the three most prominent elements of this approach. First, the seasoned patrolman seeks to acquire a richly particularized knowledge of people and places in the area. Second, he gives the consideration of strict culpability a subordinate status among grounds for remedial sanction. Third, his use and choice of coercive interventions is determined mainly by exigencies of situations and with little regard for possible long range effects on individual persons.

The particularization of knowledge.

The patrolman's orientation to people on skid row is structured basically by the presupposition that if he does not know a man personally there is very little that he can assume about him. This rule determines his interaction with people who live on skid row. Since the area also contains other types of persons, however, its applicability is not universal. To some such persons it does not apply at all, and it has a somewhat mitigated significance with certain others. For example, some persons encountered on skid row can be recognized immediately as outsiders. Among them are workers who are employed in commercial and industrial enterprises that abut the area, persons who come for the purpose of adventurous "slumming," and some patrons of second-hand stores and pawn shops. Even with very little experience, it is relatively easy to identify these people by appearance, demeanor, and the time and place of their presence. The patrolman maintains an impersonal attitude toward them, and they are, under ordinary circumstances, not the objects of his attention.[26]

Clearly set off from these outsiders are the residents and the entire corps of personnel that services skid row. It would be fair to say that one of the main routine activities of patrolmen is the establishment and maintenance of familiar relationships with individual members of these groups. Officers emphasize their interest in this, and they maintain that their grasp of and control over skid row is precisely commensurate with the extent to which they "know the people." By this they do not mean having a quasi-theoretical understanding of human nature but rather the common practice of individualized and reciprocal recognition. As this group encompasses both those who render services on skid row and those who are serviced, individualized interest is not always based on the desire to overcome uncertainty. Instead, relations with service personnel become absorbed into the network of particularized attention. Ties between patrolmen, on the one hand, and businessmen, managers, and workers, on the other hand, are often defined in terms of shared or similar interests. It bears mentioning that many persons live *and* work on skid row. Thus, the distinction between those who service and those who are serviced is not a clearcut dichotomy but a spectrum of affiliations.

As a general rule, the skid-row patrolman possesses an immensely detailed factual knowledge of his beat. He knows, and knows a great deal about, a large number of residents. He is likely to know every person who manages or works in the local bars, hotels, shops, stores, and missions. Moreover, he probably knows every public and private place inside and out. Finally, he ordinarily remembers countless events of the past which he can recount by citing names, dates and places with remarkable precision. Though there are always some threads missing in the fabric of information, it is continuously woven and mended even as it is being used. New facts, however, are added to the texture, not in terms of structured categories but in terms of adjoining known realities. In other words, the content and organization of the patrolman's knowledge is primarily ideographic and only vestigially, if at all, nomothetic.

Individual patrolmen vary in the extent to which they make

themselves available or actively pursue personal acquaintances. But even the most aloof are continuously greeted and engaged in conversations that indicate a background of individualistic associations. While this scarcely has the appearance of work, because of its casual character, patrolmen do not view it as an optional activity. In the course of making their rounds, patrolmen seem to have access to every place, and their entry causes no surprise or consternation. Instead, the entry tends to lead to informal exchanges of small talk. At times the rounds include entering hotels and gaining access to rooms or dormitories, often for no other purpose than asking the occupants how things are going. In all this, patrolmen address innumerable persons by name and are in turn addressed by name. The conversational style that characterizes these exchanges is casual to an extent that by non-skid-row standards might suggest intimacy. Not only does the officer himself avoid all terms of deference and respect but he does not seem to expect or demand them. For example, a patrolman said to a man radiating an alcoholic glow on the street, "You've got enough of a heat on now; I'll give you ten minutes to get your ass off the street!" Without stopping, the man answered, "Oh, why don't you go and piss in your own pot!" The officer's only response was, "All right, in ten minutes you're either in bed or on your way to the can."

This kind of expressive freedom is an intricately limited privilege. Persons of acquaintance are entitled to it and appear to exercise it mainly in routinized encounters. But strangers, too, can use it with impunity. The safe way of gaining the privilege is to respond to the patrolman in ways that do not challenge his right to ask questions and issue commands. Once the concession is made that the officer is entitled to inquire into a man's background, business, and intentions, and that he is entitled to obedience, there opens a field of colloquial license. A patrolman seems to grant expressive freedom in recognition of a person's acceptance of his access to areas of life ordinarily defined as private and subject to coercive control only under special circumstances. While patrolmen accept and seemingly even cultivate the rough quid pro quo of informality, and while they do not expect sincerity, candor, or obedience in their dealings with the inhabitants, they do not allow the rejection of their approach.

The explicit refusal to answer questions of a personal nature and the demand to know why the questions are asked significantly enhances a person's chances of being arrested on some minor charge. While most patrolmen tend to be personally indignant about this kind of response and use the arrest to compose their own hurt feelings, this is merely a case of affect being in line with the method. There are other officers who proceed in the same manner without taking offense, or even with feelings of regret. Such patrolmen often maintain that their colleagues' affective involvement is a corruption of an essentially valid technique. The technique is oriented to the goal of maintaining operational control. The patrolman's conception of this goal places him hierarchically above whomever he approaches, and makes him the sole judge of the propriety of the occasion. As he alone is oriented to this goal, and as he seeks to attain it by means of individualized access to persons, those who frustrate him are seen as motivated at best by the desire to "give him a hard time" and at worst by some darkly devious purpose.

Officers are quite aware that the directness of their approach and the demands they make are difficult to reconcile with the doctrines of civil liberties, but they maintain that they are in accord with the general freedom of access that persons living on skid row normally grant one another. That is, they believe that the imposition of personalized and far-reaching control is in tune with standard expectancies. In terms of these expectancies, people are not so much denied the right to privacy as they are seen as not having any privacy. Thus, officers seek to install themselves in the center of people's lives and let the consciousness of their presence play the part of conscience.

When talking about the practical necessity of an aggressively personal approach, officers do not refer merely to the need for maintaining control over lives that are open in the direction of the untoward. They also see it as the basis for the supply of certain valued services to inhabitants of skid row. The coerced or conceded access to persons often imposes on the patrolman tasks that are, in the main, in line with these persons' expressed or implied interest. In asserting this connection, patrolmen note that they frequently help people to obtain meals, lodging, employment, that they direct them to welfare and health services, and that they aid them in various other ways. Though patrolmen tend to describe such services mainly as the product of their own altruism, they also say that their colleagues who avoid them are simply doing a poor job of patrolling. The acceptance of the need to help people is based on the realization that the hungry, the sick, and the troubled are a potential source of problems. Moreover, that patrolmen will help people is part of the background expectancies of life on skid row. Hotel clerks normally call patrolmen when someone gets so sick as to need attention; merchants expect to be taxed, in a manner of speaking, to meet the pressing needs of certain persons; and the inhabitants do not hesitate to accept, solicit, and demand every kind of aid. The domain of the patrolman's service activity is virtually limitless, and it is no exaggeration to say that the solution of every conceivable problem has at one time or another been attempted by a police officer. In one observed instance, a patrolman unceremoniously entered the room of a man he had never seen before. The man, who gave no indication that he regarded the officer's entry and questions as anything but part of life as usual, related a story of having had his dentures stolen by his wife. In the course of the subsequent rounds, the patrolman sought to locate the woman and the dentures. This did not become the evening's project but was attended to while doing other things. In the densely matted activities of the patrolman, the questioning became one more strand, not so much to be pursued to its solution as a theme that organized the memory of one more man known individually. In all this, the officer followed the precept formulated by a somewhat more articulate patrolman: "If I want to be in control of my work and keep the street relatively peaceful, I have to know the people. To know them I must gain their trust, which means that I have to be involved in their lives. But I can't be soft like a social worker because unlike him I cannot call the cops when things go wrong. I am the cops!"[27]

The restricted relevance of culpability. It is well known
that policemen exercise discretionary freedom in invoking the
law. It is also conceded that, in some measure, the practice is
unavoidable. This being so, the outstanding problem is whether
or not the decisions are in line with the intent of the law. On
skid row, patrolmen often make decisions based on reasons
that the law probably does not recognize as valid. The problem
can best be introduced by citing an example.

A man in a relatively mild state of intoxication (by skid-row
standards) approached a patrolman to tell him that he had a
room in a hotel, to which the officer responded by urging him
to go to bed instead of getting drunk. As the man walked off,
the officer related the following thoughts: Here is a completely
lost soul. Though he probably is no more than thirty-five years
old, he looks to be in his fifties. He never works and he hardly
ever has a place to stay. He has been on the street for several
years and is known as "Dakota." During the past few days,
"Dakota" has been seen in the company of "Big Jim." The latter
is an invalid living on some sort of pension with which he pays
for a room in the hotel to which "Dakota" referred and for
four weekly meal tickets in one of the restaurants on the street.
Whatever is left he spends on wine and beer. Occasionally, "Big
Jim" goes on drinking sprees in the company of someone like
"Dakota." Leaving aside the consideration that there is probably a homosexual background to the association, and that it is
not right that "Big Jim" should have to support the drinking
habit of someone else, there is the more important risk that if
"Dakota" moves in with "Big Jim" he will very likely walk off
with whatever the latter keeps in his room. "Big Jim" would
never dream of reporting the theft; he would just beat the hell
out of "Dakota" after he sobered up. When asked what could
be done to prevent the theft and the subsequent recriminations,
the patrolman proposed that in this particular case he would
throw "Big Jim" into jail if he found him tonight and then tell
the hotel clerk to throw "Dakota" out of the room. When asked
why he did not arrest "Dakota," who was, after all, drunk
enough to warrant an arrest, the officer explained that this
would not solve anything. While "Dakota" was in jail "Big Jim"
would continue drinking and would either strike up another

liaison or embrace his old buddy after he had been released. The only thing to do was to get "Big Jim" to sober up, and the only sure way of doing this was to arrest him.

As it turned out, "Big Jim" was not located that evening. But had he been located and arrested on a drunk charge, the fact that he was intoxicated would not have been the real reason for proceeding against him, but merely the pretext. The point of the example is not that it illustrates the tendency of skid-row patrolmen to arrest persons who would not be arrested under conditions of full respect for their legal rights. To be sure, this too happens. In the majority of minor arrest cases, however, the criteria the law specifies are met. But it is the rare exception that the law is invoked merely because the specifications of the law are met. That is, compliance with the law is merely the outward appearance of an intervention that is actually based on altogether different considerations. Thus, it could be said that patrolmen do not really enforce the law, even when they do invoke it, but merely use it as a resource to solve certain pressing practical problems in keeping the peace. This observation goes beyond the conclusion that many of the lesser norms of the criminal law are treated as defeasible in police work. It is patently not the case that skid-row patrolmen apply the legal norms while recognizing many exceptions to their applicability. Instead, the observation leads to the conclusion that in keeping the peace on skid row, patrolmen encounter certain matters they attend to by means of coercive action, for example, arrests. In doing this, they invoke legal norms that are available, and with some regard for substantive appropriateness. Hence, the problem patrolmen confront is not which drunks, beggars, or disturbers of the peace should be arrested and which can be let go as exceptions to the rule. Rather, the problem is whether, when someone "needs" to be arrested, he should be charged with drunkeness, begging, or disturbing the peace. Speculating further, one is almost compelled to infer that virtually any set of norms could be used in this manner, provided that they sanction relatively common forms of behavior.

The reduced relevance of culpability in peacekeeping practice on skid row is not readily visible. As mentioned, most arrested persons were actually found in the act, or in the state,

alleged in the arrest record. It becomes partly visible when one
views the treatment of persons who are not arrested even
though all the legal grounds for an arrest are present. Whenever such persons are encountered and can be induced to leave,
or taken to some shelter, or remanded to someone's care, then
patrolmen feel, or at least maintain, that an arrest would serve
no useful purpose. That is, whenever there exist means for
controlling the troublesome aspects of some person's presence
in some way alternative to an arrest, such means are preferen-
tially employed, provided, of course, that the case at hand
involves only a minor offense.[28]

The attenuation of the relevance of culpability is most visible
when the presence of legal grounds for an arrest could be
questioned, that is, in cases that sometimes are euphemistically
called "preventive arrests." In one observed instance, a man
who attempted to trade a pocket knife came to the attention of
a patrolman. The initial encounter was attended by a good deal
of levity and the man willingly responded to the officer's
inquiries about his identity and business. The man laughingly
acknowledged that he needed some money to get drunk. In
the course of the exchange it came to light that he had just
arrived in town, traveling in his automobile. When confronted
with the demand to lead the officer to the car, the man's
expression became serious and he pointedly stated that he
would not comply because this was none of the officer's business. After a bit more prodding, which the patrolman initially
kept in the light mood, the man was arrested on a charge
involving begging. In subsequent conversation the patrolman
acknowledged that the charge was only speciously appropriate
and mainly a pretext. Having committed himself to demanding
information he could not accept defeat. When this incident was
discussed with another patrolman, the second officer found
fault not with the fact that the arrest was made on a pretext but
with the first officer's own contribution to the creation of
conditions that made it unavoidable. "You see," he continued,
"there is always the risk that the man is testing you and you
must let him know what is what. The best among us can usually
keep the upper hand in such situations without making arrests.

But when it comes down to the wire, then you can't let them get away with it."

Finally, it must be mentioned that the reduction of the significance of culpability is built into the normal order of skid-row life, as patrolmen see it. Officers almost unfailingly say, pointing to some particular person, "I know that he knows that I know that some of the things he 'owns' are stolen, and that nothing can be done about it." In saying this, they often claim to have knowledge of such a degree of certainty as would normally be sufficient for virtually any kind of action except legal proceedings. Against this background, patrolmen adopt the view that the law is not merely imperfect and difficult to implement, but that on skid row, at least, the association between delict and sanction is distinctly occasional. Thus, to implement the law naively, that is, to arrest someone *merely* because he committed some minor offense, is perceived as containing elements of injustice.

Moreover, patrolmen often deal with situations in which questions of culpability are profoundly ambiguous. For example, an officer was called to help in settling a violent dispute in a hotel room. The object of the quarrel was a supposedly stolen pair of trousers. As the story unfolded in the conflicting versions of the participants, it was not possible to decide who was the complainant and who was alleged to be the thief, nor did it come to light who occupied the room in which the fracas took place, or whether the trousers were taken from the room or to the room. Though the officer did ask some questions, it seemed, and was confirmed in later conversation, that he was there not to solve the puzzle of the missing trousers but to keep the situation from getting out of hand. In the end, the exhausted participants dispersed, and this was the conclusion of the case. The patrolman maintained that no one could unravel mysteries of this sort because "these people take things from each other so often that no one could tell what 'belongs' to whom." In fact, he suggested, the terms owning, stealing, and swindling, in their strict sense, do not really belong on skid row, and all efforts to distribute guilt and innocence according to some rational formula of justice are doomed to failure.

It could be said that the term "curbstone justice" that is

sometimes applied to the procedures of patrolmen in skid rows contains a double irony. Not only is the procedure not legally authorized, which is the intended irony in the expression, but it does not even pretend to distribute deserts. The best among the patrolmen, according to their own standards, use the law to keep skid-row inhabitants from sinking deeper into the misery they already experience. The worst, in terms of these same standards, exploit the practice for personal aggrandizement or gain. Leaving motives aside, however, it is easy to see that if culpability is not the salient consideration leading to an arrest in cases where it is patently obvious, then the practical patrolman may not view it as being wholly out of line to make arrests lacking in formal legal justification. Conversely, he will come to view minor offense arrests made solely because legal standards are met as poor craftsmanship.

The background of* ad hoc *decision making.   When skid-row patrolmen are pressed to explain their reasons for minor offense arrests, they most often mention that it is done for the protection of the arrested person. This, they maintain, is the case in virtually all drunk arrests, in the majority of arrests involving begging and other nuisance offenses, and in many cases involving acts of violence. When they are asked to explain further such arrests as the one cited earlier involving the man attempting to sell the pocket knife, who was certainly not arrested for his own protection, they cite the consideration that belligerent persons constitute a much greater menace on skid row than any place else in the city. The reasons for this are twofold. First, many of the inhabitants are old, feeble, and not too smart, all of which makes them relatively defenseless. Second, many of the inhabitants are involved in illegal activities and are known as persons of bad character, which does not make them credible victims or witnesses. Potential predators realize that the resources society has mobilized to minimize the risk of criminal victimization do not protect the predator himself. Thus, reciprocal exploitation constitutes a preferred risk. The high vulnerability of everybody on skid row is public knowledge and causes every seemingly aggressive act to be seen as a potentially grave risk.

When, in response to all this, patrolmen are confronted with the observation that many minor offense arrests they make do not seem to involve a careful evaluation of facts before acting, they give the following explanations. First, the two reasons of protection and prevention represent a global background, and in individual cases it may sometimes not be possible to produce adequate justification on these grounds. Nor is it thought to be a problem of great moment to estimate precisely whether someone is more likely to come to grief or to cause grief when the objective is to prevent the proliferation of troubles. Second, patrolmen maintain that some of the seemingly spur-of-the-moment decisions are actually made against a background of knowledge of facts that are not readily apparent in the situations. Since experience not only contains this information but also causes it to come to mind, patrolmen claim to have developed a special sensitivity for qualities of appearances that allow an intuitive grasp of probable tendencies. In this context, little things are said to have high informational value and lead to conclusions without the intervention of explicitly reasoned chains of inferences. Third, patrolmen readily admit that they do not adhere to high standards of adequacy of justification. They do not seek to defend the adequacy of their method against some abstract criteria of merit. Instead, when questioned, they assess their methods against the background of a whole system of *ad hoc* decision making, a system that encompasses the courts, correction facilities, the welfare establishment, and medical services. In fact, policemen generally maintain that their own procedures not only measure up to the workings of this system but exceed them in the attitude of carefulness.

In addition to these recognized reasons, there are two additional background factors that play a significant part in decisions to employ coercion. One has to do with the relevance of situational factors, and the other with the evaluation of coercion as relatively insignificant in the lives of the inhabitants.

There is no doubt that the nature of the circumstances often has decisive influence on what will be done. For example, the same patrolman who arrested the man trying to sell his pocket knife was observed dealing with a young couple. Though the officer was clearly angered by what he perceived as insolence and threatened the man with arrest, he merely ordered him and his companion to leave the street. He saw them walking away in a deliberately slow manner and when he noticed them a while later, still standing only a short distance away from the place of encounter, he did not respond to their presence. The difference between the two cases was that in the first there was a crowd of amused bystanders, while the latter case was not witnessed by anyone. In another instance, the patrolman was directed to a hotel and found a father and son fighting about money. The father occupied a room in the hotel and the son occasionally shared his quarters. There were two other men present, and they made it clear that their sympathies were with the older man. The son was whisked off to jail without much study of the relative merits of the conflicting claims. In yet another case, a middle-aged woman was forcefully evacuated from a bar even after the bartender explained that her loud behavior was merely a response to goading by some foul-mouth youth.

In all such circumstances, coercive control is exercised as a means of coming to grips with situational exigencies. Force is used against particular persons but is incidental to the task. An ideal of "economy of intervention" dictates in these and similar cases that the person whose presence is most likely to perpetuate the troublesome development be removed. Moreover, the decision as to who is to be removed is arrived at very quickly. Officers feel considerable pressure to act unhesitatingly, and many give accounts of situations that got out of hand because of desires to handle cases with careful consideration. However, even when there is no apparent risk of rapid proliferation of trouble, the tactic of removing one or two persons is used to control an undesirable situation. Thus, when a patrolman ran into a group of four men sharing a bottle of wine in an alley, he emptied the remaining contents of the bottle into the gutter, arrested one man—who was no more and no less drunk than the others—and let the others disperse in various directions.

The exigential nature of control is also evident in the handling of isolated drunks. Men are arrested because of where they happen to be encountered. In this, it matters not only whether a man is found in a conspicuous place or not, but also how far away he is from his domicile. The further away he is, the less likely it is that he will make it to his room, and the more likely the arrest. Sometimes drunk arrests are made mainly because the police van is available. In one case a patrolman summoned the van to pick up an arrested man. As the van was pulling away from the curb the officer stopped the driver because he sighted another drunk stumbling across the street. The second man protested saying that he "wasn't even half drunk yet." The patrolman's response was "OK, I'll owe you half a drunk." In sum, the basic routine of keeping the peace on skid row involves a process of matching the resources of control with situational exigencies. The overall objective is to reduce the total amount of risk in the area. In this, practicality plays a considerably more important role than legal norms. Precisely because patrolmen see legal reasons for coercive action much more widely distributed on skid row than could ever be matched by interventions, they intervene not in the interest of law enforcement but in the interest of producing relative tranquility and order on the street.

Taking the perspective of the victim of coercive measures, one could ask why he, in particular, has to bear the cost of keeping the aggregate of troubles down while others, who are equally or perhaps even more implicated, go scot-free. Patrolmen maintain that the *ad hoc* selection of persons for attention must be viewed in the light of the following consideration: Arresting a person on skid row on some minor charge may save him and others a lot of trouble, but it does not work any real hardships on the arrested person. It is difficult to overestimate the skid-row patrolman's feeling of certainty that his coercive and disciplinary actions toward the inhabitants have but the most passing significance in their lives. Sending a man to jail on some charge that will hold him for a couple of days is seen as a matter of such slight importance to the affected person that it could hardly give rise to scruples. Thus, every indication that a coercive measure should be taken is accompanied by the realization "I might as well, for all it matters to him." Certain realities of life on skid row furnish the context for this belief in the attenuated relevance of coercion in the lives of the inhabitants. Foremost among them is that the use of police authority is seen as totally unremarkable by everybody on skid row. Persons who live or work there are continuously exposed to it and take its existence for granted. Shopkeepers, hotel clerks, and bartenders call patrolmen to rid themselves of unwanted and troublesome patrons. Residents expect patrolmen to arbitrate their quarrels authoritatively. Men who receive orders, whether they obey them or not, treat them as part of life as usual. Moreover, patrolmen find that disciplinary and coercive actions apparently do not affect their friendly relations with the persons against whom these actions are taken. Those who greet and chat with them are the very same men who have been disciplined, arrested, and ordered around in the past, and who expect to be thus treated again in the future. From all this, officers gather that though the people on skid row seek to evade police authority, they do not really object to it. Indeed, it happens quite frequently that officers encounter men who welcome being arrested and even actively ask for it. Finally, officers point out that sending someone to jail from skid row does not upset his relatives or his family life, does not cause him to miss work or lose a job, does not lead to his being reproached by friends and associates, does not lead to failure to meet commitments or protect investments, and does not conflict with any but the most passing intentions of the arrested person. Seasoned patrolmen are not oblivious to the irony of the fact that measures intended as mechanisms for distributing deserts can be used freely because these measures are relatively impotent in their effects.

SUMMARY AND CONCLUSIONS

It was the purpose of this chapter to render an account of a domain of police practice that does not seem subject to any system of external control. Following the terminology suggested by Banton, this practice was called keeping the peace. The procedures employed in keeping the peace are not determined by legal mandates but are, instead, responses to certain demand conditions. From among several demand conditions, we concentrated on the one produced by the concentration of certain types of persons in districts known as skid row. Patrolmen maintain that the lives of the inhabitants of the area are lacking in prospective coherence. The consequent reduction in the temporal horizon of predictability constitutes the main problem of keeping the peace on skid row.

Peacekeeping procedure on skid row consists of three elements. Patrolmen seek to acquire a rich body of concrete knowledge about people by cultivating personal acquaintance with as many residents as possible. They tend to proceed against persons mainly on the basis of perceived risk, rather than on the basis of culpability. And they are more interested in reducing the aggregate total of troubles in the area than in evaluating individual cases according to merit.

There may seem to be a discrepancy between the skid-row patrolman's objective of preventing disorder and his efforts to maintain personal acquaintance with as many persons as possible. But these efforts are principally a tactical device. By knowing someone individually the patrolman reduces ambiguity, extends trust and favors, but does not grant immunity. The informality of interaction on skid row always contains some indications of the hierarchical superiority of the patrolman and the reality of his potential power lurks in the background of every encounter.

Though our interest was focused initially on those police procedures that did not involve invoking the law, we found that the two cannot be separated. The reason for the connection is not given in the circumstance that the roles of the law officer and of the peace officer are enacted by the same person and thus are contiguous. According to our observations, patrolmen do not act alternatively as one or the other, with certain actions being determined by the intended objective of keeping the peace and others being determined by the duty to enforce the law. Instead, we have found that *peacekeeping occasionally acquires the external aspects of law enforcement*. This makes it specious to inquire whether or not police discretion in invoking the law conforms with the intention of some specific legal formula. The real reason behind an arrest is virtually always the actual state of particular social situations, or of the skid-row area in general.

We have concentrated on those procedures and considerations that skid-row patrolmen regard as necessary, proper, and
efficient relative to the circumstances in which they are employed. In this way, we attempted to disclose the conception of
the mandate to which the police feel summoned. It was entirely
outside the scope of the presentation to review the merits of
this conception and of the methods used to meet it. Only
insofar as patrolmen themselves recognized instances and patterns of malpractice did we take note of them. Most of the
criticism voiced by officers had to do with the use of undue
harshness and with the indiscriminate use of arrest powers
when these were based on personal feelings rather than the
requirements of the situation. According to prevailing opinion,
patrolmen guilty of such abuses make life unnecessarily difficult for themselves and for their co-workers. Despite disapproval of harshness, officers tend to be defensive about it. For
example, one sergeant who was outspokenly critical of brutality, said that though in general brutal men create more problems than they solve, "they do a good job in some situations for
which the better men have no stomach." Moreover, supervisory
personnel exhibit a strong reluctance to direct their subordinates in the particulars of their work performance. According
to our observations, control is exercised mainly through consultation with superiors, and directives take the form of requests rather than orders. In the background of all this is the
belief that patrol work on skid row requires a great deal of
discretionary freedom. In the words of the same sergeant
quoted above, "a good man has things worked out in his own
ways on his beat and he doesn't need anybody to tell him what
to do."

The virtual absence of disciplinary control and the demand
for discretionary freedom are related to the idea that patrol
work involves "playing by ear." For if it is true that peacekeeping cannot be systematically generalized, then, of course, it
cannot be organizationally constrained. What the seasoned
patrolman means, however, in saying that he "plays by ear" is
that he is making his decisions while being attuned to the
realities of complex situations about which he has immensely
detailed knowledge. This studied aspect of peacekeeping gen-

erally is not made explicit, nor is the tyro or the outsider made aware of it. Quite to the contrary, the ability to discharge the duties associated with keeping the peace is viewed as a reflection of an innate talent of "getting along with people." Thus, the same demands are made of barely initiated officers as are made of experienced practitioners. Correspondingly, beginners tend to think that they can do as well as their more knowledgeable peers. As this leads to inevitable frustrations, they find themselves in a situation that is conducive to the development of a particular sense of "touchiness." Personal dispositions of individual officers are, of course, of great relevance. But the license of discretionary freedom and the expectation of success under conditions of autonomy, without any indication that the work of the successful craftsman is based on an acquired preparedness for the task, is ready-made for failure and malpractice. Moreover, it leads to slipshod practices of patrol that also infect the standards of the careful craftsman.

The uniformed patrol, and especially the foot patrol, has a low preferential value in the division of labor of police work. This is, in part, at least, due to the belief that "anyone could do it." In fact, this belief is thoroughly mistaken. At present, however, the recognition that the practice requires preparation, and the process of obtaining the preparation itself, is left entirely to the practitioner.

NOTES

This essay previously appeared in *American Sociological Review* 32, no. 5 (October 1967): 699–715.

This research was supported in part by Grant 64–1–35 from the California Department of Mental Hygiene. I gratefully acknowledge the help I received from Fred Davis, Sheldon Messinger, Leonard Schatzman, and Anselm Strauss in the preparation of this paper.

1. The bill for a Metropolitan Police was actually enacted under the sponsorship of Robert Peel, the Home Secretary in the Tory Government of the Duke of Wellington. There is, however, no doubt that it was one of the several reform tendencies that Peel assimilated into Tory politics in his long career. Cf. J. L. Lyman, "The Metropolitan Police Act of 1829," *Journal of Criminal Law, Criminology, and Police Science* 55 (1964): 141–54.

2. Jerome Hall, "Police and Law in a Democratic Society," *Indiana Law Journal* 28 (1953): 133–77. Though other authors are less emphatic on this point, judicial control is generally taken for granted. The point has been made, however, that in modern times judicial control over the police has been asserted mainly because of the default of any other general controlling authority. Cf. E. L. Barrett, Jr., "Police Practice and the Law," *California Law Review* 50 (1962): 11–55.

3. A. C. German, F. D. Day, and R. R. J. Gallati, *Introduction to Law Enforcement* (Springfield, Ill.: C. C. Thomas, 1966). "One concept, in particular, should be kept in mind. A dictatorship can never exist unless the police system of the country is under the absolute control of the dictator. There is no other way to uphold a dictatorship except by terror, and the instrument of this total terror is the secret police, whatever its name. In every country where freedom has been lost, law enforcement has been a dominant instrument in destroying it" (80).

4. The point is frequently made; cf. Raymond B. Fosdick, *American Police Systems* (New York: Century Company, 1920); Bruce Smith, *Police Systems in the United States*, 2d rev. ed. (New York: Harper, 1960).

5. The executive margin of control is set mainly in terms of budgetary determinations and the mapping of some formal aspects of the organization of departments.

6. Michael Banton, *The Policeman in the Community* (New York: Basic Books, 1964), 6–7, 127ff.

7. R. Bruce Holmgren, *Primary Police Functions* (New York: William C. Copp, 1962).

8. Cf. Lyman, "Metropolitan Police Act," 153; F. C. Mather, *Public Order in the Age of the Chartists*, chap. 4 (Manchester: Manchester University Press, 1959). See also Robert H. Bremer, "Police, Penal and Parole Policies in Cleveland and Toledo," *American Journal of Economics and Sociology* 14 (1955): 387–98, for similar recognition in the United States at about the turn of this century.

9. Smith, *Police Systems*, 15ff.

10. Orlando W. Wilson, "Police Authority in a Free Society," *Journal of Criminal Law, Criminology, and Police Science* 54 (1964): 175–77.

11. Joseph Goldstein, "Police Discretion Not to Invoke the Criminal Process," *Yale Law Journal* 69 (1960): 543.

12. Jerome Skolnick, *Justice Without Trial* (New York: John Wiley & Sons, 1966).

13. Wayne LaFave, "The Police and Nonenforcement of the Law," *Wisconsin Law Review* (1962): 104–37, 179–239.

14. Nathan Goldman, *The Differential Selection of Juvenile Offenders*

for Court Appearance (Washington, D.C.: National Research and Information Center, National Council on Crime and Delinquency, 1963), 114ff.

15. Elaine Cumming, Ian Cumming, and Laura Edell, "Policeman as Philosopher, Guide, and Friend," *Social Problems* 12 (1965): 276–86.

16. There is little doubt that many requests for service are turned down by the police, especially when they are made over the telephone or by mail, cf. LaFave, "Police and Nonenforcement," n. 124. The uniformed patrolman, however, finds it virtually impossible to leave the scene without becoming involved in some way or another.

17. Hans Kelsen, *General Theory of Law and State* (New York: Russell & Russell, 1961), 278–79; H. L. A. Hart, *The Concept of Law* (Oxford: Clarendon Press, 1961), 20–21.

18. Mather, *Public Order*; see also, Jenifer Hart, "Reform of the Borough Police, 1835–1856," *English History Review* 70 (1955): 411–27.

19. Francis A. Allen, *The Borderland of Criminal Justice* (Chicago: University of Chicago Press, 1964).

20. Egon Bittner, "Police Discretion in Emergency Apprehension of Mentally Ill Persons," *Social Problems* 14 (1967): 278–92.

21. It bears mentioning, however, that differential treatment is not unique with the police, but is also in many ways representative for the administration of justice in general; cf. J. E. Carlin, Jan Howard, and S. L. Messinger, "Civil Justice and the Poor," *Law and Society* 1 (1966): 9–89; Jacobus tenBroek, ed. *The Law of the Poor* (San Francisco: Chandler Publishing Co., 1966).

22. This is, however, true only in the ideal. It is well known that a substantial number of persons who are arrested are subsequently released without ever being charged and tried, cf. Barret, *Police Practice.*

23. The literature on skid row is voluminous. The classic in the field is Nels Anderson, *The Hobo* (Chicago: University of Chicago Press, 1923). Samuel E. Wallace, *Skid-Row as a Way of Life* (Totowa, New Jersey: The Bedminster Press, 1965), is a more recent descriptive account and contains a useful bibliography. Donald A. Bogue, *Skid-Row in American Cities* (Chicago: Community and Family Center, University of Chicago, 1963), contains an exhaustive quantitative survey of a Chicago skid row.

24. One of the two cities described in this paper also employed the procedure of the "round-up" of drunks. In this, the police van toured the skid-row area twice daily, during the midafternoon and early

evening hours, and the officers who staffed it picked up drunks they sighted. A similar procedure is used in New York's Bowery and the officers who do it are called "condition men." Cf. *Bowery Project* (Bureau of Applied Social Research, Columbia University, Summary Report of a Study Undertaken under Contract Approved by the Board of Estimates, 1963, mimeo), 11.

25. An illuminating parallel to the perception of skid row can be found in the more traditional concept of vagabondage. Cf. Alexandre Vexliard, *Introduction à la Sociologie du Vagabondage* (Paris: Libraire Marcel Riviere, 1956), and "La Disparition du Vagabondage comme Fleau Social Universel," *Revue de L'Instut de Sociologie* (1963): 53–79. The classic account of English conditions up to the nineteenth century is C. J. Ribton-Turner, *A History of Vagrants and Vagrancy and Beggars and Begging* (London: Chapman and Hall, 1887).

26. Several patrolmen complained about the influx of "tourists" into skid row. Since such tourists are perceived as seeking illicit adventure, they receive little sympathy from patrolmen when they complain about being victimized.

27. The same officer commented further, "If a man looks for something, I might help him. But I don't stay with him till he finds what he is looking for. If I did, I would never get to do anything else. In the last analysis, I really never solve any problems. The best I can hope for is to keep things from getting worse."

28. When evidence is present to indicate that a serious crime has been committed, considerations of culpability acquire a position of priority. Two such arrests were observed, both involving checkpassers. The first offender was caught in flagrante delicto. In the second instance, the suspect attracted the attention of the patrolman because of his sickly appearance. In the ensuing conversation the man made some remarks that led the officer to place a call with the Warrant Division of his department. According to the information that was obtained by checking records, the man was a wanted checkpasser and was immediately arrested.

3 | *Police Discretion in Emergency Apprehension of Mentally Ill Persons*

THE OFFICIAL MANDATE of the police includes provisions for dealing with mentally ill persons. Since such dealings are defined in terms of civil law procedures, the mandate of the police is not limited to persons who for reasons of illness fail to observe the law. Rather, in suitable circumstances the signs of mental illness, or a competent allegation of mental illness, are in themselves the proper business of the police and can lead to authorized intervention. The expressed legal norms governing police involvement specify two major alternatives. On the one hand, policemen may receive court orders directing them to locate, apprehend, and convey named persons to specified hospitals for psychiatric observation and/or sanity hearings. On the other hand, policemen are authorized by statute to apprehend and convey to hospitals persons whom they perceive as ill, on an emergency basis. The first form parallels the common procedures of serving court warrants, while the second form involves the exercise of discretionary freedom that is ordinarily associated with making arrests without a warrant.[1]

The study reported in this chapter concerns the rules and considerations underlying the exercise of discretion in emergency apprehensions. The findings are based on ten months of field work with the uniformed police patrol of a large West Coast city, and on psychiatric records of the hospital receiving all police referrals.[2] We shall first consider certain attitudinal and organizational factors involved in making emergency apprehensions. Next, we shall discuss the manifest properties of cases in which emergency apprehensions are frequently made. Finally, we shall deal with procedures directed toward recognized mentally ill persons who are not referred to the hospital. In the conclusion, we shall argue that the decision to invoke the law governing emergency apprehensions is not based on an appraisal of objective features of cases. Rather, the decision is a residual resource, the use of which is determined largely by the absence of other alternatives. The domain of alternatives is found in normal peacekeeping activities in which considerations of legality play a decidedly subordinate role. We shall also allude to the fact that our interpretation has important bearing on the problem of police discretion to invoke the law in general.[3]

ORGANIZATIONAL AND ATTITUDINAL FACTORS INFLUENCING EMERGENCY APPREHENSIONS

The statutory authorization under which apprehensions of the mentally ill are made provides that an officer may take steps to initiate confinement in a psychiatric hospital when he believes "as the result of his own observations, that the person is mentally ill and because of his illness is likely to injure himself or others if not immediately hospitalized."[4] It is fair to say that under ordinary circumstances police officers are quite reluctant to invoke this law. That is, in situations where, according to their own judgment, they are dealing with an apparently mentally ill person they will generally seek to employ other means to bring the existing problem under control. This does not mean that they attempt to deal with the problem as if it did not involve a mentally ill person, or as if this person's illness were none of their business. It merely means that they will try to avoid taking him to the hospital.

The avoidance of emergency apprehensions has a background that might be called doctrinal.[5] To take someone to the hospital means giving the facts of his illness formal recognition and using them as grounds for official action. The police, however, disavow all competence in matters pertaining to psychopathology and seek to remain within the lines of restraint that the disavowal imposes. Accordingly, the diagnosis they propose is not only emphatically provisional but also, in a sense, incidental. From their point of view it is not enough for a case to be serious in a "merely" psychiatric sense. To warrant official police action a case must also present a serious problem. As a general rule, the elements that make a case a serious police matter are indications that if a referral is not made, external troubles will proliferate. Among these, danger to life, to physical health, to property, and to order in public places, are objects of prominent concern. Estimating the risk of internal deterioration of the psychiatric condition as such is perceived as lying outside of the scope of police competence and thus not an adequate basis for making emergency apprehensions.

While a narrow construction of the police mandate might have the consequence of eliminating certain cases from the purview of official police interest, it does not eliminate the possibility of liberal use of the authorization. Thus, it might be expected that officers would tend to refer relatively few persons who are "merely" very ill psychiatrically but many persons who are troublesome without being very ill. This expectation seems especially reasonable since the police recently have been denied the use of certain coercive means they have employed in the past to control troublesome persons.[6] On a practical level such procedures would simply follow considerations of expediency, with the law providing a particular method and justification for taking care of matters that need be taken care of.[7] Indeed, given the heavy emphasis that mental hygiene receives in police training, it would be scarcely appropriate to attribute devious motives to the police if they were to use the "narrow construction" of the law "widely," for in many instances of untoward, but not necessarily illegal, behavior, the evidence of more or less serious psychopathology is close to the surface.[8] In fact, however, policemen do not make such use of the law. Instead, they conform in practice very closely to the views they profess. To make an emergency apprehension they require that there be indications of serious external risk accompanied by signs of a serious psychological disorder. There exist several attitudinal and organizational factors that help to explain the reluctance of the police to take official steps on the basis of the assumption or allegation of mental illness.

First, the views and knowledge of the police about mental illness are in close agreement with the views and knowledge of the public in general. Policemen, like everyone else, appear to have a correct conception of the nature of mental illness, in terms of standards of modern psychiatry, but like everyone else they avail themselves of various forms of denial when it comes to doing something about it.[9] The facts come into consciousness, as it were, without implying practical consequences; or, at least, the import of the facts is set aside in view of other considerations. Since the police almost always act on fragmentary information, their reasons for not taking any official steps are posted, among others, in the undetermined aspects of the case that must be presumed to have some undefined relevance. For example, one of the possibilities that officers must always consider is the chance that their involvement could be exploited by unknown persons for unknown reasons. Since they are not expert in symptoms of psychopathology, their desire to avoid possible future embarrassment is quite strong.

Second, policemen confront perversion, disorientation, misery, irresoluteness, and incompetence much more often than any other social agent. They can readily point to a large number of persons who, to all appearances, are ready for the "booby hatch," but who nevertheless seem to lead such lives as they can without outside aid or intervention. Against this background the requirement that one should have a good brain and an even temper belong to the same category of wishes as that one should have a large and steady income. Thus, making emergency apprehensions is, among others, a matter of economy. Lower the standards somewhat and the number of apprehensions might be multiplied by a substantial factor. Similar considerations apply to making various types of arrests. Though the police could readily multiply the number of arrests for some petty offenses, they somehow manage to produce just the right number to keep the courts busy and the jails full. With the same uncanny instinct they burden the hospital just to the limit of its capacity.

Third, though policemen readily acknowledge that dealing

with mentally ill persons is an integral part of their work, they hold that it is not a proper task for them. Not only do they lack training and competence in this area but such dealings are stylistically incompatible with the officially propounded conception of the policeman's principal vocation. It involves none of the skills, acumen, and prowess that characterize the ideal image of a first-rate officer. Given the value that is assigned to such traits in furthering a man's career, and as grounds for esteem among his co-workers, it is a foregone conclusion that conveying a "mental case" to the hospital will never take the place of catching Willie Sutton in the choice of worthwhile activities. The opportunities for making spectacular arrests are not so widely available to the uniformed patrolman as to compete for attention with the emergency apprehensions of mentally ill persons, but the established ways of collecting credits with one's superiors work against the development of voluntary interest with patients.

Fourth, officers complain that taking someone to the psychiatric service of the hospital is a tedious, cumbersome, and uncertain procedure. They must often wait a long time in the admitting office and are occasionally obliged to answer questions of the admitting psychiatrist that appear to place their own judgment in doubt. They must also reckon with the possibility of being turned down by the psychiatrist, in which case they are left with an aggravated problem on their hands. The complaints about the hospital must be understood in the light of a strong and widely respected rule of police procedure. The rule demands that an officer bring all cases assigned to him to some sort of closure within reasonable limits of time and effort. The ability to take care of things in a way that avoids protracted and complicated entanglements and does not cause repercussions is, in fact, a sign of accomplished craftsmanship in police work that runs a close second to the ability to make important arrests. Relative to this standard, contacts with the hospital and the attitudes of psychiatrists are a source of endless frustration. Policemen are often puzzled by the hospital's refusal to lend its resources to help in keeping life outside free of violence and disorder; and, though they are relatively rarely turned down by admitting psychiatrists, many officers can cite cases in which persons who were not accepted into the hospital brought grief upon themselves and others.

Fifth, in addition to these experiences, certain other facts about the hospital exercise a restraining influence upon the making of emergency apprehensions. All officers are explicitly aware that taking someone to the hospital is a civil rather than a criminal matter. They are continually reminded of this distinction, and they employ the appropriate linguistic conventions in referring to such cases and in talking with ill persons and their relatives. The actual situation belies all this euphemizing and officers are unavoidably aware of this too. Ill persons are, indeed, arrested on account of being ill. They are not taken to the jail, to be sure, but they are nevertheless locked up. The knowledge that the mental hospital is a place in which to lock people up is inferentially prior to the making of emergency apprehensions. It is only natural that officers would infer from witnessed hospital procedures with mentally ill patients to the conditions that presumably warrant them. To think otherwise would impugn the whole system, which operates not only under medical supervision but also under the auspices of the courts. Thus, in making an emergency apprehension the officer has to consider whether the person in question presents risks of such magnitude as warrant his confinement together with the rest of the "crazy" people who apparently require this sort of treatment.[10]

CONDITIONS SURROUNDING EMERGENCY APPREHENSIONS

Despite the strong reluctance of the police, emergency apprehensions of mentally ill persons are quite frequent. Indeed, officers of the uniformed patrol make them about as often as they arrest persons for murder, all types of manslaughter, rape, robbery, aggravated assault, and grand theft, taken together; and more than one fifth of all referrals to the receiving psychiatric service of the public hospital come from this source.[11]

In only a very few instances does the emergency apprehension involve the use of physical coercion. In most cases patients are passively compliant or at least manageable by means of verbal influence. At times patients go willingly, or perhaps even voluntarily.[12] In approximately half of the cases policemen encounter the patient without any warning. This happens either when officers run into the person in the course of patrolling or when they are dispatched to some address by radio, without any indication of the nature of the problem they will have to deal with. In the other half, officers are informed that they will have to deal with a possible "mental case."[13] Though the observations on which this account is based do not permit a firm inference in this matter, it appears that prior labeling does not play a role in the formation of the policeman's decision to make an apprehension.

Five types of circumstances in which emergency apprehensions are made anywhere from often to virtually always can be isolated. It is important to define the nature of this inventory. Policemen typically do not reach the conclusion that an apprehension should be made by searching for, or finding, such features as we shall enumerate. Thus, these are not, in any real sense, criterion situations. Furthermore, each of the five types encompasses cases that are linked by the rule of analogy rather than by the rule of identity.[14] By this we do not mean merely that actual instances differ over a wide range of permissible variations. Rather, we propose that the membership of any particular case in a class, or in the scheme of classes in general, is based less on the presence or absence of specific characteristics than on the judgment that the case *amounts* to being of this or that class. If such a conclusion is to be reached, the case must not be allowed to dissolve into its particulars. Instead, the conclusion is reached as much by attending to the case as such, as it is reached by attending to its contextual background.

The following three horizons of context appear to matter in cases of referable mental illness: First, the *scenic* horizon, consisting of all the more or less stable features of the background that can be brought into play as employable resources to handle the problem, or that may assume the character of added reasons for making the emergency apprehension. Second, the *temporal* horizon, including both the changing nature of the problem as it is being attended to and what can be known or surmised about its past and future. Third, the *manipulative* horizon, which consists of considerations of practicality from the standpoint of the police officer. For example, an officer may encounter a mentally ill person in some such circumstances as we shall presently describe. He may learn that the person is a member of a stable and resourceful kinship group and that relatives can be mobilized to take care of him. In addition, there is information that the person has been in a similar state before and that he received outpatient psychiatric attention at that time. Whether this person will be moved to the hospital might then depend on whether others can take over within the limits of time the officer can allocate to waiting for them to arrive on the scene. The manipulative horizon is of particular interest and we shall discuss it more extensively in the section of this chapter dealing with persons who are not referred to the hospital.

One further explanation—our description of the five categories of cases does not imply that officers themselves employ subcategories to classify mentally ill persons when they refer them to the hospital on an emergency basis. Rather, we propose the inventory as a scheme of prototypes to which policemen analogize in practice when they are confronted with a mentally ill person.

1. When there is evidence that a person has attempted, or is attempting, suicide he is virtually always taken to the hospital. Occasionally officers have doubts about the genuineness of the attempt, but such doubts do not seem to weigh significantly against making the apprehension. In some instances the evidence in support of the presumption that an attempt has been made, or is contemplated, is ambiguous. In such cases the prevailing practice is to act on the basis of positive indications. Furthermore, the information that an attempt has been made appears to be a sufficient indication in itself for an emergency apprehension. Not only is it not necessary for the victim to exhibit other signs of a mental disorder but there is no way in which a person can demonstrate that he is not in need of psychiatric attention, once the facts of the attempt have been adequately established. Both the most playful and the most rationally considered suicide attempts are treated as suggesting

serious morbidity. The only circumstance under which officers can be dissuaded from taking a potential victim to the hospital is when a physician officially assumes responsibility for the case. Finally, when officers confront a person who shows patent signs of a mental disorder and they learn that this person has in the past attempted suicide, this information is apt to contribute significantly to the decision to make an emergency apprehension, even if the earlier attempts are not clearly connected with the present episode. In short, suicide presents the "ideal" combination of serious psychopathology and serious police business.

2. When the signs of a serious psychological disorder, that is, expressions of radically incongruous affect or thought, are accompanied by distortions of normal physical appearance, the person in question is usually taken to the hospital. Such things as injuries of unknown origin, seizures, urinary incontinence, odd posturing, nudity, extreme dirtiness, and so on, all tend to augment the import of psychological indications. All such features are perceived as signifying loss of control over one's appearance and as adequate grounds to expect a further proliferation of external problems. An apprehension will not be made, however, if the situation contains features indicating a mere momentary lapse of control. For example, in a case in which the police were summoned to deal with a severely retarded person living with her parents, the officers helped in restoring the normally functioning restraint and supervision. Scenically, the home environment offered a sufficient guarantee of control; historically, the situation was known to have been managed adequately in the past; and, manipulatively, the disruption could be remedied within reasonable time and with the cooperation of all parties who had a legitimate stake in the case.

3. When the signs of serious psychological disorder are expressed in highly agitated forms, and especially when they are accompanied by incipient or actual acts of violence, the person is often taken to the hospital. Two further conditions must be met, however, before the apprehension is seriously considered. The violence or the threat of violence must be nontrivial. For example, a feeble and senile old woman assault-

ing her normally healthy son will not be taken to the hospital, but the son may be advised about the availability of hospitalization. Furthermore, the agitated person must be largely unresponsive to efforts to pacify him.

4. Persons who appear to be seriously disoriented, or who by acting incongruously create a nuisance in a public place, are often taken to the hospital. Ordinarily policemen will make an effort to induce the person to leave the scene while helping him on his way to his normal habitat. Only when it becomes clear that such a person cannot be expediently returned to a sheltered place, or remanded to some caretaker, and when he is in danger of suffering injury due to accident or exposure, will he be taken to the hospital.

5. In the cases named so far the police act mainly on the basis of firsthand observation. Though there is always a certain amount of received information present, it plays a secondary role in the decision making. The fifth category, however, is based primarily on received information. When requests for police aid come from complainants who stand to the allegedly mentally ill person in some sort of instrumental relationship, that is, from physicians, lawyers, teachers, employers, landlords, and so on, the police generally, though by no means always, move the patient to the hospital.[15] It is usually assumed that the instrumentally related persons have exhausted their power and duty to help before calling the police and that there is little else left to do but to make an emergency apprehension. Interestingly, however, similar circumstances, made by family members, friends, roommates, or neighbors are usually not honored. Thus, for example, a severely depressed person may be taken to the hospital from his place of employment, on the urging of a doctor or his employer, both of whom presumably have already attempted alternative solutions, while he would be left in the care of his parent with the advice that the parent seek hospitalization for the patient.

The five types of circumstances in which emergency apprehensions are typically made are, of course, not mutually exclusive. Indeed, most actual cases are, in terms of their external circumstances, overdetermined. The general impression one gets from observing the police is that, except for cases of suicide attempts, the decision to take someone to the hospital is based on overwhelmingly conclusive evidence of illness. The very stringency of criteria would lead one to expect that the police often deal with persons who are also seriously ill but whom they do not take to the hospital. In our description of the five types we have already alluded to the fact that this is in fact so. We have also mentioned earlier that such persons do not fall outside the purview of police interest once it is decided that they need not be apprehended. We now turn to the description of alternative methods of handling mentally ill persons, about which no records are kept.

NONOFFICIAL WAYS OF DEALING WITH MENTALLY ILL PERSONS

The following description of police dealings with mentally ill persons concerns cases in which formal emergency apprehensions are not made. We shall concentrate on encounters in which officers explicitly recognize signs of mental illness and in which they treat the illness as the primary and, in most instances, the only business at hand. That is, we will not be dealing with cases such as, for example, those involving an offender about whom policemen say, after they have arrested him, "What a nut!" Nor will we deal with cases involving various types of troublesome persons who are perceived to be, among other things, "slightly crazy." To be sure, in actual police work there exists no clear-cut dividing line segregating persons who are blatantly mentally ill from persons who are "slightly crazy." For clarity, however, we shall concentrate on extreme cases.

De Facto Emergency Apprehensions

To begin, we must consider certain types of police involvement that straddle the borderline between making and not making apprehensions. In such cases the patient usually ends up in the hospital but the police manage to avoid taking formal action. Insofar as the officers have no official part in the decision and thus no responsibilities, these cases might be considered de facto but not de jure emergency apprehensions. Occasionally policemen are summoned to aid in the move of a recalcitrant patient. The move is actually under way and the officers are merely expected, in their own words, to "do the dirty work." Though officers cannot readily avoid responding to such requests they typically do not employ coercive means. Instead, they remain in the background as a safety precaution against the possibility that the situation might get out of hand. Beyond that, they disperse curious onlookers, and at times provide help such as calling for an ambulance or a taxi. By and large, they do nothing that will change the course of the ongoing development. They interpret their presence as having the value of making something that is already fully determined as peaceful and painless as possible. Insofar as they speak to the patient at all, they restrict their remarks to indicating that the move is legitimate and in his best interest. In fact, the officers are usually the only persons on the scene who listen attentively to the patient and who use the leverage of trust to facilitate the move. Though such cases do not involve police initiative and involve no police decisions, the successful accomplishment of these referrals actually does depend on the availability of police aid. The very fact that the person who made the decision solicited help is an indication that he could probably not have prevailed by himself, or at least not on that occasion. Generally, police officers do not accompany the patient to the hospital and their involvement is not a matter of record.

Another form of de facto apprehension occurs when officers transport a person whom they recognize as mentally ill to a medical emergency service. In such cases it is necessary, of course, that there be present some sort of physical complaint in addition to the psychiatric complaint. It is generally expected that the admitting physician will make the further referral to the psychiatric service. By this method policemen avoid taking formal action on account of mental illness and also, incidentally, avoid having to deal with psychiatric staff which they find much more cumbersome than dealing with medical staff. Only rarely are records kept of these cases; such records as do exist identify the interventions as aiding a sick person rather than making an emergency apprehension.

Restitution of Control

By far the larger number of police encounters with mentally ill persons results neither in de jure nor in de facto emergency apprehensions. Rather, the involvements begin and end in the field. No other social agency, either legal or medical, participates in these cases and the policeman acts as the terminal, all-purpose remedial agent.

While discussing typical emergency apprehension situations we mentioned that officers often try to find competent persons to whom they may relinquish the care of the patient, or they try to return the ill person to his normal habitat in which he presumably can manage his affairs with minimal adequacy. Only in rare instances is this a simple "lost persons" problem. In these relatively rare cases, persons with stable social ties and fixed positions in the community escape the normally functioning controls or suffer a breakdown away from home. Whenever circumstances indicate that this is the case, the police will bring their technical communication and transportation facilities into play to locate caretakers for the patient. Though this is by no means always easy, it is a relatively simple problem. It may not be possible to find the caretakers within the time that can be allocated to the search, but the problem at least has a solution. In fact, when the caretakers cannot be expediently located, and the ill person is taken to the hospital, the search for the caretakers continues for the sake of informing them where the patient is. As a last resort, the identity of the lost mentally ill person is entered in the lost persons record to make it possible to respond to inquiries of caretakers. In general, however, the police are ready to devote a good deal of effort to returning persons to circumstances in which they are sheltered. As might be expected, however, persons with stable social ties and fixed positions in the community only rarely depend on the aid of the police and in many such instances the fact that the person is abroad is known before he is located because of inquiries of frantic relatives.

Much more difficult are cases in which the ill person cannot be presumed to be someone's responsibility in a structured sense, and whose living arrangements are unstable. In such cases the high proficiency of the police in tracing leads and in locating viable support are noteworthy. To solve such problems the officer invokes his detailed knowledge of people and places in the district he patrols. This knowledge, as often as not, permits him to guess who the person is and where he normally belongs. Failing this, the officer will know where to look and whom to ask for information. Bits and fragments of evidence have high informational value because the officer can fill in the missing parts out of past experiences in the same locale and with related persons.

This informational advantage is useful not only in the search for caretakers but also functions as the context for the considered transfer of responsibility. For while it is true that officers generally welcome opportunities to be rid of a mentally ill person, they are not uncritical about whom they will yield to. In one observed instance, for example, a young woman in agitated distress was taken to the hospital in part because her fiancé arrived on the scene and proposed to take over. Prior to his arrival the officers were about ready to leave the patient in the care of her mother and a neighbor who appeared to have a soothing influence on her. The entry of the fiancé seemed quite innocuous to the observer, but the officers gathered from his remarks that the arrangements he had in mind were not only not feasible but even destructive. The evaluation was possible because the officers knew many factual details about the places, persons, and arrangements the man envisioned. It is important to emphasize that the critical approach is not pursued by deliberate inquiry and scrutiny of all aspects of cases and decisions. Rather, the informational advantage of the officers automatically raises the level of demand for plausibility. That is, they can judge whether some proposed solution is practical and acceptable with reference to empirical details of particular known places, at specified times, and in known social contexts. In the instance cited, this background information persuaded the officers that the patient could not be left safely unattended.

Among the types of persons to whom policemen most readily transfer responsibilities are family members and physicians. It is, however, not unusual to find neighbors, hotel clerks, landlords, bartenders, or shopkeepers entrusted with someone who is mentally ill. Especially in blighted parts of the city such persons are known to "keep an eye" on certain others. In such areas the policeman often stands in the midst of a referral and information system that is unstable and informally fluid, but the network of connections is so rich and ramified that an accredited member of the system is scarcely ever completely at a loss. For example, an officer might learn from a news vendor that a certain bartender might know someone who knows something about a senile old lady. If the bartender does not happen to be on duty, some patron in the bar, or the pawnbroker across the street might know. Here it is important to emphasize that news vendors and bartenders are not so much good sources of information, as that they become good sources of information, and incidentally also good resource persons, when the officer knows them personally and is personally known to them. The officer's superior competence is to a large extent dependent on the fact that he is accepted as a powerful and in certain ways uniquely authoritative member of a system of mutual aid.

Unfortunately, we know very little about the ways in which people in blighted areas of the city corroborate each others' identity and augment each others' feeble powers. But there is no doubt that the policeman is the only social agent who has some access to the functioning of this arrangement, and the only one who can employ it knowledgeably for the protection and aid of its members. The unique effectiveness of the officer as a quasi member of this community hinges on the fact that he can invoke the powers of coercion; the effectiveness of this resource would be, however, drastically reduced if he were not also an insider who understands the dominant interests and attitudes of the denizens. It is the officer's grasp of the stable aspects of the social structure of life in slums, in rooming house sections, and in business districts—aspects that often elude the attention of outside observers—that permits him to find alternatives to the emergency hospitalization of mentally ill persons. In certain ways, dealing with persons who inhabit blighted parts of urban areas is an easier task for a seasoned foot patrolman than dealing with persons who have stable addresses and social ties, although, of course, once the latter are located a more permanent solution is guaranteed.

The relative stability of circumstances to which a mentally ill person can be returned is, of course, distributed on a continuum. At one extreme there are those patients who need only be conveyed to worried relatives, and at the other extreme there are those who can only be returned to a status of inconspicuous anonymity. With the latter, as with those who have some tenuous ties, the problem of letting the patient slip back into his normal groove is adumbrated with questions whether the normally working controls can be entrusted with "taking care of the problem." In terms of the policeman's own standards of proper procedure it is scarcely ever sufficient to remove the patient from sight. What is intended, instead, is the achievement of a solution of some degree of permanency. Although the officer's own altruism is the main acknowledged motivational impetus for this activity, the achievement of this goal is also a practical necessity. To settle for less than an adequate solution is apt to result in repeated calls and more work.

"Psychiatric First Aid"

The involvement of the police with mentally ill persons who are not taken to the hospital is not confined to finding responsible caretakers for them, or to taking them to their normally sheltered place. Nor is this always the problem at hand, for quite often the very person who is most eligible for this role is the one who solicited police intervention. In these cases officers always administer some sort of direct "psychiatric first aid," even though they repudiate this designation. It is extremely rare that officers encounter a patient who is too passive or too withdrawn for interaction of some sort. In fact, most of the patients the police encounter are in states of relatively high agitation and can be drawn into an exchange. From the officer's point of view, his task consists of monitoring the transition of a state of affairs from its dangerous phase to a phase of relative safety and normalcy.

Although police training and literature have come to include references to the handling of mentally ill persons, it is fair to say that officers are not instructed in anything that deserves to be called a technique. With no more to go on than the maxims of kindness and caution, officers tend to fall back on being formally correct policemen. To start, seasoned officers invariably remove the patient from the immediate context in which they find him. In this they merely follow good police practice in general, applicable to all types of persons who attract police attention. The object is to establish boundaries of control and to reduce the complexity of the problem.[16] When it is not feasible to move the patient, the context is altered by removing others. The result in either case is the envelopment of the subject by police attention.

In direct dealings with the patient the policeman tries to establish and maintain the pretense of a normal conversational situation. All of the patient's remarks, allegations, or complaints are treated in a matter-of-fact manner. Policemen do not attempt to suppress or eliminate the absurd and bizarre, but rather leave them aside while concentrating verbal exchanges on the ordinary aspects of things. By this method every situation acquires a certain sense of normalcy. For example, in one observed instance a middle-aged lady complained, in highly agitated panic, that she was pursued by neighbors with an unheard-of weapon. Without questioning the lady's beliefs about what is possible in the domain of weaponry, or what might be reasonably assumed about the motives of angry neighbors, the officers went through the motions of dealing with the situation as if it involved a bona fide complaint. They searched the premises for nonexistent traces of impossible projectiles. They carefully took note of mundane particulars of events that could not have happened and advised the lady to be on the alert for suspicious occurrences in the future. The intervention, which lasted approximately one hour, terminated when the lady came to equate her predicament with the predicament of all other persons who were under some sort of threat and who apparently survive under police protection. She was visibly calmed and expressed the belief that the officers understood what she was facing and that it was within their capacity to ensure her safety. In the end, the conversation turned to such practical matters as how to summon the police quickly in situations of imminent danger and how to make doubly sure that locks on windows and doors were secure. Throughout the conversation the officers gave no hint that they doubted any part of the story. They did not challenge the statement that a projectile may travel through walls, furniture, and clothes without leaving any traces but be, nevertheless, fatal to persons. They also took pains to convince the lady that it would be tactically unwise and impractical to arrest or even interview suspected neighbors at this stage of the case.

Although the method of field work, as employed in this study, does not permit the formulation of reliable estimates of frequencies, it can be said that neither the observations nor the interviews with policemen suggested that the distribution of "psychiatric first aid" is anything but random, relative to social class. Furthermore, such interventions sometimes involve patients exhibiting signs of very serious psychopathology. In general, agitated patients receive much more careful and protracted attention than patients who are overtly passive, which accords with the fact that officers give high priority to risks of proliferation of external troubles. Finally, although the police occasionally encounter the same patient repeatedly, they tend to treat each confrontation as a separate emergency. Every precinct station has a fund of knowledge about persons who have been the subjects of past "psychiatric first aid," but there is no sustained concern for these persons. Whenever certain known persons come to the attention of officers, it is said that they are "acting up again." The avoidance of sustained concern and attention is part of the official posture of the police and an expression of the fact that the illness as such is of little interest and that it acquires relevance only through its unpredictable exacerbations.

The attitudes and procedures of "psychiatric first aid" are in a general sense representative of the overall involvement of the police with mental illness. The attitudes and procedures also play a role in cases in which emergency apprehensions are made. In the latter instances they provide, in part, the background for the decision, in the sense that if these measures do not succeed in reducing the potential of the external risk, the patient will be taken to the hospital. Thus, the practice of "psychiatric first aid" and the skill that it involves represent the core of what we earlier identified as the manipulative horizon of relevance in the decision-making process. The point to be emphasized about these interventions is that they involve no basic modification of police posture but rather its use for the particular purposes of dealing with patients. Though the officers are fully aware that they are dealing with mentally ill persons, they do not act in the manner of quasi mental health specialists.

Continuing Care

After having placed proper emphasis on the generally prevalent pattern of the episodic, emergency, and *ad hoc* involvement of policemen with mentally ill persons, we turn to a significantly less frequent type of activity practiced by a limited number of patrolmen. In contrast with "psychiatric first aid," foot patrolmen, especially when they work in the slum, tenderloin, business, or rooming house districts of the city, know some mentally ill persons with whom they have established a more or less regularized pattern of running into each other. Some of these persons are apparently chronic schizophrenics, others seem mentally defective, and others are senile. Many have a history of past hospitalization. Though the officers do not attempt to diagnose these persons, they recognize the presence of substantial psychological handicaps. Indeed, the officer's interaction with and interest in these people is basically structured by the consideration that they suffer from serious disorders.

The encounters are so highly routinized that they scarcely have an event-character of their own. It is part of the ordinary routine for a foot patrolman to meet people and to engage them in conversations. Each encounter is in its own way thematized. The themes occasionally are determined in terms of the prevailing contingencies of situations. For the most part, however, the exchanges are better understood, and often can only be understood, as episodes in long-standing relationships, with past exchanges furnishing the tacit background for presently exchanged remarks. This format of meetings holds also for the encounters with known mental patients, except that in these cases the encounters are thematized by the person's psychological handicap. Officers acknowledge that their approach and manipulation of the patient is deliberately organized around this concern.

In one observed instance a young man approached an officer in a deteriorating business district of the city. He voiced an almost textbook-type paranoid complaint. From the statements and the officer's responses it could be gathered that this was a part of a sequence of conversations. The two proceeded to walk away from an area of high traffic density to quieter parts of the neighborhood. In the ensuing stroll the officer inspected various premises, greeted passers-by, and generally showed a low level of attentiveness. After about twenty-five minutes the man bade the officer good-bye and indicated that he would be going home now. The officer stated that he runs into this man quite often and usually on the same spot. He always tries to lead the man away from the place that apparently excites his paranoid suspicions. The expressions of inattentiveness are calculated to impress the person that there is nothing to worry about, while, at the same time, the efforts the man must make to hold the officer's interest absorb his energies. This method presumably makes the thing talked about a casual matter and mere small talk. Thus, the practices employed in sustained contacts involve, like the practices of "psychiatric first aid," the tendencies to confine, to disregard pathological material, and to reduce matters to their mundane aspects.

CONCLUSION

Certain structural and organizational restraints leading to an apparent reluctance on the part of the police to invoke the law governing emergency apprehensions of mentally ill persons were discussed. Next we described the external properties of situations in which the law is often invoked. This approach left a seemingly residual category of cases in which persons are judged to be mentally ill but are not taken to the hospital. The category is residual, however, only in conjunction with one particular conception of the nature of police work.

According to this conception the police act with competence and authority only when their actions can be subsumed under the heading of some legal mandate. If the conditions for making an arrest or an emergency apprehension are not satisfied, then, presumably, an officer has no further legitimate business with the case. It is universally accepted that the police could not possibly conform fully to this rule. Not only is it inevitable, but it has been said to be desirable that officers use a variety of means in keeping the peace.

In real police work the provisions contained in the law represent a resource that can be invoked to handle certain problems. Beyond that, the law contains certain guidelines about the boundaries of legality. Within these boundaries, however, there is located a vast array of activities that are in no important sense determined by considerations of legality. In fact, in cases in which invoking the law is not a foregone conclusion, as for example in many minor offenses or in the apprehension of mentally ill persons, it is only speciously true to say that the law determined the act of apprehension, and much more correct to say that the law made the action possible. The effective reasons for the action are not located in the formulas of statutes but in considerations that are related to established practices of dealing informally with problems.[17]

The important point about the relevance of established practice is that it contains the means and considerations in terms of which judgments are made whether there is any need to invoke the law. The practices are, of course, responsive to influences from the courts, from prosecutors, and the public. They also stand in some relationship of correspondence to the intent of the law. Some problems are routinely handled by invoking the law, in other cases it is merely one of the available alternatives. In these latter cases it is possible that an officer who merely complies with the law may nevertheless be found to be an incompetent practitioner of his craft. About him it may be said that he should have been able to handle the problem in some other way. The other ways of handling are not explicitly codified and they undoubtedly depend on personal ingenuity on the part of the officer. Their foundation, however, is in a transmittable skill.

When one defines these established practices as the focal point of reference of police function, instead of ministerial law enforcement, then the cases of mentally ill persons who are not referred to hospitals do not constitute a residual category. Instead, "psychiatric first aid" appears as the standard practice that contains within the realms of its possibilities the emergency apprehension. In certain cases, as for example in cases involving suicide attempts, the apprehension is virtually a foregone conclusion, but in general it is viewed as merely one of several ways of solving problems. It happens to be the only visible alternative, but this is an artifact resulting from existing police recording systems that note only those actions that involve ministerial law enforcement. Indeed, it can safely be said that the proper understanding of recorded interventions hinges on the knowledge of cases for which there is no official record. When, for example, we say that one of the necessary conditions for the emergency apprehension is the discernment of the risk of proliferation of external troubles, then we must add that these are such perceived risks as cannot be controlled by the ordinarily available means contained in the standard practices. Thus, to understand the perception of risk it is necessary to know the structure of what can be and is normally done to control it.

In this chapter we have tried to describe briefly certain practices of dealing with mentally ill persons and we have argued that the structure and means contained in these practices determine who will be referred to the hospital on an emergency basis. The external characteristics of cases are not irrelevant to the decisions, but their import is always mediated by practical considerations of what can and need be done alternatively. We should like to propose that such procedures as finding responsible caretakers who will "look out" for the patient, or "psychiatric first aid," or the sustained interest in some patients by foot patrolmen, are part of a larger domain of police work. We further propose that this work, which has been called "keeping the peace,"[18] in differentiation from "enforcing the law," consists of occupational routines with particular procedures, skills, standards, and information, in short, of craft, that meets certain tacit public expectations.[19] Chances are that when police decisions are viewed from the perspective of the requirements of this craft, rather than with an interest in seeking to discover how well they correspond to the conventional formalities of the law, they may appear quite a bit less adventitious than they are generally perceived to be. To say, however, that there exists a body of methodically organized routines for keeping the peace, which in some sense influence police decisions to invoke the law, in no way settles the question whether the currently prevailing patterns of police discretion are desirable or not. It merely urges that the study of it will furnish a more realistic basis for appraisal.

NOTES

This essay previously appeared in *Social Problems* 14, no. 3 (Winter 1967): 278–92.

This research was supported in part by Grant 64–1–35 from the California Department of Mental Hygiene. I gratefully acknowledge the help I have received from Sheldon L. Messinger in preparing this paper.

1. See, for example, *Welfare and Institutions Code*, State of California, Division 6, pt 1, chap. 1.

2. The city has a population of approximately three-quarters of a million inhabitants and is patrolled by a uniformed police force of approximately 1,000 men. The receiving hospital is a public institution. Its psychiatric inpatient service registered a demand population of 7,500 during the period of the study, July 1, 1963, to June 30, 1964. Eighty-eight percent of this population has been accepted for observation and such short-term care as is ordinarily associated with it. The average length of stay of patients is just short of five days, with a distribution that is heavily skewed toward shorter stays. The hospital also houses a department of the court that holds sanity hearings.

3. The problem referred to is treated in Joseph Goldstein, "Police Discretion Not to Invoke the Criminal Process," *Yale Law Journal* 69 (1960): 543–94; W. R. LaFave, "The Police and Non-enforcement of the Law," *Wisconsin Law Review* (1962): 104–37, 179–239; S. H. Kadish, "Legal Norms and Discretion in the Police and Sentencing Process," *Harvard Law Review* 75 (1962): 904–31; I. Piliavin and S. Scott, "Police Encounters with Juveniles," *American Journal of Sociology* 70 (1964): 206–14; Nial Osborough, "Police Discretion Not to Prose-

cute Students," *Journal of Criminal Law, Criminology, and Police Science* 56 (1965): 241–45.

4. *Welfare and Institutions Code,* Section 5050.3.

5. The term "doctrinal" is perhaps too strong, but only in the sense that the scheme of reasoning and justification lacks explicit formulation.

6. The literature on this topic is voluminous and heavily polemical. For a general overview, see Wayne R. LaFave, *Arrest* (Boston: Little, Brown & Co., 1965); W. T. Plumb, Jr., "Illegal Enforcement of the Law" *Cornell Law Quarterly* 24 (1939): 337–93; Jim Thompson, "Police Control over Citizen Use of the Public Streets," *Journal of Criminal Law, Criminology, and Police Science* 49 (1959): 562–68; R. C. Donnelly, "Police Authority and Practices," *Annals of the American Academy of Political and Social Science* 339 (1962): 90–110; Arthur H. Sherry, "Vagrants, Rogues and Vagabonds," *California Law Review* 48 (1960): 557–73.

7. I have dealt with the practice of invoking official rules of procedure to legitimize various "necessary" activities, as a general problem in formal organizations, in "The Concept of Organization," *Social Research* 32 (1965): 239–55.

8. The problem of the devious and exploitative use of the determination of mental illness in the administration of justice is dealt with by Thomas Szasz in a number of publications. See especially his latest book, *Psychiatric Justice* (New York: Macmillan, 1965).

9. Shirley Star, "The Public's Ideas About Mental Illness" (Paper presented to the National Association of Mental Health, Indianapolis, 1955 [mimeo]); "The Place of Psychiatry in Popular Thinking" (Paper presented to the American Association of Public Opinion Research, 1957 [mimeo]).

10. We propose that the degradation ceremony of the mental patient, to which Goffman refers in his work, presents itself to the policeman as a justified necessity with certain patients.

11. During the period of the study, policemen apprehended and referred to the hospital approximately 1,600 patients. The total number of arrests for the mentioned offenses, by the uniformed patrol, was exactly 1,600, according to published statistics of the police department. However, the study covered the period from July 1, 1963, to June 30, 1964, while the published statistics of the department cover the calendar year of 1964.

12. This observation is frankly judgmental; no one can estimate realiably the extent of covert coercion standing behind compliance. It is, however, not startlingly unusual for patients to ask policemen to take them to the hospital.

13. The information comes to the officer through radio code. The code contains special designations to indicate that an assignment involves a mental case, a suicide attempt, or an assignment of unknown nature.

14. Edward H. Levi has argued that reasoning by analogy prevails generally in the administration of justice; see his *Introduction to Legal Reasoning* (Chicago: University of Chicago Press, 1949). Since police officers must be attuned to the style of proof and inference that is used in courts, it would not be unreasonable to assume that they might assimilate some of this pattern of thinking.

15. In general, policemen insist on getting a fairly detailed story from the complainant and also on seeing the patient before they decide to make an emergency apprehension. One physician who was interviewed in the course of the study complained about this with a good deal of chagrin. From his point of view the police should take the word of a doctor without questioning him. Officers, however, maintain that the doctor's judgment would not protect them in the case of future complaints; they prefer making an "honest mistake." Policemen are generally acutely aware of the requirement of personal knowledge in finding "adequate grounds" for any action.

16. One police lieutenant explained that one of the major stresses of police work has to do with the fact that officers are often forced to reach difficult decisions under the critical eye of bystanders. Such situations contain the simple hazard of losing physical control of the case as well as the risk that the officer's decision will be governed by external influence or provocation.

17. We are talking about practice, of course, but the problem stands in the midst of a debate in legal theory. If it is maintained that the substance of the law is that it contains a system of rules of conduct, informing people what they must not do, and providing sanctions for violations, then neither the policeman nor the judge has any legitimate powers to exculpate a violator. If, however, it is maintained that the substance of the law is that it contains a system of rules limiting the powers of the institutions of the polity with respect to certain offenders and offensive types of conduct, then alternative means of control are not out of order, provided that they are not explicitly forbidden. The former position is expressed in Jerome Hall, *General Principles of Criminal Law* (Indianapolis: Bobbs-Merrill, 1947); an exposition of the latter view is contained in Norberto Bobbio, "Law and Force," *The Monist* 49 (1965): 321–42.

18. Michael Banton proposed and discussed the distinction between peacekeeping and law enforcement functions in his book, *The Policeman in the Community* (New York: Basic Books, 1965).

19. Elaine Cumming and her co-workers define the policeman engaged in activities that do not relate to "keeping the law from being broken and apprehending those who break it" as an "amateur social worker." They do not consider, however, that their conception of the role of the policeman, that is, as being limited to law enforcement and restrictive control, may have been correct only "by definition and by law," and not in reality. Our own contention is that keeping the peace contains elements of control *and* support in a unique combination and that its pursuit has nothing amateurish about it. See Elaine Cumming et al., "Policeman as Philosopher, Guide and Friend," *Social Problems* 12 (1965): 276–86.

4 | *The Functions of the Police in Modern Society*

A Review of Background Factors,
Current Practices,
and Possible Role Models

INTRODUCTION

IN HIS ASSESSMENT of the police, Bruce Smith wrote in 1940 that, in spite of the still rather bleak picture, "the lessons of history lean to the favorable side."[1] He pointed to the fact that the then existing police forces had moved a long way from the past associated with the notorious names of Vidocq and Jonathan Wild,[2] and he suggested that the uninterrupted progress justifies the expectation of further change for the better. It is fair to say that this hope has been vindicated by the events of the past thirty years. American police departments of today differ by a wide margin of improvement from those Smith studied in the late 1930s. The once endemic features of wanton brutality, corruption, and sloth have been reduced to a level of sporadic incidence, and their surviving vestiges have been denounced by even generally uncritical police apologists. Indeed, police reform, once a cause espoused exclusively by spokesmen from outside the law enforcement camp, has become an internal goal, actively sought and implemented by leading police officials.

Despite these widely acknowledged advances, however, the police continue to project as bad an image today as they have in the past.[3] In fact, the voices of criticism seem to have increased. The traditional critics have been joined by academic scholars and by some highly placed judges. Certain segments of American society, notably the ethnic minorities and the young people, who have only recently acquired a voice in public debate, express generally hostile attitudes toward the police. At the same time, news about rising crime rates and widely disseminated accounts about public disorders—ranging from peaceful protest to violent rebellion—contribute to the feeling that the police are not adequately prepared to face the tasks that confront them. As a result of all of this, the police problem has moved into the forefront of public attention, creating conditions in which highly consequential and long-range decisions are apt to be formulated. For this reason, it is of utmost importance to bring as much clarity as possible to the ongoing debate now.

The survival of the unmitigatedly critical attitude toward the police, in the face of patent improvements, implies a concern of far greater complexity than the ordinary exchanges of denunciation and defense are likely to reveal. Surely the police are not bad in some such simple sense that those who have the power to eliminate existing shortcomings could do so if they would just set their minds to it. Nor is it reasonable to assume that all the persistent critics are merely devious or fickle. Instead, it would appear more probable that in the heat of polemics some facts and some judgments shifted out of line, that many polemic opponents argue from positions that are submerged in tacit and conflicting presuppositions, and the task of analysis and pending reform could only be advanced beyond its present impasse by first setting forth as unambiguously as possible the terms on which the police must be judged in general and in all the particulars of their practices. Without such prior specifications of the proper terms of critique, it will continue to take the form of a desultory array of animadversions. Moreover, such a critique, employing arbitrary and *ad hoc* criteria of judgment, will unavoidably alienate the police, will strengthen their defensive and distrustful posture, and will cause, at best, a patchwork of reform, the main effect of which will be to shift malpractice from one form to another.

The formulation of criteria for judging any kind of institutional practice, including the police, rather obviously calls for the solution of a logically prior problem. Clearly it is necessary that it be known *what* needs to be done before anyone can venture to say *how* it is to be done well. In the case of the police, this sets up the requirement of specifying the police role in society. Simple as this demand may seem on first glance, it presents difficulties that are more commonly avoided than addressed. Were such avoidance explicit it might do little harm; unfortunately it is often obscured by specious programmatic idealizations. Thus, we are often told that the role of the police is supposed to center around law enforcement, crime control, and peacekeeping. The principal import of such statements is not to inform, but to maintain the pretense of understanding and agreement. Because such statements of function are abstract and do not restrict the interpretations that can be given to them, they can be as easily invoked to serve the polemic purposes of those who find fault with existing practices as of those who sound the fanfare of praise of the police. Nor is it very helpful to elaborate the official formulas in finer detail as long as the elaborations remain on the level of abstract moral, legal, or political theory. As David Hume has demonstrated long ago, all efforts at a transition from the *ought* to the *is* can be achieved speculatively only by unwarranted and arbitrary inferences,[4] with the result that those who begin by talking amicably suddenly and unaccountably find themselves locked in bitter enmity without knowing when their seeming agreement collapsed.

The point of all this is not that programmatic idealizations are not important, but that they are important precisely to the extent that there is agreement on how they are to be interpreted in actual practice. This is not an easy matter because references to practice can easily be subverted to serve the purposes of abstract theorizing. That is, many a theoretician is fully prepared to concede that what is perceived as *in principle desirable* needs to be perceived in ways that are attuned to realities, only to go on from this concession to the formulation of subsidiary rules concerning what is *in principle practical*. For example, Joseph Goldstein argued in an immensely important and justly influential paper that the law enforcement function of the police cannot be properly understood when considered solely in terms of principles of pure legality. Far from merely applying legal maxims in a ministerial manner, police employ discretion in invoking the law. Thus, they in effect draw the outer perimeter of law enforcement, a power that is certainly not officially assigned to them. Because policemen often make decisions that are essentially "invisible" and subject to no review, especially when they decide not to make arrests, Goldstein concluded that they should be brought under the control of some subsidiary rules, compliance with which would be ensured by the scrutiny of an official agency.[5] While the proposal that discretion should be reviewable is meritorious, the hope that its scope can be curtailed by the formulation of additional norms is misguided. Contrary to the belief of many jurists, new rules do not restrict discretion but merely shift its locus.

The main reason why the abstract formulations of the police mandate cannot be brought closer to the conditions of actual practice by more detailed rulemaking, even when such more detailed rules are devised under the aegis of in-principle-practicality, is that all formal rules of conduct are basically defeasible.[6] To say that rules are defeasible does not merely admit the existence of exceptions; it means asserting the far stronger claim that the domain of presumed jurisdiction of a legal rule is essentially open ended. While there may be a core of clarity about its application, this core is always and necessarily surrounded by uncertainty. Consequently, in real life—as opposed to certain simple games—the element of mootness can never be eliminated. And since it is imponderable what either total certainty or total uncertainty might mean in rule compliance, talk about the reduction of rule ambiguity has all the earmarks of image mongering. The realization that all legal rules are defeasible need not lead to what in contemporary jurisprudence is known as rule scepticism.[7] For as Edward Levy argued, "Legal reasoning has a logic of its own. Its structure fits it to give meaning to ambiguity and to test constantly whether the society has come to see new differences or similarities."[8] But the realization of the defeasibility of rules does indicate that the discernment of the function of a public agency, in our case the police, cannot be achieved by working down from broadly conceived programmatic idealizations, or, at least, that proceeding in this manner produces a quest of highly uncertain promise. No matter how far we descend on the hierarchy of more and more detailed formal instruction, there will always remain a step further down to go, and no measure of effort will ever succeed in eliminating, or even in meaningfully curtailing, the area of discretionary freedom of the agent whose duty it is to fit rules to cases. In the final analysis, we can send even the most completely instructed patrolman out on his round only if we have grounds for believing that he will know what the instructions mean when he faces a situation that appears to call for action.[9] We cannot spare him the task of judging the correctness of the fit. And if this is so in the final analysis, we should be well advised to take account of it in the first instance as well. Accordingly, instead of attempting to divine the role of the police from programmatic idealizations, we should seek to discern this role by looking to those reality conditions and practical circumstances to which the formulas presumably apply. Naturally, we cannot afford to forget the terms of the abstractly formulated mandate. We would not know what to look for if we did. But we will keep them in mind as something to be worked back to, rather than as a point of departure. In sum, the task we have set for ourselves is to elucidate the role of the police in modern American society by reviewing the exigencies located in practical reality which give rise to police responses, *and* by attempting to relate the actual routines of response to the moral aspirations of a democratic polity.

POPULAR CONCEPTIONS ABOUT THE CHARACTER OF POLICE WORK

The abandonment of the norm-derivative approach to the definition of the role of the police in modern society immediately directs attention to a level of social reality that is unrelated to the ideal formulations. Whereas in terms of these formulations police activity derives its meaning from the objectives of upholding the law, we find that in reality certain meaning features are associated with police work that are largely independent of the objectives. That is, police work is generally viewed as having certain character traits we take for granted, and which control dealings between policemen and citizens, on both sides. Though we are lacking in adequate evidence about these matters, the perceived traits we will presently discuss are universally accepted as present and the recognition of their presence constitutes a realistic constraint on what is expected of the police and how policemen actually conduct themselves. It is important to emphasize that even while some of these ideas and attitudes are uncritically inherited from the past they are far from being totally devoid of realism. In the police literature these matters are typically treated under either euphemistic or cynical glosses. The reason for this evasion is simple, the Sunday school vocabulary we are forced to employ while talking about any occupational pursuit as dignified, serious, and necessary forces us to be either hypocritical or disillusioned, and prevents us from dealing realistically with the facts and from being candid about opinion.

Among the traits of character that are commonly perceived as associated with police work, and which thus constitute in part the social reality within which the work has to be done, the following three are of cardinal importance.

1. Police work is a tainted occupation. The origins of the stigma are buried in the distant past and while much has been said and done to erase it, these efforts have been notably unsuccessful. Medieval watchmen, recruited from among the ranks of the destitute and subject to satirical portrayals, were perceived to belong to the world of shadows they were supposed to contain.[10] During the period of the absolute monarchy the police came to represent the underground aspects of tyranny and political repression, and they were despised and feared even by those who ostensibly benefited from their services. No one can say how much of the old attitude lives on; some of it probably seeps into modern consciousness from the continued reading of nineteenth century romantic literature of the Victor Hugo variety. And it cannot be neglected that the mythology of the democratic polity avidly recounts the heroic combat against the police agents of the old order. But even if the police officer of today did not evoke the images of the past at all, he would still be viewed with mixed feelings, to say the least. For in modern folklore, too, he is a character who is ambivalently feared and admired, and no amount of public relations work

can entirely abolish the sense that there is something of the dragon in the dragon-slayer.[11] Because they are posted on the perimeters of order and justice in the hope that their presence will deter the forces of darkness and chaos, because they are meant to spare the rest of the people direct confrontations with the dreadful, perverse, lurid, and dangerous, police officers are perceived to have powers and secrets no one else shares. Their interest in and competence to deal with the untoward surrounds their activities with mystery and distrust. One needs only to consider the thoughts that come to mind at the sight of policemen moving into action: here they go to do something the rest of us have no stomach for! And most people naturally experience a slight tinge of panic when approached by a policeman, a feeling against which the awareness of innocence provides no adequate protection. Indeed, the innocent in particular typically do not know what to expect and thus have added, even when unjustified, reasons for fear. On a more mundane level, the mixture of fear and fascination that the police elicit is often enriched by the addition of contempt. Depending on one's position in society, the contempt may draw on a variety of sources. To some the leading reason for disparaging police work derives from the suspicion that those who do battle against evil cannot themselves live up fully to the ideals they presumably defend. Others make the most of the circumstance that police work is a low-paying occupation, the requirements for which can be met by men who are poorly educated. And some, finally, generalize from accounts of police abuses that come to their attention to the occupation as a whole.

It is important to note that the police do very little to discourage unfavorable public attitudes. In point of fact, their sense of being out of favor with a large segment of the society has led them to adopt a petulant stance and turned them to courting the kinds of support which, ironically, are nothing but a blatant insult. For the movement that is known by the slogan, "Support your local police," advocates the unleashing of a force of mindless bullies to do society's dirty work. Indeed, if there is still some doubt about the popular perception of police work as a tainted occupation, it will surely be laid to rest by pointing to those who, under the pretense of taking the side of the police, imply that the institution and its personnel are uniformly capable and willing to act out the baser instincts inherent in all of us.

In sum, the taint that attaches to police work refers to the fact that policemen are viewed as the fire it takes to fight fire, that they in the natural course of their duties inflict harm, albeit deserved, and that their very existence attests that the nobler aspirations of mankind do not contain the means necessary to ensure survival. But even as those necessities are accepted, those who accept them seem to prefer to have no part in acting upon them, and they enjoy the more than slightly perverse pleasure of looking down on the police who take the responsibility of doing the job.

2. Police work is not merely a tainted occupation. To draw a deliberately remote analogy, the practice of medicine also has its dirty and mysterious aspects. And characteristically, dealings with physicians also elicit a sense of trepidated fascination. But in the case of medicine, the repulsive aspects, relating to disease, pain, and death, are more than compensated by other features, none of which are present in police work. Of the compensatory features, one is of particular relevance to our concerns. No conceivable human interest could be opposed to fighting illness; in fact, it is meaningless to suppose that one could have scruples in opposing disease. But the evils the police are expected to fight are of a radically different nature. Contrary to the physician, the policeman is always opposed to some articulated or articulable human interest. To be sure, the police are, at least in principle, opposed to only reprehensible interests or to interest lacking in proper justification. But even if one were to suppose that they never err in judging legitimacy—a farfetched supposition, indeed—it would still remain the case that police work can, with very few exceptions, accomplish something *for* somebody only by proceeding *against* someone else. It does not take great subtlety of perception to realize that standing between man and man locked in conflict inevitably involves profound moral ambiguities. Admittedly, few of us are constantly mindful of the saying, "He that is without sin among you, let him cast the first stone . . .," but only the police are explicitly required to forget it. The terms of their mandate and

the circumstances of their practices do not afford them the leisure to reflect about the deeper aspects of conflicting moral claims. Not only are they required to proceed forcefully against all appearances of transgression but they are also expected to penetrate the appearance of innocence to discover craftiness hiding under its cloak. While most of us risk only the opprobrium of foolishness by being charitable or gullible, the policeman hazards violating his duty by letting generosity or respect for appearances govern his decisions.

Though it is probably true that persons who are characterologically inclined to see moral and legal problems in black and white tend to choose police work as a vocation more often than others, it is important to emphasize that the need to disregard complexity is structurally built into the occupation. Only after a suspect is arrested, or after an untoward course of events is stopped, is there time to reflect on the merits of the decision and, typically, that reflective judgment is assigned to other public officials. Though it is expected that policemen will be judicious and that experience and skill will guide them in the performance of their work, it is foolish to expect that they could always be both swift and subtle. Nor is it reasonable to demand that they prevail, where they are supposed to prevail, while hoping that they will always handle resistance gently. Since the requirement of quick and what is often euphemistically called aggressive action is difficult to reconcile with error-free performance, police work is, by its very nature, doomed to be often unjust and offensive to someone. Under the dual pressure to "be right" and to "do something," policemen are often in a position that is compromised even before they act.[12]

In sum, the fact that policemen are required to deal with matters involving subtle human conflicts and profound legal and moral questions, without being allowed to give the subtleties and profundities anywhere near the consideration they deserve, invests their activities with the character of crudeness. Accordingly, the constant reminder that officers should be wise, considerate, and just, without providing them with opportunities to exercise these virtues is little more than vacuous sermonizing.

3. The ecological distribution of police work at the level of

departmentally determined concentrations of deployment, as well as in terms of the orientations of individual police officers, reflects a whole range of public prejudices. That is, the police are more likely to be found in places where certain people live or congregate than in other parts of the city. Though this pattern of manpower allocation is ordinarily justified by references to experientially established needs for police service, it inevitably entails the consequence that some persons will receive the dubious benefit of extensive police scrutiny merely on account of their membership in those social groupings which invidious social comparisons locate at the bottom of the heap.[13] Accordingly, it is not a paranoid distortion to say that police activity is as much directed to who a person is as to what he does.

As is well known, the preferred targets of special police concern are some ethnic and racial minorities, the poor living in urban slums, and young people in general.[14] On the face of it, this kind of focusing appears to be, if not wholly unobjectionable, not without warrant. Insofar as the above-mentioned segments of society contribute disproportionately to the sum total of crime, and are more likely than others to engage in objectionable conduct, they would seem to require a higher degree of surveillance. In fact, this kind of reasoning was basic to the very creation of the police; for it was not assumed initially that the police would enforce laws in the broad sense, but that they would concentrate on the control of individual and collective tendencies toward transgression and disorder issuing from what were referred to as the "dangerous classes."[15] What was once a frankly admitted bias is, however, generally disavowed in our times. That is, in and of itself, the fact that someone is young, poor, and dark-complexioned is not supposed to mean anything whatsoever to a police officer. Statistically considered, he might be said to be more likely to run afoul of the law, but individually, all things being equal, his chances of being left alone *are supposed* to be the same as those of someone who is middle aged, well-to-do, and fair-skinned. In fact, however, exactly the opposite is the case. All things being equal, the young-poor-black and the old-rich-white doing the very same things under the very same circumstances will almost certainly not receive the same kind of treatment from policemen. In fact, it is almost inconceivable that the two characters could ever appear or do something in ways that would mean the same thing to a policeman.[16] Nor is the policeman merely expressing personal or institutional prejudice by according the two characters differential treatment. Public expectations insidiously instruct him to reckon with these "factors." These facts are too well known to require detailed exposition, but their reasons and consequences deserve brief consideration.

In the first place, the police are not alone in making invidious distinctions between the two types.[17] Indeed the differential treatment they accord them reflects only the distribution of esteem, credit, and deserts in society at large. Second, because of their own social origins, many policemen tend to express social prejudices more emphatically than other members of society.[18] Third, policemen are not merely like everybody else, only more so; they also have special reasons for it. Because the preponderant majority of police interventions are based on mere suspicion or on merely tentative indications of risk, policemen would have to be expected to judge matters prejudicially even if they personally were entirely free of prejudice. Under present circumstances, even the most completely impartial policeman who merely takes account of probabilities, as these probabilities are known to him, will feel reasonably justified in being more suspicious of the young-poor-black than of the old-rich-white, and once his suspicions are aroused, in acting swiftly and forcefully against the former while treating the latter with reserve and deference. For as the policeman calculates risk, the greater hazard is located on the side of inaction in one case, and on the side of unwarranted action in the other.

That policemen deal differently with types of people who are thought always to be "up to something" than with people who are thought to have occasional lapses but can otherwise be relied upon to conduct their affairs legally and honorably, does not come as a surprise, especially if one considers the multiple social pressures that instruct the police not to let the unworthy get away with anything and to treat the rest of the community with consideration. But because this is the case, police work tends to have divisive effects in society. While their existence and work do not create cleavages, they do magnify them in effect.

The police view of this matter is clear and simple—too simple, perhaps. Their business is to control crime and keep the peace. If there is some connection between social and economic inequality, on the one hand, and criminality and unruliness, on the other hand, this is not their concern. The problem is not, however, whether the police have any responsibilities with regard to social injustice. The problem is that by distributing surveillance and intervention selectively they contribute to already existing tensions in society. That the police are widely assumed to be a partisan force in society is evident not only in the attitudes of people who are exposed to greater scrutiny; just as the young-poor-black expects unfavorable treatment, so the old-rich-white expects special consideration from the policeman. And when two such persons are in conflict, nothing will provoke the indignation of the "decent" citizen more quickly than giving his word the same credence as the word of some "ne'er-do-well."[19]

The three character traits of police work discussed in the foregoing remarks—namely, that it is a tainted occupation, that it calls for peremptory solutions for complex human problems, and that it has, in virtue of its ecological distribution, a socially divisive effect—are structural determinants. By this is meant mainly that the complex of reasons and facts they encompass are not easily amenable to change. Thus, for example, though the stigma that attaches to police work is often viewed as merely reflecting the frequently low grade and bungling personnel that is currently available to the institution, there are good reasons to expect that it would continue to plague a far better prepared and a far better performing staff. For the stigma attaches not merely to the ways policemen discharge their duties, but also to what they have to deal with. Similarly, while it is probably true that moral naïveté is a character trait of persons who presently choose police work as their vocation, it is unlikely that persons of greater subtlety of perception would find it easy to exercise their sensitivity under present conditions. Finally, even though discriminatory policing is to some extent traceable to personal bigotry, it also follows the directions of public pressure, which, in turn, is not wholly devoid of factual warrant.

The discussion of the structural character traits of police work was introduced by saying that they were independent of the role definitions formulated from the perspective of the norm-derivative approach. The latter interprets the meaning and adequacy of police procedure in terms of a set of simply stipulated ideal objectives. Naturally these objectives are considered desirable; more importantly, however, the values that determine the desirability of the objectives are also used in interpreting and judging the adequacy of procedures employed to realize them. Contrary to this way of making sense of police work, the consideration of the structural character traits was meant to draw attention to the fact that there attaches a sense to police work that is not inferentially derived from ideals but is rooted in what is commonly known about it. What is known about the police is, however, not merely a matter of more or less correct information. Instead, the common lore furnishes a framework for judging and interpreting their work. In crudest form, the common lore consists of a set of presuppositions about the way things are and have to be. Thus, for instance, whatever people assume to be generally true of the police will be the thing that a particular act or event will be taken to exemplify. If it is believed that police work is crude, then within a very considerable range of relative degrees of sublety, whatever policemen will be seen doing will be seen as crudeness.

In addition to the fact that the normative approach represents an exercise in formal, legal inference, while the structural character traits reflect an approach of informal, commonsense practicality, the two differ in yet another and perhaps more important aspect. The normative approach does not admit the possibility that the police may, in fact, not be oriented to those objectives. Contrary to this, the sense of police activity that comes to the fore from the consideration of the character traits assigned to it by popular opinion and attitude leaves the question open.[20]

Since we cannot rely on abstract formulations that implicitly rule out the possibility that they might be entirely wrong, or far too narrow, and since we cannot depend on a fabric of common-sense characterizations, we must turn to still other sources. Of course, we can no more forget the importance of the popularly perceived character traits than we can forget the formulas of the official mandate. To advance further in our quest for a realistic definition of the police role, we must now turn to the review of certain historical materials that will show how the police moved into the position in which they find themselves today. On the basis of this review, in addition to what was proposed thus far, we will be able to formulate an explicit definition of the role of the institution and its officials.

THE CULTURAL BACKGROUND OF THE POLICE IDEA

The police, as we know it today, is a creature of English society in the second quarter of the nineteenth century.[21] The location of origin reflects the fact that England was, at that time, further advanced along the path of development as an urban-industrial society than other states. In due course, the model was adopted everywhere else, albeit with modifications required by different traditions and different forms of political organization. In the United States the first modern police department was created by the State of New York for the city of New York, in accordance with recommendations made by a committee that was earlier sent to London to study the English model. Other American cities quickly acquired similar departments. Even though older forms of policing continue to exist, notably the office of the sheriff, and some new forms were added more recently, that is, the Federal Bureau of Investigation, the municipal police department has been by far the most important way of doing police work in the United States since the turn of the century.

The most remarkable fact about the timing of the foundation of the modern police is that it is sequentially the last of the basic building blocks in the structure of modern executive government.[22] Military conscription, tax collection, economic and fiscal planning, social service, and a host of other administrative organs antedate the police by several generations. Even public education existed in a limited form in Prussia and in France long before Sir Robert Peel marshaled through Parliament the Bill establishing the Metropolitan Police of London. This seems strange because the absolute monarchies of the seventeenth and eighteenth centuries had ample reasons for creating the kind of institution that would furnish them with means for the continuous and detailed surveillance of citizens. Yet they did not develop such means, but relied on inherited methods of crime control and met such peacekeeping problems as they confronted by contingently mobilized means. The postponement of the creation of the police calls for an explanation and directs attention to the particular circumstances that surrounded it.[23]

In the years following the Peace of Vienna (1815), English society experienced what seemed to have been an alarming escalation of rates of criminality in her cities. Especially in the 1820s, the people of London were startled by a series of extremely brutal crimes of violence.[24] Though the country had a history of crime waves dating back to the beginning of the eighteenth century,[25] and resorted to a variety of means to control them, the idea of having a police force that would function as an arm of executive government was always strongly resisted. The main reason for the resistance was the fear that the existence of such a force would tip the balance of power in favor of the executive branch of government, leading ultimately to a suppression of civil liberties. Though these fears were never wholly allayed, the advocates of the police gained the upper hand in the debate when it became clear that the inherited methods were utterly incapable of handling the seemingly exploding crime problem. Furthermore, the aftermath of the Napoleonic wars brought forth a sequence of disastrous urban riots that had to be subdued by military force at great expense of life and property. This method of peacekeeping came to be viewed as inefficient as the old forms of crime control since the use of armed repression did not seem to have any noticeable deterrent effects, despite its unrestrained brutality. Reasoning along lines of efficiency was, of course, quite persuasive to a people that deliberately cultivated a spirit of hard-headed business rationality, and it would be easy to say that the police were finally accepted, despite many objections in principle, on grounds of considerations of sheer expediency. But there were other motives at work, too. The inherited methods of crime control and peacekeeping did not only fail in attaining the desired objectives, they were also perceived as incompatible with the ethos of a civil society. The corrupt and brutal thief-catcher extorting a pound of flesh from the wretch he accused of crimes and the yeomanry massacring mobs of hungry protesters in front of St. Peter's Cathedral harked back to a dark and despised past, and offended the sensibilities of a people who were at the threshhold of a period of their national history they defined as the acme of civilization.

The sentiment that could not abide the more archaic forms of repressive control of deviance and disorder was an expression of cultural and ideological change initiated in the nineteenth century. It is best described as the rise of the sustained, and thus far not abandoned, aspiration of Western society to abolish violence and install peace as a stable and permanent condition of everyday life.[26] To be sure, the history of this aspiration is by and large a history of its failures and those who count only results may judge the avowals of nonviolence as a massive display of hypocrisy. No generation would be more justified in passing this judgment than ours, for the violence we have experienced is overwhelming by the standards of any age. Yet, there can be no doubt that during the past one hundred fifty years the awareness of the moral and practical necessity of peace took hold of the minds of virtually all people. The advocacy of warfare and violence did not disappear entirely, but it grew progressively less frank and it keeps losing ground to arguments that condemn it.

The yearning for peace is, of course, not a nineteenth century invention. But it happened only after the end of the Napoleonic wars that attempts were made to develop practical measures to bring its attainment within the orbit of practical possibility. More importantly perhaps, during the nineteenth century the structure of everyday life changed, especially in the cities, in ways indicating that people relied on the efficacy of the means that were available to secure freedom from violence, despite the fact that this reliance was demonstrably hazardous.

Though these developments reflect the growth of humane sentiments, they derive more basically from a shift of values in which the virtues associated with material progress and assiduous enterprise gained ascendancy over the virtues of masculine prowess and combative chivalry.

Because the quest for peace has remained such a dubious enterprise, some of the efforts it inspired must be reviewed briefly. As will be shown, proper appreciation of these efforts furnishes the indispensable background for the understanding of the role of the police in modern society.[27]

At the international level, Europe enjoyed between 1815 and 1914 a period of historically unprecedented tranquility. The system of diplomatic consultations that controlled this state of affairs did not eliminate all belligerence and it failed completely in 1914, as did its successor, the League of Nations, in 1939. Remarkably, however, the lesson nations learned from these reversals did not lead to the abandonment of efforts, but, quite the contrary, to endeavors to form an even more binding commitment to worldwide peacekeeping through the United Nations Organization and through a variety of other regional treaty organizations.

At the level of internal governing, two developments are of particular importance. First, compliance with the demands of political authority became, after the beginning of the nineteenth century, less and less dependent on the direct presence of officials and on threats or the exercise of physical coercion, and more and more on voluntary performances of the governed. Indeed, it is the salient characteristic of modern authority implementation that it interposes distance between those who command and those who obey. It clearly makes a great difference, for example, whether taxes are collected by armed retainers or by means of written communications of demands. And it makes an equally great difference whether the recruitment of conscripts for military service is accomplished through the presence of armed might in villages or by means of mailed notices ordering eligible persons to report to induction centers. The threat of coercion is certainly not absent in modern forms of governing but its elaborate symbolization makes it more remote. The extent to which we have become accustomed to, and take for granted, the indirect ways of authority implementation and peaceful governing is perhaps best illustrated by the fact that the notorious "knock on the door," associated with totalitarian regimes, is generally viewed as the supreme political abomination.[28]

The second, even clearer indication of progressive avoidance of force in governing is evident in changes in the administration of justice. Up to the nineteenth century it was commonly taken for granted that the criminal process, from accusation, through inquiry and trial, to punishment, must properly involve the systematic mortification of defendants. Punishment for crimes meant death, mutilation, or physical pain. It is sufficient to point to the most obvious changes. The ordeal of inquisition has been entirely abandoned and its psychological forms are condemned. The atmosphere of the modern courtroom, with its emphasis on rationally argued proof and rebuttal—or even in its *sub rosa* dependence on plea bargaining—is profoundly inimical to the traffic of force between accused and accuser. Finally, modern punishment, with its emphasis on rehabilitation, partakes of the nature of an argument against evil. People are sent to prisons to persuade them to mend their ways, more than to suffer deprivation, at least in terms of the prevailing penal philosophy.[29] In fact, it would seem that the criminal process of today, at least in terms of its official script, seeks to dramatize the possibility of life without violence even under conditions where the imposition of coercive sanctions is the business at hand. Again, as in the case of international affairs, it is all too easy to show that reality often belies intentions, but surely it does make a difference whether violent methods are used because they are viewed as just and proper or by way of subterfuge.

Parallel to the admittedly insufficient efforts to conduct the affairs of governing in a pacific manner are changes in the manner of conducting private affairs. After ages of unquestioned presence, weapons ceased to be a part of expected male attire in the nineteenth century. Though we are certainly not a disarmed people, especially in the United States, we do not ordinarily consider swords, daggers, and guns as necessary accoutrements in our dealings with others and we require special reasons for carrying them around. The relatively late survival of armed life in the American West is conspicuous by contrast, not only with conditions in Europe, but also in the densely populated urban areas of the eastern part of the United States. Aside from such occasional relics of the past, the use of physical force has all but vanished as an acceptable means for defending one's honor, and certainly as an effective way of advancing interest or gaining honor. Indeed, the vestigial survival of regular patterns of interpersonal violence are perceived either as indications of personal immaturity or as features of "lower-class culture."[30] As if we were not fully satisfied with banishing the private use of force from the pale of respectability, our canons of good taste, which also originate in the nineteenth century, require us not only to avoid belligerence but "bodiliness" in general. That is, we tend to suppress, conceal, or deny matters which, through their visceralness, are related to violence. This is understandable when one considers that candor about sex, pain, and death is typically associated with styles of life in which violence is a normal part of daily existence; they are found joined in some pre-literate cultures, in our medieval past, and in "lower-class culture." Even more remarkably, the recent history of medicine reveals some of these trends. Such violent remedies as bloodletting, purging, and cauterization started disappearing from *materia medica* before the full justification for their abandonment was available, and our efforts to devise anaesthetic procedures, that is procedures that would neutralize unavoidably inflicted pain, have reached a level of complexity requiring an entire medical specialty for its proper administration.

Clearly the foregoing discussion of the pacific tendencies contained in the past century and a half contains one-sided exaggerations. We have repeatedly indicated that it would be naive to view it as an epoch of peace. Indeed, there is some question whether the several generations wanted peace above all. The times were, after all, a period of revolution of both nationalist and social nature.[31] But it was not our intention to render a balanced picture of the recent past, but merely to highlight one aspect of it. Our main point is that the trend toward the achievement of peace is basically new in Western history, even as we admit that it is continuously in danger of being overwhelmed by countertendencies.

One last comment is necessary before concluding the discussion of the importance of the ideal of peace and nonviolence in modern civilization. It is often said that our morality is based on precepts epitomized in the teachings of the Prince of Peace and on the humane wisdom of Socratic philosophy. Whatever the influence of these inspirations might have been, it appears that our quest for peace, such as it was and is, draws mainly on other sources. In the two thousand years since their announcement, neither religious faith nor humanistic concern led to even perfunctory efforts of practical implementation. The aspiration to peace that has finally led to some realistic steps toward its attainment derives from the lackluster ethic of utilitarianism. According to its maxims we are directed to sacrifice the lesser and momentary interests of personal gratification for the benefit of the greater good of the greater number. The common good, however, is not advocated as an abstract ideal because within it is located the greater advantage of every individual. Accordingly, our desire to abolish violence is fundamentally based not on the belief that it is spiritually reprehensible, but on the realization that it is foolish. Forceful attack and the defense it provokes have an unfavorable input/output ratio; they are a waste of energy. A simple, hardheaded, business-like calculus of preference dictates that coercive force, especially of a physical nature, is at best an occasionally unavoidable evil. Jeremy Bentham, the leading prophet of this outlook, taught that even legal punishment was, in and of itself, mischievous and defensible solely in such minimal forms and measures as was necessary to contain those few who could not or would not see that their advantage too was on the side of cooperation rather than conflict.[32]

Though it is always hazardous to formulate estimates of historical necessity, it would seem to be exceedingly unlikely that the idea of the modern police could have arisen in any other cultural context except that described above. In any case, though some forms of policing existed in many different societies and many different time periods, none of these forms resembled our institution even remotely.

THE COURTS AND THE POLICE

It is of the utmost importance for the understanding of the role of the police in modern society that its relations to the courts be set forth as clearly as possible. It is no exaggeration to say that much, perhaps most, of the present confusion about the police, and a great deal of empty polemic, are due to the lack of clarity on this point. Most legal writers do not know enough about police work to understand how it might relate to what the courts do, and most authors familiar with police procedure do not have an adequate appreciation of the nature of the legal process to discern the proper connection. Having indicated everybody's lack of competence, we are compelled to confess that what will be proposed below will not be offered as a proven explanation. Instead, the following remarks are offered as a possibly correct line of reasoning, in the hope that more extensive and more expert study along the proposed lines will help in casting light on what has thus far been left to loose conjecture.

Though there still attaches a great deal of esoteric mystery to the administration of justice, not only in the minds of lay people but also among jurists, its historical development in the Western world has been a movement away from unaccountable oracular judgment to a method of operation that is in all its important aspects restricted by explicit norms deriving from substantive and procedural law.[33] Indeed, there are good reasons for arguing that the modern penal law has become mainly, perhaps exclusively, a device for rationalizing courtroom procedure, and that its proscriptions and prescriptions are not addressed to anyone but the judges.[34] Contrary to the Biblical Decalogue, for example, contemporary penal statutes do not forbid or command any kind of citizen conduct. Instead, they merely stipulate that some proven actions and some proven omissions authorize and enjoin legal officials to proceed against the offending person. The powers to proceed are always set at a level of a fixed legal norm, which no legal official may exceed with impunity, regardless of circumstances. Moreover, when the presumed applicability of a legal norm specifying the imposition of a penal sanction is challenged by an accused person's plea of not guilty, or some other defense or rebuttal of charges, then this challenge must receive deliberately exhaustive consideration in open court. That is, the case the government opposes to the defendant's claim of innocence must be demonstrated by a method of reasoned proof which, in principle, calls for meticulous respect of the accused person's civil rights, even when such respect will defeat an otherwise meritorious cause. The procedural norm that requires that every indictment be left open to debate in court and that facts introduced in support of it must not only be true, but also legally admissible, points to a reluctance to invoke sanctions on any but unimpeachably reasoned grounds. And reasoned justification is required not only to convict but also to acquit or to dismiss.

It is only fair to admit two objections to the above description of the ways justice is administered in our courts. In the first place, the legalization of the criminal process is in reality not as complete as these remarks suggest. One can cite many examples of jurisdictions in which the legal rights of defendants are not only not observed in fact but to which the protections do not even extend under the law. Aside from such obvious instances of departure from the rule of law in the strict sense as the military and juvenile administration of justice, one need only point to the fact that jury deliberations are not really in accordance with the spirit of legality, if only because of their secrecy.[35] In the second place, and more importantly, it could be said that the version of the criminal process that was outlined is a mere facade. After all, the preponderant majority of cases that come before our criminal courts do not go to trial and, therefore, never receive the benefit of careful scrutiny and legal protection. Instead, they are disposed of by means of covert plea-bargaining which is based on considerations of practical expediency rather than legality.[36]

Though these objections are well taken, they can be set aside easily. As concerns the first, there can be no doubt that the progressive legalization of the criminal process has been the dominant trend for a long time and that this trend has accelerated in recent decades to the point where the rapidity of change bewilders even seasoned jurists. This movement might suffer an occasional setback, but the possibility of a reversal is imponderable without assuming a radical change in our system of government, a consideration which is beyond the scope of this analysis. With reference to the second objection, it must be said to begin with that evasions of legal restriction always have and probably always will abound in the administration of justice;[37] it is difficult to be so naive as not to recognize the fact and, indeed, its necessity. More important is that the scope, methods, and objectives of subterfuge are themselves determined by the official norm. No one can possibly understand the why, the what, and the what for, of the sub-rosa bargaining between the district attorney and defense counsel without knowing what might happen in court if the case at hand went to trial. No district attorney in his right mind would offer a reduction in charges when he has conclusive and admissible evidence. And no responsible defense counsel will offer a plea of guilty in trade for a reduced charge when he knows that there is no legal case against his client. Considerations of expediency, such as the desire to save time and work, certainly play a part in plea bargaining, but only totally corrupt lawyers base settlements entirely on such considerations, though it must be admitted that totally corrupt lawyers are probably not quite as rare as one would hope. In general, however, the norms observable in open court reach down and govern even the processes of its evasion. In the criminal process, like in chess, the game is rarely played to the end, but it is a rare chess player who concedes defeat merely to save time. Instead, he concedes because he knows or can reasonably guess what would happen if he persisted to play to the end. And thus the rules of the endgame are valid determinants of chessplaying even though they are relatively rarely seen in action. It is for these reasons that we hold to our description of the criminal process against the objections.

Now, the flow of business of the criminal courts is virtually completely supplied by the police. According to the common law, judges were not obliged, nor were they entitled, to inquire how the police secured this flow of business in the first place. That is, how the policeman learned about the delict, how he apprehended the putative culprit, and how he collected evidence to support his allegations had no bearing on the subsequent trial. While no judge would allow that a defendant be compelled to testify against himself during his trial, he cared not what the police did to obtain the evidence as long as there were no compelling reasons for assuming that it might be false in substance. This rule was reversed in the United States in 1914. Since then the U.S. Supreme Court has issued a series of rulings requiring the police to observe certain legal restrictions in questioning, detention, and search and seizure.[38] To all appearances, therefore, the judges have become the custodians of the legality of police procedure, even as they are the custodian of the legality of courtroom procedure. In point of fact, however, the appearances are deceiving and nothing could be further from the truth. Our courts have no control over police work, never claimed to have such control, and it is exceedingly unlikely that they will claim such powers in the foreseeable future, all things being equal.[39] Indeed, the courts have, today, even less control over the police than they have over attorneys in private practice.

Since the assertion that the courts have no power to compel the police to comply with norms of legality is a strong assertion that flies in the face of widespread assumption, it deserves further documentation. Let us begin with an example. It is generally correctly taken for granted that a policeman may, on the basis of no more than intuited suspicion, stop a person in a public place (actually, he may effectively do so anywhere, but we let this point pass) and demand of this person that he identify himself and explain the nature of his business on the scene. It is also rightly assumed that the officer may place such a person under arrest if the answers he receives do not satisfy him. All this does not seem such an unreasonable power considering that evil stalks our streets under the guise of innocence, and considering that the cost of inconvenience and possible error might be a small price to pay for the prevention of a possibly much greater disaster. Yet it is remarkable nevertheless that such inquiries cannot be addressed anywhere in the entire criminal process by any official of the administration of justice without the suspect's explicit consent. And that the legal norm forbidding inquiries without consent also forbids using the suspect's refusal to give an account of himself as grounds for a decision against him. In point of fact, not even the policeman himself is permitted to insist on questioning a suspect *after* he has arrested him and *if* he intends to see him prosecuted. The "if" emphasized in the preceding sentence is of absolutely crucial importance. It signifies that in many instances of police intervention there exists the possibility, which in some instances becomes a virtual certainty, that the case at hand will become the business of prosecutors and judges. Only when and only insofar as this possibility is envisioned does the police come under the rule of some of the restrictions that bind the administration of justice. If the policeman fails to comply adequately with these restrictions then the courts will not accept the case. This and this alone will be the consequence of his failure.

To be sure, having cases dismissed in court is no small matter. Many kinds of police activity have, after all, the sole objective of setting the criminal process into motion. What is the use of staffing a robbery detail that investigates robberies and arrests robbers who are subsequently released even though guilty, merely because the constable blundered? Thus, to say that the courts have no control over the police surely could not mean that what they say and do about police activity is of no consequence. Indeed, it is rather obvious that the series of U.S. Supreme Court decisions concerning admissibility of evidence has influenced police practices. But there is momentous difference between influence and control. For example, it would constitute at least a small measure of control if judges issued permanent injunctions against illegal searches and seizures, in which case every proven instance of it would constitute the culpable offense of contempt of court. But judges have not done this, nor is it likely that they will do it.[40] Instead, the present arrangement between prosecutors and judges, on the one hand, and the police, on the other hand, is not unlike that between any set of independent consumers and suppliers of services. The latter are constrained to respect what the former want because this is the only way they can do business. In the open competitive market, purveyors hue closely to the demands lest they lose their source of revenue. But in the marketplace of public service there would appear to be need for another kind of coordinating mechanism.

The prevailing form of coordination between public agencies in a receiving and supplying relationship to one another is the hierarchical control of the former over the latter. For example, if the Internal Revenue Service collected taxes in some such manner that would force their return to the taxpayer, then the Secretary of the Treasury would simply order a revision of the procedure. Nothing of the sort exists between the courts and the police. Since the judge is not the policeman's superior there is nothing that prevents the latter from doing as he pleases while forwarding cases on a take it or leave it basis. Nothing, that is, except two powerful considerations that put emphasis on the court's influence in the absence of control: the police really want to make use of the powers of the courts to punish, *and* they are fearful of scandals.

Saying that the police really do want to see offenders punished probably does not do their case justice. Though it is probably true that there attaches a certain degree of punitive zealotry to what Skolnick called the working personality of policemen,[41] cooperation with the courts is more than the product of occupational psychology. Most policemen do in fact conceive of their mandate as involving the law as it exists, and though they voice objections about the restrictions that this entails,[42] they have even greater misgivings about disregarding the restrictions entirely. Their attitude is basically American. Like all of us, the police have a love-hate affair with the administration of justice; they distrust lawyers, including judges, profoundly and they have an indomitable faith in "The Law."[43] Thus, it is probably fairer to say that the police want to see offenders punished by the courts because they feel that this is in the public interest. With respect to this, it is interesting to note that every generation of policemen appears to accept those legal restrictions as just and practical which the generation of their predecessors deemed unwarranted and destructive of police efficacy.[44]

As concerns the second consideration, the fear of scandals, it is a mixed blessing. Though it is undoubtedly true that it helps in bringing police work patterns closer to legality, it also can and often does have untoward consequences because the fear of scandal gives rise to hypocrisy, secretiveness, and mendacity.

In general it is far easier to err on the side of overestimating, rather than on the side of underestimating, the influence of the courts on what the police do in their daily work routines. While it is probably true that judges exert strong influence on *some* kinds of police procedure—as in cases involving major crimes in which resolute defense is anticipated—its extent is quite limited for several reasons. First, it generally does not touch the vast domain of charges involving disorderly conduct and other minor offenses. This is so because in such cases the merits of the police decision ordinarily are not questioned by either the defendants or the judges.[45] Second, because the police are often exposed to strong pressures to take some action against conditions that offend the public, they sometimes have to proceed in ways that could not be sustained on grounds of legality. Police officials are quite frank about it, referring to public opinion as one source of their authority.[46] Third, policemen in many jurisdictions proceed against some types of illegal activity—notably those involving the so-called sumptuary crimes—with deliberate neglect of rules of legal restraint. In most of these cases arrests are made without intent to prosecute and primarily for harassment purposes. By such means they hope to make plying some unsavory occupation more hazardous and less profitable.[47] Fourth, judicial influence is totally irrelevant for the immense variety of activities that have nothing to do with law enforcement or legality but is primarily oriented to easing some social strains.[48] For instance, no court has thus far presumed to inquire whether police service should be authorized and made available for helping to settle marital disputes.

In sum, the much heralded discovery that policemen are not merely ministerial officers, applying the laws as interpreted by the courts, must be considered the understatement of the decade. In point of fact, they not only exercise discretion in carrying out the mandates of the law, but they do even that much only as an incidental part of their more general responsibilities.

THE INSTITUTIONAL INDEPENDENCE
OF THE POLICE

It is important to emphasize that the institutionalized segregation of the police from the courts is a relatively recent phenomenon and that it is particularly characteristic of English and American methods of law enforcement. To understand this situation, it is necessary to review some of its historical, doctrinal, and practical background.

Under the Common Law, the Justice of the Peace was at once the magistrate and the chief police officer in his jurisdiction.[49] Though the office of the Justice of the Peace never functioned well in urban settings, the general principle that those who busied themselves with catching criminals should work under the direction of those who judged them was carried over into municipal law enforcement without question. Accordingly, as late as the first decades of the nineteenth century, the licensing of some police operations invariably involved the elevation of the head of the agency to the post of magistracy. This was true for all those kinds of agencies of which the Bow Street Runners were the best known example.[50] Even where this model was not followed literally, as for example in the police system of the city of Boston in the first quarter of the nineteenth century, there was a tendency to restrict the activities of staff to the role of process servers for the courts.[51] Moreover, the planners of the Metropolitan Police of London, though they anticipated that the officers of the force would engage in some activities that would not involve invoking the law, did not challenge the principle. Thus, the first two superintendents of Scotland Yard were named Justices of the Peace.[52] Since, however, the London force was created against strong opposition and operated under a cloud of suspicion that it might develop into an uncontrolled and arbitrary tyranny, the superintendents were divested of their powers of magistracy in 1839.[53] When the London model was copied elsewhere, including in the United States, it was copied as it actually functioned, that is, without the provision for any direct connections with the judiciary. Aside from following the model of English experience, the separation of the police from the courts in the United States was based on other reasons. From the middle of the nineteenth century to the 1930s, running the police establishment was part of the patronage system of urban politics in America. Though the lower judiciary was part of this system too, it was in the nature of the situation that strong institutional connections could not develop. As long as tenure depended on political favors, prudent office holders tended to stick to their knittings. Consequently, police chiefs and magistrates felt independently "responsible" to the city bosses.[54]

Historical developments in the climate of urban politics were not the sole reason for the institutional segregation. The progressive formal legalization of the criminal process during the past one hundred years meant in the United States, among other things, that the courts took less and less part in the inquisitorial part of it.[55] This decline reflected a growing commitment to the principle of adversary proceedings. According to this doctrine, justice is best served by allowing accusation and defense a maximum amount of freedom of expression. The role of the judge became restricted to hearing the evidence presented by the opposing parties and to safeguarding the legality and decorum of the exchanges before the bench. Only after the parties rest does the judge have a chance to act, but prior to that he is not supposed to interfere in any way that might possibly have the effect of strengthening or weakening the case of either the defense or the prosecution. Since it is difficult to foresee what consequences judicial involvement might have, disciplined judges tend to act on their own motions or ask questions only in extreme circumstances to prevent gross injustice. Above all, judges attempt to avoid maintaining one-sided connections with parties before them. Now, the police are of course always a party in matters pending before the court and they are always on the side of prosecution. Thus, if judges were to maintain any kind of direct supervisory control over them, then this would create a strangely incongruous situation. For it could be argued that if judges have real power to determine how police work should be done then they are implicitly responsible for the way it is done. Would it then still be reasonable to assume that judges will review disinterestedly the merits of cases presented by the police? Surely, there would be at least the impression created that whatever is done by a judicially controlled agency is done with implied consent and therefore immune to scrutiny. In sum, judicial control is apparently less compatible with the principles of adversary procedure than institutional segregation.[56]

In addition to the historical and doctrinal reasons for police independence from the courts, there are the practical limitations resulting from the commitment of the judiciary to a pacific and rational administration of justice. In order for the criminal process to enjoy an atmosphere of calm deliberation, where everything that needs to be accomplished can be accomplished by mere talk, logical inference, and careful assessment of facts, it is necessary to expel from its purview all those exigencies that are incompatible with it. The long-range objective is to abolish these exigencies, of course, but human life being what it is, whatever is left of them can only be made to disappear by shifting them from one place to another and creating a wall between the two. It is all too easy to point to hypocrisy inherent in the arrangement; practical idealism requires one to recognize, however, that the progress from a dirty house to a clean house may require a phase in which dirt is swept under the rug.

The need for procedures that fall short of the ideal of peacefulness and rationality expected of the criminal process is all too obvious to require extensive documentation. In fact, in many cases the criminal process cannot even be set into motion without violent and intuitive action. Before a person can be tried in court he or she has to be arrested. To make arrests the police need the kind of discretionary freedom that is difficult to reconcile with those observances of civil rights that are guaranteed in the courtroom. Police officers must apprehend suspects, in most instances, on the basis of evidence that would not be sufficient, in and of itself, for a conviction. The fact that officers must act on the basis of surmise rather than proof is not remarkable. In fact, time permitting, they can obtain judicial authorization to proceed on just such grounds. After all, the process of meticulous forensic scrutiny has to begin somewhere and it proceeds from lesser to greater certainty.[57] Even in the civil law one who seeks to avail himself of legal remedies by entering a suit against someone else initiates the action with less than full justification and with the mere hope that his claim will be vindicated. And civil suits, too, impose inconvenience and expense on the defending party. Far more important than the authorization to abridge the freedom of citizens on the grounds of merely suspected justification, is the expectation that the police will use force to achieve their objectives. To make the point quite clear, once an officer feels justified in making an arrest he has the duty to overcome the suspect's resistance and he may not retreat in the face of risks or threats of retaliation.[58] The authorization and the obligation to use force on the basis of no more than reasonable belief that the undertaken action is justified is the exclusive monopoly of the police. No other official in any branch of civil government has this right or this duty. To say, however, that the police have a monopoly on force means that this is their unique role in society, one which, on the basis of practical considerations, neither the government nor the citizenry could presumably do without.

Thus, the institutional independence of the police from the judiciary is ultimately based on the realization that policemen are inevitably involved in activities that cannot be fully brought under the rule of law. Only a limited set of legal restrictions can be conditionally imposed on the police which, however, still do not make it impossible for the police to proceed as they see fit.[59] Judges do not review the cases in which these restrictions have been violated. They have resorted to simple dismissals even though this might possibly injure the effectiveness of crime control. The reasons the courts gave for dismissals are that they see no other way of ensuring police compliance with demands of legality but to teach them a lesson.[60] Nothing can explain this exceedingly subtle pedagogy except the fact that the courts are in fact powerless vis-à-vis the police establishment.[61] Of course, it cannot be disregarded that judges, contrary to widely advocated views, probably do not really desire to "handcuff" the police. But insofar as this is the case, it would merely constitute a case of compatibility between the personal inclinations of certain officials with institutional constraints.[62]

THE CAPACITY TO USE FORCE AS THE CORE
OF THE POLICE ROLE

We have argued earlier that the quest for peace by peaceful means is one of the culture traits of modern civilization. This aspiration is historically unique. For example, the Roman Empire was also committed to the objectives of reducing or eliminating warfare during one period of its existence, but the method chosen to achieve the *Pax Romana* was, in the language of the poet, *debellare superbos,* that is, to subdue the haughty by force. Contrary to this, our commitment to abolish the traffic of violence requires us to pursue the ideal by pacific means. In support of this contention we pointed to the development of an elaborate system of international diplomacy whose main objective it is to avoid war, and to those changes in internal government that resulted in the virtual elimination of all forms of violence, especially in the administration of justice. That is, the overall tendency is not merely to withdraw the basis of legitimacy for all forms of provocative violence, but even from the exercise of provoked force required to meet illegitimate attacks. Naturally this is not possible to a full extent. At least, it has not been possible thus far. Since it is impossible to deprive responsive force entirely of legitimacy, its vestiges require special forms of authorization. Our society recognizes as legitimate three very different forms of responsive force.

First, we are authorized to use force for the purpose of self-defense. Though the laws governing self-defense are far from clear, it appears that an attacked person can counterattack only after he has exhausted all other means of avoiding harm, including retreat, and that the counterattack may not exceed what is necessary to disable the assailant from carrying out his intent. These restrictions are actually enforceable because harm done in the course of self-defense does furnish grounds for criminal and tort proceedings. It becomes necessary, therefore, to show compliance with these restrictions to rebut the charges of excessive and unjustified force even in self-defense.[63]

The second form of authorization entrusts the power to proceed coercively to some specifically deputized persons against some specifically named persons. Among the agents

who have such highly specific powers are mental hospital attendants and prison guards. Characteristically, such persons use
force in carrying out court orders; but they may use force only
against named persons who are remanded to their custody and
only to the extent required to implement a judicial order of
confinement. Of course, like everybody else, they may also act
within the provisions governing self-defense. By insisting on
the high degree of limited specificity of the powers of custodial
staffs, we do not mean to deny that these restrictions are often
violated with impunity. The likelihood of such transgressions
is enhanced by the secluded character of prisons and mental
institutions, but their existence does not impair the validity of
our definition.

The third way to legitimize the use of responsive force is to
institute a police force. Contrary to the cases of self-defense
and the limited authorization of custodial functionaries, the
police authorization is essentially unrestricted. Because the
expression "essentially" is often used to hedge a point, we will
make fully explicit what we mean by it. There exist three formal
limitations of the freedom of policemen to use force, which we
must admit even though they have virtually no practical consequences. First, the police use of deadly force is limited in most
jurisdictions. Though the powers of a policeman in this respect
exceed those of citizens, they are limited nevertheless. For
example, in some jurisdictions, policemen are empowered to
shoot to kill fleeing felony suspects, but not fleeing misdemeanor suspects. It is scarcely necessary to argue that, given
the uncertainties involved in defining a delict under conditions
of hot pursuit, this could hardly be expected to be an effective
limitation.[64] Second, policemen may use force only in the performance of their duties and not to advance their own personal
interest or the private interests of other persons. Though this
is rather obvious, we mention it for the sake of completeness.
Third, and this point too is brought up to meet possible
objections, policemen may not use force maliciously or frivo-
lously. These three restrictions, and nothing else, were meant
by the use of the qualifier "essentially." Aside from these
restrictions there exist no guidelines, no specifiable range of
objectives, no limitations of any kind that instruct the police-

man what he may or must do. Nor do there exist any criteria that would allow the judgment whether some forceful intervention was necessary, desirable, or proper. And finally, it is exceedingly rare that police actions involving the use of force are actually reviewed and judged by anyone at all.

In sum, the frequently heard talk about the lawful use of force by the police is practically meaningless and, because no one knows what is meant by it, so is the talk about the use of minimum force. Whatever vestigial significance attaches to the term "lawful" use of force is confined to the obvious and unnecessary rule that police officers may not commit crimes of violence. Otherwise, however, the expectation that they may and will use force is left entirely undefined. In fact, the only instructions any policeman ever receives in this respect consist of sermonizing that he should be humane and circumspect, and that he must not desist from what he has undertaken merely because its accomplishment may call for coercive means. We might add, at this point, that the entire debate about the troublesome problem of police brutality will not move beyond its present impasse, and the desire to eliminate it will remain an impotent conceit, until this point is fully grasped and unequivocally admitted. In fact, our expectation that policemen will use force, coupled by our refusals to state clearly what we mean by it (aside from sanctimonious homilies), smacks of more than a bit of perversity.

Of course, neither the police nor the public is entirely in the dark about the justifiable use of force by the officers. We had occasion to allude to the assumption that policemen may use force in making arrests. But the benefit deriving from this apparent core of relative clarity is outweighed by its potentially misleading implications. For the authorization of the police to use force is in no important sense related to their duty to apprehend criminals. Were this the case then it could be adequately considered as merely a special case of the same authorization that is entrusted to custodial personnel. It might perhaps be considered a bit more complicated, but essentially of the same nature. But the police authority to use force is radically different from that of a prison guard. Whereas the powers of the latter are incidental to his obligation to implement a legal command, the police role is far better understood by saying that their ability to arrest offenders is incidental to their authority to use force.

Many puzzling aspects of police work fall into place when one ceases to look at it as principally concerned with law enforcement and crime control, and only incidentally and often incongruously concerned with an infinite variety of other matters. It makes much more sense to say that the police are nothing else than a mechanism for the distribution of situationally justified force in society. The latter conception is preferable to the former on three grounds. First, it accords better with the actual expectations and demands made of the police (even though it probably conflicts with what most people would say, or expect to hear, in answer to the question about the proper police function); second, it gives a better accounting of the actual allocation of police manpower and other resources; and, third, it lends unity to all kinds of police activity. These three justifications will be discussed in some detail in the following.

The American city dweller's repertoire of methods for handling problems includes one known as "calling the cops." The practice to which the idiom refers is enormously widespread. Though it is more frequent in some segments of society than in others, there are very few people who do not or would not resort to it under suitable circumstances. A few illustrations will furnish the background for an explanation of what "calling the cops" means.[65]

Two patrolmen were directed to report to an address located in a fashionable district of a large city. On the scene they were greeted by the lady of the house who complained that the maid had been stealing and receiving male visitors in her quarters. She wanted the maid's belongings searched and the man removed. The patrolmen refused the first request, promising to forward the complaint to the bureau of detectives, but agreed to see what they could do about the man. After gaining entrance to the maid's room they compelled a male visitor to leave, drove him several blocks away from the house, and released him with the warning never to return.

In a tenement, patrolmen were met by a public health nurse who took them through an abysmally deteriorated apartment inhabited by four young children in the care of an elderly woman. The baby-sitter resisted the nurse's earlier attempts to remove the children. The patrolmen packed the children in the squad car and took them to Juvenile Hall, over the continuing protests of the elderly woman.

While cruising through the streets a team of detectives recognized a man named in a teletype received from the sheriff of an adjoining county. The suspect maintained that he was in the hospital at the time the offense alleged in the communication took place, and asked the officers to verify his story over their car radio. When he continued to plead innocence he was handcuffed and taken to headquarters. Here the detectives learned that the teletype had been canceled. Prior to his release the man was told that he could have saved himself grief had he gone along voluntarily.

In a downtown residential hotel, patrolmen found two ambulance attendants trying to persuade a man, who according to all accounts was desperately ill, to go to the hospital. After some talk, they helped the attendants in carrying the protesting patient to the ambulance and sent them off.

In a middle-class neighborhood, patrolmen found a partly disassembled car, tools, a loudly blaring radio, and five beer-drinking youths at the curb in front of a single-family home. The homeowner complained that this had been going on for several days and the men had refused to take their activities elsewhere. The patrolmen ordered the youths to pack up and leave. When one sassed them they threw him into the squad car, drove him to the precinct station, from where he was released after receiving a severe tongue lashing from the desk sergeant.

In the apartment of a quarreling couple, patrolmen were told by the wife, whose nose was bleeding, that the husband stole her purse containing money she earned. The patrolmen told the man they would "take him in," whereupon he returned the purse and they left.

What all these vignettes are meant to illustrate is that whatever the substance of the task at hand, whether it involves protection against an undesired imposition, caring for those who cannot care for themselves, attempting to solve a crime, helping to save a life, abating a nuisance, or settling an explosive dispute, police intervention means above all making use of the capacity and authority to overpower resistance to an attempted solution in the native habitat of the problem. There can be no doubt that this feature of police work is uppermost in the minds of people who solicit police aid or direct the attention of the police to problems, that persons against whom the police proceed have this feature in mind and conduct themselves accordingly, and that every conceivable police intervention projects the message that force may be, and may have to be, used to achieve a desired objective. It does not matter whether the persons who seek police help are private citizens or other government officials, nor does it matter whether the problem at hand involves some aspect of law enforcement or is totally unconnected with it.

It must be emphasized, however, that the conception of the centrality of the capacity to use force in the police role does not entail the conclusion that the ordinary occupational routines consist of the actual exercise of this capacity. It is very likely, though we lack information on this point, that the actual use of physical coercion and restraint is rare for all policemen and that many policemen are virtually never in the position of having to resort to it. What matters is that police procedure is defined by the feature that it may not be opposed in its course, and that force can be used if it is opposed. This is what the existence of the police makes available to society. Accordingly, the question, "What are policemen supposed to do?" is almost completely identical with the question, "What kinds of situations require remedies that are non-negotiably coercible?"[66]

Our second justification for preferring the definition of the police role we proposed to the traditional law enforcement focus of the role requires us to review the actual police practices to see to what extent they can be subsumed under the conception we offered. To begin we can take note that law enforcement and crime control are obviously regarded as calling for remedies that are non-negotiably coercible. According to available estimates, approximately one-third of available manpower resources of the police are at any time committed to dealing with crimes and criminals. Though this may seem to be a relatively small share of the total resources of an agency ostensibly devoted to crime control, it is exceedingly unlikely that any other specific routine police activity, such as traffic regulation, crowd control, supervision of licensed establishments, settling of citizens' disputes, emergency health aids, ceremonial functions, or any other, absorb anywhere near as large a share of the remaining two-thirds. But this is precisely what one would expect on the basis of our definition. Given the likelihood that offenders will seek to oppose apprehension and evade punishment, it is only natural that the initial dealings with them be assigned to an agency that is capable of overcoming these obstacles. That is, the proposed definition of the role of the police as a mechanism for the distribution of non-negotiably coercive remedies entails the priority of crime control by direct inference. Beyond that, however, the definition also encompasses other types of activities, albeit at lower level of priority.

Because the idea that the police are basically a crimefighting agency has never been challenged in the past, no one has troubled to sort out the remaining priorities. Instead, the police have always been forced to justify activities that did not involve law enforcement in the direct sense by either linking them constructively to law enforcement or by defining them as nuisance demands for service. The dominance of this view, especially in the minds of policemen, has two pernicious consequences. First, it leads to a tendency to view all sorts of problems as if they involved culpable offenses and to an excessive reliance on quasi-legal methods for handling them. The widespread use of arrests without intent to prosecute exemplifies this state of affairs. These cases do not involve errors in judgment about the applicability of a penal norm but deliberate pretense resorted to because more appropriate methods of handling problems have not been developed. Second, the view that crime control is the only serious, important, and necessary part of police work has deleterious effects on the morale of those police officers in the uniformed patrol who spend most of their time with other matters. No one, especially he who takes a positive interest in his work, likes being obliged to do things day in, day out that are disparaged by his colleagues. Moreover, the low evaluation of these duties leads to neglecting the development of skill and knowledge that are required to discharge them properly and efficiently.

It remains to be shown that the capacity to use coercive force lends thematic unity to all police activity in the same sense in which, let us say, the capacity to cure illness lends unity to everything that is ordinarily done in the field of medical practice. While everybody agrees that the police actually engage in an enormous variety of activities, only a part of which involves law enforcement, many argue that this state of affairs does not require explanation but change. Smith, for example, argued that the imposition of duties and demands that are not related to crime control dilutes the effectiveness of the police and that the growing trend in this direction should be curtailed and even reversed.[67] On the face of it this argument is not without merit, especially if one considers that very many of those activities that are unrelated to law enforcement involve dealing with problems that lie in the field of psychiatry, social welfare, human relations, education, and so on. Each of these fields has its own trained specialists who are respectively more competent than the police. It would seem preferable, therefore, to take all those matters that belong properly to other specialists out of the hands of the police and turn them over to those to whom they belong. Not only would this relieve some of the pressures that presently impinge on the police, but it would also result in better services.[68]

Unfortunately, this view overlooks a centrally important factor. While it is true that policemen often aid sick and troubled people because physicians and social workers are unable or unwilling to take their services where they are needed, this is not the only or even the main reason for police involvement. In fact, physicians and social workers themselves quite often "call the cops." For not unlike the case of the administration of justice, on the periphery of the rationally ordered procedures of medical and social work practice lurk exigencies that call for the exercise of coercion. Since neither physicians nor social workers are authorized or equipped to use force to attain desirable objectives, the total disengagement of the police would mean allowing many a problem to move unhampered in the direction of disaster. But the non-law-enforcement activities of the police are by no means confined to matters that are wholly or even mainly within the purview of some other institutionalized remedial specialty. Many, perhaps most, consist of addressing situations in which people simply do not seem to be able to manage their own lives adequately. Nor is it to be taken for granted that these situations invariably call for the use, or the threat of the use, of force. It is enough if there is need for immediate and unquestioned intervention that must not be allowed to be defeated by possible resistance. And where there is a possibility of great harm, the intervention would appear to be justified even if the risk is, in statistical terms, quite remote. Take, for instance the presence of mentally ill persons in the community. Though it is well known that most live quiet and unobtrusive lives, they are perceived as occasionally constituting a serious hazard to themselves and others. Thus, it is not surprising that the police are always prepared to deal with these persons at the slightest indication of a possible emergency. Similarly, though very few family quarrels lead to serious consequences, the fact that most homicides occur among quarreling kin leads to the preparedness to intervene at the incipient stages of problems.

In sum, the role of the police is to address all sorts of human problems when and insofar as their solutions do or may possibly require the use of force at the point of their occurrence. This lends homogeneity to such diverse procedures as catching a criminal, driving the mayor to the airport, evicting a drunken person from a bar, directing traffic, crowd control, taking care of lost children, administering medical first aid, and separating fighting relatives.

There is no exaggeration in saying that there is topical unity in this very incomplete list of lines of police work. Perhaps it is true that the common practice of assigning policemen to chauffeur mayors is based on the desire to give the appearance of thrift in the urban fisc. But note, if one wanted to make as far as possible certain that nothing would ever impede His Honor's freedom of movement, he would certainly put someone into the driver's seat of the auto who has the authority and the capacity to overcome all unforeseeable human obstacles. Similarly, it is perhaps not too farfetched to assume that desk sergeants feed ice cream to lost children because they like children. But if the treat does not achieve the purpose of keeping the youngster in the station house until his parents arrive to redeem him, the sergeant would have to resort to other means of keeping him there.

We must now attempt to pull together the several parts of the foregoing discussion in order to show how they bring into relief the main problems of adjusting police function to life in modern society, and in order to elaborate constructively certain consequences that result from the assumption of the role definitions we have proposed.

At the beginning we observed that the police appear to be burdened by an opprobrium that did not seem to lessen proportionately to the acknowledged improvements in their practices. To explain this puzzling fact we drew attention to three perceived features of the police that appear to be substantially independent of particular work methods. First, a stigma attaches to police work because of its connection with evil, crime, perversity, and disorder. Though it may not be reasonable, it is common that those who fight the dreadful end up being dreaded themselves. Second, because the police must act quickly and often on mere intuition, their interventions are lacking in those aspects of moral sophistication which only a more extended and more scrupulous consideration can afford. Hence their methods are comparatively crude. Third, because it is commonly assumed that the risks of the kinds of breakdowns that require police action are much more heavily concentrated in the lower classes than in other segments of society, police surveillance is inherently discriminatory. That is, all things being equal, some persons feel the sting of police scrutiny merely because of their station in life. Insofar as this is felt, police work has divisive effects in society.

Next, we argued that one cannot understand how the police "found themselves" in this unenviable position without taking into consideration that one of the cultural trends of roughly the past century and a half was the sustained aspiration to install peace as a stable condition of everyday life. Though no one can fail being impressed by the many ways the attainment of this ideal has been frustrated, it is possible to find some evidence of partially effective efforts. Many aspects of mundane existence in our cities have become more pacific than they have been in past epochs of history. More importantly for our purposes, in the domain of internal statecraft, the distance between those who govern and those who are governed has grown and the gap has been filled with bureaucratically symbolized communication. Where earlier compliance was secured by physical presence and armed might, it now rests mainly on peaceful persuasion and rational compliance. We found the trend toward the pacification in governing most strongly demonstrated in the administration of justice. The banishment of all forms of violence from the criminal process, as administered by the courts, has as a corollary the legalization of judicial proceedings. The latter reflects a movement away from peremptory and oracular judgment to a method in which all decisions are based on exhaustively rational grounds involving the use of explicit legal norms. Most important among those norms are the ones that limit the powers of authority and specify the rights of defendants. The legalization and pacification of the criminal process was achieved by, among other things, expelling from its purview those processes that set it into motion. Since in the initial steps, where suspicions are formed and arrests are made, force and intuition cannot be eliminated entirely, purity can be maintained by not taking notice of them. This situation is, however, paradoxical if we are to take seriously the idea that the police is a law enforcement agency in the strict sense of legality. The recognition of this paradox became unavoidable as early as in 1914, in the landmark decision of *Weeks* v. *U.S.* In the following decades the United States Supreme Court issued a series of rulings affecting police procedure which foster the impression that the judiciary exercises control over the police. But this impression is misleading, for the rulings do not set forth binding norms for police work but merely provide that *if* the police propose to set the criminal process into motion, *then* they must proceed in certain legally restricted ways. These restrictions are, therefore, conditional, specifying as it were the terms of delivery and acceptance of a service and nothing more. Outside of this arrangement the judges have no direct concerns with police work and will take notice of its illegality, if it is illegal, only when offended citizens seek civil redress.

Because only a small part of the activity of the police is dedicated to law enforcement and because they deal with the majority of their problems without invoking the law, a broader definition of their role was proposed. After reviewing briefly what the public appears to expect of the police, the range of activities police actually engage in, and the theme that unifies all these activities, it was suggested that *the role of the police is best understood as a mechanism for the distribution of non-negotiably coercive force employed in accordance with the dictates of an intuitive grasp of situational exigencies.*

It is, of course, not surprising that a society committed to the establishment of peace by pacific means and to the abolishment of all forms of violence from the fabric of its social relations, at least as a matter of official morality and policy, would establish a corps of specially deputized officials endowed with the exclusive monopoly of using force contingently where limitations of foresight fail to provide alternatives. That is, given the melancholy appreciation of the fact that the total abolition of force is not attainable, the closest approximation to the ideal is to limit it as a special and exclusive trust. If it is the case, however, that the mandate of the police is organized around their capacity and authority to use force, that is, if this is what the institution's existence makes available to society, then the evaluation of that institution's performance must focus on it. While it is quite true that policemen will have to be judged on other dimensions of competence, too—for example, the exercise of force against criminal suspects requires some knowledge about crime and criminal law—their methods as society's agents of coercion will have to be considered central to the overall judgment.

The proposed definition of the police role entails a difficult moral problem. How can we arrive at a favorable or even accepting judgment about an activity which is, in its very conception, opposed to the ethos of the polity that authorizes it? Is it not well nigh inevitable that this mandate be concealed in circumlocution? While solving puzzles of moral philosophy is beyond the scope of this analysis, we will have to address this question in a somewhat more mundane formulation: namely, on what terms can a society dedicated to peace institutionalize the exercise of force?

It appears that in our society two answers to this question are acceptable. One defines the targets of legitimate force as enemies and the coercive advance against them as warfare. Those who wage this war are expected to be possessed by the military virtues of valor, obedience and esprit de corps. The enterprise as a whole is justified as a sacrificial and glorious mission in which the warrior's duty is "not to reason why." The other answer involves an altogether different imagery. The targets of force are conceived as practical objectives and their attainment a matter of practical expediency. The process involves prudence, economy, and considered judgment, from case to case. The enterprise as a whole is conceived as a public trust, the exercise of which is vested in individual practitioners who are personally responsible for their decisions and actions.

Reflection suggests that the two patterns are profoundly incompatible. Remarkably, however, our police departments have not been deterred from attempting the reconciliation of the irreconcilable. Thus, our policemen are exposed to the demand of a conflicting nature in that their actions are supposed to reflect military prowess and professional acumen.

In the following, we will review certain well-known aspects of police organization and practice in an attempt to show that the adherence to the quasi-military model by our police forces is largely a self-defeating pretense. Its sole effect is to create obstacles in the development of a professional police system. On the basis of this review we will attempt to formulate an outline of a model of the police role in modern society that is recognizably in accord with existing practices but which contains safeguards against the existence and proliferation of those aspects of police work that are generally regarded as deplorable. In other words, the proposed suggestions will be innovative only in the sense that they will accent already existing strength and excise impeding ballasts.

THE POLICE AND "WAR ON CRIME"

Mr. Justice Reed of the United States Supreme Court once drew attention to the dangers inherent in the tendency to develop maxims of judgment and conduct from figures of speech. The matter of his concern was the proverbial "wall between church and state" and the confusion of logic resulting from this metaphor.[69] Needless to say, the warning fell on deaf ears because the intent of rhetoric is to appeal to associations that are established below the level of rational discourse and to evoke responses that would ordinarily not issue from sober analysis. The use of imagery in public debate is, of course, not simply a regrettable state of affairs, conflicting with a more composed attitude. In mobilizing sentiment and support for causes, an aptly chosen phrase may do the work of a thousand good reasons. Regrettable is only the total abdication of the supervisory role of rational scrutiny over the flight of the imagination which sometimes feeds on its own popular appeal.

A figure of speech that has recently gained a good deal of currency is the "war on crime." The intended import of the expression is quite clear. It is supposed to indicate that the community is seriously imperiled by forces bent on its destruction and it calls for the mounting of efforts that have claims on all available resources to defeat the peril. The rhetorical shift from "crime control" to "war on crime" signifies the transition from a routine concern to a state of emergency. We no longer face losses of one kind or another from the depredations of criminals; we are in imminent danger of losing everything! The perception of such risks does not abide patient study; as long as the envisioned doom is held up as a realistic possibility there is no need to show its impending certainty nor to estimate its likelihood with precision. It matters little that the metaphor, like many metaphors, contains a contradiction in terms. For in truth a community can no more wage war on its internal ills than an organism can "wage war" against its own constitutional weaknesses. Though it may seem paradoxical on first glance, the existence of crime in society is like the existence of organic malfunction, a normal aspect of human life.[70] Both are properly subject to vigilant control. But the conceit that they can be ultimately vanquished, which is the implicit objective of war, involves a particularly trivial kind of utopian dreaming. Out of control malfunction and crime could possibly overcome life, but control can never succeed in more than keeping them to a level appropriate to the prevailing form of human life. But vigilance waxes and wanes; to ensure that it does not fall below a level of minimally necessary tension it must be fed a diet of rhetorical illuminations.

The recognition of the positive role of rhetorical figures of speech in public life also forces the realization that their effects are not easily confined. Insofar as they involve exaggeration, they appear to sanction more than calculating advocates intend. Worse yet, they project unrealistic hopes. The expression "war on crime," not only implicitly extends the stamp of legitimacy to methods that would not be acceptable on moral and legal grounds, but it also encompasses the impossible. Professor Harold Lasswell observed long ago that under certain demands "police action . . . becomes military action, requiring for efficiency a will to ruthlessness which cannot, in fact, be mobilized in the situation."[71]

Lasswell's formulation, though exhaustively correct as stated, requires some elaborations to fully grasp its import. The "situation" to which he refers is never definable solely in terms of those forms of disorder and crime the police face. Instead, it always encompasses the whole range of interlocking relations to other aspects of life in which these targets of police action are located and from which they cannot be extricated. Thus, the absence of the "will to ruthlessness" is not predicated on tender and charitable sentiments toward offenders, but on devotion to the principle that dealing with them must not be allowed to affect adversely the context in which offenses are located. The price we are prepared to pay to defeat crime and disorder does not include visiting incidental suffering on innocents. Not to observe this stricture would turn crime control into a handmaiden of crime. Second, the "will to ruthlessness" involves not only attitudes toward the adversary but also the organization of the struggle against him. It is characteristic of the posture of the military establishment that it is as unsparing of its own as it is of the enemy. Its ferocity in engagement is preceded by a ferocity in preparedness, achieved by means of an unapologetically depersonalizing discipline among the ranks. Though one could conceivably organize police forces along such lines, the result would bear no resemblance to the institution as it exists. Finally, the "ruthlessness" of the military enterprise is a matter of coldly calculated expediency. It is deliberately produced and maintained with full regard to the exigencies of warfare against an alien enemy. To be sure, its maintenance involves appeals to spontaneous sentiments of manliness and patriotism but these feelings must not be allowed to escape the harness of strategy. The objectives and strategies involved in fighting off internal attacks are, however, different from those related to confronting an external foe, and while "ruthlessness" is the method of choice in the latter, it is not in the former. In sum, Lasswell is not overly sanguine about the capacity of policemen to be as unscrupulously belligerent against criminals as soldiers are against alien enemies. He only denies the structural feasibility of the approach.

Professor Allan Silver argues the same point even more forcefully in proposing that "the replacement of intermittent military intervention in a largely unpoliced society by continuous professional bureaucratic policing meant that the benefits of police organization—continual pervasive moral display and lower long term costs of official coercion for the state and the properties classes—absolutely required the moral cooperation of civil society." He recognizes and emphasizes that the police, like the military, are instituted for purely coercive tasks. But he also makes it clear that there issue radically different organizational needs from the objectives of military victory, on the one hand, and from "the penetration and continual presence of central political authority through daily life," on the other hand.[72] To cite one more authority, Professor Morris Janowitz pointed out that even when the tasks of policing are taken over by the military establishment it involves a reorientation of their normal posture. "The constabulary function as applied to urban violence emphasizes a fully alert force committed to a minimum resort to force and concerned with the development and maintenance of conditions for viable democratic institutions."[73]

Though it may seem like quibbling about words whether one calls the concerns of the police with lawlessness and disorder an effort to control them or war against them, the ambiguities of expression are symptomatic of deeper confusion. While most informed observers will readily agree that there is a difference between the military and the police they would also adhere to the view that the police are in some sense a quasi-military establishment. What the qualification "quasi" is supposed to mean is, however, not clear. In some countries with national police forces, notably in certain western European states, the problem is solved by maintaining parallel organizations, one with a distinctly military cast and the other free of constraints of military organization.[74] Something like this situation is also evident in the United States where some aspects of policing sometimes devolve on the National Guard. Contrary to the situation prevailing in European states, the National Guard is, however, not continually available. Consequently, American police forces have broader responsibilities than the civilian police forces of France, Spain, or Italy. In an apparent effort to meet these responsibilities, our police are more generally militarized than is the case elsewhere. This causes profound organizational problems. On the one hand, the military model does seem to furnish a form of control and supervision that helps to overcome laxness and corruption where it exists. On the other hand, the core of the police mandate is profoundly incompatible with the military posture. On balance, the military-bureaucratic organization of the police is a serious handicap.

THE QUASI-MILITARY ORGANIZATION OF THE POLICE

The conception of the police as a quasi-military institution with a war-like mission plays an important part in the structuring of police work in modern American departments. The merits of this conception have never been demonstrated or even argued explicitly. Instead, most authors who make reference to it take it for granted or are critical only of those aspects of it, especially its punitive orientation, that are subject of aspersion even in the military establishment itself.[75] The treatment the topic receives in the Task Force Report on the Police of the President's Commission on Law Enforcement and Administration of Justice is representative of this approach. The authors note that "like all military and semi-military organizations, a police agency is governed in its internal management by a large number of standard operating procedures."[76] This observation is accompanied by remarks indicating that the existence of elaborate codes governing the conduct of policemen relative to intradepartmental demands stands in stark contrast to the virtual absence of formulated directives concerning the handling of police problems in the community. The imbalance between proliferation of internal regulation and the neglect of regulations relative to procedures employed in the field leads to the inference that the existing codes must be supplemented by substantive instructions and standards in the latter area. The question whether such an expansion of regulation might not result in a code consisting of incompatible elements is not considered. Instead, it is implicitly assumed that policemen can be instructed how to deal with citizens by regulations that will not affect the existing system of internal disciplinary control.

The lack of appreciation for the possibility that the developments of professional discretionary methods for crime control and peacekeeping may conflict with the enforcement of bureaucratic-military regulations is not merely a naive oversight; more likely, it represents an instance of wishful thinking. For the military model is immensely attractive to police planners, and not without reason. In the first place, there exist some apparent analogies between the military and the police and it does not seem to be wholly unwarranted to expect methods of internal organization that work in one context to work also in the other. Both institutions are instruments of force and for both institutions the occasions for using force are unpredictably distributed. Thus, the personnel in each must be kept in a highly disciplined state of alert preparedness. The formalism that characterizes military organization, the insistence on rules and regulations, on spit and polish, on obedience to superiors, and so on, constitute a permanent rehearsal for "the real thing." What sorts of rules and regulations exist in such a setting are in some ways less important than that there be plenty of them and the personnel be continually aware that they can be harshly called to account for disobeying them.[77] Second, American police departments have been, for the greater part of their history, the football of local politics, and became tainted with sloth and corruption at least partly for this reason. Police reform was literally forced to resort to formidable means of internal discipline to dislodge undesirable attitudes and influences, and the military model seemed to serve such purposes admirably. In fact, it is no exaggeration to say that through the 1950s and 1960s the movement to "professionalize" the police concentrated almost exclusively on efforts to eliminate political and venal corruption by means of introducing traits of military discipline. And it must be acknowledged that some American police chiefs, notably the late William Parker of Los Angeles, have achieved truly remarkable results in this respect. The leading aspiration of this reform was to replace the tragicomic figure of the "flatfoot cop on the take" by cadres of personally incorruptible snappy operatives working under the command of bureaucrats-in-uniform. There is little doubt that these reforms succeeded in bringing some semblance of order into many chaotic departments and that in these departments "going by the book" acquired some real meaning.

Finally, the police adopted the military method because they could not avail themselves of any other options to secure internal discipline. For all its effectiveness, the military method is organizationally primitive. At least, the standard part of the method can be well enough approximated with a modicum of administrative sophistication. Moreover, since most of the men who go into police work have some military experience, they need not go to outside resources to obtain help in building a quasi-military order. This is important because a century of experience taught American police forces that outside intervention into their affairs—known as the "shake-up"—was almost always politically inspired. Because the suspicion of high-level chicanery is still very much alive, and not without reasons, the police is the only large scale institution in our society that has not benefited from advances in management science. In the absence of lateral recruitment into supervisory positions and developed technical staff skills, changes had to be achieved mainly by means of rigid enforcement of regulations of internal procedure and by emphasizing external trappings of discipline. In a situation where something had to be done, with little to do it with, this was no mean accomplishment.[78]

Acknowledging that the introduction of methods of military-bureaucratic discipline was not without some justification, and conceding that it helped in eliminating certain gross inadequacies, does not mean, however, that the approach was beneficial in larger and longer range terms. Even where the cure succeeded in suppressing many of the diseases of earlier times, it brought forth obstacles of its own to the development of a model of a professional police role, if by professional role is meant that practice must involve technical skill and fiduciary trust in the practitioner's exercise of discretion. The reason for this is simple. While in early police departments there existed virtually no standards of correct procedure at all and no inducement to do well—since rewards were scant and distributed along lines of personal favoritism—one can now distinguish between good and bad officers, and engaging in what is now defined as correct conduct does carry significant rewards. But since the established standards and the rewards for good behavior relate almost entirely to matters connected with internal discipline, the judgments that are passed have virtually nothing to do with the work of the policeman in the community, with one significant exception. That is, the claims for recognition that have always been denied to the policeman are now respected, but recognition is given for doing well *in* the department, not *outside* where all the real duties are located.

The maintenance of organizational stability and staff morale require that praise and reward, as well as condemnation and punishment, be distributed methodically, that is, predictably in accordance with explicit rules. Correspondingly, it is exceedingly difficult to assign debits and credits for performances that are not regulated by rule. Because the real work of the policeman is not set forth in the regulations, it does not furnish his superior a basis for judging him.[79] At the same time, there are no strongly compelling reasons for the policeman to do well in ways that do not count in terms of official occupational criteria of value. The greater the weight placed on compliance with internal departmental regulation, the less free is the superior in censoring unregulated work practices he disapproves of, and in rewarding those he admires, for fear that he might jeopardize the loyalty of officers who do well on all scores that officially count—that is, those who present a neat appearance, who conform punctually to bureaucratic routine, who are visibly on the place of their assignment, and so on. In short, those who make life easier for the superior, who in turn is restricted to supervising just those things. In fact, the practical economy of supervisory control requires that the proliferation of intradepartmental restriction be accompanied by increases in license in areas of behavior in unregulated areas. Thus, one who is judged to be a good officer in terms of internal, military-bureaucratic codes will not even be questioned about his conduct outside of it. The message is quite plain: the development of resolutely careful work methods in the community may be nice, but it gets you nowhere!

There is one important exception to the priority of intradepartmental quasi-military discipline in the judging of the performances of policemen. Police departments have to produce visible results of their work. The most visible results are arrested persons who keep the courts busy. This demand naturally devolves on individual officers. The question about the expected contribution of individual policemen to the statistical total of crimes cleared, summonses delivered, and arrests made is a matter of heated controversy. The problem is usually addressed as to whether or not there exist quotas officers must meet. Of course, the question can always be so framed that one can answer it truthfully either way.[80] But more fundamentally it is quite clear that individual policemen must contribute to the sum total of visible results, unless they have some special excuse, such as being assigned to a desk job. Moreover, how could any police superior under present conditions of supervision ever know whether the men assigned to the traffic division or to the vice squad are on the job at all, if they did not produce their normal share of citations or arrests?

Clearly, therefore, there is added to the occupational relevance of the military-bureaucratic discipline the demand to produce results.[81] While the emphasis on stringent internal regulation, taken alone, merely discourages the elaboration of careful approaches to work tasks, it exercises in combination with production demands a truly pernicious influence on the nature of police work. There are several reasons for this but the most important is based on the following consideration. Though the explicit departmental regulations contain little more than pious sermonizing about police dealings with citizens, whether they be offenders, an unruly crowd, quarreling spouses, accident victims, or what not, it is possible that a policeman could, despite his discretionary freedom, act in some such way as to actually come into conflict with some stated rule, even though the rule is not topically relevant to the situation at hand. Since he knows that his conduct will be judged solely with respect to this point he must be attuned to it, avoiding the violation even if that involves choosing a course of action that is specifically wrong with respect to the realities of the problem. For example, it is far from unusual that officers decide whether to make an arrest or not on the basis of their desire to live within departmental regulation rather than on the merits of the case at hand. In these situations the military-bureaucratic discipline regulates procedure speciously; it does not provide that in such-and-such a situation such-and-such a course of action is indicated. On the contrary, the regulations are typically silent about such matters; but in insisting on specific ways for officers to keep their noses clean they limit the possibilities of desirable intervention and they encourage transgression. Thus, it has been reported that in the New York Police Department, known for its stringently punitive discipline, officers who violate some official rules of deportment while dealing with citizens simply arrest potential complainants, knowing the complaints of persons charged with crimes are given no credence. Incongruously, while in New York the Police Department is much more likely to discipline an officer for brutalizing a citizen than elsewhere, it in fact rarely gets a chance to do it. For whenever there is a situation in which it is possible that an officer could have an infraction entered in his record, an infraction against an explicit regulation, he will redefine it into an instance of police work that is not regulated. Thus, while citizens everywhere run the risk of receiving a beating when they anger a policeman, in New York they run the added risk of being charged with a crime they did not commit, simply because its officers must keep their records clean.[82]

As long as there are two forms of accounting, one that is explicit and continually audited (internal discipline), and another that is devoid of rules and rarely looked into (dealings with citizens), it must be expected that keeping a positive balance in the first might encourage playing loose with the second. The likelihood of this increases proportionately to pressures to produce. Since it is not enough that policemen be obedient soldier-bureaucrats, but must, to ensure favorable consideration for advancement, contribute to the arrest total, they will naturally try to meet this demand in ways that will keep them out of trouble. Thus, to secure the promotion from the uniformed patrol to the detective bureau, which is highly valued and not determined by civil service examinations, officers feel impelled to engage in actions that furnish opportunities for conspicuous display of aggressiveness. John McNamara illustrates this tactic by quoting a dramatic expression of cynicism, "If you want to get 'out of the bag' into the 'bureau' shoot somebody."[83] Leaving the exaggeration aside, there is little doubt that emphasis on military-bureaucratic control rewards the appearance of staying out of troubles as far as internal regulations are concerned, combined with strenuous efforts to make "good pinches," that is, arrests that contain, or can be managed to appear to contain, elements of physical danger. Every officer knows that he will never receive a citation for avoiding a fight but only for prevailing in a fight at the risk of his own safety. Perhaps there is nothing wrong with that rule. But there is surely something wrong with a system in which the combined demands for strict compliance with departmental regulation and for vigorously productive law enforcement can be met simultaneously by displacing the onus of the operatives' own misconduct on citizens. This tends to be the case in departments characterized by strong militaristic-bureaucratic discipline where officers do not merely transgress to make "good pinches," but make "good pinches" to conceal their transgressions.[84]

No matter how elaborate and no matter how stringently enforced codes of internal regulations are, they do not impinge on all segments of police departments with equal force. By and large the highly visible uniformed patrol is exposed to far greater disciplinary pressures than personnel in the detective bureaus, which Arthur Niederhoffer aptly described as "mock bureaucracies."[85] While this situation is viewed as unavoidable, because the conduct of detectives cannot be as closely scrutinized as the conduct of patrolmen, and necessary because detectives need more freedom than patrolmen,[86] it tends to demean uniformed assignments. Because patrolmen perceive military discipline as degrading, ornery, and unjust, the only motive they have for doing well—which, of course, involves, among others, the devious practices we have just described—is to get out of the uniformed assignments.[87] Thus, the uniformed patrol suffers from a constant drain of ambitious and enterprising men, leaving it generally understaffed and, incidentally, overstaffed with men who are regarded as unsuitable for more demanding tasks. Though by no means all competent personnel take advantage of opportunities to leave the patrol for the detective bureaus, those who remain are dispirited by the conditions under which they are obliged to work and by the invidiously low level of prestige connected with their performance.[88] In consequence the outwardly snappy appearance of the patrol hides a great deal of discontent, demoralization, and marginal work quality.

Another complex of mischievous consequences arising out of the military bureaucracy relates to the paradoxical fact that while this kind of discipline ordinarily strengthens command authority it has the opposite effect in police departments. This effect is insidious rather than apparent. Because police superiors do not direct the activity of officers in any important sense they are perceived as mere disciplinarians.[89] Not only are they not actually available to give help, advice, and direction in the handling of difficult work problems, but such a role cannot even be projected for them. Contrary to the army officer who is expected to lead his men into battle—even though he may never have a chance to do it—the analogously ranked police official is someone who can only do a great deal *to* his subordinates and very little *for* them. For this reason supervisory personnel are often viewed by the line personnel with distrust and even contempt.[90] It must be understood that this character of command in police departments is not due solely to its administrative incompetence. It is exceedingly rare that a ranking police officer can take positive charge of police action, and even in the cases where this is possible, his power to determine the course of action is limited to giving the most general kinds of directions.[91] But like all superiors, police superiors, do depend on the good will of the subordinates, if only to protect their own employee interests within the institution. Thus, they are forced to resort to the only means available to ensure a modicum of loyalty, namely, covering mistakes. The more blatantly an officer's transgression violates an explicit departmental regulation the less likely it is that his superior will be able to conceal it. Therefore, to be helpful, as they must try to be, superiors must confine themselves to whitewashing bad practices involving relatively unregulated conduct, that is, those dealings with citizens that lead up to arrests. In other words, to gain compliance with explicit regulations, where failings could be acutely embarrassing, command must yield in unregulated or little regulated areas of practice. It is almost as if patrolmen were told, "Don't let anyone catch you sleeping on the job; if they do I'll get it in the neck and you will too. So, please, keep walking; in return I'll cover for you if you make a false arrest." Superiors, needless to say, do not speak in such terms. They probably do not even communicate the message covertly. Indeed, it is quite likely that most police officials would honestly view the suggestion with contempt. But this is the way things work out and the more a department is organized along military-bureaucratic lines the more likely it is that they will work out this way. Naturally, the situation is not conducive to the development of relations of genuine trust, respect, and loyalty.

Finally, emphasis on elaborate codes of internal regulation of a military kind tends to subvert police training, at least wherever this training is administered in departments, as is commonly the case. In the very best existing training programs instruction consists of three parts. There are some lectures concerning criminology, criminal law, human relations, mental health, and so forth given by visiting social scientists and lawyers. The second part consists largely of homilies about the social importance and dignity of police work, which emphasize that the occupation makes the highest demands on integrity, wisdom, and courage. The third part, to which the bulk of instructional time is devoted, relates to the teaching of departmental regulation. Since this is the only practical part of the course of instruction, it is abundantly clear that the overall purpose of the training is to turn tyros into compliant soldier-bureaucrats rather than competent practitioners of the craft of peacekeeping and crime control.[92] But since there exists no direct relation between knowing the regulations and maintaining the appearance of complying with them, the first thing graduates learn on their first assignment is that they must forget everything they have been taught in the academy. The immediate effect of the "reality shock" is a massive increase in the attitude of cynicism among first year policemen, not surprisingly since their introduction to the occupation was not only inadequate as far as their work duties are concerned, but also misleading.[93]

It could be said, of course, that the argument proposed thus far merely shows that efforts to professionalize police work by means of importing traits of outward military discipline is apt to create tendencies to displace misconduct into unregulated areas because the pertinent regulations have not yet been formulated. In time, these areas too will come under the scope of the existing discipline. It is our view that it is exceedingly unlikely that this development will take place. The charting of realistic methods of peacekeeping and crime control is profoundly incompatible with the style of current regulations of internal discipline. One simply cannot bring under the same system of control rules relating to dress and bureaucratic formalities, on the one hand, and norms governing the discretionary process of handling an instance of disorderly conduct on the streets, on the other. Emphasis on the first defeats care for the other. This does not imply that all presently existing regulations must be rescinded to encourage a methodical approach to police work tasks. Quite the contrary, the majority of present expectations will probably retain value in any alternative system of control. But their relevance, mode of presentation, and enforcement will have to be made subsidiary to a system of procedure that charts professionally responsible decisionmaking under conditions of uncertainty. In simplest terms, if policemen can be induced to face problems in the community and to deal with citizens in ways that meet at once criteria of purposeful efficiency and will correspond to the expectations of the kind of public trust commonly associated with the exercise of professional expertise, then there will be no need to treat them like soldier-bureaucrats. Correspondingly, as long as policemen will be treated like soldier-bureaucrats, they cannot be expected to develop professional acumen, nor value its possession.

It must be said, however, that the true professionalization of police work, in and of itself, is no weapon against sloth and corruption, no more than in the case of medicine, the ministry, law, teaching, and social work. That is, the professionalization of police work still leaves open the matter of its control. But if we are not willing to settle for having physicians who are merely honest, and who would frankly admit that in curing diseases and dealing with patients they have to rely entirely on "playing by ear," it is difficult to see why we would devote all our energies to trying to make the police honest without any concern whatever for whether or not they know, in a technical sense, how to do what they are supposed to do. Some people say it is foolish to demand technical proficiency and professional ethics where none exists. This view is certainly premature and probably wrong. We know far too little about the way police work is actually done to say with assurance that what we desire could not exist. What we know is that policemen have not written any scholarly tracts about it. We also know that presently good and bad work practices are not distinguishable, or, more precisely, are not distinguished. Worst of all, we have good reasons to suspect that if some men are possessed by and act with professional acumen, they might possibly find it wiser to keep it to themselves lest they will be found to be in conflict with some departmental regulation. The pending task, therefore, has less to do with putting external resources of scholarship at the disposal of the *police departments*, than with discovering those good qualities of police work that already exist in the skills of some *individual practitioners*. It is not enough to discover them, however, they must be liberated and allowed to take their proper place in the scheme of police organization. By making the possession and use of such skills the controlling consideration in the distribution of rewards, we will have a beginning of a professional system for controlling police practices. The prospect of such a control is in strict competition with presently existing methods of military-bureaucratic regulation.[94]

ESPRIT DE CORPS AND THE CODE OF SECRECY

In addition to the style of internal regulation and control, the quasi-military character of the police is evident in the esprit de corps that pervades the institution. Like the methods of enforcing soldierly discipline, the esprit de corps has some basis in the realities of police work and is, in its own way, purposeful. Policing is a dangerous occupation and the availability of unquestioned support and loyalty is not something officers could readily do without. In the heat of action it is not possible to arrange, from case to case, for the supply of support, nor can the supply of such support be made dependent on whether the cooperating agents agree about abstract principles. The governing consideration must be that as long as "one of us" is in peril, right or wrong, he deserves help. Moreover, manly pursuits ordinarily are associated with a spirit of close knit comradery that not only pervades personal relations but adds traits to the pursuit it does not necessarily have in and of itself. In fact, it is not unusual that some activities that are unpleasant as such are sought after if they are attended in a spirit of brotherly solidarity. Police officers often remark that one of the most cherished aspects of their occupation is the spirit of "one for all, and all for one."

To the extent that the fraternal spirit binds members of the police it also segregates them from the rest of society. It is therefore not an unmixed blessing even at first sight. But the fraternalism among policemen has come under critical scrutiny for other reasons as well. The late Chief William Parker considered it to be a major obstacle against police reform and he did everything in his power to break it up in the Los Angeles Police Department.[95] Naturally, Chief Parker was not opposed to the laudable practice of rushing to one another's aid; in fact he demanded that much of his subordinates in any case. Instead, his opposition was based on the realization that just as one can always count on the fact that personnel will close ranks and present a united front against outside critics, so one must also expect that similar tactics will be employed inside of the department. That is, functional parts of departments close ranks in dealing with each other, creating obstacles against integration of work, and subordinates close ranks against their superiors, preventing effective control. Thus, what appears on first glance as a uniform esprit de corps functions mainly as an infinite variety of contingently collusive arrangements that always bind the entire personnel against outsiders but also solidify a plethora of internal schisms and conspiracies.[96]

Despite the fact that the fraternal loyalty of the police is not what it appears to be to the naive beholder who thinks the "cops are one great happy family," it remains a fact that officers must work with men they can trust. This is so not only because it helps in making performance look better than it actually was, one man being always ready to attest to the excellence of his associate, but also because of the manifold dangerous uncertainties that inhere in the occupation. But the kind of trusting relations with one another policemen seem to require on a continuing basis are easily met by pervasive silence. Teams of partners do not talk about each other in the presence of nonteam members, line personnel do not talk about their peers in the presence of ranking officers and, of course, no members of the department talk about anything remotely connected with police work with any outsiders. Obviously the rule of silence is not uniform throughout these levels. Thus, matters that could never be mentioned to outsiders can be topics of shoptalk among peers. But this reflects only gradations of secretiveness. In a larger sense police departments accommodate a colossally complicated network of secret sharing, combined with systematic information denial.

The principal characteristic of this network of relations is that while secret sharing creates a state of mutual dependency and a semblance of lateral organization of cooperation on various levels of the institution, this result is held to a minimum by the overriding rule that no one tells anybody else more than he absolutely has to. In consequence, solidarity is based mainly on, and limited to the perception of, some external risk to a unit, regardless whether this risk is located outside or inside the institution. Beyond that, every man and every part of the force is on its own. The lack of cooperation between independent police organizations in the United States is well recognized,[97] and the bad relations between federal and local police agencies have reached a state of near notoriety. The hostility and information denial between bureaus and details of departments is occasionally admitted. But that every individual officer has important information that he does not share with anyone is virtually never mentioned in the literature. Yet this is a central fact of police work and every officer learns about it in the first year of his practice. By this we do not mean that individual officers have information which if revealed would compromise someone. Instead, we mean substantive factual information about crime, people, social areas, conditions, etc., which are of use in getting the work of policing done. That his brother officer might need access to such information for a specific purpose, or that he might benefit from having access to it in general, is his problem; he may receive informational help as a favor, but he has no claim on it.

The fact that all police officers are in some sense individual entrepreneurs while they are also dependent on one another gives their fraternal unity a particular cast. While all types of such solidarity are at the peak of their strength in confrontations with outsiders, that of the police is *only* outward oriented. Beyond that the solidarity does not lead to effective lateral cooperation between departments, between parts of departments, and between individual officers above the level of two-partner teams. Indeed, it appears that the most seasoned policemen who approach their work in the most craftsmanlike manner are most often acting as if they were independent practitioners who merely credit the department with the products of their work and who merely use their membership in the police force as the basis of their activity. For example, several detectives assigned to the fraud detail in a large West Coast city police department each had his separate files. Not only was the exclusive access to these files guaranteed by a tacit respect for privacy, but what they contained would probably not have been of much use to anyone but the men who collected them. They were meant to be a nonshareable resource, and their correct employment was impossible without the knowledge the detective kept in his head. Moreover, every detective had his private sources of information in the community who kept him abreast of new fraudulent practices and about the life and activities of known swindlers. These informants are under instructions not to speak to other policemen and it is considered to be a breach of professional ethic for one officer to trespass on another officer's informational domain.[98] Similarly, patrolmen assigned to stable beats are known to possess an enormous amount of factual information about their areas and about the people living in them, but they do not communicate this information to one another. Even the patrolmen who work the same streets do not share information. For example, one officer observed patrolling a skid-row area in a large Rocky Mountain city kept a card file of transients passing through his territory in the back room of a local bar. The supervising sergeant knew about it but made it clear that he would not dream of demanding access to it. His explanation was that "if you want a man to do a good job you have to let him do it in his own way."

It is important to emphasize that the pervasive information denial, which seems to make a mockery of the fraternal spirit, is not based solely on capricious secretiveness or on fear of disclosure of potentially embarrassing facts, though both of these factors are probably relevant to some extent. It appears that effective peacekeeping and crime control require the maintenance of personal ties with persons active in, or living on the fringes of, illegal activities. Since these ties involve an intricate exchange of secrets for favors they can be easily jeopardized by being open to others. Only the long-range symbiotic dependency between a policeman and his informer furnishes the security the latter craves. The informant has no reason to think that a third policeman who does not depend on him for a steady flow of information will have his interest at heart, and thus he will refuse to cooperate. If he has reasons to believe that his identity has been betrayed by the officer he once trusted, he will probably refuse to cooperate with him too. In addition to the fact that sources tend to dry up when they are not secretively cultivated, officers have understandably proprietary interest in exclusive access to them. Having a good informer is a substantial asset to an enterprising policeman. In the competitive struggle for advancement in the department it would be foolish for an officer not to maximize the advantage that accrues from exclusive access to information, especially since the development of a trusting source sometimes involves a good deal of work.

This method of working is generally accepted by policemen as a routine part of their occupation and those who depend on it close ranks to defend it against others in the department whose interests are opposed to it. Thus, for example, intelligence units in police departments are frequently isolated and distrusted. The one kind of intelligence that is not available to such units is the information from those community resources individual officers use in their work. Typically, the detectives assigned to intelligence units must develop their own contacts, and they avoid seeking the cooperation of other personnel out of fear that this would antagonize them. One important consequence of this state of affairs is that even the most advanced among our police departments are not anywhere near the objective of developing adequate information storage and retrieval systems. Even if the present efforts to make use of modern electronic technology would succeed in coding existing information, this would not encompass the knowledge that is currently neither shared nor recorded. But this information is incomparably more important in getting the practical tasks of police work done than all the materials contained in the now obligatory narrative reports. Talks with detectives assigned to intelligence units make it quite clear that the information denial from which they now suffer is not exclusively, nor even mainly, based on considerations of career expediency seen from the vantage point of officers who wish to protect their advantage. The interest of these units is to ensure that this information is made use of wherever it might be useful and they would be willing to make every provision to protect the advantage of the officer who would supply it by calling him into cases where his help is desired. The real obstacle is a fraternal understanding among those who have information not to cooperate. That is, the uniformed patrol as a whole, and the various bureaus, are opposed to having any of their members hobnobbing with detectives from the intelligence unit in accordance with the most general maxim of brotherly obligation to keep things one knows to himself.[99]

It is part of the pathological influence of the military bureaucratic approach to the "professionalization" of the police that it actually strengthens tendencies toward the combination of occupational individualism and defensive fraternal solidarity even though it is opposed to it in principle. The proliferation of formal regulation and the singleminded care that is given to their enforcement—even if only in appearance—creates a flow of communication that moves almost exclusively downwards through the chain of command. Though most of this communication does not actually relate to the realities of police work, or relates to it only in the most superficial way, it floods, so to speak, all the channels to capacity. Despite the fact that police departments depend almost entirely on the perceptiveness and judgment of their individual members to get the work of policing done, despite the fact that citizens who solicit police intervention always deal with individual officers whose decisions about the merits of the case are final,[100] there is virtually no feedback to the institution beyond the kind of record keeping that barely serves statistical purposes. Even if personnel would not have reasons of their own to deny the department vital information, the system would continue to encourage it because it contains no routinely open channels for return communication. This is not to say that those in command positions would not like to know what their subordinates know. Quite the contrary, they decry secretiveness. But they don't seem to realize that they cannot expect an upward flow of communications of any kind from the soldier-bureaucrat-policeman who is conditioned to respond to the incessant voice of regulation with "Yes, Sir!" and who will inevitably reply to even the well meant question, "What do you think?" with an obligatory "Whatever you say, sir!"

Even the military method of debriefing of field personnel

would be a substantial improvement over the existing state of affairs. By means of this device departments would be in a position of gathering at least a modicum of intelligence about conditions in specific territories and in specific problem areas. Optimally, police departments should institute the practice of regular staff conferences in place of the present largely meaningless roll call at which officers stand in military formation listening to the order of the day. Under present conditions such conferences are not feasible, nor are they likely to be productive of results. But this is in no way due to the nature of police work as such, but merely to the definition of the policeman's role as a small cog in a large quasi-military machine. Some people might say that the idea of "burly" policemen having staff conferences at every change of the watch in the precinct house is absurd, presumably because they are by the nature of their background, especially their low education and inarticulateness, not prepared for it. This view is almost certainly mistaken. Whenever police officers are furnished an opportunity to discuss their work problems around a conference table, they generally display a thoughtful approach that amazes outsiders. Naturally not all policemen contribute to discussions nor do all benefit from them. But in this respect they are not very different from teachers, some of whom might also not attend faculty meetings without much loss.[101]

People with high educational attainment often have a remarkably naive opinion of what can be expected of persons who did not attend college, and they never cease to marvel when they discover that such people are informed and resolute. There is perhaps no better example of this experience than what happened in this respect in many psychiatric hospitals. The initial impulse to have low-level psychiatric personnel, that is, attendants and practical nurses, attend staff conferences was to try to improve their performance by association with their betters. It was soon learned, however, that such persons, whose educational attainment is often below that of policemen, were not only fully competent participants in discussions but their contribution to conferences went far beyond what was expected. There is one more reason why the view that policemen could not benefit from ways of exchanging information and coordinating activity that are characteristic of the higher professions must be a travesty. For if it is in fact true that they are so crude as not to be able to discuss their work profitably, then surely they should not be entrusted with responsibilities that involve making decisions that literally involve the very existence of a great many people. Strangely, however, many of the same people who hold that police work is of the nature of a semiskilled occupation and ought to be organized accordingly, have absolutely no scruples in giving policemen powers that can save or destroy their own lives.

It is ironic that duties that arise out of a sense of fraternal obligation should be divisive in their effects. The duties to which we refer are, of course, to spring to the aid of one's fellow officer in case of an external attack, combined with the enjoinder not to stick one's nose into his business. It is difficult to see how relations between policemen can be anything but superficial and uneasy. For they have very little control over one another, contrary to what is commonly the case among work associates. Once accepted into his community, a police-man can be as different from the rest as he desires. The only rule he must observe scrupulously is not to go against his kind. Naturally, certain similarities of attitude develop from similari-ties of circumstance and from the common interest in opposing outside critics. Within these limits, however, reciprocal toler-ance is virtually unlimited. And they do tolerate the worst of their kind in their midst without a murmur of protest. Thus, Isidore Silver can say with full justification, "Police secrecy and suspicion even in 'professionalized forces' preclude 'ratting' on those violent and sadistic officers held in revulsion by their votaries."[102]

Our critique of the military-bureaucratic form of internal regulation and of the particular kind of fraternal spirit was mainly directed to show that they are specious forms of orga-nization of police departments. The former does not in any serious sense govern what policemen do in their work and the latter does not bring forth true understanding and cooperation among officers. Indeed, they not only create a mere semblance of order and cohesion that is actually unconnected with the real concerns of peacekeeping and crime control, but they are a positive impediment to the development of methodical approaches to it. It is no exaggeration to say that whatever good and responsible work some policemen do, they do despite the handicaps created by the department of which they are members. How little the existing forms of regulation mean is perhaps best highlighted by considering what the practices of medicine and nursing would be like if they were patterned solely by those bodies of bureaucratic rules that facilitate the operations of hospitals, that is, by rules concerning duty assignments, dress, punctuality, routine paper work, hierarchy, etc., while such matters as recognizing symptoms of illness, choosing and administering remedial treatment, and the whole rest of substantive concerns with the health and illness of patients were left entirely to the personal wisdom, integrity, and compassion of practitioners without being determined in any other way. If a body of medical and nursing skills did not exist, would anyone seriously expect that it could be extrapolated from hospital regulations? Would anyone believe that if such skill and knowledge existed in only a vestigial and largely unformulated form that they could flower under conditions where compliance with bureaucratic regulation was given unqualified priority over everything else? Could anyone hope that careful approaches to problems will develop where staff feel encouraged to attempt as many dramatic feats as possible without regard to substantive merit? Naturally the answer to these questions is a resounding no, and there can be no disagreement on the point that though hospitals must be well regulated, their regulation is necessarily subordinated to the craft of healing.

It could be said that the analogy is contrived because while we already have an elaborate and highly sophisticated craft of healing, there does not exist an even remotely similar craft of policing. This view, while true as far as it goes, is profoundly misleading. Healing was a professional craft long before a single element of its modern knowledge and technique was in existence. Though academies of medicine existed for centuries, most practitioners acquired whatever little knowledge they possessed through an apprenticeship system of training. And, of course, the requirement that licensed nursing be based on a background of academic training is of most recent origin. That is, the healing arts became professions not because they possessed a firmly formulated body of information and technique but because they cultivated the development of methodically informed craftsmanship. It was on this basis that they became emancipated from magic and came to operate on the foundation of a secular social trust.

No one knows, of course, how to set the development of a profession into motion, and therefore no one should presume to talk about the professionalization of the police in any but the most tentative terms. With this reservation in mind, some problems of development can be explored in the hope that they might lead to movement in the desired direction. In this undertaking it is useful, to some extent, to dwell on analogies with existing professions, provided that it be kept in mind that conditions that accompanied their birth no longer exist, and provided that full recognition be given to the substantive differences of tasks.

In the following we will discuss the formation of the professional police role under four general headings: first, the personal accreditation of police practitioners; second, the relationship of policing to scholarship; third, recruitment and professional training; and fourth, several specific topics of police practice. It must be emphasized that this discussion is not offered as exhaustive of the problem; in fact, it is not only incomplete, but to an extent desultory. These are simply some things that can be said now with some justification. If this discussion will be proven wrong in every point, but will have given rise to discussion, then the purpose for which it is offered will have been achieved. Should some of the things proposed be found acceptable, that much the better.

ACCREDITATION OF POLICE SKILL

The mandate of policing is assigned to police organizations as corporate entities and not to particular staff members. Specific duties of individual officers are, therefore, wholly derivative and determined by internal schemes of division of labor. While this kind of work organization is characteristic of all corporate structures, the police differ from others in one important aspect. Because all personnel enter their respective police departments with identical qualifications—more precisely, because differences of background do not receive official recognition in recruitment—the work distribution is largely arbitrary. That is, all members of police departments are eligible for all assignments at the outset of their careers and most remain in this status throughout their careers. Of course, some allocations of personnel to positions are stabilized. The hierarchy of command position, which can be attained through a system of civil service examinations is the most important way of fixing a differentiation of responsibility on a permanent basis. However, since the duties of sergeants, lieutenants, and captains are not clearly delineated, it is often merely a matter of departmental politics whether a position will be occupied by a man in one rank or another. Only in the uniformed patrol have command positions been routinized to some extent, but even here practice often conflicts with policy. In any case, the idea that underlies the hierarchical differentiation of command is that the best among equals move to levels of greater responsibility, with practically no regard for specific competence requirements either of substantive or managerial nature. Consequently it is not unusual that an officer who has commanded the traffic division will be shifted to assume command of, let us say, the juvenile detail. A modicum of technical specialization tends to develop through assignments to detective bureaus, assignments which are generally not governed by civil service rules, and men with several years of service in some crime control area will ordinarily not be called upon to do work outside their fields of activity. Moreover, seniority in terms of years of service tends to give some men an informal moral right to expect that their choice of work assignments will be given favorable consideration in the overall division of labor. These are, however, merely exceptions to the more general rule that being a policeman is basically an undifferentiated employment status, as many officers learn to their grief in the not infrequent department "shake-ups," if they do not already know it.

All members of police departments, without regard to rank or assignments, benefit from a certain occupational franchise. That is, by virtue of simply being a policeman one is officially licensed to undertake actions from which other citizens are barred. But this franchise is strictly derivative of actual employment. Contrary to the case of the social worker, teacher, or nurse, a policeman out of employment is merely an ex-policeman. In fact, the projection of a career in police work means virtually always spending one's working life in a single department. Though it happens occasionally that men occupying intermediate ranks in large departments will be lured away to head smaller departments, the occupation is generally characterized by the absence of opportunities for lateral movement among organizations. Thus, police officers are, in a sense, captives of departments and must restrict their career planning and social life to opportunities that are available locally. Consequently, aspirations to advancement cannot be oriented merely to objective features of good work in the occupation but must necessarily contain a more heavy admixture of regard for interpersonal relations with one's peers and superiors than is the case in occupations that have a marketable value outside the present employment situation. Thus, because in police work "what you know" unavoidably matters far less than "whom you know" than elsewhere, the realization of aspirations involves recourse to a ramified network of empire building, collusive arrangements, and informal politicking.[103]

Because the preponderant majority of policemen are in an undifferentiated employment status in terms of their official job classification and in terms of informal realities, and because there exists no open employment market for their occupational skill and experience, departments find it easy to order officers to do anything at all that according to the lights of the command needs to be done or will help to keep the system going. Thus, for example, when departments need mechanics, record clerks, messengers, laboratory technicians, ambulance drivers, switchboard operators, etc., they often assign officers to these jobs. Moreover, being assigned to the uniformed patrol might mean being ordered, in the course of a single day, to direct traffic, to investigate a reported crime, to transport a prisoner, to chaperone a teenage affair, to pacify a group of boisterous conventioneers, to do some clerical work in the station house, to escort a foreign dignitary, and more. While this gives police departments a great deal of organizational flexibility and, incidentally, makes the lives of those in command so easy as to make understandable why they do not need to possess managerial skills, it clearly conveys that men who can be ordered to do whatever comes up will not be expected to be good at anything in particular.

As a consequence of this situation it remains possible to define the role of the policeman at the level of the meanest task associated with his work. After all, it can always be said that a performance that can be replaced by a traffic light—something often mentioned by patrolmen with bitter humor—or driving a locked van full of drunks, does not require elaborate preparation and scarcely deserves a high level of recognition. But the same men who do this nonskilled or semiskilled work are also empowered to coerce citizens to obey their orders, are obligated to make decisions that can ruin a person's life, and are expected to help in keeping families intact and peaceful. Now, it is clearly vain and hopeless to claim professional status for such an occupation, especially when its more serious and more consequential parts are far less visible than its simple parts.

One reason why the more serious aspects of police work suffer from low visibility is that they center around the lives of people whose voice is either not heard or does not count on the forum of public opinion. It is exceedingly rare that policemen make decisions that have a direct and lasting effect on the circumstances of existence of members of the middle and upper classes. This segment of society experiences police presence mainly in the form of traffic control and similar low level service. But for the rest of the community—the poor, the powerless, the ghetto, the slum dwellers, the devious, the deviant, and the criminals—the policeman is a figure of awesome power and importance. What he does or fails to do literally shapes their destiny on a day to day basis. In this area of society an officer is continually in the position to save, let destruction take its course, or to destroy, and thus his role is at least as important as that of the physician, lawyer, or social worker. The only way one could possibly deny validity to this estimate of the importance and seriousness of police work is to take the view that whatever is done for or against the wretched is by definition unimportant and therefore not deserving of serious concern.[104] But this view is clearly inconsistent with the ethos of a civil polity. Surely even the most bigoted opinion will allow that dealings with skid-row derelicts, drug addicts, spouses at each other's throats, juvenile delinquents, and even hardened criminals, constitute a demanding and complex concern, and that, therefore, these tasks should be attended with motives and a degree of sophistication commonly associated with professional vocations. In the light of such considerations the professionalization of police work is a nondeferrable necessity and every alternative to it is nothing short of the betrayal of democratic ideals.

To elevate peacekeeping and crime control to the level of a professional vocation, indeed to create a favorable condition for this development, it would appear absolutely unavoidable that those who are assigned to such duties be freed of all tasks that are not connected with it, or only incidentally connected with it. It is inconceivable, or at least exceedingly unlikely, that this freeing could be attained within the framework of the present employment situation and organizational structure. That is, the present franchise that functions through membership of the force will have to be augmented by personal certifications of competent personnel. Certified or licensed policemen should not be required, nor are they likely to be willing, to do anything but policing. By the same token, they, and they alone, should be empowered, in accordance with the definition of the police role proposed earlier, to "exercise non-negotiably coercive force against citizens in the light of situational exigencies." The endless variety of routines that are currently part of police work, but which in the ordinary course of events do not require the competence mentioned in the definition, must be assigned to other kinds of staffs. It is after all most unlikely that the mayor's travels will be significantly impeded by protesting citizens and, accordingly, it is difficult to justify making a licensed policeman his chauffeur to ensure the freedom of movement he needs. To free licensed policemen to do police work the departments must cease to be miniature military establishments, in which the soldiers can be expected to do whatever needs doing, and they have to begin to be like every other corporate enterprise. They will have to develop, just as schools, hospitals, airlines, the post office, and so forth had to develop, a large variety of supportive services of a managerial, technical, clerical, skilled, and unskilled nature. Of course, management may have to be recruited in part from among licensed policemen, not unlike the case in schools and hospitals where it involves educators and physicians respectively, in addition to professional managerial personnel.

The way of attaining the objective of limiting the duties of policemen to policing is by making the license to engage in the activity analogous to the certification of teachers. In education the license to teach is granted to the person, and while the duty to provide an educational program is vested in school systems, the mandate is discharged by competing for, and employing the services of, individually competent teachers. Like policemen, teachers function in corporate settings and are to some extent under bureaucratic regulation. But it is understood that what they do in classrooms, that is what they do specifically *qua* teachers, is mainly determined by the skill and knowledge they are certified to possess. And, of course, they are substantially free of duties that have nothing to do with teaching. Naturally complete freedom from bureaucratic regulation and incidental duties cannot be attained in practice. Even physicians are often obliged to engage in, or desist from, certain practices merely to comply with some hospital regulation. The point always involves the location of emphasis.

In the long run the issuing of police credentials, like the issuing of teaching credentials, must become the function of professional schools. But the beginning of the certification does not need to await the development of such schools. Large police departments could very well begin right now to function as selective licensing institutions in the manner in which large hospitals have in the past, and do even to some extent now function as licensing institutions for registered nurses.

The beginning of licensing will undoubtedly create troublesome problems and perhaps even dangerous tensions. Since large departments should begin the process, before professional schools will take over, and since they differ greatly, the procedure that might be appropriate in Los Angeles will not work in Chicago or New York. In any case, it is more than likely that the greater danger is on the side of being too hesitant about it than on the side of making mistakes. One way in which departments could set the licensing procedure into motion would be to adopt the distinctions of relative competence recommended in the Report of the President's Commission on Law Enforcement and Administration of Justice.[105] Though this recommendation does not intend the creation of personally certified professional policemen because it is far too closely attuned to administrative needs of existing police systems, it could, precisely for this reason, serve as a transitional phase in the transformation from soldier-bureaucrat to professional.

THE RELATIONS OF POLICE WORK TO SCIENTIFIC SCHOLARSHIP

It is often said that the *sine qua non* of a modern profession is that it be founded on a body of technical, scholarly knowledge.[106] That is, the public trust in the efficacy of professional practices is based in part on the assumption that what a practitioner decides to do is related to information contained in books and taught in classrooms. Such knowledge is arcane, at least in the sense that it is not accessible to lay people, its acquisition involves protracted and assiduous study, and its validity is determined by scientific criteria, rather than by standards of common sense reasonableness.

In our times the connection between this kind of arcane information and professional practice is justified entirely on the basis of secular and pragmatic considerations. But it is a matter of some importance that the tie between professional knowing and professional doing antedates this understanding of its significance. At their beginnings, the great professions of healing and teaching were founded on sacred knowledge and their procedures were closely related to religious ritual and priestly functions. Thus, their intellectual, or more properly perhaps, spiritual character is not a modern invention. Instead, they have from the time of their outset been, so to speak, inspired vocations. But modern physicians and modern teachers have become what they are today only after they turned into an exhaustively secular "priesthood." The conversion of these professions from their archaic to their contemporary form involved a complete emancipation from the sources of their origin. The turn to secular-scientific scholarship, in lieu of earlier recourse to divination and revelation, was in large measure due to the fact that the former is superior to the latter in the attainment of worldly purposes. But the archaic sense of the connection between arcane knowledge and professional practice did not disappear entirely. Science merely took the place of sacred knowledge. For this to be possible it is necessary to claim more on behalf of science than can be actually justified. Thus, though everyone knows that as a merely technical resource available scientific information is often not adequate to handle many specific problems, its use is nevertheless attended by the hopeful belief that somehow, in yet unknown ways, science cannot fail. Consequently, to claim for some professional procedure that it is scientific constitutes an ambiguous claim, or, at least, as ambiguous a claim as to invoke divine sanction in its favor. In this framework the belief in the connection between scientific truth and professional practice can remain intact even though specific justifications are often lacking and for the rest only of passing merit. In sum, the professionalization of modern medicine and teaching involved the severance of ties with their beginning, that is, the transfer from sacred to secular knowledge, *and* a hefty dose of faith in the ultimate value of scientific scholarship.

Not all the modern professions trace their origins to associations with religious wisdom and priestly functions, however, and hence not all begin with arcane knowledge. Engineering, for example, springs from the other end of the sacred-secular spectrum. It was from the outset geared to the mundane objectives of converting forms of work from lower to higher input-output ratios, and to changing matter from worthless to valued forms. The practitioners of this craft remained shop craftsmen roughly up to the end of the last century. Despite notable achievement the craft did not attain professional status until it became emancipated from exclusive concerns with situational work problems and from apprenticeship methods of training and turned to bookish knowledge and to academic instruction.[107] Similarly, social work arose out of humanitarian and political motives. But its helping functions remained a lay pursuit until it became dissociated from these inspirations and went on to basing its practices on a body of information and precepts that at least aspire to recognition as scientific.

In an earlier section of this chapter we have criticized at length the quasi-military character of modern American police forces. We can now put this critique in yet another perspective. In some inchoate sense all police forces trace their origin to the role of men of arms, as is, indeed, still reflected in the term gendarme. Certainly this is the guiding sense of the occupational self-conception of many policemen. Now, in abandoning this conception, and the entire framework of militaristic associations that come with it, the police would move along the path of development of all the professions which received recognition only after severing connections with their respective sources of origin and gained new public trust and legitimacy on the basis of association with secular scientific scholarship.

The transformation of the conception of policing from the model of the man of arms to the model of the trained professional, whose training stands in some relationship to scientific scholarship, naturally involves the mobilization of specifically delineated programs of study and instruction. The development of such programs requires decisions of what should be studied and what should be taught. But the consideration of these questions can go on indefinitely. The only way out of this situation is to form some institutions that can assume at least provisional jurisdiction over the solution of these problems. Drawing on analogies with the existing professions, such institutions are the post-graduate professional schools.

It may seem preposterous to suggest the formation of post-graduate professional schools of police work—graduation from which will ultimately be a condition of employment for all licensed policemen—at a time when most of those who practice the occupation have no more than a high school education. Worse yet, it may seem cynical to suggest that such schools be formed prior to the time the field of study can be defined or even adumbrated. But if these objections are taken at their face value then none of the existing professional schools could have been founded in the first place, and some might lose their right to existence even today. The presumption that the research programs and curricula of the existing schools have unexceptionally well founded relevance to professional practice is simply a presumption.[108] A good deal of what physicians, lawyers, teachers, social workers, and so forth study in their respective institutions is of no sensible use and is either simply forgotten or abandoned because it is dated before the hard won knowledge can be applied. Moreover, in some professions, such as engineering or social work, practitioners without educational credentials still abound and the possession of a degree is not yet an enforceable condition of employment. None of this, however, alters the fact that professional schools in these occupations function as legitimizing institutions of the professional status of the occupations as a whole.

Though it is not true of all professional schools, in some it matters less that they have a well-defined field of study and a well-justified program of instruction than that they be the foci of scholarly pursuits oriented to some field practice. As far as the students of these schools are concerned it is less important that they learn a body of specific facts and specific techniques, than that they acquire a complex of generalized methods and approaches to facts and problem solving. Preferably professional education should be as rich in substance as medicine and engineering are. But in the absence of knowledge of such richness and complexity, the education is valuable even if it merely imparts studiousness and the habits of inquisitively dispassionate reasoning. Above all, however, the importance of professional schools resides in that they constitute links between occupations and scientific scholarship. It is difficult to overestimate the practical and symbolic significance of this fact. For better or for worse, in our society occupations progress in efficiency, sophistication, importance and dignity proportionately to the strength of the connections they maintain with academic scholarship.

It is important to emphasize that the transformation of meaning to which we refer—from gendarme to professional policemen—cannot be accomplished by merely infusing police work with some fruits of scientific research or by requiring policemen to secure academic degrees within the existing programs of instruction. Thus, for example, the various existing programs of instruction for policemen offered in association with college departments of social science will almost certainly not produce the desired result. Such programs are valuable only as temporary expedients and because they might help some persons who are active in the police establishment to acquire the stature and the interest to lay the foundations for independent police work– education. But even this much is perhaps too much to expect. For in the existing programs the students are taught by academicians and left to their own resources to establish the connection between what they learn and what they must do. Often such instruction causes resentment rather than enlightenment. Furthermore, student-policemen are the recipients of watered-down wisdom because instructors tend to assume that men who joined the police are probably not very desirous of learning. The depressing effect of this assumption is augmented by the belief instructors and students share that taking courses will make but a slight and uncertain impact on the student's standing in the police department. Finally, the existing programs are generally designed to service existing police systems. Though they are greatly superior to what is offered in departmental police academies, they turn out men who are neither prepared nor equipped to oppose the soldier-bureaucrat role that awaits them.

It is clearly not for lawyers, sociologists, or psychologists to develop an intellectually credible version of what police work should be like. This must be left to scholarly policemen, just as the analogous task is left to scholarly physicians, social workers, or engineers. Of course, lawyers, sociologists, and psychologists will retain a role in the professional police work curriculum; but it will be an auxiliary role of the kind that chemists, physiologists, and psychologists now have in medical schools. For the main reason for having professional schools of police work is to make a home for police work-study. It must be their own home, or the enterprise will be dispirited and doomed to failure. The development of a fully reasoned meaning of the police role in society, that might give rise to a range of rationally methodical work procedures, must be worked out from within the occupation, it cannot be imparted to it by outsiders.[109] Outsiders can help in this task, but they cannot take it over. The main reason for this is not that outsiders are not adequately informed but that supplying knowledge from external sources would leave police work intellectually inert. The main purpose of having professional schools of police work (and it is not a matter of great importance whether they be of a postgraduate nature as was argued above and as is the case for schools of social work, or of an undergraduate nature as is the case for schools of engineering) is not to produce educated policemen but to make *specific education,* and the range of meaning associated with it, part of the conception of the occupation.[110] This can only be achieved by independent degree granting institutions functioning within the framework of existing universities, in the maintenance of which the practicing profession will have a realistic interest.

It takes little imagination to anticipate the formidable difficulties that will attend the formation of a connection between police work and scientific scholarship by means of independently functioning professional schools. The universities will undoubtedly balk at having such schools in their midst, as they have in the past opposed the establishment of other such schools. Even after a foothold is gained the relations will remain strained, as they are generally between academicians and professionals. But all this is a relatively minor difficulty. Professional police schools can buy their way into the university as was done by others who brought financial endowments with them. That this is possible may be sad, but it is true. No matter how painful it is to admit it, the modern university is no longer a bastion of pure learning; the ivory tower is merely its *inner sanctum.* A more serious difficulty is created by the need to staff the schools with faculties drawn from within the occupation. Though the number of persons who are capable of taking such positions is not great, it is quite probable that there are more of them than is generally known. The only possible solution of this problem is for some groups of policemen with respectable credentials to get together, work out some program jointly with some interested scholars and lawyers, and approach a university with a request for acceptance. In this way, schools will be created as viable prospects for them to emerge. But the greatest problem of all is to mobilize, in the existing police establishment, the conviction that the development proposed here is absolutely necessary and will not abide any delays. Since we do not propose to run out of solutions in this study, and because the proposed solution requires a background argument, we will deal with it in the next section.

RECRUITMENT AND EDUCATION

Though we have argued in all seriousness that the licensing of professional policemen and the establishment of professional police schools are nondeferrable projects, they are clearly of a long-range nature. Even if the proposals were to be accepted, it will take years for them to gain momentum. But changes could be instituted in existing methods of police training and recruitment that would enhance this development immeasurably. They also are meritorious without regard for this consideration. Indeed, virtually all we will propose has been recommended as desirable by the President's Commission on Law Enforcement and Administration of Justice; we merely wish to put a new cast on these matters.

In simplest terms: it must be made clear as unambiguously as possible that education does matter in police work. This demand has a certain obvious meaning which we do not and indeed could not possibly intend. We do not propose that education be made to matter in the sense that what is taught be specifically relevant to practice. Naturally this would be highly desirable; but because very little knowledge exists that could conceivably serve this purpose, the limitation would merely show that study does not really matter. Instead, we merely propose that the need for protracted and assiduous study be firmly associated with the occupation of policing. The main objective of the recommendation is to abolish permanently the idea that is all too prevalent in our society that if one does not want to take the trouble of becoming something worthwhile, he can always become a cop. Of the many ways in which the relevance of education can be asserted in practice, the following four appear to be feasible without placing an unduly heavy tax on available resources.

First, the possession of a regular college degree should be made a minimum prerequisite for employment as a policeman. This standard will be later changed as professional schools begin to turn out graduates. The main argument that is ordinarily marshaled against recruiting at the college level is that police departments find it difficult to fill vacancies even through recruiting at lower educational levels. The argument has a certain surface cogency, but is faulty on several counts. For one thing, by recruiting at the level of the high school diploma, police departments in effect lower their standards from year to year. While it must certainly not be assumed that all those young people who decide not to go to college are necessarily lacking in intelligence or aspirations, it is only reasonable to expect that as progressively larger percentages of high school graduates do continue their education, the remaining pool of eligibles will decline in average quality. Thus, it should not come as a surprise that many police departments find it impossible to accept more than a ridiculously small fraction of applicants.[111] Next, the fact that an occupation recruits at the high-school level and cannot find sufficient numbers of eligible applicants does not, in and of itself, compel the conclusion that it would do worse by recruiting at the college level. In fact, it makes a good deal of sense to suppose that, given the rather attractive remuneration—in comparison with teaching or social work—many a young man with a college degree does not choose to become a policeman *because* his diploma is not required.[112] Furthermore, many occupations suffer from personnel shortages, but they do not meet this problem by taking in whoever they can get. For example, registered nurses are in even shorter supply than policemen and they are paid considerably less, but the entrance requirements have been increased. The shortages are coped with by purging nursing of menial tasks that require no professional competence, and employing attendants for this purpose. We have pointed to the desirability of an analogous development in police work while discussing the problem of licensing. Naturally, college graduates do not relish the prospect of being station clerks or animated street signs, but policemen should not have to do this kind of work anyway; it must be granted, though, that many who do it now should probably continue doing it, without, however, being empowered to do real police work. Finally, and perhaps most importantly, an occupation that cannot find sufficient numbers of candidates of adequate background and quality, and yields to the compulsion to take what it can get, obviously veers into a course of decline. There is no use in having policemen if they are not the ones we need.

Though it may be unkind, it is difficult to suppress the suspicion that the high-school level of entrance into the police is retained not for any realistic reasons, but because those who set the standards, those who do the recruiting, and those who run the police departments, do not wish to be educationally outranked by their subordinates and risk all sorts of disciplinary problems on that account.

Second, in-service training should be extended to at least two years. Of course, this also will change with the advent of the professional schools. In the meantime it is simply silly to quibble whether police training should last six or twelve weeks. In either case the recruit learns nothing about police work and acquires the firm conviction that he doesn't need to know anything about it. In place of this, recruits should be exposed to regular four semesters of half-time college work, involving textbooks, exams, grades, and all the other accouterments of academic study. According to calculations made by college students who have to work while they go to school, this should leave approximately six hours daily for work assignments, without undue stress. During the first semester, the work assignment should involve tasks that do not involve contacts with citizens, while the remaining three semesters of class work would be accompanied by supervised practice. During vacations, the recruits would of course be available on a full-time basis to the department. Since, according to the International Association of Police Chiefs, some departments can now afford as much as twenty weeks of full-time training, what we propose does not seem to put excessive pressure on manpower resources.[113] But it would convey the clear message that becoming a policeman involves protracted study. It is rather obvious that there will be no great problems in devising a course curriculum, since class work will be mainly broadly *educational* in such areas as law, sociology, psychology, accompanied by some more technical courses, such as criminalistics. The *training* aspect will be left entirely to supervised practice. Needless to say the student will remain in a probationary status during the four semesters, without any powers of a licensed policeman, and aware that the grades he receives and the evaluations his supervisors make will have a bearing on his career.

Third, all presently employed personnel should be required to pass, at a pace of one course per semester, the curriculum offered for recruits, or to take an analogous course curriculum at a college. Licensure of present staff should be made conditional on this requirement. Since people in other occupations often have to go to school on their own time to keep up with changes in their occupation, there are no reasons why one could not expect the same of policemen. In any case, those who do not desire to avail themselves of this opportunity should be assured of continued employment in some capacity other than the licensed policeman. It must be admitted, however, that this requirement is probably not enforceable without making some exception on the basis of considerations of rank and age.

Fourth, successful study should be rewarded by increases in pay and career advancement. It is scarcely necessary to argue the merits of this recommendation. There are few people who will undertake the ardors of study for the love of learning alone, and if they feel that love they typically do not join any profession.

Though it was mentioned before, a point deserves repeated emphasis: the insistence on study and education, expressed in this section, was not meant to be technically specific. What they will learn will not make the students any better policemen in a practical sense. But they will be different kinds of policemen both through selection and through the educational experience. For example, to have an understanding of law will enable them at least to seek a rational understanding of the recent court decisions.[114] In particular, making the college degree a requirement for admission to police work should not be misunderstood: four years of a liberal arts education of any kind will not prepare a young man for police work. And it would be absolutely pernicious to encourage the belief, either in the minds of the new recruits or of existing personnel, that a B.A. in sociology or psychology equips a person to do peacekeeping or crime control. Quite the contrary, until the time that the professional schools will get into a full swing of operation, the college graduates will have to learn the craft of policing from the old hands. What the recruitment of college graduates will accomplish, however, is to impel the occupation in the direction of becoming a social mechanism functioning at the level of complexity, sophistication, and responsibility commensurate with the gravity of the problems it is meant to meet. Such an impulse can be expected of college graduates not because they are invariably more idealistic or more resolute than their high school counterparts, but because they will find it in their own selfish interest. College graduates will naturally tend to resist mechanical discipline and work assignments that are below the level of their qualifications; they will naturally demand opportunities for advanced training and explore new possibilities of practice in place of the tired old routines; and they will demand recognition of their professional status over and above whatever recognition accrues from having employment ties with a police department. But this kind of militancy would, in effect, make the implementation of desired reforms a self-implementing process, simply because the ordinary career aspirations of college graduates are in line with them. Above all, college graduates will accept the idea of professional police schools with enthusiasm, will provide the cadres of students and teachers and, last but not least, will make the idea of professional police schools acceptable to the university.

Of course there will be problems in making education matter in police work. Not the least of them will be the resistance of old personnel. But this can be overcome, in part by making certain that the institution of the new requirements will not jeopardize the employment security and income of present staff. Administrative devices like "grandfather clauses" have this effect. Beyond that it will be necessary to convince present personnel that making a college degree a condition of licensed police work cannot but help the status of the occupation as a whole, benefiting even those who do not have it.

SOME ELEMENTS OF METHODICAL POLICE WORK

The role components of policing discussed in the preceding sections are all of a formal nature. That is, neither the restriction of occupational duties to serious police work and its licensing as a marketable occupation, nor the severance of ties with military origins and alignment with academic scholarship, nor the institution of the emphasis on educational requirements, specify what a policeman must know and what he must be able to do, in substantive terms. It was merely proposed that the introduction of these formal role components will further the development of a disciplined and explicit body of knowledge and technical skill, and that without introducing them such a development is not likely to take place. But it is possible to go beyond that to the tracing of fragmentary outlines of substantive knowledge and technique, albeit merely in a tentative manner and mainly for purposes of further exploration.

In the following remarks, we will attempt to sketch several elements or aspects of what appears to be professional, purposeful, and responsible police work. It is important to emphasize that, in accordance with our earlier expressed view, the substance of police professionalism must issue mainly from police practice and police experience; none of the points discussed is based on purely invented desiderata. Indeed, the following features of police work are not being presented as necessary and proper in the same sense as the formal role components discussed in the foregoing three sections. Instead, they are presented because there seems to attach to them a sense of rationality and methodicalness. What commends them is not that they are right but that they are based on reason, rather than on feeling, and in this sense professional. All of the following topics are based on observations of police practice and on extended conversations with policemen of all ranks and all kinds of assignments. That is, the to-be-described knowledge and methods are already in use. But what will be said is merely descriptive of some policemen and not of others. The possession of this information and skill, and its use, are optional in police work under present conditions. They are usually perceived as elements of a personal style of work and they are neither urged upon others nor recognized as superior to alternatives. In fact, even the officers of whom what we will have to say is descriptive typically do not undertake to advocate the propriety and usefulness of their own ways, nor do they express disapproval of alternative ways. They recognize that in the present system they can have their own peace only by leaving everybody else in peace, even if this goes against their better judgment.

The Use of Area Knowledge

As is well known, there are two schools of thought concerning the organization of activities of the uniformed patrol. One emphasizes the need for familiarity with the area that is patrolled and frequent contact with people, and the other a high degree of motorized mobility. Both sides agree that both objectives are desirable. In general, however, arguments favoring mobility have the advantage, and the overall tendency in most departments is to put as many members of the patrol as possible into radio-monitored vehicles, where they can be readily reached and quickly dispatched to troublespots. Continuous connection with dispatchers requires that officers do not leave their cars except to handle assigned incidents. It is readily granted that this reduces contacts with citizens, makes surveillance more cursory, and attenuates the officers' opportunities to become familiar with the areas they patrol. But it is felt that this is not an excessive sacrifice to achieve the ability to respond rapidly to distant needs for services and a high mobilization potential in general.[115] It is possible, however, that this felt preference is due to an inadequate appreciation of the importance of area knowledge in police work.

For rather obvious reasons, the effectiveness of both control and help is greatly enhanced when specific situational factors can be taken into account. To be sure, it is always possible to cite some needs that can be met by universalistic approaches in which the helping and controlling agents can act, or at least can pretend to act, "according to the book," regardless of circumstances. More generally, however, the neglect of situational realities produces the impact of inconsiderateness as far as the subjects of the interventions are concerned, which in itself impairs the effectiveness of the agent.[116] Beyond that, and all policemen will agree on this point, methods that *simply* follow universalistic rules are also ordinarily ill considered. Thus, very often one hears officers explaining that while some procedure is *normally* indicated, in "this particular situation" the norm must be suspended in favor of certain particular considerations. Since this kind of explanation is exceedingly frequent, it seems quite clear that what is referred to as *the* norm is merely a formalized paradigm of action, that "departures" from it are not exceptions or evasions, and that the proper application of the norm always involves attuning it to circumstantial factors.[117] To give circumstantial factors their correct weight in decision making it is necessary that they be intelligently appraised. That is, patrolmen must be able to draw on background information to be able to discern what particular constellations of facts and factors mean. In the case of the carefully deliberate policeman—by which is meant a man who organizes his activities with a view toward long-range peacekeeping and crime control objectives in the area of his patrol, knowing that what he does from case to case can create more or less calculable advantages or liabilities for himself in the future—the background information consists of an enormously detailed factual knowledge.[118] When one accompanies such a man in his patrol duties, he can hear countless variations of stories like, "This is Jack S. He used to own a Dime Store, but for the past ten years he has been working for the T Company. His marriage has been on the rocks ever since his daughter got married. He owns several old automobiles and he quarrels with his neighbors on account of taking up all the curbside parking. He and his wife spend a couple of evenings a week in the X Bar. But when I see him there alone, I know that more likely than not he will get dead drunk and I will have to take him home. We once had him up on receiving stolen property, with one of his cars, but they let him go," and so on. Ordinarily such stories are told with minute precision, mentioning specific names, places, and dates, and they are told in great profusion. That is, many people are known in considerable detail. In addition to this, patrolmen know the shops, stores, warehouses, restaurants, hotels, schools, playgrounds, and all other public places in such a way that they can recognize at a glance whether what is going on in them is within the range of normalcy.

No matter how rich such factual knowledge of an area and its residents is, however, it can never encompass more than a fraction of reality. Many places have not been visited and most persons are not recognized. Thus it appears that though interest is directed to the accumulation of factually descriptive information, as opposed to the desire to achieve a theoretically abstract understanding, the ulterior objective is to be generally knowledgeable rather than merely being factually informed. That is, patrolment seek to be sufficiently enlightened to be able to connect the yet unknown with the known through extrapolation and analogy. By this method they are always in the position to reduce the open and unrestricted variety of interpretative possibilities that baffles outsiders to a far more restricted range. They always have, as it were, something to go on. Thus, the factual area knowledge, far from being merely a desultory array of data, functions as a powerful scheme of interpretation. It partakes of the nature of a good ethnographic grasp in that it employs typifications without sacrificing interest in and respect for individual variation. Every person and every event is always seen as a particular instance of a class, that is, neither merely unique nor merely a type.

In calling the patrolman's area knowledge ethnographic we intend to indicate that it is methodical in ways quite akin to the knowledge of sociologists and social anthropologists.[119] Social scientists, of course, engage in participant observation field work for limited periods of time and for the purpose of writing scholarly work about it, while the policeman acquires his knowledge on an indefinitely continuing basis for practical purposes. Moreover, since policemen ordinarily do not write books, they feel no compulsion to formulate their methods explicitly. Thus, many of those who are obviously methodical in their orientation and practice tend to say that what they do "comes naturally when you like working with people." This view is not entirely mistaken. Many people could probably never become either good ethnographers or area-knowledgeable patrolmen. But it is established that the competence of those who want to be ethnographers can be vastly increased by study and guided experience. There is every reason to suppose that this could also be true of area knowledge in police work. But under present conditions every patrolman is left to his own devices in mobilizing and using this resource.

There is a particular reason why the cultivation of area knowledge in existing police departments is left entirely to the initiative of individual officers, and is treated as a noncommunicable style of work. It does not possess any recognizable high value as far as departments as a whole are concerned. The drunk whom the patrolman escorts home, knowing who he is and where he lives, will be neither the victim nor the perpetrator of an assault. How should one measure credit for the prevention of relatively rare and unforeseeable contingencies? Moreover, area knowledge helps "only" the officer who uses it. Though knowledgeable patrolmen could be "the eyes and ears" of their departments, in fact they are not. This is due to the pervasive information denial and the absence of upward communication channels which we described earlier as characteristic of military-bureaucratic police systems. Of course, no one objects when individual policemen do well on their own and many high police officials applaud it, but only if it doesn't involve any special costs.

Technical Concerns

Closely associated with area knowledge is a range of types of information about, and approaches to, problems that are typically associated with specialization in police work. It is important to emphasize that while this complex of knowledge, technique, and attitude is presently observable almost exclusively among officers assigned to specific crime control fields, there is no necessary connection between the two.

Perhaps it is best to explain what is meant by technical con-

cern through an illustration. An officer whose duties are limited to dealing, let us say, with shoplifting will tend to develop
knowledge about it of the kind that can be found in the book
by Mary Owen Cameron.[120] That is, he will know the varieties
of techniques associated with the crime, the types of persons
who engage in it, and the opportunities that exist for it in the
community. Beyond that, however, he will seek to be continually apprised of changes in the population of shoplifters operating in his jurisdiction by keeping tabs on roving gangs of
shoplifters who move from city to city and by investigating the
ever-changing patterns of association between shoplifting and
other kinds of illegal activities, such as prostitution or the sale
of stolen goods. Finally, he will be observant of innovations in
merchandizing with a view to whether or not they lend themselves to theft. In a manner of speaking, his interest is not
unlike that of the "professional" criminal and his attitude is
businesslike. While the activity of some daring criminal causes
indignation in everybody else, it presents a technical challenge
to the policeman to whom we refer. But contrary to the sleuth
celebrated in detective fiction, our man does not concentrate
on a particular case by carefully assembling the plot of an
individual crime. Instead, he focuses on a crime problem in
general and he is moved by the desire to achieve maximum
control over it. He may be occasionally zealous in his work, but
he guards against letting his pursuits develop into a vendetta.[121]
He is apt to feel that "you can't let things get to you if you don't
want to end up with a bleeding ulcer." He knows that criminals
are not nice people and he expects neither politeness nor
candor from them. He also knows that they will try to elude
him and outwit him, and he prepares to meet these difficulties
rather than relying on a strenuous chase or a head-on clash.

Such officers, whose description we have already idealized
for purposes of emphasis, are certainly not above losing their
patience and striking out in anger. But contrary to the crusad-
ers against crime who act mainly on impulse, they consider
impulsive action sometimes excusable, occasionally even useful
to put the fear of God into someone, but generally inferior to
calculated and informed procedure. That is, for them the

preference for wits over brawn is a matter of principle, which, once accepted, becomes a fixed habit in decision making.

In crime control technical concerns are of direct and readily understandable importance. The more an officer knows about shoplifting the more likely he will be to solve such crimes by arresting offenders. But the attitude of dispassionate interest that is naturally associated with technical concerns is perhaps more important than the resulting volume of arrests. The point is simply this: in an occupation that is directed principally to dealing with things that stir up feelings of hatred, indignation, contempt, and fear in most people, it is doubly important to bring such feelings under control. A policeman who acts merely in ways everybody else would act naturally forfeits the claim to practicing a specialized occupation of any kind, let alone a profession. For in this case it is not he, as a person, who is employed by society, but merely the deeper and more visceral levels of his psyche; it is scarcely possible to imagine a more degrading status, no matter what the objectives behind it.

A policeman who hits a verbally abusive suspect and turns to an outside observer to ask, "Wouldn't you have done the same thing?" might well get the answer, "Yes, but *you* shouldn't!" The assertion, "*you* shouldn't," though it might be fundamentally determined by legal and moral considerations, cannot be argued exclusively, or even principally, on these grounds. People always tell others to be ethical and high-minded! To draw an analogy, physicians refrain from sexually exploiting access to their patients' bodies not so much because it is immoral but more because eroticism wreaks havoc with sobriety needed for good judgment. Similarly, the interdiction, "You shouldn't act impulsively," directed to a policeman must be related to practical occupational interests. That is, it must finally rest on the realization that in any kind of purposeful work, impulsive action is inefficient, uncontrollable, and obstructive of the attainment of the worker's own interest. It might be a source of emotional gratification but it defeats every kind of other purpose the agent might have in mind. It submits the impulsive person to the control of anyone who has a mind to provoke him and it makes the impulsive person to that extent unfree. Only the resolutely calculating approach, that is, a technical concern, leaves the options in the hand of the agent. A detective sergeant with twenty-two years of work experience in one of the great American police departments put this view into words upon which it is difficult to improve: "In all these years as a cop I was always up to my ass in things that would turn your stomach and make your blood boil. But to me they don't mean anything but work. I might have lost my patience more often than I should have, but I am not proud of it. I have learned a long time ago that in this racket it is always better to be smart than to do things in ways that make you feel good at the moment. A lot of guys don't know that, and when they get to be forty years old and no longer feel like wrestling in the gutter with everybody who calls them a dirty son of a bitch, they figure there is nothing left for them to do."

COPING WITH RESISTANCE
AND THE USE OF FORCE

The control over compliance with normative expectations is a diffuse social function most of which is embedded in the everyday network of interpersonal transactions. Within this network even the lowliest member of his community has the capacity to create conditions that will in effect compel others to live up to standards. Such powers are, however, always limited. Among the limitations, the most important is that we cannot compel compliance, even when it is recognizably due, by recourse to illegitimate means. For example, we are not permitted to collect a debt with force. In other societies and in earlier times this method was unobjectionable, but in our society and in our times he who "takes the law into his own hands" commits a culpable offense, even though his claim might be just. In place of the freedom of self-help we have devised an exceedingly cumbersome and time-consuming method of dealing with transgressions and omissions, known as the administration of justice. For most purposes this method works, if not well, at least well enough. Thus, if I desire to prevent my neighbor's dog from tearing up my flower bushes, I can go to court to obtain some satisfaction for past damages and an injunction against future trespasses. But if the neighbor sicks his dog on me and threatens to do it again, then I can scarcely be expected to wait for the wheels of justice to turn. Instead, I will do what every American would, namely, "Call the cops!"

What are the duties of the police in a case of this nature? Let us explore the incident further to discover the answer. Two policemen drive up approximately one-half hour after my call for help and while walking up to my house they observe the dog in my neighbor's yard. I explain that I have been bitten by the animal, which has been a nuisance for quite some time, and that I am fearful that I might be bitten again. I know that I cannot prove that the neighbor sicked the dog on me but our city has a leash ordinance that clearly has been violated and therefore I want the owner arrested and the dog confiscated. After all, the animal could be rabid and should be checked. The patrolmen, who kept asking many questions while I was reciting my tale, find the suggestion that they arrest the neighbor too strong. People are not ordinarily arrested for violating city ordinances; besides, since the violation could certainly be no more than a misdemeanor, they lack the power to make an arrest as they did not witness the offense. But they agree that the dog should probably be quarantined and they will see what can be done about it. Before taking leave they suggest that the bite should be treated and they offer to make arrangements for transportation to a medical aid station. After I turn down their offer they proceed to my neighbor's house. On the way one of the officers goes to the car to call the dispatcher, requesting that the city animal pound send someone to pick up the animal. Then there follows a prolonged conversation during which my neighbor manages to explain that he is a taxpayer and law abiding citizen, whose dog has never bitten anyone, and who has the misfortune of living next door to a troublemaker. Well, say the officers, whatever the case might be, the dog will have to be quarantined. Over his dead body, replies the dog owner. At this moment the van from the animal pound arrives and the driver joins the group. No matter what is said, however, my neighbor will not yield; he becomes more and more acrimonious as he is being told that his pet will have to go and that he himself could be arrested for interfering with an officer in the performance of his duty.

As it happens a sociologist was doing research about the police in the city and he arranged to accompany the sergeant supervising the patrol watch of which our officers were members. They heard the initial assignment over the radio and after attending first to some other incident they decided to drop in on the case. They arrived at the moment when the officers were about to arrest the man. The sergeant received a quick briefing from one of the officers, after which he walked up to the door of the house, which was blocked by my neighbor. He introduced himself by rank, name, and station and continued by remarking that he caught a glance of the dog through the fence and thought he was a clean and healthy looking animal, could he see him, please. The sergeant and my neighbor walked through the house into the yard where they talked about pets for a while. The sergeant took the dog off the chain and, while fondling him, remarked that it would be a lot cheaper to have the animal checked at the city pound than by a private veterinarian. There is no reason to worry about the dog, he added, because he will personally sign the receipt which will make it clear that the dog is in his custody while being examined. My neighbor did not protest when the sergeant handed the dog to the pound attendant.[122]

The case was cited at such length because it contains several elements that pervade routine police peacekeeping. First, there is a complainant with a real grievance who in calling the police hopes, openly or secretly, to invite doom upon his adversary. Though it can be argued in such cases that the complaint is of a civil rather than criminal nature and, thus, strictly speaking, not within police jurisdiction, there is often the risk that what is merely a private quarrel among citizens could escalate into violence. Thus it cannot be left unattended. Second, the officers who handled the case were competent. They recognized that the situation involved bad blood among neighbors. They also knew the law and took the trouble of explaining the limitations of their powers to the complainant. Third, the officers made a serious effort to gain compliance with their decision by means of persuasion. Since the person upon whom they were intent to impose their will was uncooperative and truculent, they limited themselves to formal explanations of the reasons for their decision and to warnings about the possible consequences of continued resistance. Fourth, having failed in arguing their case they were prepared to use force to bring the case to a conclusion. Though they were probably hesitant to lay their hands on the man who opposed them, considering the nature of the case, they knew not what else they could do but arrest him. Fifth, the mere resolution not to use force, though an important asset in peacekeeping, is not enough. The peaceful disassembly of resistance through the means of formal explanation and warning is sufficient in some cases; in other cases other means have to be used. The sergeant employed an apparently efficient two-step technique. To begin, he broached the troublesome topic in an unprejudiced manner. That is, he attempted to structure the conversation about the dog in ways that did not presuppose the complaint as the occasion for it. What the two men talked about in the yard could have been an ordinary conversation any two men could have had anywhere at any time. Thus the impact of the irritant was mitigated. Next, after the conversation had gained some integrity and sensibility of its own, he introduced the need for confining the dog not by asserting what needed to be done but by commenting about the options that were presumably available to the person whose compliance he sought to monitor. With this, the subject's interests move away from the alternatives of either continuing to resist or submitting to orders, to choosing between a private veterinarian or a public animal pound. The effectiveness of this tactic does not depend on whether the proposed options are realistically available. It is possible to offer alternatives of which all but one are quite absurd. For this too makes compliance with the necessary option appear to be based on reasoned choice, rather than mere submission.[123] Sixth, had the sergeant's method failed, and the man continued to resist, force would have been used to overcome his resistance.

The possibility of using force entered the case at the moment the officers decided to become involved in it, and it remained present all along the course of its development. The likelihood that force would be used was at all time commensurate with the skill of the officers. But it would be a mistake to think that techniques of avoiding the use of physical coercion are confined to methods of verbal persuasion. Quite often it is necessary first to create conditions in which this is possible. One important feature of the illustration is that the case was confined. Though some neighbors observed the ongoings by peeking through curtains, there was no risk of them meddling in the incident. Another example will explain this risk and how it can be handled in some instances. An officer was dispatched to investigate a complaint from a merchant in a downtown business section. Upon arriving he found two longhaired young men in an ugly confrontation with a small crowd. The complainant stated that the "hippies" were pestering people by attempting to pass handbills and by soliciting money. The patrolman made a perfunctory attempt to disperse the crowd, which was not possible in the heavy pedestrian traffic, and moved the two young men into the store of the complainant. Inside, he asked for a copy of the handbill, talked about its contents, about the freedom of speech and about rights to do what the Salvation Army does. After this amiable colloquy, he informed them that he could not let them go back into the street, for their own protection. But, he offered, they might be free of jeopardy in a nearby park where people are given to airing their views freely. After the men left, the patrolman explained that the most important "trick" in police work is not to make people obey but to make it possible for them to obey. Few people do not mind losing face and therefore it is exceedingly difficult to solve any problem in an open environment. Thus, the first choice of a patrolman confronting an incident is to isolate it from onlookers. Whenever this is at all possible it should not be neglected.

The technique of isolation naturally brings to mind a caveat. While it is a powerful resource in the hands of a policeman seeking to abate a peacekeeping problem with a minimum resort to coercion, it can also set the stage for the most flagrant abuses. The most hideous and perverse police transgressions occur in sheltered backrooms. But this circumstance merely highlights the dilemma inherent in all kinds of professional practice. Whatever increases the powers of purposeful intercession on the part of the remedial agent also appears to increase opportunities for corruption. Thus, the technique of isolation should be endorsed with caution and with a view to adding safeguards to it that would eliminate even the appearance of possible deviousness.

Aside from the abuses isolation is capable of sheltering, the tactic is of limited usefulness because it cannot always be achieved. Indeed, officers often fail in their attempts to isolate an incident precisely because the person or persons involved in it fear police abuses. We will now present a case of this nature. But before proceeding to it we must acknowledge that in most such instances most policemen tend to act with little consideration. That is, their actions are more likely than not apt to be both inconsiderate and ill-considered. But for purposes of exposition we will discuss a case in which the officers did attempt to proceed with methodical purposefulness, at least at the level of the officers handling the dog complaint mentioned earlier.[124]

Two patrolmen cruising in a black neighborhood were flagged down by a citizen and directed to an altercation in a nearby bar. On the scene they found a small crowd, some members of which were locked in a bitter quarrel. While one officer addressed two men, the other turned to an agitated woman who appeared to be the star of the event. The woman disregarded the officer's attention and attempted to push through to the two men conversing with his partner. At this, the patrolman pinned her arm behind her back, turned her around forcefully, and pushed her into the crowd blocking the exit. This produced shouts of protest from several people, who demanded to know why the woman was being pushed around. There is no need to describe the incident further. It led to several arrests, made with the aid of additional policemen summoned by the bartender, who realized that the incident was slipping out of control.

The feature of the case we wish to highlight has been called "alter-casting."[125] It consists of doing something that has the effect of shifting the participation of people from one kind of interest to another. In this case the officer's act of pushing the woman recast the participation of some persons from the role of spectators to the role of partisans of the victim. It is no exaggeration to say that in peacekeeping where isolation cannot be achieved, alter-casting is the leading risk and the major obstacle to purposeful abatement of troubles. It appears that as long as people have access to a situation, they can be controlled only by assimilating their interest to the intended solution. This is an enormously difficult task, requiring the utmost of relational sophistication and almost heroic composure. Since such virtuosity cannot be demanded as an element of average skill, the prevention of alter-casting must draw on other resources, namely, area knowledge. It is characteristic of patrolmen with good area knowledge that they not only know many people in the area they patrol but that they are also known to many people. Thus, their interventions usually have the character of episodes in an ongoing relationship in which some roles are at least partly fixed. Consequently the officer can always count on a modicum of prior understanding between himself and the people. This background makes him better equipped to prevent the inadvertent mobilization of sentiments against himself.

All the cases we have discussed thus far involve citizen-solicited police intervention. That is, the situation is defined, at least in part, by the knowledge that someone has "called the cops." Though this accounts for the bulk of peacekeeping interventions,[126] patrolmen also find cause to intervene in the course of normal surveillance. Virtually all such "on-sight" actions occur in blighted areas of the city and they ordinarily involve clearing the streets or other public places. Again, it must be mentioned that very many of these interventions are, in fact, ill conceived, impulsive, and mainly harassment oriented. Indeed, it appears that all police departments employ some officers who like to harass people solely on the basis of their own gratuitous fascination with power and tend to assign these officers disproportionately to districts populated by alienated and powerless people. Not satisfied with spontaneous opportunities to meet the slightest challenge, they are not above provoking tests of strength, the outcome of which is, of course, a foregone conclusion.[127] Leaving these indefensible practices aside, however, there are some situations in which the order to "break it up and move on" is reasonably justified.[128] In such situations all the tactics of peacekeeping mentioned are obviously indicated. The most important among them is to leave the persons who must be moved some semblance of freedom of option. For example, a patrolman ordered a group of lounging youths to vacate a street corner. They grumbled and moved on at an expressively slow pace. The patrolman explained, "I don't like sass any better than anyone else; but when I tell kids like that to break it up and they don't sass me I get worried." What would he have done had they not complied? He would have told them that he will be back in fifteen minutes; that should give them enough time to figure out why they didn't want to stay there in the first place. But, suppose they had not moved, what then? Well, they had their chance and if they don't go now some of them will have to be taken in. That is, here too procedure is continually informed by the awareness that it may come to having to use force and it is geared to obviating this necessity.[129]

It is possible, certainly not unthinkable, that at some future time policemen may be able to compel the desired outcome of any problem without ever resorting to physical force. But it appears that in the existing structure of communal life in our society such force is not wholly avoidable. This being the case, not only its avoidance, but its employment must be methodically normalized.

It is, or should be, a source of embarrassment to everybody who undertakes to talk about police practice that he has virtually nothing to say about the exercise of physical coercion. Only the use of firearms is somewhat regulated. Policemen usually receive some instruction on how to use firearms and many departments require regular marksmanship practice. All this is of slight importance, however, because in the United States the pistol is not mainly a tool but an emblem the symbolic value of which draws on history and myth. Thus, the discussion about the role of firearms cannot refer only to practical need or use.[130] Ultimately, the armed policeman in America is a reflection of popular interest in arms and of the symbolic significance the gesture of the drawn gun has retained in folklore, games, fiction, and reality. A disarmed policeman might well be a stylistically incongruous figure to many people, despite the fact that in practical terms it is more than likely—we lack data about it—that the preponderant majority of officers have in years of service either never used their guns or used them so rarely that the number of cases in which use was instrumental in solving a problem could not possibly have a significant effect on the cumulative outcome of crime control and peacekeeping. Leaving the ineffable attitudes toward firearms aside, however, police concern with them contains one glaring omission. While in the administration of justice every effort is made to keep defendants alive and healthy so that they can stand trial and fully suffer the punishment they will be sentenced to suffer if found guilty, the police do not seem to be constrained by this consideration. Contrary to what is reported about other countries, markmanship training in the United States does not emphasize the duty of, and skills in, avoiding the infliction of fatal injury.[131] It is beside the point to say that as long as policemen are required to shoot one must expect some deaths. What matters is that marksmanship could be, but is not, taught and rated to develop skills in hitting nonvital areas of the human body.

Accepting the use of firearms as a normal part of police practice still leaves open the need for systematic evaluations. Thus, it could be said that all things being equal, policemen who kill, or policemen who resort to the use of firearms more often than is normal for their assignment, ought to have their credentials reviewed. Very many departments already have such review procedures and in some an officer who causes death is suspended from duty pending the outcome of an investigation. Unfortunately, the effectiveness of such scrutiny is reduced by the fact that the peers of the officer whose action is questioned invariably rally to his support, and superiors who fear just this response are half-hearted in their efforts to avoid jeopardizing the morale of their subordinates.

The use of force not involving firearms is almost entirely unchartered. There exists some vestigial lore about the comparative merits of short versus long batons, about the application of handcuffs, and about the relative value of skill in boxing, wrestling, and judo. Withal, the exercise of physical coercion is remarkably devoid of models, precepts, or rules. Perhaps the main reason why this area has been left unregulated—and to recognize that it is even a little regulated involves recognizing the few existing pieties about the use of "minimum necessary force" as having the import of regulation—is the belief that he who risks life and limb ought not to be unduly restricted. There are other reasons, most of which are related to an exacerbated sense of masculine pride and soldierly prowess according to which insults and attacks must be met in kind, in the hope that fear will inspire respect, and in ignorance of the fact that it causes only hatred. In any case, whatever defenses one might raise on behalf of a "gutsy" response to challenge, they could not possibly have anything to do with workmanship, and at best make it excusable that an officer, being only human, may occasionally lose his patience, abandon resolute purposefulness, and strike out in anger.[132]

The normalization of the exercise of physical force involves two relatively distinct problems. One has to do with the decision to resort to it and the other with techniques of application. It is important to recognize that the moment of application is not always a matter of choice. At times, it is the attacking offender who makes the decision for the policeman. While it may be reasonable to expect that officers will take certain risks it is absurd to expect that they should risk certain injury. Second, the process of skilled preventive persuasion is limited by time considerations that derive in part from situational exigencies and in part from the temporal structure of police work. For example, most peacekeeping problems in public places have a potential for proliferation and require quick solutions. Thus, the last resort may have to follow the outset with little delay. In situations where these pressures do not exist it still remains necessary to solve problems within some economy of time allocations. Finally, the question when force should be applied may depend on whether postponement might not contribute to the development of conditions that will require greater force. Thus, it is common practice to put handcuffs on all felony suspects to prevent attack or flight. In consequence it is quite likely that more persons are handcuffed than is necessary, but it is equally probable that this procedure reduces the number of those who might otherwise be clubbed or shot. Within the limits of these considerations, the decision to use force must follow exhausting all alternatives.

The only observation that can be made with some warrant about techniques of using force is this: Some policemen have developed ways of restraining certain persons, notably, the mentally ill and women, that result in a minimum of pain and injury. They do this, even though they occasionally encounter formidable resistance, because they do not define such cases as contests. At present the choice of these methods is based mainly on feelings of compassion or chivalry. But there are no reasons why these techniques of achieving restraint could not be adopted to all situations on the basis of their technical superiority to ordinary brawling. It is also possible that much could be gained through adaptations of ancient oriental techniques of defeating attack or resistance.

In the past, and in some places even now, policemen often used physical force as part of so-called curbstone justice. That is, physical punishment was administered by policemen in lieu of the remedies of the penal code. Today force is generally associated with making arrests. This does not mean that policemen now use force only to arrest persons suspected of having committed crimes, but only that when they use force they also make arrests; that not all of these arrested persons go to trial is another matter with which we will deal presently. One important exception to this rule is found in the handling of large-scale civil disorders. To compel the compliance of a mass of people, policemen often simply inflict pain. Leaving aside questions of moral, legal, and political justification, there can be little doubt that existing police forces are, without exception, most scandalously inefficient by thus handling the problem. To arrive at this judgment one need not draw on the accounts of outside critics; the police stand condemned by their own accounts. In the urban upheavals of the recent past they have acted almost invariably in utter confusion, with prodigious waste of manpower and energy, and with no other apparent purpose in mind than to visit punishment on the people they sought to subdue. This response has become so predictable that the provocation of police frenzy was developed into a standard tactic of revolutionary groups.[133] The purpose of this tactic is quite apparent to everyone but the police; namely, by entrapping the police into actions that are repugnant to a large segment of the community, radical groups gain sympathies and support they could not otherwise receive. That this situation has reached the point of near absurdity is evident in the fact that the administrations of our colleges and universities are in effect not in the position to avail themselves of police help. They must suffer the impositions of small groups of belligerents because they know that police action against, let us say, a sit-in demonstration, far from solving the problem at hand, would aggravate it by throwing the support of the neutral and moderate majority to the rebels.[134]

Many observers believe that the gross inadequacy of the police in handling civil disorders is due primarily to the fact that their political attitudes and opinions are opposed to the causes of these protests. Thus, they act not as deputized officials of the state but as representatives of one political faction of society opposing another. Insofar as this view is correct it constitutes a fully adequate reason for not involving the police in the handling of this problem. It is, of course, not possible to isolate the police entirely from politics, but carrying the isolation as far as possible is surely part of the democratic creed. Thus it would seem that any time a simple breach of the peace acquires the character of factional strife, the function of the police should be taken over by some other peacekeeping force—perhaps the National Guard. Aside from the need to isolate the police from political involvements, there is another reason why they should not be required—or allowed—to handle mass upheavals. Such phenomena are best handled by methods of a military constabulary consisting of highly disciplined troops. But the police are a military institution only in the most superficial aspects of their organization. Their daily work involves processes of individualistic discretionary action and they are not accustomed to being led in these activities. Nor are the ranking officers of the police accustomed to leading their men. To make the police more capable than they presently are in handling civil strife one would have to increase their military discipline and turn them from quasi soldiers into real soldiers, which is, as we have proposed, inimical to the professionalization of police work.

In sum, the fundamental maxim of the methodical exercise

of coercion by the police is that, just as society as a whole attempted to restrict the legitimate use of force by creating a special institution, so, in turn, resorting to it in police practice must be restricted to an unavoidable minimum. Above all, force must not be used for any other purpose except to effect restraint. This objective can be attained only by making the use of coercion a technical element of professional peacekeeping and crime control. To return to an earlier analogy once more, policemen must acquire the attitude of physicians who take pride in employing all available means to avoid surgery, and who, when surgery is unavoidable, take pride in making the smallest possible incision. With this assumption of what is proper and necessary, the policeman who has a history of heroic exploits against "cop-haters" and "resisters" will not be admired by his peers—ambivalently because most policemen see through the sham of his heroics but cannot afford to disparage it in the existing system of fraternal obligation and reward distribution. He will be viewed as an occupational failure, someone who cannot do his work without continually getting into trouble.

ARREST AND DETENTION

No other aspects of police practice have received more scholarly attention in the recent past than the procedures and decisions connected with invoking the law. The principal result of these inquiries was the discovery that policemen have, in effect, a greater degree of discretionary freedom in proceeding against offenders than any other public official. This is so because an officer's decision not to make an arrest is not a matter of record, contrary to the decision of the prosecutor not to prosecute, and the decision of the judge to dismiss or to acquit. The condition creates something of a legal paradox because, according to the discovered facts, the policeman who is in terms of the official hierarchy of power, competence, and dignity, on the lowest rung of the administration of justice, actually determines the "outer perimeter of law enforcement," and thus actually determines what the business of his betters will be.[135] The vexation increases when one realizes that this situation is not the result of simple misunderstandings or evasions, which could be remedied by direct corrective measures, but is deeply rooted in the nature of the law itself. For example, the penal codes of many states contain provisions that make gambling a culpable offense. Yet, according to prevailing interpretations, these statutes, though they were drafted in ways allowing no exception, were directed only against some forms of gambling. Since writing this interest into the law would have created loopholes permitting the activity the control of which was desired to elude prosecution, it becomes necessary to rely on the good judgment of the arresting policeman to put the legislative intent into effect.[136] Thus, when a policeman comes upon a gathering of citizens engaged in a game of chance, it is his duty to consider first whether this is an instance of what the legislators had in mind before he makes an arrest. Accordingly, all the courts can consider in the realm of gambling offenses is what the police have found, according to their understanding, to be suitable for their concerns.

The problem does not end, however, with the duty of the police to discern tacit legislative intent implied in a large number of the provisions of the penal codes. Associated with it is another difficulty of at least equal seriousness. Since the reasons the officer has to invoke the law selectively are implied, rather than explicit, there is no way of ascertaining whether his reasons are in accord with legislative intent. For example, a group of youths tossing coins on the sidewalk can be arrested and charged with gambling even though the legislature supposedly did not intend to bar such games. In such cases the decision to invoke the law could be based on the officer's desire to get at these people because they are troublesome in some other ways. Perhaps they are known panderers, but evidence cannot be secured to charge them with pandering. The point is, laws, the enforcement of which is meant to be discretionary, do not impinge only on a specifically intended area of application. Instead, they become all-purpose control devices.[137] As long as even a moderately sizable inventory of such laws is available, any policeman worth his salt ought to be able to arrest almost anyone on formally defensible grounds, with relatively little effort. Naturally, this condition creates favorable conditions for the expression of personal prejudice and for the advancement of corrupt interest. But even if no policeman ever invoked the discretionary law outside the scope of its intended application with any but reputable purposes in mind, a condition in which most people appear to have a license to transgress that can be denied to some by no more than an officer's fiat must obviously trouble the legal mind. Panderers should be arrested for pandering. If they can be arrested for merely pitching pennies, then everybody who merely pitches pennies should be arrested. It is one thing to say that the legislature implicitly exempted friendly games from prosecution and quite another to say that they exempted only some friendly games and not others and it is for the policeman to decide which ones they meant.

The main reason why policemen do not follow a simple rule of impartiality in the enforcement of laws is that their conception of the import of law differs from that which lawyers entertain. To be sure, these two conceptions have an area of overlap encompassing all major crimes that are universally proscribed. Here, for policemen and lawyers alike the rule is that whatsoever transgresses will be arrested for that reason and that reason alone. Outside of this area policemen follow the explicit or implicit instructions of the law only occasionally. That is, people who are thought to have committed a robbery are arrested for that reason, but people who are arrested and charged with begging are rarely so treated because they were caught begging and virtually never for that reason alone. To put it bluntly, in discretionary law enforcement involving minor offenses, policemen use existing law largely as a pretext for making arrests. This makes it specious to inquire whether arrest practices conform with the law; in most cases they do, without, however, the law being the determining factor for making the arrest. Because persons who in the judgment of the police should be detained must be charged with something the law recognizes as valid grounds for detention, many arrests have the outward aspects of adhering to principles of legality. In point of fact, however, the real reasons for invoking the law are wholly independent of the law that is being invoked.[138] The point to be emphasized is not that this procedure is illegal, though it often enough is, but that it has nothing to do with considerations of legality. The earlier mentioned panderers were really gambling, but the reason why they were arrested was that they were panderers, a fact that is not legally recognizable in the charge lodged against them. Is this procedure justifiable? It certainly cannot be easily impugned, for there is no question about the fact that the charged offense has taken place. But the practice has some remarkable consequences. For instance, the suspension of vagrancy statutes need not in any way affect the rates of persons who were earlier arrested under these provisions. They are simply charged with some other kind of offense. Similarly, it could not possibly matter less that the New York State "Stop and Frisk" law is surrounded by rules that are supposed to govern its application.[139] It is impossible to imagine a situation in which a patrolman could not cite these rules to justify invoking the law, whatever the real reasons were that motivated him. This puts lawmakers in a curious position. They are not unlike the engineer who develops a screwdriver that is marvelously designed for a specific purpose only to find that people use it to open cans, to knock holes into walls, to chastise children, to spread mayonnaise, and to do all sorts of other things that need doing, occasionally even to tighten a screw.

While for the lawyer police detention is justifiable only as a first link in a chain of legal processes,[140] for the policeman it is, in the large majority of cases, merely a practical device, the legal aspects of which are a pure outward formality about which he has little if any care. He might wish that the people he arrests would receive harsher treatment in the courts than they do, but knowing that this will not come to pass, that, indeed, a large number of people whom he arrests will either not be prosecuted at all or discharged if prosecuted, does not stop him from making arrests. This is so because in all cases but those involving major crimes, arrests are remedies with an immediate import, they are attuned to situational exigencies, they are not preliminary to punishment but punishment in themselves. Thus, even when a trial follows such arrests it "becomes not the determiner of guilt or innocence but a procedure for release of the accused from punishment previously meted out."[141]

Throwing people into jail for periods of time ranging anywhere from a few hours to a few days, without any intention of prosecuting them, is probably the oldest police routine in existence. No one knows the true extent to which this practice exists today, whether it is on the increase or the decline. Some jurisdictions seem to have succeeded, or nearly succeeded, in abolishing it and in them all arrestees are presented to magistrates. But we also have data indicating that in some cities more than ninety-five percent of all persons detained because of allegation of prostitution or gambling are simply released from custody after a day or two.[142] The larger picture of how many people are in police jails across the country on any particular night, who they are, and why they are there cannot be estimated in even terms of a rough guess.

What we do know, however, is that it has been argued for a long time that policemen need the power to place some persons in temporary detention.[143] For example, the so called "Golden Rule" directs the overnight detention of inebriates for their own protection.[144] It is very likely that the net cast to catch the drunk also takes in persons who are simply sick, feeble, disoriented, and without a place to stay. And there are some persons who are jailed for short periods on the request of their relatives who, however, do not wish to go so far as instituting prosecution.[145] Finally, large numbers of persons, such as known prostitutes, gamblers, and con-artists, are detained temporarily for the sole purpose of inducing them to be less brazen and to impede their illegal activities, that is, as part of a harassment program.[146]

Clearly the powers of the police to abridge the freedom of citizens temporarily is not simply a legal problem and, therefore, not solvable by increasing the volume and specificity of legal regulation. Only on the police blotter or in the court record does it appear that detained persons were detained because they engaged in some specific illegal activity. For some this reflects reality well enough. But from the vantage point of police interest and in consideration of the real reasons that determined the decision to take someone into custody, the vast majority of detained persons appear to have been perceived as diffusely troublesome, inappropriate in their manner, vaguely dangerous, dissolute, disruptive, or in various other ways a bane.[147] The presently prevailing opinion of most knowledgeable legal students of police practice is that discretionary law enforcement should be brought into closer accord with legal norms.[148] But it is virtually certain that this approach, by itself, will produce no more than a specious kind of correctness. It is, after all, inconceivable that an officer could not find some label in any code to justify detention,[149] and the more comprehensive the code, the more likely that he will be devious about it. In the last analysis, it will remain the officer's judgment that must be evaluated when he makes an arrest; and because judgment is inherently difficult to control we must see to it that we have officers whom we can trust not only because they are personally honest but also because they are expert.

Many of the practices encompassed by the discretionary freedom policemen enjoy are revolting, but the pressures to do something about it should not lead to fruitless efforts. Moreover, for the moment at least, it is certainly profoundly regrettable but not altogether repugnant that a man who is so lacking in self-control as to risk squandering his weekly earnings on drink, depriving his family of its livelihood, be kept in jail for a short period. Nor is it inhuman of an officer to arrest a skid-row derelict for no other reason than to spare him from the risks of exposure or assault. It is easy to say that other kinds of services should be made available to serve such needs. In fact, very little movement in this direction is discernible. And there are good reasons for saying that making other resources available will become a viable prospect only if and when the police will establish continuous cooperative relations with medicine, psychiatry, and social work. At present, these relations could scarcely be worse.[150] Policemen are generally hostile and distrustful toward physicians and welfare workers, and the latter make no attempt to conceal their often less than well founded feelings of superiority. This condition will not change until the policeman achieves the status that is in a real sense equal to that of other remedial agents, that is, until he actually becomes, and will be recognized as, a licensed professional. Though this will not answer the question whether panderers should be arrested because they violated gambling laws, nor whether prostitutes should be jailed for purposes of harassment, it will at least create conditions in which such questions can be addressed jointly by all concerned agents and discussed without aspersions and acrimony.

In sum, police recourse to temporarily abridging the freedom of citizens deserves recognition as a practical peacekeeping method that has only in its most outward aspects the character of a legal action. Though it is often resorted to for inadequate or deplorable reasons, it is not wholly without justification. In its seemingly justified form the procedure involves a good deal of knowledge and considerate judgment.[151] Like the use of physical force, temporary detention is a measure of last resort, and no policeman who is methodical in his work uses it in any other way.

COMMUNITY RELATIONS

One of the most vigorously advocated new developments in the field of policecraft is known under the heading of "Community Relations." The endeavors thus designated deserve consideration at two relatively distinct levels of analysis. First, in terms of their proximal causes and objectives and, second, as possibly part of an incipient shift in the overall orientation of all systems of remedial social control functioning in modern society.

Like most other recent accretions to police work, community relations activities take the form of a special assignment. Accordingly, departments have created Community Relations Units or appointed Community Relations Officers, whose task it is to achieve and maintain an ongoing exchange of views between the police and all segments of society, *especially* those groups whose aggrievement and disadvantage expresses itself in the waves of demonstrations of discontent that have been sweeping our cities in this decade.[152] Though one could probably not show that every effort in this direction has been mounted only after some specific incident of civil strife, there can be no doubt that the undertaking as a whole has been reactive in the sense that it followed external pressure rather than the spontaneous appreciation of the need. There is no strong argument against the police to be built on this observation. After all, they were not the only ones to learn the hard way, nor were they the last ones. But the emergency nature of the timing gave rise to serious difficulties. In the first place, the response to outside conditions came to be viewed by many policemen as a coerced concession to rebellion. These men, who view themselves as custodians of the official order, consider it deplorable to enter any kind of negotiations with parties that dared to challenge this order. Second, because of the haste in which community relations work was undertaken the units were carelessly staffed and they suffered from a great deal of personnel turnover. This strengthened the argument of those who felt that the whole thing was unworkable in the first place. Finally, even though the units received broadly formulated mandates, it has not been made clear what sort of activities they should engage in.[153] Under the combined pressure of these difficulties, and under the pressure to do something, the work of the units tended to follow one or the other of the following two models.

The simpler of the two options consists of implementing a public relations program along lines of least resistance. To transcend the limitations of past public relations efforts which consisted mainly of furnishing speakers on invitation, the Community Relations Units proceeded to organize committees of citizens in various parts of cities, which were supposed to function as market places for the exchange of ideas. Organizationally, the resulting set-up is not unlike the PTA in being closely attuned to the needs of the existing system. But it actually never came to function even as well as the PTA. The shortcoming of the approach has been stated in these terms: "The formalized program is impressive on paper but in action we found a serious communication blockage. It is difficult to clearly determine the reasons for this blockage but certainly the defensive attitude of the police is a contributing factor and has inhibited the productivity of the district committees. Additionally, selection of committee members is based on those whom the police consider 'responsible' and our discussion of this issue with top police commanders brought forth a feeling that those people were responsible if they 'agreed' with police thinking. This line of thought is a major stumbling block toward community involvement in the program."[154] It must, of course, not be assumed that responsible citizens in the above sense are wholly unrepresentative of community sentiments, but in view of the fact that the program was primarily oriented to those groups with whom relations were strained, the outcome scarcely qualifies as a success. It merely displays the availability of already existing support and it leaves all existing misunderstandings and animosities intact. Indeed, alienated groups tend to view such activities as further evidence of the refusal of the police to hear their grievances and as an underhanded ploy that forces them further into estrangement from the "establishment."

The more ambitious alternative is for Community Relations Units to reach to the grassroots of discontent. While this does lead to the establishment of genuinely trusting relations between some policemen and some leaders of alienated groups, it results, where it succeeds, in the isolation of the effort within the police department. Officers who manage to establish viable and reciprocally understanding ties with people living in ghettos, skid rows, and tenderloin districts are often viewed by their colleagues as having joined "the opposition,"[155] or, somewhat more sanely, as being engaged in an activity that has nothing to do with police work and should be left to social workers. Thus, while the first approach fails because it leaves out those groups to which the program is primarily directed, the second fails because it leaves out the police department.

Neither of the two programs should be judged a total failure, however, and there is at least a chance that the second may learn to cope with internal resistance as it learns to overcome external opposition. In a situation where success is hard to come by, every small gain counts. But realism requires the recognition that the gap community relations work was intended to bridge still exists. At best, a few lines of communication have been strung across it. Whether they will avail when they are truly needed is highly uncertain. Surely the effort must be strengthened as far as possible under conditions of abated stress, and in this respect the recommendations of the

President's Commission on Law Enforcement and Administration of Justice are highly meritorious. In this it is of utmost importance that the perimeter of police interest be as all encompassing as possible. Some groups may remain permanently beyond reach, but as the endeavor contains no room for hurt feelings or indignation, there can be no end to trying. In particular, and this is far more serious risk to the enterprise than is allowed, those men in the Community Relations Units who are strongly impressed by the grievances against their institution must not yield to the temptation to give up on the police.

But police community relations work can be conceived as having an import that goes beyond its function of, so to speak, helping to "keep the lid on." Leaving the public relations–type programs entirely out of consideration, let us first take note that the activities do not constitute a social service in the ordinary sense. Though they often take the form of finding jobs for persons with police records who cannot obtain employment otherwise, or of organizing recreational facilities for youth who might otherwise turn to delinquency, they are merely instrumentalities to reach an ulterior objective. That is, on the surface it is always some individual or group of individuals whose descent into misery or transgression is intercepted. The real targets of the interventions are, however, networks of social relations. More than changing persons, it is the changing of alignments among persons, and between parts of society, that is the aim of community relations work. This involves a profound reorientation in the direction of police interest. According to inherited conceptions of remedial control, risks to the social order are always found in individuals and the preferred way of handling the problems they create is to do something for them or against them. The police are not unique in focusing on individuals; the whole spectrum of preventive and remedial control in our society is principally person-oriented. Every problem always turns to something being the matter with someone in particular. Thus, physicians and psychiatrists combat diseases in patients, and lawyers and social workers aid clients, and policemen deal with delinquents and derelicts. But recently a new and not yet well formulated

interest has come to the fore—of which we take police community relations work to be a part—which directs its interests less
to the sick, the incompetent, and the deviant as individuals,
and more to conditions of existence, to the social fabric, and to
cultural change. Though this interest draws support from
scholarly sources, mainly social science research, and is in this
sense well founded, it has been, thus far, an uncertain quest.[156]
Because the critique of the social order is a matter of political
concern and because professionals seek to remain aloof of
politics, they have not found any fully acceptable ways of
dealing with what they discern to be the ills of society. Nor are
there any easy solutions of this dilemma in sight. The main
direct result of the new interest has been that the person who
creates difficulties, or who is failing, is perceived as presenting
a far more complex problem than when he was considered as
an isolated case. Thus, for example, from the vantage points of
this new interest, a diabetic patient is no longer viewed as
merely a case of a diseased pancreas, but someone with inherited dietary habits, occupying a role in a network of reciprocal
obligations, encumbered by certain culturally set prejudices
about health and illness, and commanding limited resources
for his care, all of which becomes a part of the picture and
plays a role in setting a course of remedies. In short, the
changes were not earthshaking and have been largely confined
to making care more careful. This is, by and large, what is
meant by social medicine, social psychiatry, and is what Judge
Allen appears to have in mind when he calls for the "socializa-
tion" of the administration of criminal justice.[157]

In sum, the interest in situations, in circumstances, in background, in relatedness, or broadly speaking, in the sociocul-
tural—as opposed to concern for individual and isolated
cases—has not led to radical changes in professional practice;
instead, it functioned mainly as a general educative influence.

It does not seem too far fetched to suppose that police
community relations work might be the vehicle for such broadening educational experiences. The men assigned to the units
could retain the specific role assigned to them in the administrative scheme of things. In addition to this, however, all recruits could have a protracted period of supervised practice in

the field at an early point in their training. This experience contains opportunities for learning three lessons that cannot be taught adequately in formal courses of instruction. The first concerns the dynamics of community organization. The second has to do with deviance as a cultural rather than an individual phenomenon.[158] The third pertains to the effects of policy on the lives of the people to whom it applies. Of these the last is by far the most important because it affords the policeman the opportunity to look at the effects of his own activity. In the professionalization of the police it is, of course, of decisive significance that the practitioner gain a firm understanding of the product of his interventions. In the past policemen have disavowed such concerns under the pretense that they merely enforce the law and that it is not their business to decide whether this is good or bad in the long run. But we know that this is a misconception; that they, in fact, have an enormous degree of freedom in setting peacekeeping and law enforcement policies. Thus they cannot be allowed to evade the question raised long ago by social scientists about the extent to which defining someone officially as a deviant has the effect of solidifying his deviant identity and of contributing to the proliferation of deviance in society.[159] Unfortunately such questions are deeply embedded in long-standing ideological conflict. But avoiding them for this reason is also an evasive tactic. For if knowledge and clarity is the hallmark of the professional, then obscurantism cannot be permitted any defense at all.

CONCLUSION

The psalmist spoke truly for all times when he said, "except the Lord keep the city, the watchman waketh but in vain."[160] One of the greatest risks in all attempts to define the role of the police in society is to overestimate their significance. They are surely not the "thin blue line" that saves us from being inundated by depredation and chaos. Order and safety depend primarily on other factors and, in real peril, they could not be saved even if half of us took to policing the other half. In fact, it has been said that, "one might reasonably maintain that society would not go to pieces even if the state should exercise no coercion whatever."[161] This opinion is probably as misleading in its implications as are the truculent and imperious voices which say that unless we let the police have their way they will refuse to play ball and leave us facing destruction. A more pragmatic view is forced to acknowledge that the availability of the police does make life safer and more orderly than it would be otherwise, but it refuses to accept that we are at their mercy.

The approach that avoids apocalyptic visions is called upon to give a practical interpretation to the belief that the police are of one cloth with the society they service. Certainly it does not compel the conclusion that whatever exists, exists for adequate reasons. The test of time, which a conservative view is apt to emphasize, is a tricky standard. It sometimes protects arrangements that have lasted merely because fear or neglect have prevented scrutiny. There is little doubt that many aspects of the modern police are just such survivals.

At an earlier time, when most of the people were illiterate or barely literate, when physicians knew less about diseases than a modern practical nurse, when lawyers barely knew how to use a few forms and were considered educated if they had a cursory acquaintance with Blackstone, policemen with a background of eight years of school were adequately prepared for the job. In any case, the definition of their tasks virtually never brought them into contact with people who were superior to them in any important respect. But all this has changed in the past two generations, and the police, by hewing to old standings, is falling back from year to year, increasingly becoming a field of opportunities for those who can do no better than join the simpler service occupations.

The failure of the police to keep up with the general upgrading of all occupations is augmented by the fact that, whereas at one time a certain degree of crudeness was acceptable, it can no longer be tolerated. In the first place, the policeman of the past had fewer matters to attend to. Under conditions where the vast majority of those official regulations of conduct we now take for granted were unheard of, keeping the peace and enforcing the law were relatively simple matters. This does not mean that social controls did not function, but only that they typically did not involve police interventions. Those problems that were beyond the scope of informal remedies and self-help, that is, the problems that did require police attention, were ordinarily quite clear-cut and required no great subtleties of perception. Precisely the opposite is the case today. For a variety of reasons the number of problems people no longer feel competent to attend to themselves has multiplied enormously. Moreover, under conditions of anonymity prevailing in urban life, order in public life can be maintained only by formal means of control. Thus, while it once may have been sufficient if an officer knew the difference between a corpse and a live body, he must now, owing to the fact that he is inevitably involved in handling vast arrays of all sorts of human problems, be knowledgeable and judicious about virtually everything. In any case, crudeness on his part becomes quickly apparent, and it frustrates both him and the one who depends on his service.

In addition to the earlier grossness of the police task, the admissibility of crude police work in the past was connected with the then prevailing view that people on whom police attention centered deserved no better handling. Nothing the police could conceivably do to them would appreciably worsen their lot. People who were fair and considerate did not attract police interest, and those who did could not lay claim to being dealt with fairly and considerately. Nor did "those people" seem to object to the treatment they received; at least, the voice of their objections was not heard, let alone acknowledged. But this too is a thing of the past. Today policemen direct, control, and discipline persons from all walks of life, and crudeness on their part places them in a position of significant disadvantage. To be sure, crudeness can yet prevail but only at a cost sober judgment would find intolerable. Fear may prevent me from protesting the traffic patrolman's vulgarity but it will not inspire my trust in him as a public official. Nor will my feeling change by knowing that his manner was "provoked" by what he took to be uncooperativeness on my part. Waiters, psychiatrists, cab drivers, and teachers know that the handling of uncooperativeness is a necessary part of their occupational skill and it is not too much to expect the same of policemen. But it is not good manners that I expect. Instead, I should like, in my deal-

ings with policemen, to be able to perceive them as qualified
to do the serious and important work I know they have to do.
To be sure, politeness does not indicate this, but the man who
does not know that he should avoid offending me, or who
works up more feeling than he can safely contain, is surely not
the one to be trusted with anything more demanding than
some simple service routine. But the sensitivity of the likes of
me is the least important argument against police crudeness.
Far louder than our voice sounds the voice of those who have
until recently suffered the impositions of crudeness in silence.
Here crudeness is not a simple mistake but specifically subver-
sive. A policeman who appreciates the likely consequences of
an approach that will cause resentment and indulges in it
nevertheless contributes to what he is paid to prevent. It will
not do to say that in police work the causing of resentment is
often unavoidable. Precisely for that reason it must be avoided
wherever possible.

It is sometimes said that the police must adopt as their work
ethic the belief that no man's claim to dignity and civil rights is
smaller than any other man's claim, and that neither age nor
social status, nor race, nor even deviant conduct diminishes
entitlement to decent treatment. Though this certainly appears
desirable, it is possible that it matters less than the simple
empirical fact that in degrading others they must stoop to the
level of the degraded.

While civility and humaneness are desirable qualities in any
person, and their possession may be indispensable for competent police work, they do not suffice. The opposite of the crude
policeman is not one imbued with civic virtues and possessed
of a polite manner; instead, he is the informed, deliberating,
and technically efficient professional who knows that he must
operate within the limits set by a moral and legal trust.

It has been urged in this study that the only way open toward
the professionalization of the police leads through institutions
of higher learning, more specifically, through professional
schools of police work. This was urged not because academic
scholarship has now much to offer that will make police work
more methodical than it is but because in our society the
university has become the sole home of every form of research,

study, and exercise of critical reason. No occupation can hope to achieve dignity, seriousness, and importance that does not go this route. Of course, an occupation that has roots in the university can no longer encompass menial duties. But this will merely remove the incongruity of requiring that men who have the power and the duty to make decisions that affect permanently the welfare, prosperity, even the very existence of citizens, do work that can be safely entrusted to unskilled labor.

The public trust that authorizes and restricts police practices can be simply stated. A society committed to the achievement of peace by pacific means has created an institution with the monopoly to employ non-negotiably coercive force in situations where its use is unavoidably necessary. Procedures that go against the ideal may perhaps be excused occasionally, but they can never be defended. Above all, force may not be used for any other purpose but to effect restraint. To use it to teach someone a lesson is not only a violation of trust; it is also silly, for there are scarcely any other two things that are as completely opposed as violence and teaching.

It has been said that the creation of a highly trained, elite police force magnifies the danger of tyranny.[162] This warning must not be taken lightly. It should be entered on the list of warnings against the other possible tyrannies of psychiatrists, engineers, and social workers.[163] The simple fact is that we have become dependent on the availability of these professionals and we continually expect them to improve their methods, and thus become more powerful. Every power to do good is also a power to do harm and everything that can save life can also destroy it. This is the paradox of technique—the better it is perfected, the more neutral it becomes, and the more readily it is available for both good and evil. But in the last analysis this is not a peculiarly modern phenomenon. One of the greatest and one of the oldest themes of humanistic reflection concerns the tragic puzzle that men who seek to do right sometimes do wrong. Thus, having begun this section by invoking the psalmist, it might perhaps be fitting to close it with an ancient Pythagorean prayer:[164]

> King Zeus, grant us good whether prayed for or unsought by us;
> But that which we ask amiss, do thou avert.

NOTES

This essay previously appeared in the National Institute of Mental Health, Crime and Delinquency Issues Series (Rockville, Md.: Center for Studies of Crime and Delinquency, 1970).

Some of the observations about the crime control activities of the police reported in this essay derive from research Sheldon Messinger and I conducted on behalf of the President's Commission on Law Enforcement and Criminal Justice. My understanding of it owes a great deal to our discussions and the memoranda we wrote, a debt I acknowledge gratefully.

1. Bruce Smith, *Police Systems in the United States,* 2d rev. ed. (New York: Harper & Row, 1960), 8.

2. For descriptions of early European police practices, see Patrick Pringle, *The Thief-Takers* (London: Museum Press, 1958); and P. J. Stead, *Vidocq* (London: Staples Press, 1958). Early American urban police is described in Roger Lane, *Policing the City: Boston 1822–1855* (Cambridge, Mass.: Harvard University Press, 1967); and in the literature cited therein.

3. J. Q. Wilson cites evidence that improvements undertaken under the leadership of America's foremost police reformer, O. W. Wilson, did not result in better public attitudes; see "Police Morale, Reform, and Citizen Respect: The Chicago Case," in *The Police: Six Sociological Essays,* ed. D. J. Bordua (New York: John Wiley & Sons, 1967), 137–62.

4. David Hume, *A Treatise of Human Nature,* ed. L. A. Selby Bigge, bk. 3, pt. 1, section 1 (Oxford: Clarendon Press, 1896).

5. Joseph Goldstein, "Police Discretion Not to Invoke the Criminal Process: Low Visibility Decisions in the Administration of Justice," *Yale Law Journal* 69 (1960): 543–94; see also H. L. Packer, "Two Models of the Criminal Process," *University of Pennsylvania Law Review* 113 (1964): 1–68; S. H. Kadish, "Legal Norm and Discretion in the Police and Sentencing Process," *Harvard Law Review* 75 (1962): 904–31; and W. R. LaFave, "The Police and Non-enforcement of the Law," *Wisconsin Law Review* (1962): 104–37, 179–239.

6. L. G. Boonin, "Concerning the Defeasibility of Legal Rules," *Philosophy and Phenomenological Research* 26 (1966): 371–78.

7. The term "rule-scepticism" is part of the polemics of modern American jurisprudence; see F. S. Cohen, "Transcendental Nonsense and the Functional Approach," *Columbia Law Review* 35 (1935): 809–49; see also Jerome Frank, *Courts on Trial: Myth and Reality in American Justice* (Princeton, N.J.: Princeton University Press, 1949).

8. E. H. Levi, *An Introduction to Legal Reasoning* (Chicago: University of Chicago Press, 1948), 104.

9. F. J. Remington writes, "Even the most careful revision, such as those accomplished in Wisconsin, Illinois, and Minnesota, will not produce a criminal code which is capable of mechanical application to the wide variety of situations which arise. Legislatures expect that law enforcement agencies will exercise good judgment in developing an enforcement program" ("The Role of Police in a Democratic Society," *Journal of Criminal Law, Criminology and Police Science* 56 [1965]: 361–65).

10. Werner Dankert, *Unehrliche Menschen: Die Verfehmten Berufe* (Bern: Francke Verlag, 1963).

11. G. S. McWatters wrote about the typical policeman, after many years of being one himself: "He is the outgrowth of a diseased and corrupted state of things, and is, consequently, morally diseased himself" (Lane, *Policing the City*, 69).

12. Erle Stanley Gardner, the prolific detective story writer, reports being troubled by the apparent need for the "dumb" cop in fiction. When he attempted to remedy this and depicted a policeman in favorable colors in one of his books, book dealers and readers rose in protest; see "The Need for New Concepts in the Administration of Criminal Justice," *Journal of Criminal Law, Criminology, and Police Science* 50 (1959): 20–26; see also, G. J. Falk, "The Public's Prejudice against the Police," *American Bar Association Journal* 50 (1965): 754–57.

13. V. W. Piersante, chief detective of the Detroit Police Department, has juxtaposed with remarkable perceptiveness the considerations which, on the one hand, lead to dense and suspicious surveillance of certain groups because of their disproportionate contribution to crime totals, while on the other hand, these tactics expose the preponderant majority of law-abiding members of these groups to offensive scrutiny. He stated, "In Detroit in 1964 a total of 83,135 arrests were made . . . of this 58,389 were Negroes. . . . This means that 89 percent of the Negro population were never involved with the police" (Harold Norris, "Constitutional Law Enforcement Is Effective Law Enforcement," *University of Detroit Law Journal* 42 [1965]: 203–34).

14. Gilbert Geis, *Juvenile Gangs*, A Report Produced for the President's Committee on Juvenile Delinquency and Youth Crime (Washington, D.C.: U.S. Government Printing Office, 1965); Carl Werthman and Irving Piliavin, "'Gang Membership and the Police," in *The Police*, ed. Bordua, 56–98.

15. Allan Silver, "The Demand for Order in Civil Society: A Review of Some Themes in the History of Urban Crime, Police, and Riot," in *The Police*, ed. Bordua, 1–24.

16. J. Q. Wilson writes, "The patrolman believes with considerable justification that teenagers, Negroes, and lower-income persons commit a disproportionate share of all reported crimes: being in those population categories at all makes one, statistically, more suspect than other persons; but to be in those categories *and* to behave unconventionally is to make oneself a prime suspect. Patrolmen believe that they would be derelict in their duty if they did not treat such persons with suspicion, routinely question them on the street, and detain them for longer questioning if a crime has occurred in the area. To the objection of some middle-class observers that this is arbitrary and discriminatory, the police are likely to answer: 'Have you ever been stopped and searched? Of course not. We can tell the difference; we have to tell the difference in order to do our job. What are you complaining about?' " (*Varieties of Police Behavior: The Management of Law and Order in Eight Communities* [Cambridge, Mass.: Harvard University Press, 1968], 40–41).

17. Of primary significance in this respect is that the courts make the same kinds of invidious distinctions even as they follow the law; see J. E. Carlin, Jan Howard, and S. L. Messinger, "Civil Justice and the Poor," *Law and Society* 1 (1966): 9–89, and Jacobus ten-Broek, ed., *The Law of the Poor* (San Francisco, Calif.: Chandler Publishing Co., 1966).

18. Reference is made to the evidence that persons of working class origin are more prone than others to harbor attitudes that are favorable to politics of prejudice and authoritarianism; see S. L. Lipset, "Democracy and Working Class Authoritarianism," *American Sociological Review* 24 (1959): 482–501; "Social Stratification and Right Wing Extremism," *British Journal of Sociology* 10 (1959): 346–82; "Why Cops Hate Liberals—and Vice Versa," *Atlantic Monthly* (March 1969).

19. Arthur Niederhoffer, a former ranking police official, writes, "The power structure and the ideology of the community, which are supported by the police, at the same time direct and set boundaries to the sphere of police action" (*Behind the Shield: The Police in Urban Society* [New York: Anchor Books, 1969], 13). Niederhoffer cites an even stronger statement to that effect from Joseph Lohman, a former sheriff of Cook County, Ill., and later Dean of the School of Criminology at the University of California at Berkeley.

20. The normative approach is perhaps best exemplified in Jerome Hall, "Police and Law in a Democratic Society," *Indiana Law Journal* 2

(1953): 133–77, where it is argued that the structure of police work must be understood as decisively determined by the duty to uphold the law and every police action must be interpreted in relation to this objective. The man on the street, however, approaches police work from a different vantage point. He probably supposes that police work has something to do with law enforcement, but to him this is mainly a figure of speech which does not limit his freedom to decide what the police are really for from case to case.

21. The leading historian of the police is Charles Reith; see *A New Study of Police History* (Edinburgh: Oliver & Boyd, 1956). A brief review of American development is contained in S. A. Chapman and T. E. St. Johnston, *The Police Heritage in England and America* (East Lansing, Mich.: Institute for Community Development and Services, Michigan State University, 1962), and in Lane, *Policing the City*, 69.

22. Ernest Barker, *The Development of Public Services in Western Europe, 1660–1930* (London: Oxford University Press, 1944).

23. J. L. Lyman, "The Metropolitan Police Act of 1829," *Journal of Criminal Law, Criminology and Police Science* 55 (1964): 141–54.

24. Christopher Hibbert, *The Roots of Evil* (Boston: Little, Brown & Co., 1963).

25. Leon Radzinowicz, *A History of English Criminal Law* (New York: Macmillan Co., 1957).

26. A perhaps overly optimistic review of this trend is contained in Paul Reiwald, *Eroberung des Friedens* (Zürich: Europa Verlag, 1944).

27. The following remarks are not intended as a "well-rounded" picture of the problem of peace and violence during the past 150 years. Instead, they deliberately accent a single trend.

28. Indirect and symbolic forms of authority implementation can be, of course, even more oppressive in their effects than the permanent presence of the fist at the scruff of the neck. But while political power that rests only on means of violence is repugnant on its face, indirect authority contains at least the possibility of consensual governing.

29. Egon Bittner and A. M. Platt, "The Meaning of Punishment," *Issues in Criminology* 2 (1966): 79–99.

30. W. B. Miller, "Lower-Class Culture as a Generating Milieu of Gang Delinquency," *Journal of Social Issues* 14 (1958): 5–19; Oscar Lewis, "The Culture of Poverty," *Scientific American* 215 (October 1966); 19–25.

31. E. J. Hobsbawm entitled his book dealing with the first one-third of the period, *The Age of Revolution* (London: Weidenfeld & Nicolson, 1962). American developments have been superbly reviewed

in *Violence in America,* ed. H. D. Graham and T. R. Gurr (New York: Signet Books, 1969); the preparation of this collection of studies was undertaken for the National Commission on the Causes and Prevention of Violence.

32. For a review of Bentham's teachings concerning penal law and punishment, see James Heath, *Eighteenth Century Penal Philosophy* (London: Oxford University Press, 1963), 219–20. The sources, mainstream, and influence of Benthamite philosophy are described in Elie Halevy, *The Growth of Philosophical Radicalism* (Boston: Beacon Press, 1955).

33. The history of the administration of justice, even only in the West, is of course a far more complex matter than this statement allows. For a statement of the ascendancy of what he calls the "formal rationalization" of the law, see Max Weber, *On Law in Economy and Society,* ed. Max Rheinstein (Cambridge, Mass.: Harvard University Press, 1954).

34. This position is espoused by the so-called Scandinavian School of Jurisprudence, whose main representatives are Karl Olivercrona and Alf Ross. An exposition of their views is contained in Norberto Bobbio, "Law and Force," *The Monist* 49 (1965): 321–41.

35. Weber wrote, "The jury, as it were, thus took the place of the oracle, and indeed it resembles it inasmuch as it does not indicate rational grounds for its decisions" (*On Law in Economy,* 79); see also Patric Devlin, *Trial by Jury* (London: Methuen, University Paperbacks, 1966).

36. D. J. Newman, *Conviction: The Determination of Guilt or Innocence without Trial* (Boston: Little, Brown & Co., 1966).

37. Egon Bittner, "The Concept of Mental Abnormality in the Administration of Justice Outside the Courtroom," in *The Mentally Abnormal Offender: A Ciba Foundation Symposium,* ed. A. V. S. de Reuck and Ruth Porter (London: A. & J. Churchill, 1968), 201–213.

38. The rule that overturned common law doctrine concerning the admissibility of evidence regardless of the illegality of means by which it was obtained was first formulated in the celebrated case of *Weeks* v. *United States,* 232 U.S. 383 (1914). Though the decision was binding only upon Federal Courts, it was extended to all jurisdiction 47 years later in *Mapp* v. *Ohio,* 81 Sup. Ct. 1684 (1961). For a review of the entire field of problems concerning the admissibility of evidence, see *Police Power and Individual Freedom,* ed. Claude Sowle (Chicago: Aldine Publishing Co., 1962). A more popular, though generally reliable, account is contained in Alan Barth, *Law Enforcement versus the Law* (New York: Collier Books, 1961).

39. W. R. LaFave and F. J. Remington call judicial control of police practice a "fiction" which possibly detracts from the likelihood that policemen will do what judges expect them to do; see "Controlling the Police: The Judge's Role in Making and Reviewing Law Enforcement Decisions," *Michigan Law Review* 63 (1965): 987–1012. Mr. Justice Brennan states that judges "have little or no direct authority to require police and other law enforcement agencies to comply with the rules of the game" ("Judicial Supervision of Criminal Law Administration," *Crime and Delinquency* 9 [1963]: 227–34). Fred Inbau asserts without qualification: "The courts have no right to police the police. This is an executive not a judicial function" (*Journal of Criminal Law, Criminology and Police Science* 52 [1961]: 209–12). See also R. C. Donnelly, "Police Authority and Practices," *The Annals of the American Academy of Political and Social Sciences* 339 (January 1962): 90–110.

40. It has been said that the U.S. Supreme Court issued the rulings concerning police practices in "desperation," and that judicial control over the police cannot be expected of the courts. See H. L. Packer, "Policing the Police: Nine Men Are Not Enough," *New Republic* 153 (4 September 1965): 17–21, H. J. Friendly, "The Bill of Rights as a Code of Criminal Procedure," *California Law Review* 53 (1965): 929–79. W. R. LaFave cites the chief judge of the U.S. Court of Appeals for the Second District: "It is not by judicial action that the intelligence and effectiveness of local police work can be improved. It is not for the judges to define the powers of investigation and inquiry. . . . In these important areas only Congress and the state legislatures can redress the balance and provide due process for all the people" ("Improving Police Performance through the Exclusionary Rule—Part II: Defining the Norms and Training the Police," *Missouri Law Review* 30 [1965]: 566–610). Herman Goldstein, recognizing that neither the courts nor the legislatures can be expected to set norms for police procedure, urges that the police themselves develop binding policy guidelines, see "Police Policy Formulation: A Proposal for Improving Police Performance," *Michigan Law Review* 65 (1967): 1123–46.

41. J. H. Skolnick, *Justice without Trial: Law Enforcement in Democratic Society,* chap. 3 (New York: John Wiley & Sons, 1967).

42. D. J. Dalby, "Alice in a Patrol Car," *FBI Law Enforcement Bulletin* (July 1966): 9–27.

43. H. S. Commager commented that while Americans have a cavalier disrespect of laws and an abiding suspicion of lawyers, they venerate The Law; see *The American Mind: An Interpretation of American Thought and Character since the 1880s* (New Haven: Yale University Press, 1950), 19ff.

44. Police fears that Mapp, Escobedo, Miranda, etc., will destroy law enforcement effectiveness have not been borne out, according to figures made available by police departments; see Neiderhoffer, *Behind the Shield*, 174. D. M. McIntire cites evidence that the rates at which confessions were used to obtain convictions after Escobedo either increased or remained unchanged for all offenses except burglary, in his *Law Enforcement in the Metropolis* (Chicago: American Bar Foundation, 1967), 65. It may take some time for the police to assimilate these facts, but they will accept them, just as they have in the past accepted that the "third degree" was not really an essential part of police work.

45. T. R. Brooks observed correctly that there is a "rough understanding between the police and the derelict population." The arrested person accepts his or her fate, knowing that a plea of guilty before the magistrate will usually induce a disposition of the case he or she is willing to accept; see "New York's Finest," *Commentary* 40 (August 1965): 29–36. Similarly, A. L. Stinchcombe noted, "Hearings before a police court magistrate in these cases are generally purely formalities; it is assumed by all concerned, including the defendant, that the presumed offender is guilty. The only question that remains to be decided is how much noblesse oblige the magistrate should show" ("Institutions of Privacy in the Determination of Police Administrative Practice," *American Journal of Sociology* 69 [1963]: 150–60). In the same vein, B. J. George, Jr., advises, "Please note that the judge-made exclusionary rules of evidence are of no help here. The case is never contested either in the trial court or in an appellate court, and the police conduct is never attacked" ("Police Practices and the Citizen," *Police* 10 [March–April 1966]: 38–42).

46. W. R. LaFave writes, "Police administrators assert that 'there is a wide discrepancy between what the people expect the police to do and what the police are permitted to do under the law,' and then frankly admit that under the circumstances they choose to respond to the public demand. Thus, Superintendent Wilson of Chicago declared, 'If we follow some of our court decisions literally, the public would be demanding my removal as Superintendent of Police and—I might add—with justification.' Chief Parker of Los Angeles has taken the view that, 'it is anticipated that the police will ignore these legal limitations when the immediate public welfare appears to demand police lawlessness.' And Chief Schrotel of Cincinnati has stated the dilemma of the policeman in these terms: 'Either he abides by the prescribed rules and renders ineffective service, or he violates or circumvents the rules and performs the service required of him' "

("Improving Police Performance through the Exclusionary Rule—
Part I: Current Police and Local Court Practices," *Missouri Law Review*
30 [1965]: 391–458). (Footnotes and emphases omitted.) Herman
Goldstein illustrates public pressure with the example of "residents
of a community terrorized by a serious murder, by the strangling of
a series of women, or by the rape of a child will urge that no stone be
left unturned in the search for the offender. Such pressures are taken
by individual police officers as a mandate to employ techniques which
they might otherwise not employ in attempting to identify and apprehend the offender" ("Administrative Problems in Controlling the
Exercise of Police Authority," *Journal of Criminal Law, Criminology and
Police Science* 58 [1967]: 160–72). There are, however, reasons to
believe that the police may be factually mistaken in invoking the
support of public demand. J. P. Clark has shown that the police
generally tend to overestimate the public's desire for forceful intervention; see table 6 in "Isolation of the Police: A Comparison of the
British and American Situation," *Journal of Criminal Law, Criminology
and Police Science* 56 (1965): 307–19.

47. There exists, of course, no legal justification for harassment
arrests; see E. L. Barrett, Jr., "Police Practices and the Law—From
Arrest to Release or Charge," *California Law Review* 50 (1962): 11–55,
and the voluminous literature cited therein. Yet, the practice is widespread. To cite but one example, in Detroit, "The police department
conducts what is commonly recognized as a harassment program in
dealing with gamblers and prostitutes. Under this program, individuals suspected of taking part in the gambling syndicate operations
are subject to frequent street questioning and frisking. Should gambling paraphernalia be found on their person, they are usually
arrested and later released. There is no prosecution in such cases,
since the evidence is inadmissible." That is, "From the beginning of
such procedure, the officers have no intention of taking the case into
court." During a six-month period, Detroit policemen made 3047
arrests for prostitution and 606 arrests for gambling; of these, 75 and
24 respectively resulted in prosecution. McIntire, *Metropolis*, 21, 41,
84; see also LaFave, "Improving Police Performance," 441ff. E. L.
Barrett, Jr., speculated that the court decisions restricting the admissibility of evidence may have had the effect of encouraging harassment arrests. According to this view, policemen probably increase the
number of times they arrest certain persons to compensate for the
inability to prosecute them; see "Personal Rights, Property Rights,
and the Fourth Amendment," *Supreme Court Review*, ed. Kurland
(1960), 53–57.

48. According to the International Association of Police Chiefs, "the percentage of police effort devoted to the traditional criminal law matters probably does not exceed ten percent" as quoted in Niederhoffer, *Behind the Shield*, 75. According to its own Annual Report of 1963, the Los Angeles Police Department responded to more than two million service calls of which less than 200,000 involved investigations of reported crimes, as quoted by E. L. Barrett, Jr., in "Criminal Justice: The Problem of Mass Production," in *The Courts, the Public, and the Law Explosion*, ed. H. W. Jones (Englewood Cliffs, N.J.: Prentice-Hall, 1965), 85–123. See also Elaine Cumming, Ian Cumming, and Laura Edell, "Policeman as Philosopher, Guide, and Friend," *Social Problems* 12 (1965): 276–86; Michael Banton, *The Policeman in the Community* (New York: Basic Books, 1964); and Egon Bittner, "Police Discretion in Emergency Apprehension of Mentally Ill Persons," *Social Problems* 14 (1967): 278–92.

49. C. A. Beard, *The Office of the Justice of Peace in England in its Origin and Development* (New York: B. Franklin, 1904); J. F. Stephen, *A History of the Criminal Law of England*, vol. 1 (London: Macmillan & Co., 1883), 112f., 190f.

50. Gilbert Armitage, *History of the Bow Street Runners* (London: Wishart & Co., 1932).

51. Lane, *Policing the City*, 154; see also G. L. Haskins, *Law and Authority in Massachusetts* (New York: Macmillan, 1960), 174f.

52. F. W. Maitland, *Justice and Police* (London: Macmillan & Co., 1885), 100.

53. Ibid.

54. R. B. Fosdick, *American Police Systems* (New York: Century Co., 1920). See also Raymond Moley, *Our Criminal Courts* (New York: Minton, Balch & Co., 1930), where it is argued that the independence of American police systems is in some part traceable to the power and prestige of the sheriff in frontier communities. T. C. Esselstyn has shown that sheriffs in rural counties even today are more responsive to the weight of community sentiment than to the dictates of the law; see "The Social Role of the County Sheriff," *Journal of Criminal Law, Criminology and Police Science* 44 (1953): 177–83.

55. Several states confer powers of investigation upon judicial officers who function in the manner of the French *juge d'instruction*. Lewis Mayers comments: "Even though the judicial officer who conducts the investigation does not preside at the subsequent trial of the persons accused as a result of his investigations, his investigative activities have associated him in the public mind, and perhaps, even though unconsciously, in his own mind, with the prosecution, and to that extent

derogated from the complete impartiality of the judicial character which our tradition demands" (*The American Legal System,* rev. ed. [New York: Harper & Row, 1964], 74).

56. When asked whether they would suggest to the police proper ways of acquiring evidence in the future, some judges assert that it would be unethical for them to do so unless they also 'coached' the defense" (President's Commission on Law Enforcement and Administration of Justice, *Task Force Report: The Police* [Washington, D. C.: U.S. Government Printing Office, 1967], 31). Hereafter cited as *Task Force Report.*

57. C. D. Breitel, in arguing against Jerome Hall's legalistic view, which he regards as "an unexceptional statement of what Professor Hall himself might call paper law," urges a flexible approach to police discretion which "must operate to separate the inconsequential and harmless from the consequential and harmful" ("Controls in Criminal Law Enforcement," *University of Chicago Law Review* 27 [1960]: 427–35). Needless to say, it is far easier to assert the need for such an approach than to develop it.

58. "If he [a policeman] is justified in making an arrest, he is not obliged to retreat in the face of force but may stand his ground and, if he believes that deadly force is necessary to protect himself, he may employ it" (Donnelly, "Police Authority," 96). See also R. J. Bowers, "Nature of the Problem of Police Brutality," *Cleveland Marshall Law Review,* 14 (1965): 601–09.

59. For evidence that policemen often do not comply fully with exclusionary rules, see McIntire, *Metropolis,* 65. D. J. Black and A. J. Reiss, Jr., *Studies of Crime and Law Enforcement in Major Metropolitan Areas,* A Report Produced for the President's Commission on Law Enforcement and Administration of Justice, vol. 2, section 1 (Washington, D. C.: U.S. Government Printing Office, 1966, 85; R. J. Medalie, L. Zeitz, and P. Alexander, "Custodial Police Interrogation on Our Nation's Capital: The Attempt to Implement Miranda," *Michigan Law Review* 66 (1968): 1347–1422; J. Griffiths and R. E. Ayres, "A Postscript to the Miranda Project: Interrogation of Draft Protestors," *Yale Law Journal* 77 (1967): 300–29.

60. That the principal purpose of the exclusionary rules is to induce a higher level of police performance (despite the famous objection of the late Mr. Justice Cardozo who saw folly in the principle that "the criminal is to go free because the constable blundered") is frequently emphasized; see LaFave, "Improving Police Performance," 391–96.

61. Alfred Hill pointed to a paradox inherent in the situation. He

writes: "The exclusionary rule benefits only the criminal, or at least only the person who is in fact incriminated by what is found or seized. If other remedies are as ineffective as is claimed, this means that innocent victims of illegal searches and seizures are now substantially without recourse" ("The Bill of Rights and the Supervisory Power," *Columbia Law Review* 69 [1969]: 181–215 n. 17). Civil remedies are, of course, theoretically available. In practice, however, the likelihood of obtaining satisfaction is quite remote; see *Task Force Report*, 31; Donnelly, "Police Authority," 101; Goldstein, "Police Discretion," 168; Bowers, "Police Brutality," 604.

62. Isidore Silver proposes "One possible solution to the problem of unreviewable discretion would be the integration of the police function with the prosecutorial one. If the police department were a part of the district attorney's office, presumably there would be closer supervision of police practices" ("The President's Crime Commission Revisited," *New York University Law Review* 43 [1968]: 916–66). This would call for radical transformation of existing police systems. More limited moves in this direction were ill-fated, resulting in a partial breakdown of cooperation between the police and prosecutorial offices; see *Task Force Report*, 81–82.

63. "Justification for the Use of Force in the Criminal Law," *Stanford Law Review* 13 (1961): 566–609.

64. "At common law, the rule appears to have been that an officer was entitled to make a reasonable mistake as to whether the victim had committed a felony, but a private person was not so entitled. Thus strict liability was created for the private arrester, and he could not justifiably kill, if the victim had not actually committed a felony. Several modern cases have imposed this standard of strict liability even upon the officer by conditioning justification of deadly force on the victim's actually having committed a felony, and a number of states have enacted statutes which appear to adopt this strict liability. However, many jurisdictions, such as California, have homicide statutes which permit the police officer to use deadly force for the arrest of a person 'charged' with felony. It has been suggested that this requirement only indicates the necessity for reasonable belief by the officer that the victim has committed a felony" (ibid., 599–600).

65. The illustrations are taken from field notes I have collected over the course of fourteen months of intensive field observations of police activity in two large cities. One is located in a Rocky Mountain state, the other on the West Coast. All other case vignettes used in the subsequent text of this chapter also come from this source.

66. By "non-negotiably coercible" we mean that when a deputized

police officer decides that force is necessary, then, within the boundaries of this situation, he is not accountable to anyone, nor is he required to brook the arguments or opposition of anyone who might object to it. We set this forth not as a legal but as a practical rule. The legal question whether citizens may oppose policemen is complicated. Apparently resisting police coercion in situations of emergency is not legitimate; see Hans Kelsen, *General Theory of Law and State* (New York: Russel & Russel, 1961), 278–79, and H.A.L. Hart, *The Concept of Law* (Oxford: Clarendon Press, 1961), 20–21. Common law doctrine allows that citizens may oppose "unlawful arrest," *Corpus Juris Secundum* 6, Arrest #13, 613; against this, the Uniform Arrest Act, drafted by a committee of the Interstate Commission on Crime in 1939, provides in section 5, "If a person has reasonable grounds to believe that he is being arrested by a peace officer, it is his duty to refrain from using force or any weapons in resisting arrest regardless of whether or not there is a legal basis for the arrest"; see S. B. Warner, "Uniform Arrest Act," *Vanderbilt Law Review* 28 (1942): 315–47. At present, at least twelve states are governed by case law recognizing the validity of the Common Law doctrine, at least five have adopted the rule contained in the Uniform Arrest Act, and at least six have case law or statutes that give effect to the Uniform Arrest Act rule. That the trend is away from the Common Law doctrine and in the direction of the Uniform Arrest Act rule is argued in Max Hochanadel and H. W. Stege, "The Right to Resist an Unlawful Arrest: An Outdated Concept?" *Tulsa Law Journal* 3 (1966): 40–46. I am grateful for the help I received from 35 of the 50 State Attorney General offices from whom I sought information concerning this matter.

67. Smith, *Police Systems*, 8.

68. The authors of the *Task Force Report* note that little has been done to make these alternative resources available as substitutes for police intervention; see p. 14.

69. M. DeWolfe Howe, *The Garden and the Wilderness: Religion and Government in American Constitutional History* (Chicago: University of Chicago Press, 1965), 1.

70. The argument about the "normalcy" of crime and other forms of social pathology is contained in Emile Durkheim, *The Rules of Sociological Method*, chap. 3 (Chicago: University of Chicago Press, 1938).

71. H. D. Lasswell, *World Politics and Personal Insecurity* (Glencoe, Ill.: Free Press, 1950), 228.

72. Silver, "Demand for Order," 12–14.

73. Morris Janowitz, *Social Control of Escalated Riots* (Chicago: Uni-

versity of Chicago Center for Policy Studies, 1968), 8. For a general discussion of the concept of the military constabulary see *The Professional Soldier: Political and Social Portrait* (New York: Free Press of Glencoe, 1960), 417–40. Some armed forces appear to exist solely for constabulary purposes; a case in point is the Irish army; see J. A. Jackson, "The Irish Army and the Development of the Constabulary Concept" (Paper presented to the Sixth World Congress of Sociology, September 1966, mimeo).

74. P. J. Stead, "The Police of France," *Medico-Legal Journal* 33 (1965): 3–11.

75. Recently some authors have expressed doubts about the merits of organizing the police along military lines. Wilson takes issue with Smith's assertion that the police have "disciplinary requirements of a quasi-military body." *Varieties of Police Behavior,* 79 nn. 16, 24. Similarly, A. J. Reiss and D. J. Bordua have questioned the adequacy of the idea of the police as a military organization; see "Environment and Organization: A Perspective on the Police," in *The Police,* ed. Bordua, 46ff.

76. *Task Force Report,* 16.

77. The tendency of police departments to adopt outward military rigidities has been frequently emphasized; see *Task Force Report,* 29; J. D. Lohman and G. E. Misler, *The Police and the Community,* A Report Prepared for the President's Commission on Law Enforcement and Administration of Justice (Washington, D.C.: U.S. Government Printing Office, 1966), 1:152, 2:196; Banton reports that American police chiefs admire Scottish officers who "bore themselves well, and were smartly and uniformly dressed" *(The Policeman in the Community),* 123.

78. In addition to the rigors of outward discipline, military establishments also rely on "command charisma," a feature observed in American police departments by D. J. Bordua and A. J. Reiss; see "Command, Control and Charisma: Reflections on Police Bureaucracy," *American Journal of Sociology* 72 (1966): 68–76. The term indicates a leadership principle in which subordinates are moved to obedience by a high regard for, and trust in, the person in command.

79. See *Task Force Report,* 20; Goldstein, "Administrative Problems," 162; and Wilson, *Varieties,* 16.

80. Niederhoffer, *Behind the Shield,* 68–69.

81. The most illuminating and extensive discussion of pressures to produce is contained in Skolnick, *Justice without Trial,* 164–81.

82. Paul Chevigny explains that New York policemen sometimes rebut allegations of brutality by maintaining that they are obviously fabrications since the complainant would have been arrested had the

officer laid hands on him. Chevigny reports numerous instances of arrests following altercations with citizens which were ineptly or deviously provoked by policemen, and he comments, "Many lawyers think it a triumph for a felony to be reduced to a mere offence, but the truth is that it requires only two simple ingredients: guiltless clients and infinite patience" (*Police Power: Police Abuses in New York City* [New York: Pantheon Books, 1969]).

83. J. H. McNamara, "Uncertainties in Police Work: The Relevance of Police Recruits' Background and Training," in *The Police*, ed. Bordua, 163–252.

84. McNamara cites the following case: "A patrolman directing traffic in the middle of an intersection . . . fired his revolver and hit an automobile whose driver had not heeded the officer's hand signals. The driver immediately pulled over to the side of the street and stopped the car. The officer realized the inappropriateness of his action and began to wonder what he might offer as an explanation to his supervisor and to the citizen. The patrolman reported that his anxiety was dissipated shortly upon finding that the driver of the car was a person convicted of a number of crimes. The reader should understand that departmental policy did not specify that any person convicted of crimes in New York City thereby became a target for police pistol practice" (ibid., 171). Nevertheless, as the officer's feeling of relief indicates, the transgression was apparently construable as an instance of aggressive crime control.

85. Niederhoffer, *Behind the Shield,* 85.

86. Wilson notes, however, that this view is probably mistaken. The patrolman deals with matters that are ill defined and ambiguously emergent, while detectives deal with more precisely defined crimes and only after they have been committed; *Varieties,* 8–9.

87. "A high arrest record reinforces the cynicism that inspired it in the first place, while often establishing a policeman's reputation for initiative and efficiency. His superiors recommend him for assignment to the detective division. This route to promotion appeals to many young policemen who have little hope of passing a written competitive test for promotion, and impels many of them to adopt cynicism as a rational and functional way to advancement" (Niederhoffer, *Behind the Shield,* 76–77.

88. "At present the principal rewards are promotion, which takes a patrolman off the street, or reassignment to a detective or specialized unit, which takes him out of order maintenance altogether; not surprisingly, patrolmen wanting more pay or status tend to do those things . . . that will earn them those rewards" (Wilson, *Varieties,* 292–93).

89. On the pervasiveness of purely punitive discipline, see McNamara, "Uncertainties," in *The Police,* ed. Bordua, 178–83. Wilson reports that regulations are so framed that they do not instruct but "give the brass plenty of rope with which to hang us" (*Varieties,* 279 n. 16).

90. McNamara reports attitudes of patrolmen toward their superiors and concludes, "Regardless of their accuracy, these assertions strongly support the feeling that the 'bosses' of the department do not deserve the respect which the organization requires or demands" ("Uncertainties," in *The Police,* ed. Bordua, 187–88.

91. Banton views the absence of instructions and supervision as a main characteristic distinguishing American police from their British counterpart, *The Policeman in the Community,* 115–16. The absence of supervision is frequently noted; see McNamara, "Uncertainties," in *The Police,* ed. Bordua, 183; and *Task Force Report,* 28, 52, *et passim.*

92. McNamara speaks about the dilemma, "whether to emphasize training strategies aimed at the development of self-directed and autonomous personnel or to emphasize strategies aimed at developing personnel over whom the organization can readily exercise control. It appears that the second strategy is the one most often emphasized" ("Uncertainties," 251). Niederhoffer similarly states, "At the Academy he [the recruit] masters and simultaneously succumbs to, the web of protocol and ceremony that characterizes any quasi-military hierarchy" (*Behind the Shield,* 45).

93. Niederhoffer speaks about the "reality shock" and documents the rapid rise of cynicism among first year policemen; see especially ibid, 239.

94. The competitive nature of ideals of military discipline and methodical discretion has been noted in a survey of the Boston police department undertaken in 1934: "Too often the military aspect of organization pushes the essentially individual character of police work into the background" (*Task Force Report,* 136).

95. Chief Parker said, perhaps too optimistically, "One thing we have done is to break down a false sense of fraternal obligation. If there is even the beginning of a dereliction on the part of an officer, we hear about it from others within the department" (*The Police,* An Interview by Donald McDonald with William H. Parker [Santa Barbara: Center for the Study of Democratic Institutions, 1962] 10–11).

96. Concerning disunity, jealousies, and recriminations in police departments, see *Task Force Report,* 53. McNamara remarks that the "cohesiveness is not only related to difficulties associated with handling citizens or police problems but also extends to the difficulties

associated with a patrolman's relations with other officers, particularly his superiors" ("Uncertainties," 246).

97. The fragmentation of American police systems could scarcely be expected to yield other results; see A. C. Breckenridge, "The Constitutional Basis for Cooperative Crime Control," *Journal of Criminal Law, Criminology and Police Science* 39 (1949): 565–83. The actual extent of uncooperativeness is something of a "well-guarded secret."

98. Niederhoffer understates the case in saying, "It is also true that ambitious detectives strive to build up a *private* circle of informants" (*Behind the Shield,* 84). The fact is that no detective can even begin to solve cases without it. Werthman and Piliavin write about officers assigned to juvenile details: "Although the officer may consult *his* files on populations of suspects and offenders located during previous investigations, these files are used largely as memory aids. Most of this information is in his head" ("Gang Membership," 69).

99. Remarkably, the President's Commission on Law Enforcement and Administration of Justice did not recognize this point even though it devoted considerable attention to the problems of police intelligence.

100. K. C. Davis writes about the police, "No other federal, state, or local agency, as far as I know, delegates so much power to subordinates. No other agency, so far as I know, does so little supervising of vital policy determination which directly involves justice and injustice to individuals" (*Discretionary Justice: A Preliminary Inquiry* [Baton Rouge, La.: Louisiana University Press, 1969], 88). Davis should have added that there is no room for supervision of, and interest in, policy determinations in a system that is permanently flooded with petty military and bureaucratic regulations.

101. Dr. Harry A. Willmer, of the Langley Porter Neuropsychiatric Institute in San Francisco, conducted and videotaped problem centered conferences involving patrolmen. Most viewers of these tapes expressed astonishment at the thoughtfulness and articulateness of the participants.

102. Silver, "The President's," 932. Silver also cites support from a statement by W. A. Westley that the few sadists, who seem isolated, and who arouse fear and revulsion among their associates, are safe because it is exceedingly difficult to mobilize support against them. My own observations confirm this. It seems that the only aspersions one officer can honorably cast upon another is that the latter breached the code of silent fraternity. See also J. Q. Wilson, "The Police and Their Problems: A Theory," *Public Policy,* ed. C. J. Friedrich and S. Harris, vol. 12, 1963, 189–216.

103. New York patrolmen believe that advancement in the department can be secured through the good offices of a "rabbi," i.e., a senior officer who is favorably disposed to the patrolman on a personal basis; see McNamara, "Uncertainties," 189.

104. This view is associated with archaic forms of control of vagabondage. See Alexandre Vexliard, "La Disparition du Vagabondage comme Fleau Social Universelle" *Revue de l'Institut de Sociologie* (1963): 53–79; and A. H. Sherry, "Vagrants, Rogues and Vagabonds—Old Concepts in Need of Revision," *California Law Review* 48 (1960): 557–73.

105. See *Task Force Report* 122ff. The recommendation as it stands does little more than sanction distinctions that already are made informally in *some* departments between detectives, patrolmen, and cadets.

106. H. M. Volmer and D. L. Mills, eds., *Professionalization* (Englewood Cliffs, N.J.: Prentice-Hall, 1966).

107. Professionalization of engineering is a fascinating story; see B. M. Fisher, *Industrial Education: American Ideals and Institutions* (Madison, Wis.: University of Wisconsin Press, 1967), 60–71, where F. A. Walker, who took over the presidency of MIT in 1875, is quoted as having stated, "We assert that the disinterestedness of study does not depend on the immediate usefulness or uselessness of the subject matter, but upon the spirit with which the student takes up and pursues his work. If there be zeal in investigation, if, there be delight in discovery, if there be fidelity to truth as it is discerned, nothing more can be asked by the educator of highest aims" (62).

108. Schools of medicine are a possible exception in this respect. Law schools were certainly not founded to answer needs of professional practice; W. F. Murphy and C. Pritchett report about admission standards to legal practice that, as late as 1953, "only twenty states demanded a law degree; three required merely a high-school education and two set no minimal standards whatever" (*Courts, Judges, and Politics: An Introduction to the Judicial Process* [New York: Random House, 1961], 125). It is also a well-known fact that law schools have a long history of struggles in attempting to bring curricula into some sort of functional relationship with practice; see Erwin Griswold, *Law and Lawyers in the United States* (Cambridge, Mass.: Harvard University Press, 1964). The problems of defining the field of academic study and its relevance to practice are even more acute in schools of education and in schools of social work.

109. Thus, for example, the definition of the role of police in modern society offered in the foregoing remarks, even if it appeals

to social scientists, will be of no practical value unless the practitioners recognize it, and elaborate it further, as the leading maxim of their methods.

110. The leading example of how unimportant "mere" education can be, as opposed to specific professional education, is diplomacy. It appears that even though most members of the foreign service have academic credentials, they are scandalously unprepared for their assignments. Smith Simpson writes, "Diplomacy and foreign policy, like the law involve justice and order. Like medicine, they involve people's lives, and on a very large scale. Diplomacy, therefore, should demand the most thorough, the most grueling professional preparation. Yet the State Department moseys along, requiring no more than was required fifty or sixty years ago. It takes the position that any adult, aged twenty-one, can make a good diplomatic officer if he has but personality, character, a high IQ and a smattering of a liberal arts education" (*Anatomy of the State Department* [Boston: Houghton Mifflin Co., 1967], 10).

111. See *Task Force Report*, in which it is stated: "In 1961, only 22.3 percent of applicants for positions in 368 police departments were accepted. The applicant success rate in many departments is far lower. For example, in 1965, only 2.8 percent of the candidates for the Los Angeles Police Department were eventually accepted into the force. In 1966, only 29 of 3,033 applicants were hired by the Dallas Police Department" (134).

112. "Departments that have college requirements, such as the Multnomah County Sheriff's Department, have reported that the elevation of standards has enhanced, not hindered, recruiting efforts" (ibid., 133).

113. Ibid., 138. The recruit training of the Los Angeles County Sheriff's Department consisted of 820 hours in 1966. According to time allocations we have proposed, departments would "lose" only 780 hours, on the basis of six-hour work days during the 78 weeks four semesters take up. Though for the students the six hours will be a learning experience, the departments will actually receive almost all the benefits they now expect of tyro policemen.

114. D. J. Dalby, a severe critic of the Supreme Court decisions restricting police practice, has urged that policemen should receive legal training beyond what is now given; he said, "An officer so unfamiliar with the law that he cannot understand its requirements will lose heart; he will quit trying" ("New Concepts in Criminal Law," *FBI Law Enforcement Bulletin* [August 1964]: 1–9).

115. See the arguments contained in *Task Force Report*, 54ff., 190.

The prevailing American view is that the foot patrol is useful but too costly. This opinion is not sustained by the results of experimental studies conducted in England, which show that the presence of a patrolman on the beat results in very substantial reduction in the incidence of indictable offenses; see Ben Whitaker, *The Police* (Baltimore, Md.: Penguin Books, 1964), 33.

116. Frank Elmes points to the seemingly trivial mistakes English policemen sometimes make—such as calling "a 'Sir' type 'mate' and a 'mate' type 'Sir' "—which are sources of nontrivial consequences ("The Police: 1954–1963," *Criminal Law Review*, [July 1964]: 505–28).

117. As a point of methodological interest, it may be mentioned that researchers who study police activities are almost always given legalistic explanation by policemen. But careful probing reveals, as Nathan Goldman observed, that "their interpretation and enforcement of the law cannot be considered in any way as constant" (*The Differential Selection of Juvenile Offenders for Court Appearance* [New York: National Council on Crime and Delinquency, 1963], 97).

118. Egon Bittner, "The Police on Skid Row: A Study of Peace Keeping, *American Sociological Review* 32 (1967): 699–715.

119. The patrolman's information gathering contains certain elements of the type of inquiry described in B. G. Glaser and A. L. Strauss, *The Discovery of Grounded Theory: Strategies for Qualitative Research* (Chicago: Aldine Publishing Co., 1967), without, of course, leading to theory formulation.

120. M. O. Cameron, *The Booster and the Snitch: Department Store Shoplifting* (New York: The Free Press, 1964).

121. J. H. Skolnick and J. R. Woodworth describe a case of conflict between two officers assigned to the "morals detail." One of the officers zealously treats all persons accused of statutory rape as serious sex offenders. The other avoids treating young men whom he recognizes as being merely amorous Lotharios in this way, explaining, "Not that I care if he has to register; but I hate to clutter up our file of pictures with these non–sex-criminal guys" ("Bureaucracy, Information, and Social Control," in *The Police*, ed. Bordua, 115).

122. I beg forgiveness for switching roles for the sake of narrative fluency. Naturally, I was the sociologist. The story is actually the composite of two observed cases. In the first case, I accompanied the team of officers and the offending animal was surrendered after the officers asked the owner to accompany them to the station. The rest of the story, after the entry of the sergeant, happened as stated, except that I am not quite certain that the officers "were about to arrest the man."

123. The value of offering alternatives to persons whose compliance is monitored by policemen is discussed by McNamara, "Uncertainties," in *The Police*, ed. Bordua, 173.

124. Black and Reiss point out that policemen are far more likely to encounter nonisolable incidents, involving crowds of onlookers, in black neighborhoods than in any other parts of the city; see *Studies of Crime*, 23.

125. The term "alter-casting" was suggested by E. A. Weinstein in a paper read at the American Sociological Association Meetings, Washington, D. C., 1962, as quoted by McNamara, "Uncertainties," in *The Police*, ed. Bordua, 169.

126. Black and Reiss report that 86 percent of police interventions are directed either by radio dispatches (81 percent) or by on-the-street requests of citizens (5 percent); see *Studies of Crime*, 17.

127. Reports about such incidents are frequent. But no one can say how many officers are involved in them. Most researchers who have studied the police tend to agree that their number is quite small. My own experience leads me to think that they are probably not more numerous than cruel teachers.

128. The legal justification of orders to "move on" is another matter. The police have, according to common law doctrine and many statutes, the authority to compel the peaceful dispersal of assemblies in incipient stages of disorder; see Hall, "Police and Law," 147ff. But authorities are divided on the question whether refusal to obey police orders to "move on" constitutes disorderly conduct; see J. V. Henry, "Breach of Peace and Disorderly Conduct Laws: Void for Vagueness?" *Howard Law Journal* 12 (1966): 318–31, 321ff. The District of Columbia has an ordinance making refusal to comply with an order to "move on" a misdemeanor, but 90 percent of persons who are arrested on this account are discharged by the courts "for lack of prosecutorial merit"; see *On the Metropolitan Police Department*, A Report of the President's Commission on Crime in the District of Columbia (Washington, D. C.: U.S. Government Printing Office, 1966), 67, 94; see also Jim Thompson, "Police Controls over Citizen Use of the Public Streets," *Journal of Criminal Law, Criminology and Police Science* 49 (1959): 562–69.

129. Illuminating accounts of police interaction with young people on the streets of blighted areas of the city are contained in Werthman and Piliavin, "Gang Membership," in *The Police*, ed. Bordua, 56–98; and Irving Piliavin and Scott Briar, "Police Encounters with Juveniles," *American Journal of Sociology* 70 (1964): 206–14.

130. It should be borne in mind, however, that while an average of

four policemen are killed annually in New York City in the line of duty, only one policeman is killed, on the average, every four years in the city of London, Whitaker, *The Police,* 24.

131. George Berkley, "How the Police Work: In Western Europe and in the U.S.," *New Republic* (12 August 1969): 15–18.

132. The fact that the police often resort to violence in response to what they perceive as disrespectful defiance of authority is widely recognized; see W. A. Westley, "Violence and the Police," *American Journal of Sociology* 59 (1953): 34–41; W. R. LaFave, *Arrest: The Decision to Take a Suspect into Custody* (Boston: Little, Brown & Co., 1965), 146f.; and McIntire, *Metropolis,* 61. By the same token, members of juvenile gangs tend to define officers who do not respond forcefully to provocation as "chicken," but they exempt juvenile officers from this judgment. It appears that the juvenile officer's businesslike approach obviates the need for force without a decline in effectiveness; see Werthman and Piliavin, 66 n. 15, 94. O. W. Wilson mentioned rather superfluously that there is "no law against making a policeman angry" (*Police Administration* [New York: McGraw-Hill, 1963]); but "fighting words" directed against a policeman "have been held not within the first and fourteenth amendments' protection" (Henry, "Breach of Peace," 322n. 128).

133. James Ridgeway, "The Cops and the Kids," in Walt Anderson, ed., *The Age of Protest* (Pacific Palisades, Calif.: Goodyear Publishing Co., 1969), 174–80.

134. Stinchcombe argues that because American police forces lack the military character of, for example, the Spanish *Guardia Civil,* they lack the capability of handling militant, politically inspired mass upheavals; see "Institutions of Privacy," 158. The actual performance of American police forces in such situations is described in the *Report of the National Advisory Commission on Civil Disorders* (New York: Bantam Books, 1968), 299–322. To meet the newly arisen need to control street disorders some police departments have organized highly mobile "tactical squads." In Philadelphia, such a unit has not only engendered the hostility of citizens but also is viewed with disfavor within the Police Department. Lohman and Misner quote a "high-ranking police officer" as referring to the unit in these terms: "They are a skull-cracking division. . . . The Department would be much better off (sic!) without this unit and I wish that these men could be reassigned and transferred back to the District station under the command of each captain" (*The Police and the Community*), 2:46.

135. Goldstein, "Police Discretion," 543f.

136. Concerning "Noninvocation [of the law] because the legisla-

ture may not desire enforcement as to the conduct in the ordinary case," see LaFave, *Arrest,* 188ff.

137. Herman Goldstein writes, "Broadly-stated laws are, after all, one of the lesser concerns of the police. Most attention of law-enforcement officers in recent years has focused upon legal provisions which are too narrow. The average police official is not very concerned about having the authority to enforce adultery statutes and not having the manpower or the community support necessary to do so. He is much more concerned because of his inability to attack organized crime effectively. And there may be an occasion upon which he can use an obscure or otherwise unenforced law to launch an oblique attack against a situation or activity which he feels warrants action on his part. His attitude is often that the law should be left on the books; it may come in handy sometime. Why impose self-limitations on police authority beyond those established by the legislature?" ("Dealing with Crime: Can All Laws Be Enforced?" *Current* 46 [February 1964]: 39–42).

138. For an account of how patrolmen avail themselves of whatever laws exist to make life on skid row somewhat more bearable than it would otherwise be, by temporarily removing perilous persons, but also persons in peril, see Bittner, "Police on Skid Row," 699–715.

139. *Task Force Report,* 38–41. J. A. Ronayne, "The Right to Investigate and New York's 'Stop and Frisk' Law," *Fordham Law Review* 33 (1964): 211–38; S. L. Sindell, "Stop and Frisk: Police Protection or Police State," *Intramural Law Review-New York University School of Law* 21 (1966): 180–90.

140. The law appears to allow a genuine error. If it is learned that an arrest was a mistake, the suspect can be released without having been presented before a magistrate. This raises the question of how freely policemen may err. Barrett urged that, "Police departments should be measured and compared not only in terms of 'arrests' and 'clearances' and 'convictions,' but also in terms of their effectiveness in reducing the incidence of arrests and the amount of police custody. Police departments should boast of their ability to reduce the percentage of persons arrested who are released without charge" ("Police Practices," 50).

141. C. D. Robinson, "Alternatives to Arrest of Lesser Offenders," *Crime and Delinquency* (January 1965): 8–21.

142. See the figures quoted above in n. 47.

143. Even Hall, the most uncompromising advocate of the principle of legality, writes, "When we consider that the vast majority of persons subjected to illegal imprisonment are vagrants, drunkards,

and derelicts, we realize that the police conduct serves as a crude prophylaxis and as a minor benefit to the arrestees, in providing a night's lodgings and time to become sober" ("Police and Law," 156).

144. The term "golden rule" refers to the practice of overnight detention of derelicts in city jails. The practice was once advocated as part of an urban reform movement. See R. H. Bremmer, "The Civic Revival in Ohio: Police, Penal and Parole Policies in Cleveland and Toledo," *American Journal of Economics and Sociology* 14 (1955): 387–98.

145. In these cases arrests are ordinarily made only when the offending person also fails in being as obsequious toward the intervening officer as the latter expects. At other times, officers bring the quarreling parties to a "hearing" at the police station; see R. L. Parnas, "Police Response to Domestic Disturbance," *Wisconsin Law Review* (1967): 914–60.

146. A high-ranking police official stated, "I don't know of any official endorsement of the program, but I am sure that on more than one occasion it has happened, because we could not have continued this practice over these many years without at least the tacit approval of the courts. There would have been something done by this time to eliminate the practice. In combating prostitution, particularly, this must be done." The same officer gave the following illustration for the necessity of the program, "Our patrol finds two women. . . . They are prostitutes. Yet, there has been no offense committed by them in the presence of the officers. They make the arrest to get them off the street. These particular women are not only prostitutes but are decoys for the 'Murphy Game.' Persons who come in contact with them have been murdered. As a general rule, in fact almost invariably, these women are out there at two o'clock when the saloons close, and the prospective customers have a lot of liquor in them. Now what should we do under those circumstances?" (McIntire, *Metropolis*, 85).

147. This problem has an obverse facet that deserves mention. Just as police often arrest persons on specious grounds, they often do not arrest others who should, according to principles of legality, be charged with crimes. When this policy, which exists everywhere, was once officially proclaimed (in England), it resulted in the dismissal of the candid police official; W. N. Osborough, "Immunity for the English Supermarket Shoplifter?" *American Journal of Comparative Law* 13 (1964): 291–99. Osborough quotes Lord Morris of Borth-y-Gest with reference to this way of exculpating offenders: "The fact that prosecutions have been, and doubtless will continue to be, infrequent demonstrates that the law is the handmaiden of reason" (ibid., 297).

148. See the literature cited above in n. 5.

149. See Lohman and Misner, *The Police and the Community*, 2:169; J. E. Carlin and Jan Howard, "Legal Representation and Class Justice," *UCLA Law Review* 12 (1965): 381–437; Bittner, "Police on Skid Row," 710.

150. See Clark, "Isolation, 307–19. The isolation of the police is also in some measure due to their exacerbated sensitivity to criticism; see Whitaker, *The Police*, 135f.; and Niederhoffer, *Behind the Shield*, 13, where the police fear of criticism is referred to as "the principle of equilibrium," presumably to emphasize its great significance.

151. Bittner, "Police on Skid Row," 709f., contains a lengthy description detailing the complex consideration that leads up to making an arrest in which the formal charge was a mere outward label, hiding, rather than revealing the real reasons.

152. The desire of the police to open consultative contacts with ethnic minorities and lower class groups is part of a larger drive in this direction. Mayor A. J. Cervantes of St. Louis explained it in these terms: "We have found out that ghetto neighborhoods cannot be operated on from the outside alone. The people within them should have a voice, and our experience has shown that it is often a voice that speaks with good sense, since the practical aspects of the needs of the ghetto people are so much clearer to the people there than they are to anyone else." As quoted in the *Report of the National Advisory Commission on Civil Disorders*, 287.

153. See *Task Force Report*, 149–63.

154. *A National Survey of Police and Community Relations* (Report prepared by the National Center on Police and Community Relations, School of Police Administration and Public Safety, Michigan State University, East Lansing, Mich., for the President's Commission on Law Enforcement and Administration of Justice [Washington, D. C.: U.S. Government Printing Office, 1967], 72).

155. In one department a unit of this nature is referred to by some officers as the "Commie Unit."

156. The formulation of the new interest is most advanced in psychiatry where a specialty known as Social Psychiatry has developed; its drift is described in Egon Bittner, "The Structure of Psychiatric Influence, *Mental Hygiene* 5 (1968): 423–30.

157. F. A. Allen, "The Borderland of the Criminal Law: Problems of 'Socializing' Criminal Justice," *Social Service Review* 32 (1958): 107–19.

158. The study of deviance as a cultural phenomenon is perhaps best exemplified in the papers collected in *The Other Side*, ed. H. S.

Becker (New York: The Free Press, 1964). It is rather obvious that policemen doing community relations work are in a uniquely advantageous position to engage in such studies.

159. E. M. Lemert, *Social Pathology* (New York: McGraw-Hill, 1951); see also R. D. Schwartz and J. H. Skolnick, "Two Studies of Legal Stigma," *Social Problems* 10 (1962): 134–42.

160. Psalm 127:1.

161. Eugene Ehrlich, *Fundamental Principles of the Sociology of Law* (Cambridge, Mass.: Harvard University Press, 1936), 71.

162. See Clark, "Isolation," 308; Donnelly, "Police Authority," 110; and Hall, "Police and Law," 176.

163. Silver writes with reference to a suggestion made by the President's Commission on Law Enforcement and Administration of Justice that the policeman of the future may well be a member of a team including social workers, psychiatrists, and doctors acting as an intake screening unit for all kinds of antisocial and disturbing behavior: "This is a frightening description of a 'Brave New World' ruled by professional *Wunderkinder* pulling 'antisocial' or 'disturbed' people off the street with, we can only hope, some kind of warrant" ("The President's," 940).

164. *The Dialogues of Plato,* trans. B. Jowett (New York: Random House, 1937), 2:798.

5 | *Florence Nightingale in Pursuit of Willie Sutton*

A Theory of the Police

AMONG THE INSTITUTIONS of modern government the police occupies a position of special interest: it is at once the best known and the least understood. Best known, because even minimally competent members of society are aware of its existence, are able to invoke the services it provides with remarkable competence, and know how to conduct themselves in its presence. How and how well the police is known, and the ways it matters in the lives of people, vary considerably over the spectrum of social inequality. But to imagine people who are not at all touched by the police one must conjure images of virtually complete isolation or of enormous wealth and power. Least understood, because when people are called upon to explain on what terms and to what ends police service is furnished they are unable to go beyond the most superficial and misleading commonplace which, moreover, is totally unrelated to the interactional skill that manifestly informs their dealings with policemen. What is true of people generally is true of the police as well. Policemen have not succeeded in formulating a justification of their existence that would recognizably relate to what they actually do (not counting those activities the doing of which they disavow or condemn). The situation is not unlike that of a person who, asked to explain how he speaks, offers an account which, while itself linguistically in perfect order, does not even come close to doing justice to the skill involved in producing the utterance.

In this chapter I propose to explain the function of the police by drawing attention to what their existence makes available in society that, all things being equal, would not be otherwise available, and by showing how all that policemen are called upon to do falls into place when considered in relationship to it. My thesis is that police are empowered and required to impose or, as the case may be, coerce a provisional solution upon emergent problems without having to brook or defer to opposition of any kind, and that further, their competence to intervene extends to every kind of emergency, without any exceptions whatever. This and this alone is what the existence of the police uniquely provides, and it is on this basis that they may be required to do the work of thief-catchers and of nurses, depending on the occasion. And while the *chances* that a policeman will recognize any problem as properly his business depend on some external regulation, on certain structured social interest, and on historically established patterns of responsiveness and responsibility, every stricture arising out of these factors is defeasible in every *specific case* of police work. This means that the appropriateness of police action is primarily determined with regard to the particular and actual nature of the case at hand, and only secondarily by general norms. The assessment whether the service the police are uniquely competent to provide is on balance desirable or not, in terms of, let us say, the aspirations of a democratic polity, is beyond the scope of the argument. But in reviewing practice and organization I will weigh what is against what ought to be, by certain criteria internal to the enterprise.

The chapter is frankly argumentative and intended to furnish grist for the mills of debate. Hence, I shall not attempt to view all questions from all sides, and I will especially avoid giving consideration to mere administrative expediency or yielding to those demands of reasonableness that are connected with taking a live-and-let-live attitude. All this counts, to be sure, but I will try not to let it count in what I have to say; and in arguing as strongly as I know how, I do not aim to dismiss polemic opponents but to pay tribute to them. My plan is to begin with a cursory review of some preliminaries—dealing mainly with the police idea—in ways I consider indispensable for what will follow. Next I shall sketch a rather ordinary and common event in police work, and use it to explain what a policeman is required to do in this situation, in such situations, and by extension, in any situation whatever. Finally, I will attempt to characterize the problems that appear to summon police intervention and to define the role force plays in these interventions. In wrapping things up I will comment about the practical significance of police work in society and about the skills that come into play, or should come into play, in this regard.

THE OFFICIAL BASIS OF
LAW ENFORCEMENT MANDATES

While we use the term police to refer to specific corps of public officials, it bears mentioning that original usage embraced the entire field of internal government, as distinct from the conduct of foreign affairs. Sir Francis Bacon, for example, asserted that in being "civil or policied," a nation acquired the right to subdue others that were "altogether unable or indign to govern" (Bacon 1859, 29). In time this usage gave way to one restricted to the exercise of proscriptive control in matters affecting the public interest. Blackstone stated that "public police and economy . . . mean the due regulation and domestic order of the Kingdom, whereby the individuals of the state, like members of a well governed family, are bound to conform their general behavior to the rules of propriety, good neighborhood and good manners, and to be decent, industrious and inoffensive in their respective stations" (Blackstone n.d., 161). This definition is located in the volume dealing with public wrongs, in relation to a specific class of delicts, called offenses against the public police and economy. By the end of the nineteenth century this class of delicts is treated by Sir James Fitzjames Stephen as lying outside of the scope of criminal law, but is, nevertheless, explicitly related to the existence of the then existing police forces in England (Stephen 1833, 246). Though both Blackstone and Stephen treat the category of police offenses cursorily, they do furnish *legal authority* for each item discussed. The intent at scrupulous legalization of proscriptive control also inheres in the "idiom of apologetics which belongs to the vocabulary of constitutional law" (Hamilton and Rodee 1937, 192), commonly invoked to justify abridgements of civil liberties in the interest of "public health, morals, and safety" (Mugler v. Kansas 1887). Indeed, in keeping with American concepts of legality, Mr. Justice Harlan, speaking for the majority in Mugler, reserved the right of judicial review of statutes enacted in the exercise of police power.

Most of the offenses against the public police mentioned by Blackstone are no longer regarded as culpable. But the domain of legally sanctioned proscriptive control he discussed has expanded enormously since the commentaries appeared, as have the provisions of criminal law. There are scarcely any human activities, any interpersonal relations, any social arrangements left that do not stand under some form of governmental regulation, to the violation of which penalties are attached. To say that modern life is thus controlled does not mean saying that it is more controlled than earlier life. Tribesmen, peasants, or citizens of colonial townships most assuredly did not live in a paradise of freedom. In fact, the most widely accepted explanation of the proliferation of formal control, which associates it with the growth of a market-oriented, industrial, and urban order, implies primarily a shift from reliance on informal mechanisms of traditional authority to reliance on legal rational means (Weber 1947, 324).

Urbanism brought with it the need for explicitly formal regulations because the lives of the people living in cities are replete with opportunities of infringing upon one another and virtually devoid of incentives to avoid it. The former is due to the sheer congestion of very large numbers of people, the latter to the social distance between them. More importantly, perhaps, urban strangers cannot entrust their fate to the hope of somehow muddling through because of the manner in which they attend to the business of making a living, and because of the permanent significance of this interest in their lives.

Two conditions must be met to satisfy the need for formal governmental control that would bind effectively the behavior of individuals to rules of propriety. The first, already recognized in the treatment Blackstone accorded to the matter, is that all controls rest on specific authorization set forth in highly specific legal norms. The second, explicitly acknowledged by Stephen, is that the implementation of the authorizing norm must be entrusted to impersonal enforcement bureaucracies. In sum, "the due regulation and domestic order" in our times is the task of a host of law enforcement bureaucracies, each using procedures legitimized by, and incidental to, the attainment of explicitly formulated legal objectives.

Naturally, the actual interests and practices of enforcement officials are rarely as specific or explicit as the verbal formulations of their respective mandates. Hence, for example, while the formal authorization of the work of a health inspector may be clear and specific, things are apt to become a bit sticky when he undertakes to match factual realities with provisions of statutes. The amount of discretionary freedom it takes to fill the interstices of the legal formulation of law enforcement competence probably varies from one bureaucracy to the next. Agents concerned with weights and measures are probably less free than building inspectors. On the whole, however, it is safe to assume that none will busy himself, nor be permitted to busy himself, outside of the sphere of his mandate. More importantly, there is no mystery about the proper business of such law enforcement agents, and citizens are generally quite able to hold them to their limits. For example, though a truant officer's enforcement activities could be rich and varied, especially if he happens to be dedicated to his tasks, he can claim legitimate interest in the child's health, the conditions of his home, or some such matter, only insofar as they can be linked with school attendance. In practice it can be debated whether the connection he sees is defensible or not, but there is not debate about the terms on which the question must be decided. Because it is known what a truant officer is supposed to do, therefore he can be held to account for doing more or doing less than his mandate authorizes or requires him to do, and by the same token, the officer can reject demands he deems *ultra vires.*

It would seem reasonable to expect that the proper business of the police—that is, of the corps of officials who inherited the name once used to refer to the entire domain of internal, proscriptive regulation—should be determined in the manner in which the business of all other law enforcement bureaucracies is determined. That is, one would expect that their service and powers be derivative from some substantive authorizing norm. And, indeed, it is commonly assumed that the penal code contains this authorization, in addition to which the police are required to enforce other laws, in particular laws regulating vehicular traffic, and beyond that may have some responsibilities concerning such matters as the licensing of the possession of firearms or the operation of certain business enterprises, which vary greatly from place to place. All in all, however, activities relating to crime control are generally considered basic to the mandate of the police by both citizens and police officials, at least in the sense that its needs are regarded as having priority over other needs (Gorman et al. 1973; Leonard and More 1971).[1] Though I will argue that this presumption is misguided and misleading, and that one could not possibly understand or control what policemen actually do by assuming it, it must be said that it is not without some carefully laid foundations, the import of which is difficult to overcome.

The following considerations appear to justify the presumption that the police are a law enforcement agency whose mandate is basically derivative of the provisions of penal codes. First, the police, together with many others, cultivate and propagate the image of the policeman as the vanguard fighter in the war on crime. Americans from the members of congress to readers of tabloids are convinced that what the police do about crime is the main part of the struggle against it and that, therefore, doing something about it is the policeman's main care. Second the formal bureaucratic organization of police work stringently reinforces the view that the police are primarily dedicated to criminal law enforcement. Police training, such as it is, heavily emphasizes criminalistics, criminal law, and related matters; the internal administrative differentiation of departments tends to reflect primarily formal criminal enforcement specializations and units are designated by names of species of offenses; and police recordkeeping is almost wholly dedicated to the recording of law enforcement activity as a result of which crime control is the only documentable output of police work. Most importantly, perhaps, career advancement in departments is heavily determined by an officer's show of initiative and ability in criminal law enforcement or, at least, an officer who has some so-called good pinches to his credit can always count that this will weigh more heavily in his favor when it comes to assessing his overall performance than any other factor. Third, the criminal process is virtually always set into motion by the police, and prosecutors, judges, and correctional personnel are heavily dependent on the police to remain occupied. Moreover, the part the police play in the administration of justice is very specific and indispensable. They are charged with the responsibility of conducting investigations leading to the identification of suspects and with securing the evidence required for successful prosecution. And they are obliged to apprehend and detain identified suspects, in the course of which they are empowered to use force if force is necessary. Fourth, the work of a certain number of policemen—the number is probably not very large but large enough to be significant—is in fact quite plainly determined by the provisions of the penal code in more or less the same manner in which the work of building inspectors is determined by building codes. These are officers assigned to various detective bureaus, whose daily routines consist of investigating crimes, arresting offenders, and of otherwise being engaged with matters related to efforts to obtain convictions.

In sum, the exercise of internal, proscriptive control by modern governments has been highly legalized, at least since the end of the eighteenth century. The exercise of this control is assigned to specifically authorized bureaucracies, each of which has a substantively limited field of enforcement competence. Even though it is allowed that officials retain a measure of discretionary freedom, the terms on which substantive decisions can be made are not in dispute. In accordance with this view the police often are viewed as one of several enforcement bureaucracies whose domain of competence is determined by penal codes and certain other statutory delegations.

THE POLICE AND CRIMINAL LAW ENFORCEMENT

With all this admitted as true, why can the police mandate not be conceived as embodying the law enforcement mandate inhering in criminal law enforcement? The answer is quite simple. Regardless of how strenuously criminal law enforcement is emphasized in the image of the policeman and in police administration, and regardless of how important police work might actually be for keeping the administration of criminal justice in business, the activity of criminal law enforcement is not at all characteristic of day-to-day, ordinary occupational practices of the vastly preponderant majority of policemen. In other words, when one looks at what policemen actually do, one finds that criminal law enforcement is something that most of them do with the frequency located somewhere between virtually never and very rarely.

Later in this chapter I will address this paradox directly and try to assign to criminal law enforcement its proper place within police work. Before moving on to this, however, I must touch on some matters connected with manpower allocation, opportunity for crime control, and routine work orientation. Unfortunately the data base on which the first two observations rely is poor, partly because the information available on these matters is not as good as it could be, but in larger measure because the actuarial ratios and frequencies I shall mention are drawn from data produced to meet requirements of accountability rather than strictly factual reporting. A word of caution is in order here; it is all too easy to fall into an attitude of supercilious critique concerning the poverty of data. The fact is that neither the police nor functionaries in other practical endeavors should be expected to keep records that would make it convenient for scholars to study them. Indeed, they usually have good reasons for keeping what in the scholar's view appear to be poor records (Garfinkel and Bittner 1967, 186–207).

According to a survey of municipal police departments of cities in the 300,000 to 1,000,000 population range which is, alas, neither exhaustive nor complete, 86.5 percent of all police line personnel—that is, excluding officers occupying supervisory positions from sergeant up—are assigned to uniformed patrol (Kansas City Police Department 1971; Wilson 1963, 293).[2] Though this figure excludes persons holding the civil service rank of patrolman while assigned to detectives' bureaus, it probably overestimates the relative size of the force of patrolmen actually working on the streets. But it would certainly seem safe to assume that four out of five members of the line personnel do the work of patrolmen, especially since patrol sergeants, whose work is essentially of the same nature as the work of those they supervise, are not included in the 86.5 percent. But the importance of the uniformed patrol in the police is not altogether derivative from the preponderance of their number. They represent, in even greater measure than their numbers indicate, the police presence in society. In fact, I will argue that all the other members of the police—in particular, the various special plainclothes details—represent special refinements of police-patrol work that are best understood as derivative of the mandate of the patrol, even though their activities sometimes take on forms that are quite unlike the activities of the patrol. But I should like to make clear now that in subordinating the work of the detectives to the work of the patrol *conceptually,* I do not intend to cast doubts on the special importance the work of the former has for the prosecutors and judges. Indeed, I hope to make clear by dint of what circumstance prosecutors and judges come to be the beneficiaries of a service they ordinarily take for granted but for which—in rather rare moments of candor—they profess to lack understanding.

For the reasons I indicated, and because of reasons I hope to add as I go along, the following remarks will concern primarily the work of the uniformed patrol. But I do intend to make references to other parts of the police wherever such references are called for. In fact, the first observation about criminal law enforcement pertains equally to the work of detectives and patrolmen.

It is well known that the penal codes the police are presumed to enforce contain thousands of titles. While many of these titles are obscure, unknown, or irrevelant to existing conditions, and the administration of criminal justice is concentrated around a relatively small fraction of all proscribed acts, the police select only some, even from that sample, for enforcement. Relying mainly on my observations, I believe the police tend to avoid involvement with offenses in which it is assumed that the accused or suspected culprits will not try to evade the criminal process by flight. Characteristically, for example, they refer citizens who complain about being defrauded by businesses or landlords directly to the prosecutor. The response is also often given in cases involving other types of allegations of property crimes involving persons, real or fictional, who own substantial property. To be sure, in some of these instances it is possible that the wrong is of a civil rather than a criminal nature, and it also should be taken into account that a principle of economy is at work here, and that the police disavow responsibility for some delicts simply because of lack of resources to deal with them. It is at least reasonable to suggest, however, that police interest in criminal law enforcement is limited to those offenses in which the perpetrator needs to be *caught* and where catching him *may* involve the use of physical force. The point in all this is not that the police are simply ignorant of, and uninterested in, the majority of the provisions of the penal code, but that their selectivity follows a specific principle, namely, that they feel called upon to act only when *their* special competence is required, and that special competence is related to the possibility that force *may* have to be used to secure the appearance of a defendant in court. This restriction is certainly not impermeable, and it happens often enough that policemen are for a variety of circumstantial reasons required to proceed in cases in which the voluntary appearance of a defendant in court is not in doubt. Interestingly, however, in many of these cases the police are likely to put on a symbolic show of force by gratuitously handcuffing the arrested person.

It has become commonplace to say that patrolmen do not invoke the law often. But this is not a very good way of putting things because it could also be said that neurosurgeons do not operate often, at least not when compared with the frequency with which taxi drivers transport their fares. So it might pay to try to be a bit more specific about it. According to estimates issued by the research division of the International Association of Chiefs of Police, "the percentage of the police effort devoted to the traditional criminal law matters probably does not exceed ten percent" (Niederhoffer 1969, 75). Reiss, who studied the practices of the patrol in a number of American metropolitan centers, in trying to characterize a typical day's work, stated that it defies all efforts of typification "except in the sense that *the modal tour of duty does not involve an arrest* of any person" (Reiss 1971, 19). Observations about arrest frequency are, of course, not a very good source of information about law enforcement concerns. Yet, while they must be viewed skeptically, they deserve mention. According to the Uniform Crime Reports, 97,000 detectives and patrolmen made 2,597,000 arrests, including 548,000 for Index Crimes.[3] This means that the average member of the line staff makes twenty-six arrests annually, of which slightly more than five involve serious crimes. Though it is admittedly no more than a rough guess, it would seem reasonable to say, allowing for the fact that detectives presumably do nothing else, that patrolmen make about one arrest per man per month, and certainly no more than three Index Crime arrests per man per year. In any case, these figures are of the same order of magnitude as reported in the draft of a report on police productivity, where it was said that patrolmen assigned to New York City's Anti-Crime Squad average about fifteen felony arrests per man per year, while a "typical uniformed patrolman makes only about three felony arrests per year." In Detroit members of the Special Crime Attack Team make ten felony arrests per man per year, "considerably more than the average patrolman" (National Commission on Productivity 1973, 39f.). And the figures are also in good accord with estimates reported by the President's Commission on Law Enforcement and Administration of Justice, where it was calculated on the basis of data drawn from the operations of the Los Angeles Police Department that "an individual patrol officer can expect an opportunity to detect a burglary no more than once every three months and a robbery no more than once every fourteen years" (Institute for Defense Analysis 1967, 12).

It could be said, and should be considered, that the mere frequency of arrest does not reflect police work in the area of

criminal law enforcement adequately. Two points deserve attention in this regard: first, that clearing crimes and locating
suspects takes time; and second, that policemen frequently do
not invoke the law where the law could be invoked and thus *are*
involved in law enforcement, albeit in an unauthorized way.

In regard to the first point, it is certainly true that there are
some cases that are subject to dogged and protracted investigation. It is even not unheard of that uniformed patrolmen
work on some crime for long periods while attending to other
duties. This, however, is not characteristic of the work of either
detectives or patrolmen generally. For instance, in the majority
of reported burglaries, a patrolman or a team of patrolmen are
dispatched to survey the scene; this is followed by investigations
done by detectives, who, after writing up a report of their
investigation, in the majority of cases simply move on to the
next case (Conklin and Bittner 1973, 206–23).[4] Along these
lines, Conklin reports that criminal *investigations* of robberies
produce clearances only in one out of fifty cases (Conklin 1972,
148f.). And even if it were to be assumed that detectives engage
in five investigations for every one they conclude successfully—
no doubt a gross exaggeration—it would still remain that in the
run-of-the-mill crime the kind of investigation common lore
associates with detective work is not characteristic of the police,
and could not be, if only because the press of new business
pushes old cases into the dead file. I must add that the whole
matter of crime investigation is complicated, involving activities
that I did not mention. But I only intended to show that the
spacing of arrests is not due to the fact that the policemen need
time to work out a solution. All this means is that cases are
solved, when they are solved, either at the time the offense
takes place or shortly thereafter or, by and large, not at all.
The information required for such solution must be mobiliz-
able in short order, or the quest will be abandoned. In other
words, either a detective knows quite clearly in the case where
to turn or he will not try to pursue the matter. That he often
knows where to turn is part of his craft (Bittner 1970: 65ff.).[5]

The other point, that policemen make law enforcement
decisions of "low visibility," is the topic of a fairly substantial
body of literature.[6] According to the prevailing view expressed

in this literature, patrolmen usurp the rights of judges in a host
of minor offenses and, by not invoking the law, exculpate the
offender. While most authors find such practices reasonable
and for the most part desirable, they also recommend that the
exercise of such discretion should be placed under administrative, if not statutory, regulation (Davis 1971). They urge that,
though it appears to make good sense that policemen do not
enforce statutes pertaining to gambling literally and in every
applicable case, it is not right that the decision when to proceed
and when to desist should be left entirely to the lights of the
individual officers. Provided with more detailed instructions
officers would be, presumably, on firmer grounds and, hope-
fully, less arbitrary. Unfortunately, underlying the approach is
a presumption that begs the principal question; namely,
whether in making the arrests they make, and not making the
arrests they do not make, policemen are acting as the *functionaries of the law* they invoke or fail to invoke, as the case may be.
All available information about the practices of patrolmen place
this presumption in grave doubt, especially in regard to laws
pertaining to minor offenses. I am not aware of any descriptions of police work on the streets that support the view that
patrolmen walk around, respond to service demands, or intervene in situations, with the provisions of the penal code in
mind, matching what they see with some title or another, and
deciding whether any particular apparent infraction is serious
enough to warrant being referred for further process. While it
does happen occasionally that patrolmen arrest some person
merely because they have probable cause to believe that he has
committed crimes, this is not the way all but a small fraction of
arrests come about. In the typical case the formal charge *justifies*
the arrest a patrolman makes but is *not* the *reason* for it. The
actual reason is located in a domain of considerations to which
Professor Wilson referred as the need "to handle the situation,"[7] and invoking the law is merely a device whereby this is
sometimes accomplished. Since the persons who are arrested
at a backyard game of craps are not arrested because they are
gambling but because of a complex of situational factors of
which no mention is made in the formally filed charge, it would
seem specious to try to refine the law pertaining to the charge,

since any policeman worth his salt is virtually always in a position to find a bona fide charge of some kind when he believes the situation calls for an arrest. If criminal law enforcement means acting on the basis of, and in accordance with, the law's provisions, then this is something policemen do occasionally, but in their routine work they merely avail themselves of the provisions as a means for attaining other objectives.

In sum, the vastly preponderant number of policemen are assigned to activities in which they have virtually no opportunities for criminal law enforcement, and the available data indicate that they are engaged in it with a frequency that surely casts doubts upon the belief that this is the substance, or even the core, of their mandate. Moreover, criminal law enforcement by the police is limited to those offenses in which it is assumed that force may have to be used to bring the offender to justice. Finally, in the majority of cases in which the law is invoked, the decision to invoke it is not based on considerations of legality. Instead, policemen use the provisions of the law as a resource for handling problems of all sorts, of which *no mention* is made in the formal charge.

THE ELEMENTS OF ROUTINE POLICE PRACTICE

To explain by what conception of duty policemen feel summoned into action, and what objectives they seek to attain, I should like to use an example of ordinary practice. One of the most common experiences of urban life is the sight of a patrolman directing traffic at a busy street intersection. This service is quite expensive and the assignment is generally disliked among policemen. Nevertheless it is provided on a regular basis. The reason for this is not too difficult to divine. Aside from the private interests of citizens in maintaining safe and otherwise suitable conditions for the use of their automobiles, there is the consideration that the viability of urban life as we know it depends heavily on the mobility of vehicular traffic. No one knows, of course, how helpful police traffic control is in general, much less in the special case of a single patrolman directing traffic at a particular place and time. However uncertain the value of traffic control, the uncertainty is resolved in favor of having it simply because of the anticipated gravity of the consequences its absence might engender. In sum, traffic control is a matter of utmost seriousness. Despite its seriousness and presumed necessity, despite the fact that assignments are planned ahead and specifically funded, no assignment to a traffic control post is ever presumed to be absolutely fixed. The assigned officer is expected to be there, all things being equal, but he is also expected to have an independent grasp of the necessity of his presence. The point is not that this opens the possibility of a somewhat more casual attitude toward traffic control than the police care to admit, but rather that there exists a tacit understanding that no matter how important the post might be, it is always possible for something else to come up that can distract the patrolman's attention from it and cause him to suspend attending to the assigned task.

This understanding is not confined to traffic control assignments, but functions in all prior assigned tasks without any exceptions whatever, regardless whether the assignment involves investigating a heinous crime or feeding ice cream to a lost child, and regardless whether the prior assignment derives from the most solemn dictates of the law or whether it is based on mundane commands of immediate superiors. I am saying more than merely that patrolmen, like everybody else, will suspend the performance of an assigned task to turn to some extraordinary exigency. While everybody might respond to the call of an emergency, the policeman's vocational ear is *permanently and specifically attuned* to such calls, and his work attitude throughout is permeated by preparedness to respond to it, whatever he might happen to be doing. In the case at hand, it is virtually certain that any normally competent patrolman would abandon the traffic post to which he was assigned without a moment's hesitation and without regard for the state of the traffic he was supposed to monitor, if it came to his attention that a crime was being committed somewhere at a distance not too far for him to reach in time either to arrest the crime in its course, or to arrest the perpetrator. And it is virtually certain that all patrolmen would abandon their posts even when the probability of arresting the crime or its perpetrator was not very high, and even when the crime was of the sort which when reported to the police in the ordinary manner— that is, some time after it happened—would receive only the most cursory attention and would tend to remain unsolved in nine out of every ten reported cases. Finally, there is no doubt that the patrolman who would not respond in this manner, would thereby expose himself to the risk of an official repri- mand, and to expressions of scorn from his co-workers, and from the public.

Yet there exists no law, no regulation, no formal requirement of any kind that determines that practice. Quite the contrary, it is commonly accepted that crime control cannot be total, must be selective, and that policemen cannot be expected to rush to the scene of every crime and arrest every offender. Why then should all concerned, inside and outside the police, consider it entirely proper and desirable that a patrolman abandon his post, exposing many people to serious inconve- nience and the whole city to grave hazards, to pursue the dubious quest of catching a two-bit thief?

At the level of reason the patrolman himself might advance, the action merely follows the impulse to drop everything and catch a crook. And it seems perfectly reasonable that policemen should follow this impulse more readily than others, since they presumably are being paid for it. Thus considered, the action draws its justification from the public sentiment that a crime must not be allowed to pass without at least an attempt to oppose it and from the policeman's special obligation in this regard. This sentiment is certainly a very important aspect of the policeman's frame of mind; it directs his interests, estab- lishes priorities, furnishes justification for action, governs the expectations of reward and honor, and ultimately supplies the rhetoric with which his ready aggressiveness is explained.

But I have argued earlier that, the strength of this sentiment notwithstanding, criminal law enforcement could not possibly be the fulcrum on which the police mandate rests. How then do I explain the alacrity of the patrolman's response? Let me begin with an aside which is in its own way important but not central to the argument. For the patrolman, rushing to the scene of a crime is an opportunity to do something remarkable that will bring him to the attention of his superiors in a way that might advance his career. This aspect of his vocational interest is not rooted in the work he does but in the administrative setting within which it is done. Skolnick (1966, 231) has furnished extensive documentation for the importance of this factor in police work. Still, however important the explanation is, it fails in explaining police routines generally.

When I stated in the vignette that the patrolman will abandon his assignment to rush to the scene of a crime, I assumed without saying that the crime would be something like an act of vandalism, an assault, or a burglary. But if the crime that came to the attention of the officer had been something like a conspiracy by a board of directors of a commercial concern to issue stock with the intention of defrauding investors, or a landlord criminally extorting payments from a tenant, or a used-car dealer culpably turning back an odometer on an automobile he was preparing for sale, the patrolman would scarcely lift his gaze, let alone move into action. The real reason why the patrolman moved was not the fact that what was taking place was a crime in general terms, but because the particular crime was a member of a class of problems *the treatment of which will not abide.* In fact, the patrolman who unhesitatingly left his post to pursue an assailant would have left his post with just a little hesitation to pull a drowning person out of the water, to prevent someone from jumping off the roof of a building, to protect a severely disoriented person from harm, to save people in a burning structure, to disperse a crowd hampering the rescue mission of an ambulance, to take steps to prevent a possible disaster that might result from broken gas lines or water mains, and so on almost endlessly, and entirely without regard to the substantive nature of the problem, as long as it could be said that it involved *something-that-ought-not-to-be-happening-and-about-which-someone-had-better-do-something-now!* These extraordinary events, and the directly intuited needs for control that issue from them, are what the vocational interests of patrolmen are attuned to. And in the circumstances of such events citizens feel entitled and obliged to summon the help of the police. Naturally, in retrospect it is always possible to question whether this or that problem should or should not have become the target of police attention, but most people will agree that urban life is replete with situations in which the need for such service is not in doubt, and in which, accordingly, the service of the police is indispensable.

It is scarcely possible not to notice that the definition of the police mandate escaped Ockham's Rasor. It cannot be helped; I have seen policemen helping a tenant in arrears gain access to medication which a landlord held together with other possessions in apparently legal bailment, I have seen policemen settling disputes between parents as to whether an ill child should receive medical treatment, I have seen a patrolman adjudicating a quarrel between a priest and an organist concerning the latter's access to the church. All this suggests more than the obvious point that the duties of patrolmen are of a mind-boggling variety, it compels the stronger inference that no human problem exists, or is imaginable, about which it could be said with finality that this certainly could not become the proper business of the police.

It is fair to say that this is well known even though police work is not thought of in these terms. It must be assumed to be well known because in almost all instances the police service is a response to citizen demands, which must be taken as reflecting public knowledge of what is expected of the police. But evidently it is not thought of in these terms when it comes to writing books about the police, to making up budgets for the police, and to training policemen, administering departments, and rewarding performance. And even though the fact that policemen are "good" at helping people in trouble and dealing with troublesome people has received some measure of public recognition recently,[8] the plaudits are stated in ways reminiscent of "human interest stories" one finds in the back pages of the daily papers. More importantly, when it is asked on what terms this police service is made available in every conceivable kind of emergency, the usual answer is that it happens by default because policemen are the only functionaries, professionals, officials—call them what you will—who are available around the clock and who can be counted on to make house calls. Further, it is often said that it would be altogether better if policemen were not so often called upon to do chores lying within the spheres of vocational competence of physicians, nurses and social workers, and did not have to be all things to all men. I believe that these views are based on a profound misconception of what policemen do, and I propose to show that no matter how much police activity seems like what physicians and social workers might do, and even though what they actually have to do often could be done by physicians and social workers, the service they perform involves the exercise of a unique competence they do not share with anyone else in society. Even if physicans and social workers were to work around the clock and make house calls, the need for the police service in their areas would remain substantial, though it certainly would decline in volume. Though policemen often do what psychologists, physicians, or social workers might be expected to do, their involvement in cases is never that of surrogate psychologists, physicians, or social workers. They are in all these cases, from the beginning, throughout, and in the last analysis, policemen, and their interest and objectives are of a radically distinct nature. Hence, saying that policemen are "good at" dealing with people in trouble and troublesome people does not mean that they are good at playing the role of other specialists. Indeed, only by assuming a distinct kind of police competence can one understand why psychologists, physicians, and social workers run into problems in *their* work for which they seek police assistance. In other words, when a social worker "calls the cops" to help him with his work, he mobilizes the kind of intervention that is characteristic of police work even when it looks like social work.

To make clear what the special and unique competence of the police consists of I should like to characterize the events containing "something-that-ought-not-to-be-happening-and-about-which-somebody-had-better-do-something-now," and the ways police respond to them. A word of caution: I do not intend to imply that everything policemen attend to can be thus characterized. That is, the special and unique police competence comes into play about as often as practicing medicine, doing engineering, or teaching—in the narrow meanings of these terms—come into play in what physicians, engineers, and teachers do.

First, and foremost, *the need to do something* is assessed with regard for actually existing combinations of circumstances. Even though circumstances of need do become stereotyped, so that some problems appear to importune greater urgency than others, the rule *it depends* takes precedence over typification, and attention is directed to what is singular and particular to the here-and-now. Policemen often say that their work is almost entirely unpredictable; it might be more correct to say that anything unpredictable that cannot be dismissed or assimilated to the usual is pro tanto a proper target of police attention. That experience plays an important part in the decision making goes without saying, but it is not the kind of experience that lends itself easily to the systemization one associates with a body of technical knowledge. Most often the knowledge upon which patrolmen draw is the acquaintance with particular persons, places, and past events. Patrolmen appear to have amazingly prodigious memories and are able to specify names, addresses, and other factual details of past experiences with remarkable precision. Indeed, it is sometimes difficult to believe that all this information could be correct. However this may be, the fact that they report their activities in this manner, and that they appear to think in such terms, may be taken as indicative of the type of knowledge they depend on in their work. It could be said that while anything at all could become properly the business of the police, the patrolman can only decide whether anything in particular is properly his business after he "gets there" and examines it.

Second, the question whether some situational need justifiably requires police attention is very often answered by persons who solicit the service. Citizen demand is a factor of extraordinary importance for the distribution of police service, and the fact that someone did "call the cops" is, in and of itself, cause for concern. To be sure, there are some false alarms in almost every tour of duty, and one reason why police departments insist on employing seasoned policemen as dispatchers is because they presumably are skilled in detecting calls which lack merit. Generally, however, the determination that some development has reached a critical stage, ripe for police interest, is related to the attitudes of persons involved, and depends on common sense reasoning. For example, in a case involving a complaint about excessive noise, it is not the volume of the noise that creates hazards for life, limb, property, and the public order, but that the people involved say and otherwise show that the problem has reached a critical stage in which something-had-better-be-done-about-it. Closely connected with the feature of critical emergency is the expectation that policemen will handle the problem "then-and-there." Though it may seem obvious, it deserves stressing that police work involves no continuances and no appointments, but that its temporal structure is throughout of the "as soon as I can get to it" norm, and that its scheduling derives from the natural fall of events, and not from any externally imposed order, as is the case for almost all other kinds of occupations. Firemen too are permanently on call, but the things they are called upon to do are limited to a few technical services. A policeman is always poised to move on any contingency whatever, not knowing what it might be, but knowing that far more often than not he will be expected to *do something*. The expectation to do something is projected upon the scene, the patrolman's diagnostic instinct is heavily colored by it, and he literally sees things in the light of the expectation that he somehow *has* to handle the situation. The quick-witted and decisive activism of the police is connected with the fact that they are attuned to dealing with emergencies; and in many instances the response-readiness of the policeman rounds out the emergency character of the need to which the response was directed.

Third, though police departments are highly bureaucratized and patrolmen are enmeshed in a scheme of strict internal regulation, they are, paradoxically, quite alone and independent in their dealings with citizens. Accordingly, the obligation to do something when a patrolman confronts problems—that is, when he does police work—is something he does not share with anyone. He may call for help when there is a risk that he might be overwhelmed, and will receive it; short of such risks, however, he is on his own. He receives very little guidance and almost no supervision; he gets advice when he asks for it, but since policemen do not share information, asking for and giving advice is not built into their relations; his decisions are reviewed only when there are special reasons for review, and records are kept of what he does only when he makes arrests. Thus, in most cases, problems and needs are seen in relationship to the response capacity of an individual patrolman or teams of two patrolmen, and not of the police as an organized enterprise. Connected with the expectation that he will do what needs to be done by himself is the expectation that he will limit himself to imposing provisional solutions upon problems. Though they often express frustration at never solving anything—especially when they arrest persons and find them quickly back on the street—they do what they do with an abandon characteristic of all specialists who disregard the side effects of their activities. As they see it, it is none of their concern that many provisional solutions have lasting consequences. In fact, it would be quite well put to say that they are totally absorbed with making arrests, in the literal sense of the term. That is, they are always trying to snatch things from the brink of disaster, to nip untoward development in the bud, and generally to arrest whatever must not be permitted to continue; and to accomplish this they sometimes arrest persons, if circumstances appear to demand it.

Fourth and finally, like everybody else, patrolmen want to succeed in what they undertake. But unlike everybody else, they never retreat. Once a policeman has defined a situation as properly his business and undertakes to do something about it, he will not desist till he prevails. That policemen are uniquely empowered and required to carry out their decisions in the "then-and-there" of emergent problems is the structurally central feature of police work. There can be no doubt that the decisive and unremitting character of police intervention is uppermost in the minds of people who solicit it, and that persons against whom the police proceed are mindful of this feature and conduct themselves accordingly. The police duty not to retreat in the face of resistance is matched by the duty of citizens not to oppose them. While under common law citizens had the right to resist illegal police action, at least in principle, the recommendations contained in the Uniform Arrest Act, the adoption of which is either complete or pending before most state legislatures, provides that they must submit.

To be sure, the act pertains only to arrest powers, but it takes little imagination to see that this is sufficient to back up any coercive option a policeman might elect.[9]

The observation that policemen prevail in what they undertake must be understood as a *capacity* but not a necessarily invariant practice. When, for example, a citizen is ordered to move or to refrain from what he is doing, he may actually succeed in persuading the policeman to reverse himself. But contrary to judges, policemen are not required to entertain motions, nor are they required to stay their orders while the motion receives reasoned consideration. Indeed, *even* if the citizen's objection should receive favorable consideration in *subsequent* review, it would still be said that "under the circumstances" he should have obeyed. And even if it could be proved that the policeman's action was injudicious or in violation of civil liberties, he would be held to account only if it could also be proved that he acted with malice or with wanton frivolity.[10]

In sum, what policemen do appears to consist of rushing to the scene of any crisis whatever, judging its needs in accordance with canons of common sense reasoning, and imposing solutions upon it without regard to resistance or opposition. In all this they act largely as individual practitioners of a craft.

THE SPECIFIC NATURE OF POLICE COMPETENCE

The foregoing considerations suggest the conclusion that what the existence of the police makes available in society is a unique and powerful capacity to cope with all kinds of emergencies: unique, because they are far more than anyone else permanently poised to deal with matters brooking no delay; powerful, because their capacity for dealing with them appears to be wholly unimpeded. But the notion of emergency brings a certain circularity into the definition of the mandate. This is so because, as I have indicated, the discernment of the facts of emergency relies on common sense criteria of judgment, and this makes it altogether too easy to move from saying that the police deal with emergencies, to saying that anything the police deal with is, ipso facto, an emergency. And so, while invoking the notion of emergency was useful to bring up certain observations, it now can be dispensed with entirely.

Situations like those involving a criminal on the lam, a person trapped in a burning building, a child in desperate need of medical care, a broken gas line, and so on, made it convenient to show why policemen move decisively in imposing constraints upon them. Having exploited this approach as far as it can take us, I now wish to suggest that the specific competence of the police is wholly contained in their capacity for decisive action. More specifically, that the feature of decisiveness derives from the authority to overpower opposition in the "then-and-there" of the situation of action. *The policeman, and the policeman alone, is equipped, entitled, and required to deal with every exigency in which force may have to be used, to meet it.* Moreover, the authorization to use force is conferred upon the policeman with the mere proviso that force will be used in amounts measured not to exceed the necessary minimum, as determined by an intuitive grasp of the situation. And only the use of deadly force is regulated somewhat more stringently.[11]

Three points must be added in explanation of the foregoing. First, I am *not* saying the police work consists of using force to solve problems, but only that police work consists of coping with problems in which force *may have to be used.* This is a distinction of extraordinary importance. Second, it could not possibly be maintained that everything policemen are actually required to do reflects this feature. For a variety of reasons— especially because of the ways in which police departments are administered—officers are often ordered to do chores that have nothing to do with police work. Interestingly, however, the fact that a policeman is quite at the beck and call of his superior and can be called upon to do menial work does not attenuate his powers vis-à-vis citizens in the least. Third, the proposed definition of police competence *fully embraces* those forms of criminal law enforcement policemen engage in. I have mentioned earlier that the special role the police play in the administration of criminal justice has to do with the circumstance that "criminals"—as distinct from respectable and propertied persons who violate the provisions of penal codes in the course of doing business—can be counted on to try to evade or oppose arrest. Because this is so, and to enable the police to deal effectively with criminals, they are said to be empowered to use force. They also engage in criminal investigations whenever such investigations might be reasonably expected to be instrumental in making arrests. But the conception of the police role in all this is upside down. It is *not* that policemen are entitled to use force because they must deal with nasty criminals. Instead, the duty of handling nasty criminals devolves on them *because* they have the more general authority to use force *as needed* to bring about desired objectives. It is, after all, no more than a matter of simple expediency that it should be so; and that is is so becomes readily apparent upon consideration that policemen show little or no interest in all those kinds of offenders about whom it is not assumed that they need to be caught, and that force may have to be used to bring them to the bar of justice.

CONCLUSIONS

There is a threefold paradox in the awesome power of the policeman to make citizens obey his command, both legitimately and effectively. First, how come such a power exists at all? Second, why has the existence of this power not received the consideration it deserves? Third, why is the exercise of this power entrusted to persons recruited from a cohort from which all those with talent and ambitions must be assumed to have gone on to college and then to other occupations? I shall attempt to answer these questions in the stated order.

The hallmark of the period of history comprising the past century and a half is a succession of vast outbreaks of internal and international violence, *incongruously combined* with an unprecedently sustained aspiration to install peace as a stable condition of social life.[12] There can be no doubt that during this period the awareness of the moral and practical necessity of peace took hold of the minds of almost all the people of our world, and while the advocacy of warfare and of violent revolution has not disappeared, it has grown progressively less frank and arguments in their favor seem to be losing ground to arguments condemning violence. The sentiments in favor of peace draw in part on humane motives, but they derive more basically from a profound shift of values, away from virtues associated with masculine prowess and combativeness, and toward virtues asssociated with assiduous enterprise and material progress. There is still some glamor left in being an adventurer or warrior, but true success belongs to the businessman and to the professional.[13] Resorting to violence—outside of its restricted occasions, notably warfare and recreation—is seen as a sign of immaturity or lower-class culture (Miller, 1958, 5–19; Adorno et al. 1950). The banishment of violence from the domain of private life—as compared, for instance, with its deliberate cultivation in medieval chivalry—is the lesser part of the story. More important is the shift in the methods of government to an almost complete civil and pacific form of administration. Physical force has either vanished or is carefully concealed in the administration of criminal justice, and the use of armed retainers to collect taxes and to recruit into the military are forgotten. Paper, not the sword, is the instrument of coercion of our day. But no matter how faithfully and how methodically the dictates of this civil culture and of the rule of law are followed, and no matter how penetrating and far-reaching the system of peaceful control and regulation might be, there must remain some mechanism for dealing with problems on a catch-as-catch-can basis. In fact, it would seem that the only practical way for banishing the use of force from life generally is to assign its residual exercise—where according to circumstances it appears unavoidable—to a specially deputized corps of officials, that is, to the police as we know it. Very simply, as long as there will be fools who can insist that their comfort and pleasure take precedence over the needs of firemen for space in fighting a fire, and who will not move to make room, so long will there be a need for policemen.

I must leave out one possible explanation for the neglect of the capacity to use force as the basis of the police mandate; namely, that I am wrong in my assessment of its fundamental importance. I have no idea why the authors of many superb studies of various aspects of police work have not reached this conclusion. Perhaps they were either too close to, or too far from, what they were researching. But I believe I know why this feature of police work has escaped general notice. Until recently the people against whom the police had cause to proceed, especially to proceed forcefully, came almost exclusively from among the blacks, the poor, the young, the Spanish-speaking, and the rest of the urban proletariat, and they still come preponderantly from these segments of society. This is well known, much talked about, and I have nothing to add to what has already been said about expressions of class and race bias. Instead, I should like to draw attention to a peculiar consequence of this concentration. The lives of the people I mentioned are often considered the locus of problems in which force may have to be used. Not only do most of the criminals with whom the police deal hail from among them, but they, more often than other members of society, get into all sorts of troubles, and they are less resourceful in handling their problems. And so it could be said that the police merely follow troubles into trouble's native habitat and that no further inferences can be drawn from it, except, perhaps, that policemen are somewhat too quick in resorting to force and too often resort to it for what seem to be inadequate reasons, at least in retrospect. Of course, the rise of the counterculture, the penetration of drug use into the middle classes, the civil rights movements of the 1960s, and the student movement have proven that the police do not hesitate to act coercively against members of the rest of society. But that too has been mainly the target of critique, rather than efforts to interpret it. And the expressions of indignation we hear have approximately the effect "gesundheit" has on whatever causes a person to sneeze. The police are naturally baffled by the response; as far as they can see they did what they always did whenever they were called upon to intervene. In point of fact policemen did, mutatis mutandis, what physicians do under similar circumstances. Physicians are supposed to cure the sick through the practice of medicine, as everyone knows. But when they are consulted about some problem of an ambiguous nature, they define it as an illness and try to cure it. And teachers do not hesitate in treating everything as an educational problem. It is certainly possible to say that physicians and teachers are just as likely to go overboard as policemen. This does not mean, however, that one cannot find in these instances the true nature of their respective bags of tricks more clearly revealed than in the instances of more standard practice. In the case of the police, it merely obscures matters to say that they resort to force only against powerless people, either because it is more often necessary or because it is easier—even though these *are* important factors in determining frequency—for in fact, they define every summons to action as containing the possibility of the use of force.

The reasons why immense powers over the lives of citizens are assigned to men recruited with a view that they will be engaged in a low-grade occupation are extraordinarily complicated, and I can only touch on some of them briefly. Perhaps the most important factor is that the police were created as a mechanism for coping with the so-called dangerous classes (Silver 1967, 1–24). In the struggle to contain the internal enemy and in the efforts to control violence, depredation, and evil, police work took on some of the features of its targets and became a tainted occupation. Though it may seem perverse, it is not beyond comprehension that in a society which seeks to banish the use of force, those who take it upon themselves to exercise its remaining indispensable residue should be deprecated. Moreover, in the United States the police were used blatantly as an instrument of urban machine-politics, which magnified opportunities for corrupt practices enormously. Thus, the American urban policeman came to be generally perceived as the dumb, brutal, and crooked cop. This image was laced by occasional human interest stories in which effective and humane police work was portrayed as the exception to the rule. The efforts of some reformers to purge the police of brutality and corruption have inadvertently strengthened the view that police work consists of doing what one is told and keeping one's nose clean. To gain the upper hand over sloth, indolence, brutality, and corruption, officials like the late Chief William Parker of Los Angeles militarized the departments under their command. But the development of stringent internal regulation only obscured the true nature of police work. The new image of the policeman as a snappy, low-level, soldier-bureaucrat created no inducement for people who thought they could do better to elect police work as their vocation. Furthermore, the definition of police work remained associated with the least task that could be assigned to an officer. Finally, the most recent attempts to upgrade the selection of policemen have been resisted and produced disappointing results. The resistance is in large measure due to the employee interests of present personnel. It seems quite understandable that the chiefs, captains, and even veteran patrolmen would not be happy with the prospect of having to work with recruits who outrank them educationally. Furthermore, few people who have worked for college degrees would want to elect an occupation that calls only for a high school diploma. And those few will most likely be the least competent among the graduates, thereby showing that higher education is more likely to be harmful than helpful. And it is true, of course, that nothing one learns in college is particularly helpful for police work. In fact, because most college graduates come from middle-class backgrounds, while most of police work is directed toward members of the lower classes, there is a risk of a cultural gap between those who do the policing and the policed.

But if it is correct to say that the police are here to stay, at least for the foreseeable future, and that the mandate of policemen consists of dealing with all those problems in which force may have to be used, and if we further recognize that meeting this task in a sociallly useful way calls for the most consummate skill, then it would seem reasonable that only the most gifted, the most aspiring, and the most equipoised among us are eligible for it. It takes only three short steps to arrive at this realization. First, when policemen do those things only policemen can do, they invariably deal with matters of absolutely critical importance, at least to the people with whom they deal. True, these are generally not the people whose welfare is carefully considered. But even if democratic ideals cannot be trusted to ensure that they will be treated with the same consideration accorded to the powerful, practicality should advise that those who never had a voice in the past now have spoken and succeeded in being heard. In sum, police work, at its core, involves matters of extraordinary seriousness, importance, and necessity. Second, while lawyers, physicians, teachers, social workers, and clergymen also deal with critical problems, they have bodies of technical knowledge or elaborate schemes of norms to guide them in their respective tasks. But in police work there exists little more than an inchoate lore, and most of what a policeman needs to know to do his work he has to learn on his own. Thus, what ultimately gets done depends primarily on the individual officer's perspicacity, judiciousness, and initiative. Third, the mandate to deal with problems in which force may have to be used implies the special trust that force will be used only in extremis. The skill involved in police work, therefore, consists of retaining recourse to force while seeking to avoid its use, and using it only in minimal amounts.

It is almost unnecessary to mention that the three points are not realized in police work. Far too many policemen are contemptuous toward the people with whom they deal and oblivious to the seriousness of their tasks. Few policemen possess the perspicacity and judiciousness their work calls for. And force is not only used often where it need not be used, but gratuitous rudeness and bullying is a widely prevalent vice in policing. While all this is true, I did not arrive at those points by speculating about what police work could be. Instead I have heard about it from policemen, and I saw it in police work. I say this not to make the obvious point that there exist, in many departments, officers whose work already embodies the ideals I mentioned. More important is that there are officers who know what police work calls for far better than I can say, and from whom I have learned what I said. As far as I could see they are practical men who have learned to do police work because they had to. No doubt they were motivated by respect for human dignity, but their foremost concern was effectiveness and craftsmanship. Perhaps I can best describe them by saying that they have in their own practices placed police work on a fully reasoned basis, moving from case to case as individual practitioners of a highly complex vocation.

Though I cannot be sure of it, I believe I have written as a spokesman of these officers because I believe one must look to them to make police work what it should be. But the chances that they will prevail are not very good. The principal obstacle to their success is the presently existing organization of police departments. I cannot go into details to show how the way police work is administratively regulated constitues a positive impediment in the path of a responsible policeman, quite aside from the fact that most of his work is unrecognized and unrewarded.[14] But I would like to conclude by saying that, far from providing adequate disciplinary control over patent misconduct, the existing organizational structures encourage bad police work. Behind this is the ordinary dose of venality and vanity, and the inertia of the way things are. But the principal cause is an illusion. Believing that the real ground for his existence is the perennial pursuit of the likes of Willie Sutton—for which he lacks both opportunity and resources—the policeman feels compelled to minimize the significance of those instances of his performance in which he seems to follow the footsteps of Florence Nightingale. Fearing the role of the nurse or, worse yet, the role of the social worker, the policeman combines resentment against what he has to do day in, day out with the necessity of doing it. And in the course of it he misses his true vocation.

One more point remains to be touched upon. I began with a statement concerning the exercise of proscriptive control by government, commonly referred to as law enforcement. In all instances, except for the police, law enforcement is entrusted to special bureaucracies whose competence is limited by specific substantive authorization. There exists an understandable tendency to interpret the mandate of the police in accordance with this model. The search for a proper authorizing norm for the police led to the assumption that the criminal code provided it. I have argued that this was a mistake. Criminal law enforcement is merely an incidental and derivative part of police work. They do it simply because it falls within the scope of their larger duties—that is, it becomes part of police work exactly to the same extent as anything else in which force may have to be used, and only to that extent. Whether the police should still be considered a law enforcement agency is a purely taxonomic question of slight interest. All I intended to argue is that their mandate cannot be interpreted as resting on the substantive authorizations contained in the penal codes or any other codes. I realize that putting things this way must raise all sorts of questions in the minds of people beholden to the ideal of the Rule of Law. And I also realize that the rule of law has always drawn part of its strength from pretense; but I don't think pretense is entitled to immunity.

NOTES

This essay previously appeared in *The Potential for Reform of Criminal Justice*, vol. 3, ed. Herbert Jacob, Sage Criminal Justice System Annuals (Beverly Hills, Calif.: Sage Publications, 1974). A shorter version of this essay was delivered as the August Backus Memorial Address at the University of Wisconsin Law School in 1971. I am deeply indebted to Professor Herman Goldstein for his mentorship in all matters concerning the police. But he is, of course, in no way responsible for my errors.

Florence Nightingale is the heroic protagonist of modern nursing; Willie Sutton, for those who are too young to remember, was in his day a notorious thief.

1. Most textbooks on the police emphasize this point and enumerate the additional law enforcement obligations; see, for example, A. C. Gorman, F. D. Jay, and R. R. J. Gallati (1973); V. A. Leonard and H. W. More (1971).

2. Kansas City Police Department (1971). The survey contains information on 41 cities of 300,000 to 1,000,000 population. But the percentage cited in the text was computed only for Atlanta, Boston, Buffalo, Dallas, Denver, El Paso, Fort Worth, Honolulu, Kansas City, Memphis, Minneapolis, Oklahoma City, Pittsburgh, Portland, Ore., St. Paul, and San Antonio, because the data for the other cities were not detailed enough. The estimate that detectives make up 13.5 percent of line personnel comports with the estimate of O. W. Wilson (1963, 293), who stated that they make up approximately 10 percent of "sworn personnel."

3. Federal Bureau of Investigations, Uniform Crime Reports (1971). The data are for 57 cities of over 250,000 population, to make the figures correspond, at least roughly, to the data about manpower drawn from sources cited in n. 2, above. I might add that the average arrest rate in all the remaining cities is approximately of the same order as the figures I use in the argument. The so-called Index Crimes comprise homicide, forcible rape, robbery, aggravated assault, burglary, larceny, and auto theft. It should also be mentioned that arrests on Index Crime charges are not tantamount to conviction and

it is far from unusual for a person to be charged, e.g., with aggravated assault, to induce him to plead guilty to simple assault, quite aside from failure to prosecute, dismissal, or exculpation by trial.

4. I have accompanied patrolmen and detectives investigating burglaries in two cities and should like to add on the basis of my observation and on the basis of interviews with officers that, in almost all of these cases, there is virtually no promise of clearance, that in most of them the cost of even a routine follow-up investigation would exceed the loss many times over, and that, in any case, the detectives always have a backlog of reported burglaries for which the reporting victims expect prompt consideration. I might also add that it seemed to me that this largely fruitless busywork demoralizes detectives and causes them to do less work than I thought possible. See J. E. Conklin and E. Bittner (1973).

5. I have reference to the ramified information systems individual detectives cultivate, involving informants and informers, which they do not share with one another. I have touched on this topic in E. Bittner (1970).

6. The work that brought this observation into prominence is J. Goldstein (1960); a comprehensive review of the problem is contained in W. LaFave (1965).

7. J. Q. Wilson (1968, 31, chap. 2). The observation that policemen make misdemeanor arrests most often on practical rather than legal considerations has been reported by many authors; cf., for example J. D. Lohman and G. E. Misner (1966, 1968ff.). I have discussed this matter extensively in E. Bittner (1967a). Wistfully illuminating discussions of the topic are to be found, among others, in J. Hall (1953); J. V. Henry (1966); C. D. Robinson (1965).

8. The first expression of recognition is contained in E. Cumming, I. Cumming and L. Edell (1965); cf. also E. Bittner (1967b).

9. S. B. Warner (1942); Corpus Juris Secundum (vol. 6, 613ff.); M. Hochnagel and H. W. Stege (1966).

10. There exists legal doctrine supporting the contention that resisting or opposing the police in an emergency situation is unlawful, see H. Kelsen (1961, 278ff.), and H. L. A. Hart (1961, 20ff.). I cite these references to show that the police are legally authorized to do whatever is necessary, according to the nature of the circumstances.

11. "Several modern cases have imposed [a] standard of strict liability . . . upon the officer by conditioning justification of deadly force on the victim's actually having committed a felony, and a number of states have enacted statutes which appear to adopt this strict liability. However, many jurisdictions, such as California, have

homicide statutes which permit the police officer to use deadly force for the arrest of a person 'charged' with a felony. It has been suggested that this requirement only indicates the necessity for reasonable belief by the officer that the victim has committed a felony" (Note, *Stanford Law Review* [1961, 566–609]).

12. The aspiration has received a brilliant formulation in one of the most influential documents of modern political philosophy, Immanual Kant (1913); a review of the growth of the ideal of peace is contained in P. Reiwald (1944).

13. Literary glorification of violence has never disappeared entirely, as the works of authors like Nietzche and Sorel attest. In the most recent past, these views have again received eloquent expression in connection with revolutionary movements in Third World nations. The most remarkable statement along these lines is contained in the works of Franz Fanon.

14. But I have given this matter extensive consideration in E. Bittner (1970).

REFERENCES

Adorno, T. W., et al. *The Authoritarian Personality.* New York: Harper & Row, 1950.

Bacon, F. "An Advertizement Touching an Holy War." Vol. 7 of *Collected Works.* London: Spottiswood, 1859.

Bittner, E. "Police on Skid Row: A Study of Peacekeeping." *American Sociological Review* 32 (1967a): 600–715.

————. "Police Discretion in Emergency Apprehension of Mentally Ill Persons." *Social Problems* 14 (1967b): 278–92.

————. *The Functions of the Police in Modern Society.* Washington, D.C.: U.S. Government Printing Office, 1970.

Blackstone, W. *Commentaries on the Laws of England.* Vol. 4. Oxford, England: Clarendon, n.d.

Conklin, J. E. *Robbery and the Criminal Justice System.* Philadelphia: J. B. Lippincott, 1972.

————, and E. Bittner. "Burglary in a Suburb." *Criminology* 11 (1973): 206–32.

Corpus Juris Secundum. "Arrest." Vol. 6.

Cumming, E., I. Cumming, and L. Edell. "Policemen as Philosopher, Guide and Friend." *Social Problems* 12 (1965): 276–86.

Davis, K. C. *Discretionary Justice: A Preliminary Inquiry.* Urbana, Ill.: University of Illinois Press, 1971.

Federal Bureau of Investigations. *Uniform Crime Reports.* Washington, D.C.: U.S. Government Printing Office, 1971.

Garfinkel, H., and E. Bittner. "Good Organizational Reasons for 'Bad' Clinic Records." In H. Garfinkel, *Studies in Ethnomethodology*, 186–207. Englewood Cliffs, N.J.: Prentice-Hall, 1967.

Goldstein, J. "Police Discretion Not to Invoke the Criminal Process." *Yale Law Journal* 69 (1960): 543–94.

Gorman, A. C., F. D. Jay, and R. R. J. Gallati. *Introduction to Law Enforcement and Criminal Justice.* Rev. ed. Springfield, Ill.: C. C. Thomas, 1973.

Hall, J. "Police and the Law in a Democratic Society." *Indiana Law Journal* 23: 133–77, 1953.

Hamilton, W. H., and C. C. Rodee. "Police Power," in *Encyclopedia of the Social Sciences.* Vol. 12. New York: Macmillan Co., 1937.

Hart, H. L. A. *The Concept of Law.* Oxford, England: Clarendon Press, 1961.

Henry, J. V. "Breach of Peace and Disorderly Conduct Laws: Void for Vagueness?" *Howard Law Journal* 12 (1966): 318–31.

Hochnagel, M., and H. W. Stege "The Right to Resist Unlawful Arrest: An Outdated Concept?" *Tulsa Law Journal* 3 (1966): 40–46.

Institute for Defense Analysis. President's Commission on Law Enforcement and Administration of Justice. *Task Force Report: Science and Technology.* Washington, D.C.: U.S. Government Printing Office, 1967.

Kansas City Police Department. *Survey of Municipal Police Departments.* Kansas City, Mo., 1971.

Kant, I. [1795]. "Zum Ewigen Frieden: Ein Philosophischer Entwurf." In *Kleinere Schriften zur Geschichtsphilosophie, Ethik und Politik.* Leipzig: Felix Meiner, 1913.

Kelsen, H. *General Theory of Law and State.* New York: Russel & Russel, 1961.

LaFave, W. *Arrest: The Decision to Take a Suspect into Custody.* Boston: Little, Brown & Co., 1965.

Leonard, V. A., and H. W. More. *Police Organization and Management.* 3d ed. Mineola, N. Y.: Foundation Press, 1971.

Lohman, J. D., and G. E. Misner. *The Police and the Community.* Report prepared for the President's Commission on Law Enforcement and Administration of Justice. Vol. 2. Washington, D.C.: U.S. Government Printing Office, 1967.

Miller, W. B. "Lower-class Culture as a Generating Milieu of Gang Delinquency." *Journal of Social Issues* 14 (1958): 5–19.

National Commission on Productivity. "Report of the Task Force to Study Police Productivity." Mimeo. Draft. 1973.

Niederhoffer, A. *Behind the Shield: The Police in Urban Society.* Garden City, N.Y.: Anchor Books, 1969.

Note. "Justification for the Use of Force in Criminal Law." *Stanford Law Review* 13 (1961): 566–609.

Reiss, A. J., Jr. *The Police and the Public.* New Haven: Yale University Press, 1971.

Reiwald, P. *Eroberung des Friedens.* Zurich: Europa Verlag, 1944.

Robinson, C. D. "Alternatives to Arrest of Lesser Offenders." *Crime and Delinquency* 11 (1965) 8–21.

Silver, A. "The Demand for Order in Civil Society: A Review of Some Themes in the History of Urban Crime, Police, and Riot." In *The Police: Six Sociological Essays,* ed. D. J. Bordua, 1–24. New York: John Wiley & Sons, 1967.

Skolnick, J. H. *Justice without Trial: Law Enforcement in a Democratic Society.* New York: John Wiley & Sons, 1966.

Stephen, J. F. *A History of Criminal Law in England.* Vol. 3. London: Macmillan & Co., 1883.

Warner, S. B. "Uniform Arrest Act." *Vanderbilt Law Review* 28 (1942): 315–47.

Weber, M. *The Theory of Social and Economic Organization.* Translation edited by T. Parsons. Glencoe, Ill.: Free Press, 1947.

Wilson, J. Q. *Varieties of Police Behavior: The Management of Law and Order in Eight Communities.* Cambridge, Mass.: Harvard University Press, 1968.

Wilson, O. W. *Police Administration.* 2d ed. New York: McGraw-Hill, 1963.

6 | *Emerging Police Issues*

IN THE PAST fifteen years police departments in the United States have undergone a remarkable transformation. While the past has been a period of abundant resources and optimism, the present and probably the immediate future will be marked by a more conservative mood. Thus, it is likely that police departments will have less freewheeling experimentation, less exploration in new areas of activity, and probably a great deal less freedom in the use of resources. In some ways the change of mood constitutes a setback; a cutback atmosphere seldom is a reform atmosphere. On the other hand, the new situation offers an opportunity for taking stock. Those who have been active in the police field over the decade of the seventies can now catch up with one another; the value of their endeavors can be assessed; and programs can be put into some sort of order. This means that now is the time for synthesis; it is necessary to explore what the whole complex of policing, the old and the new parts of it, adds up to.

In the past, the nature and necessity of policing were implicitly understood. In the 1960s these implicit understandings came under severe attack. But even the demolition of old myths has not led to a notable clarification of the police mandate. Instead, the changes that have taken place usually have been responses to situational demands of all sorts. It may have been fortunate that the recent past has seen numerous poorly coordinated and inadequately justified projects. We learned more from this, and probably accomplished more, than we would have by implementing a rigorously formulated plan of action that left no room for mistakes or waste. But while expansion and growth benefit when enterprising innovators are given a free hand, consolidation is possible only when basic principles are understood. To make something lean and strong it is necessary to know what is fat and what is muscle. In the absence of a clear definition of the basic purpose of the police, the activities of police departments will be determined solely by political expediency. Determinations whether to cut back a given program will follow the sentiments of the moment. Alliances with citizens' groups, with various institutions, and with other units of government will be formed, cultivated, or neglected depending on what seem to be the balances of momentary advantage and disadvantage. And in all this the gains of the past decade and a half are sure to be lost.[1]

The formulation of the terms in which all parts of the vast complex we call policing could be assessed for their value and necessity is an essentially theoretical task. Not surprisingly, practitioners are rarely thrilled by theoretical analyses. They may allow that such efforts bring some spiritual comfort, but they do not find them immediately helpful in dealing with day-to-day problems. Police officers are not alone in this attitude. Practitioners of all vocations prefer dealing with questions that arise spontaneously and that must be answered without delay. In well-established professions such as teaching, the ministry, or medicine such neglect is relatively harmless. In a profession like policing, which has just passed through a period of beneficial but uncoordinated growth and is facing either a rational consolidation or a disorganized retreat, such neglect is very harmful indeed.

Some people think that it is quite enough that no one believes any longer that policing is a rather unsophisticated game of cops and robbers. These people need to be reminded that such revised beliefs will not be given full credit until the statement of what policing *is not* is accompanied by a strong and clear statement of what it *is*. None of the major questions about the conduct of policing in the years to come can be answered rationally without such definitional clarity. One cannot expect urban governments to underwrite programs for which only inchoate and *ad hoc* justifications are available. Nor will city hall accept empirical data of success, knowing how rarely such success is repeated. And while city hall will refuse to give in to demands, it will be in a good position to make demands of its own. After all, police departments traditionally have been available for assignments for which no other resources seem to exist.

The lack of clarity about the definition of its mandate not only hampers the police department in its dealing with urban government but also prevents the formation of any long-range cooperative understandings between police departments and citizens. The vagueness with which citizens perceive what they may expect of the police and the uncertainty with which the police respond to such expectations have created a situation in which even the best-organized efforts at cooperation disintegrate after the emergency that has led to their formation has passed. It must not be assumed that knowing exactly what the police provide to a community can solve all police–community relations problems. How can there be trust and reliance when the police convey to the people, directly or by implication, that they themselves are not entirely certain what can be expected of them?

Although uncertainties about the nature of the mandate clearly affect the external relations of the police, their effects are even more devastating internally. The following three illustrations of this impact all involve matters about which some decisions will have to be made in the near future.

First, as long as it can be maintained more or less legitimately that policing is done in an inchoate way and that it defies all efforts at conceptual formulation, the vocation of policing will be perceived as a low-grade occupation. It does not matter that policing properly done is most demanding, and it does not matter that a surprisingly large number of officers do a good job of it. The assumption that police officers do not need a firm intellectual grasp of their vocation leads to a staffing pattern in which bright and prudent officers may have only marginally competent co-workers.

Second, with no good way of specifying basic work responsibilities, there can be no justifiable way of discriminating between good and bad performance. In the absence of clear standards of workmanship, rewards must go either to those who follow orders and stay out of trouble or to those whose activities are highly visible. In either case, there are few incentives for resolute and skilled work.

Third, when officers are unsure which parts of policing are necessary and must assume that this is decided by rule of thumb, then job assignments, especially changes in job assignments, tend to be perceived as arbitrary. It is quite possible, therefore, that the notorious resistance of police officers to change results from the perception that so-called reforms are based primarily on managerial expediency.

One could easily extend this litany, but these examples should suffice to make the point that none of the problems facing policing today can be addressed properly, let alone dealt with effectively, without settling the question of what sort of activity policing essentially is. Instead, solutions to problems will have to be merely *ad hoc,* and police departments will continue to be buffeted by the tides of urban politics.

This chapter presents a definition of the mandate of the police, not in the abstract but in terms of concrete objectives, responsibilities, procedures, and capacities. The formulation is descriptive rather than prescriptive. It is based on observation of all kinds of police work, observation focused on discovering what police officers themselves consider to be serious and important police work well done. Thus the proposed formulation is no more than a way of offering suggestions about the possible definition of the police mandate and about approaches to investigating these matters further. In any case, the definition of the function of the police will have to come from within the institution, in dialogue with society. Everything else is preparatory.

Because the explicit formulation of the police mandate is practical—even though the task itself is theoretical—it will be allowed to emerge in the discussion of four prominent problems that face police institutions today in the United States. None of these problems is of recent origin. All of them have become critical because the current shift from expansive growth to consolidation will force some decisions about the direction of future development. The four problems are (1) the specific significance of criminal law enforcement in the total universe of police activity; (2) the determination of the outer boundaries of police responsibility; (3) relations between the police and members of disadvantaged segments of society; and (4) the nature of police work viewed as a vocation with special regard for educational and training expectations, the internal organization of police departments, and unionization. These matters are in various ways related and deserve a unified approach in preference to the kinds of tinkering adjustments they ordinarily receive.

THE POLICE AND CRIMINAL
LAW ENFORCEMENT

The question of what the police do—both what they *actually do* and what they are *supposed to do*—is often answered by giving lists of their activities. For example, in an excellent review of police functions in western Europe and North America, one author identifies no less than twenty fields of activity, each comprising its own complexities.[2] With one or two possible exceptions, all these activities are encountered in most police departments in the United States. Such lists are practically endless, and their content and priorities would vary with departments and with particular ideological positions. In all such lists, however, criminal law enforcement would appear either as the highest or as a very high priority.

Conditional versus Unconditional Responsibilities

While there may be some police officials who consider the settling of domestic disputes to be as important as catching criminals, it is unlikely that any of them would regard it as more important. Moreover, it is certain that police officials consider the obligations arising out of the provisions of the criminal law as unconditional and would quote the penal codes to support this belief. But duties connected with such problems as domestic disputes tend to be viewed as conditional, though it is not quite clear what is meant by the term. If one asks whether an officer has a duty to intervene in a domestic dispute, the answer is likely to start with some form of "it depends." But if one asks whether an officer has a duty to arrest an offender, the answer is affirmative without qualification, even though in practice various unstated considerations are known to play a part in the decision to make an arrest, even in cases where probable cause evidently exists.[3]

Saying that police officers might properly become involved in domestic disputes under certain conditions draws attention to some contingent features; if such features are present, the duty to intervene is unconditional. That is, obligations not connected with criminal law enforcement can be regarded as conditional only because the relevant situations are not sufficiently specified. For example, the mere fact that two or more family members are quarreling is not, in and of itself, a sufficient reason for police intervention; but if the dispute implies a threat of serious harm, injury, or loss, then it must be stopped. The perception of this threat involves the exercise of informed judgment and is therefore complicated.

Discretion in Law Enforcement

It is well known that police officers do not invoke the law mechanically. This is so in part because they must assess the value of their information relative to certain standards of proof. Accordingly, an officer cannot act on an inner sense of certainty if this certainty cannot be converted into admissible evidence. In addition, officers are expected to consider some general policy interests in deciding whether or not to invoke the law. For example, it is commonly understood that the law is not to be invoked against citizens with unblemished records who are suspected of technical and relatively trivial breaches of the law. The extent to which discretionary latitude exists and is regarded as legitimate and desirable varies considerably with the type of crime and the type of suspect. Almost certainly any police officer would arrest a homicide suspect regardless of circumstances or the identity of the suspect. It is equally certain that four elderly women caught playing penny-ante poker in the church basement will not be arrested and charged with violating the state's gambling laws.

Ever since this fact became openly acknowledged, people have worried about the extent of discretion and urged that it be restricted by additional rules of procedure.[4] But this is easier said than done. If, for example, it were determined that arrests must be made in all felony cases, but judgment could be exercised for misdemeanors, then judgment could merely be exercised in a different way—it is not difficult to justify referring to the same set of facts as either felonious auto theft or misdemeanor joyriding. By defining the case as one or the other, the officer complies with the rule that was supposed to reduce the scope of discretionary freedom without actually losing any of it. Thus, criminal law enforcement is in practice conditional, even though it is commonly regarded as unconditional.

Common versus White-Collar Crimes

Police duties relative to crime are also conditional in another way that is neglected in the literature, even though the facts are well known. Police officers are expected and expect to be involved in the control of certain crimes, especially common crimes (burglary, robbery, assault, and prostitution, for example), but they usually do not feel called upon to be involved in other crimes, especially white-collar crimes. The decision whether or not to invoke the law in cases involving common crimes is made by the individual officer or sometimes by departmental policy. But questions of whether or not to intervene in cases from the large complex of white-collar crime ordinarily do not even come up in police work. This fact raises additional questions about police discretion and about class bias in enforcement.

The designations *common crime* and *white-collar crime* are imprecise, and it is hard to separate the two. Embezzlement is a good example of this difficulty, for it seems to be both a common and a white-collar crime. Still, at the extremes the distinction is fairly clear. That is, there is general agreement that a police officer has a duty to move against a suspected mugger, assuming that conditions of probable cause are met. But a police officer is not expected to act in a case involving a state banking statute violation that is punishable by fine and/or imprisonment, regardless of the strength of probable cause. Police noninvolvement in most crimes committed in connection with the conduct of business, in the practice of a profession, or in politics seems to be based on a policy choice that, even though not always clearly articulated, is commonly understood among police agencies. According to this understanding, the police have refrained from developing enforcement capacities in these areas of criminal conduct because special enforcement agencies were created when the various crimes were defined in legislation.

Not surprisingly, there is ambiguity and overlap here, but it would be extraordinary indeed if a patrol officer initiated the prosecution of a group of steel manufacturing companies on charges involving price-fixing; it is not certain whether the officer would arrest a physician suspected of performing an illegal abortion; but it is virtually assured that he or she would nab the assistant manager of a supermarket loading pilfered merchandise into a car after closing hours, even though that too might be regarded as a white-collar crime. The fact that price-fixing may involve a federal crime does not seem to be decisive, because the same officer would surely move against a person hijacking a U.S. Postal Service truck, even though this too is a federal crime. Nor can it be argued that the police have responsibilities only if the acts in question have been regarded as criminal from time immemorial. So-called victimless crimes are virtually all of recent origin, while the crime of bribery is of great antiquity. The former are a routine target of police interest; the latter rarely is.

The Possible Need for Force

In addition to explicit or implicit conventions in the way the criminal law enforcement pie is divided, another principle also appears to explain who does what and why. In general, the people who commit common crimes are likely to try to evade arrest and may have to be caught and brought to face justice forcibly, while people who commit white-collar crimes are likely to appear in court in response to a written court order. This is so, common sense suggests, because the former have nothing to lose in trying to evade prosecution illegally, while the latter might thereby risk a business, a profession, or a career. By and large it is assumed that burglars, rapists, robbers, and prostitutes, for example, act as if their cases are won or lost in a contest of wits, strength, or speed between themselves and the police officers who are trying to nab them. But congressmen charged with accepting bribes, brokers suspected of investment fraud or lawyers accused of misapplying entrusted funds win or lose their cases only when the last judicial appeals are exhausted. On the other hand, of course, not all persons accused of common crimes actually try to flee even if they can; and some South American countries are said to be havens for fugitive white-collar offenders.

The police maintain a special readiness and capacity to act in cases where by common assumption force may have to be used, and in maintaining this readiness and capacity they reduce the likelihood of opposition and of the need for the actual use of force. Naturally, readiness is not limited to giving chase and subduing suspects. Readiness also involves the use of investigative techniques appropriate to the crime in question, although the kind of detective work romanticized in the figure of Sherlock Holmes is the exception rather than the rule.[5]

Thus, the responsibilities of the police in criminal law enforcement also are conditional. Officers are not expected to act wherever and whenever any kind of crime has taken place. Instead, the mandate restricts them to dealing with those crimes whose clearance *may* require force. When this is the case, then the duty becomes unconditional. This is not to say that officers always or even often have to use force in clearing crimes. Yet there is a sphere of criminal conduct, a group of crimes, in which it is commonly assumed that force may have to be used. The absence of the assumption about the possible need for force identifies the alternative sphere of criminality, with which the police have no business to be involved.

The boundaries of the sphere of common crimes cannot be drawn sharply, but the area is very large and most of it is quite clear. Moreover, it becomes even clearer when one considers the types of criminality that are excluded. The decisive characteristic of the excluded kind of criminal conduct—that is, white-collar crime—is that it can be committed only by taking advantage of one's position in business, in the professions, or in public life. Ordinarily such positions rank high on scales of wealth, power, and prestige, and the people occupying them are quite resourceful. Without access to such positions one cannot commit white-collar crimes. Common crimes, on the other hand, are equally accessible to all kinds of people, without regard to wealth, power, or prestige. But it is common knowledge that the vast majority of common crimes are committed by people on the bottom of the social heap. As far as the police are concerned, it makes not a whit of difference whether a mugger is a prominent person or a ne'er-do-well. That is, we do not have two police forces, one for the poor and one for the well off. We only have a police force that addresses its concerns to those crimes in which poor people happen to specialize and that leaves other crimes to the care of other law enforcement agencies. If the urban police are portrayed as society's strike force against crime generally, however, it becomes difficult to avoid the impression that this struggle is permeated by a strong class bias.

THE OUTER BOUNDARIES OF POLICE RESPONSIBILITY

Thus far it has been argued that criminal law enforcement by the police is limited to types of crime in which it is safe, or at least safest, to assume that the alleged culprit will not submit voluntarily to arrest. The tools of the police officer's trade—handcuffs, nightsticks, guns, high-speed vehicles—all imply the threat of force. Criminal law enforcement is assumed to deal with crimes against persons and property such as homicide, assault, armed robbery, and burglary. Through long experience, the police have developed procedures, skills, and resources to deal with such actions against individuals and society. In dealing with such crimes, police officers are empowered and required to use force, if necessary, to resolve the situation. This police power, especially the use of force, extends to other kinds of problems that are unrelated to criminal law enforcement.

Peacekeeping Functions

It is well known that the majority of police actions are unrelated to criminal law enforcement.[6] At times these actions are referred to as peacekeeping, order maintenance, or simply service. But none of these designations helps identify the domain of a police officer's proper business. Some informed observers believe the domain outside of criminal law enforcement is beyond the ken of police officers and that, indeed, the demands that seemingly could be made of a police officer exceed ordinary human capacities. Many police officials are especially alarmed about the possibility that police work may become swamped with demands for services that are ordinarily provided by social workers.

These apprehensions, however realistic they may seem at first glance, are based on conceptual confusion. Police activities involving peacekeeping, order maintenance, or service are not a recent development at all. They did not begin as a result of recommendations of commissions or academic researchers. Policing always has included a great number of activities through which people in trouble have been helped, troublesome people have been controlled, critical situations have been handled, and conflicts have been resolved. All of this has been done informally, without any records being kept and, in fact, without anyone's taking notice. That is, to put it colloquially, people have always called the cops, and the cops have come and taken care of whatever needed to be taken care of and left without taking any "official action." Thus, it is simply not the case that the police were suddenly burdened in the 1960s by a vast increase in duties of a social service nature. What did happen was that all these activites began receiving the attention, within and outside police departments, that was denied them in the past.[7]

As it became known—more precisely, as it became acknowledged—that police officers maintained a form of unofficial control of unruly youth, extended protection to disoriented and incompetent persons, attempted to prevent suicide, and otherwise dealt with crises, emergencies, disasters, dangers, accidents, and other unusual situations, certain of the therapeutic professions felt called upon to come to the rescue of the police. They did this partly on their own initiative and partly in response to invitation from the police establishment. Perhaps it was the invasion of professional advice and instruction from psychiatrists, psychologists, social workers, sociologists, and so on that created the impression in the minds of some police officials that police work was on the verge of turning into social work. This was a misperception, however, due no doubt to the fact that there was no conceptual clarity about the inherent purposes of police work. As there was nothing to which to relate these professional teachings, they had to be perceived either as irrelevant to police work or as subverting it. Of course, the instructors too were confused and often seemed to think that they were training police officers to be family counselors. In fact, however, police officers needed instruction in clinical psychology not to be practicing clinical psychologists but to do better police work.

An example will help clarify the point. Assume that it is in the public interest to prevent suicides. Two approaches are possible. The first calls for eliminating causes leading to suicide, a task associated with the practice of clinical psychology or psychiatry. The second calls for stopping all incipient suicides. The latter task is police work. It would seem reasonable that a police officer who has the duty of preventing suicide would benefit from knowing something about its psychodynamics and about therapeutic techniques applicable to it. Still, the officer's duty would be confined to taking potential victims off roofs, disarming them, getting them to the hospital to have their stomachs pumped, and so on, all of which are provisional solutions to long-range problems.

What the officer learned of the psychodynamics of suicide had to be useful in doing this part of police work; otherwise it was irrelevant. Psychiatric instructors, however, may neglect the officer's special task—to prevent the suicide from taking place—and emphasize psychiatric concerns, thus preventing the needed adaptation of psychodynamic knowledge to police work. Therapists tend to convey their belief that preventing suicides without getting at the causes of suicide attempts is of little use. In fact, of course, preventing suicides is a serious, important, and complex task, even if it does not get at the root causes. Officers who may have to do it need to be prepared for it. The only way they can be prepared is to adapt what is known about suicide to their own concerns with it. Anyone who thinks that social work principles are taught to police officers in order to have them do social work simply misunderstands the purpose of the instruction. The purpose is to make available to the police the knowledge and skill that will be useful in police work.

The Specific Police Mandate

Suicides are a good example because intervention is likely to be resisted, even when the victim hopes to be saved. It illustrates that what the police officer has to do may involve opposition, and here the obligation of the officer differs from that of other professionals concerned with suicide. The officer, and the officer alone, is empowered and required not to retreat in the face of opposition but to overcome it, with force if necessary. It is the thesis of this section that *all such situations, where something has to be done immediately, possibly against opposition, are the specific targets of police intervention.* The situation may involve catching a mugger who resists or tries to elude arrest, making peace between two fighting neighbors who are about to harm each other, forcing a landlord to let an emergency crew work on his property to stave off imminent tragedy, taking a mentally ill person to a hospital, or dealing with any other of an endless variety of unforeseeable problems that must be handled without delay.

In all such cases the police officer is empowered and required to use force if force is required to prevent a feared outcome or to cause the necessary to happen. The principle that gives specificity to police competence in the area of peacekeeping, order maintenance, and service is exactly the same one that identifies the specific role of the police in criminal law enforcement. Police officers are expected to deal with all problems in which force may have to be used to arrive at a provisional solution, in the expectation that others will deal with the underlying causes. As the next section will show, provisional solutions often have lasting consequences—a most troublesome matter that poses serious problems and should not be neglected.

It has been proposed here that the mandate of the police is to deal with all problems in which force may have to be used, regardless of whether the problems arise out of the criminal law or some other context. It does *not* follow that police work consists of using force to obtain certain desired results. Most skills and resources that are used in police work must be devoted to succeeding without recourse to force, but officers also must have skills and resources to use force as a last resort. This might be called the lean definition of the police mandate. No one can expect police work to be limited to matters that could be subsumed under the proposed definition. Teachers, clergymen, and nurses do many things that have nothing to do with education, the ministry, or nursing, respectively. And it seems only reasonable to expect that police officers will do many things that are not policing in its narrow sense.

Two other important reasons why police work should not be defined narrowly involve the *essential* nature of police work. First, police officers must be available when and where their specific skills are needed. This includes not only those critical situations where force may be required but also many police calls that turn out to be trivial. Second, police officers are the only helping hand available twenty-four hours a day, seven days a week, fifty-two weeks a year. One needs no appointment to see them and they make house calls in every part of the city. But it is not merely the fact that they are there that counts; it is also that they are viewed by most people as a trusted source of help.

It is essential that the specific police mandate be the governing criterion for judging the appropriateness of all police activities. Moreover, while there is nothing intrinsically wrong in having a police officer ease the movement of traffic at the county fair, it is crucial that police work not be understood to be this kind of job. By the same token, a person who might be regarded as capable of living up to the demands of this kind of job must not be judged capable of living up to all the other occupational demands of police work. The mandate must be clearly and explicitly defined not in terms of things police officers might do, often or rarely, because they happen to be available, but in terms of those activities in which they alone are competent and those that make the greatest demands on their skill and judgment.

THE POLICE AND THE URBAN POOR

The duty to intervene—with force if need be—is connected with signs of impending disaster. At times these signs are clear enough. More often, however, the interpretation of signs is a difficult and elusive art. How do officers know whether a particular gathering is dangerous and should be dispersed? How do they know whether a party is disturbingly noisy and should be quieted? How do they know whether a quarrel between two persons has reached the point where one must be ordered to leave? Moreover, how do they know when the time has come to use force to take care of a problem?

Intervention among the Poor

In present-day police work in U.S. cities, the answers to the questions of whether to intervene and whether or not the time has come to resort to force exhibit a certain pattern. Specifically, observations of police practice suggest that officers find occasion to intervene much more readily in the lives of poor people than in the lives of other members of society and that they resort to force in these encounters more readily than in other encounters. Just as criminal law enforcement by the police focuses on those crimes in which the poor specialize, so do the other activities of the police focus on poor people. Although it may appear otherwise, there is a certain peculiar impartiality in this.[8] The police direct their attention to risk, danger, violence, impending chaos, tension, uncertainty, despair; and the lives of the poor happen to be far more densely textured with these than are other lives. As a result, one is less likely to notice these problems in parts of the city inhabited by the well-to-do. This perception is justified by the knowledge that the rich, the powerful, and the prestigious have an abundance of remedial help and social strength to maintain order spontaneously. But among the poor one is inclined to expect the worst. Experience indicates that even a trivial provocation can trigger a major disaster in the blighted section of a city. Further, since violence is more prevalent among the poor it seems natural to fall back on violence early. Police officers feel that they must gain an initial advantage; they do this by acting forcefully, from which it is only a short step to acting forcibly. Finally, the lives of the poor, although rich in their own self-help mechanisms, are virtually devoid of such formal remedial resources as lawyers, psychiatrists, and marriage counselors, many of whom serve only those who can afford their services. Thus, there are objective reasons for the frequency of police interventions in the lives of the poor, and the perceptual distortion that causes greater readiness to keep the lid on does not seem unreasonable for officers acting under conditions of uncertainty, ambiguity, and possible danger.

Still, an apparent bias emerges. An officer will readily disperse a group of youths congregating noisily in front of a business and interfering with its operation, but he will do nothing when business activity inconveniences, annoys, or otherwise disrupts the lives of the poor. In fact, it seems unfair to bring up this kind of comparison. Given society's structure and values, the police officer has a duty to do the former, while the latter is within the jurisdiction of a zoning board or some other regulatory agency. But this is precisely the point, and officers who are unwilling or unable to confront these realities from the perspective of those who are oppressed by them are not really conscious of the complexity of their jobs.

Racial Prejudice

One might infer from all this that urban police forces are in some simple sense an instrument of the ruling elites to keep the proletariat down, much like the English police in the nineteenth century.[9] But as Bruce Johnson has demonstrated,

American police forces have not played this role, at least not in this century.[10] In fact, American police of the last several generations have been conscious of their origin in, and social ties to, the working class of white ethnic groups.

Unfortunately, those same ethnic groups have been and remain a source of racial prejudice, directed primarily toward blacks and Spanish-speaking people. Police practices reflect these attitudes to an extent that is a constant source of provocation to minority groups. The racist officer may feel empowered to express contempt and often to act brutally. Even in departments in which such conduct is not condoned, there is little control over it. Since such misconduct is often addressed to troublesome individuals, it is justified as aggressive police work. Of course, it is also often directed to persons who deserve courtesy and consideration. Officers often explain that in policing dangerous districts it is not always possible to act with kid gloves on. Moreover, it is argued, because police work is inherently provisional in nature, there is no permanent harm in (for example) a mistaken arrest. Unfortunately, provisional action does have lasting effects. An arrest record, even one entirely without convictions, does not open doors. But the most devastating effect of casual mistreatment of poor minority group members is their lasting hostility toward the police. Thus, while it is wrong to attribute the heavy presence of the police in the ghettos to their racism (they were sent there by all of us), the problem that cries for recognition is that even a little racism in police work does more harm than a great deal of responsible policing can repair.

All this leads to the following conclusion. Urban policing in the United States is set up to control forms of conduct that are considerably more prevalent among the poor than among other members of society. Some hold that this involves an unwarranted imposition of middle-class standards on people whose culture dictates a different kind of morality and that the burden of police control ought to be lifted entirely. Though this view is based on a desire to avoid casting aspersion on the poor and on minorities, it is biased in its own way. It is not fair to forgive a black mugger who has robbed another person of a welfare check, regardless of whether the victim was white or black. It is one thing to understand why so many minority youths become muggers; it is quite another to let it go at that.[11] Tolerance and prejudice walk hand in hand. Mugging is inexcusable, and it deserves unqualified and forceful condemnation. But the officer who thinks that mugging and other common crimes are the only evil in society, and who thinks it either is not true or does not matter that common criminals are themselves often victims of criminal exploitation, is just too simple-minded for the complicated job of policing.

There is a great risk in the police mandate. Because the mandate concentrates police activity on the poor, and because the majority of minority group members live in poverty, policing provides the racist with virtually unchecked opportunities to express racism in word and action. It is by no means necessary to assume that all, or even many, police officers are prejudiced to explain the notorious tension, anger, and distrust known to exist between the police and minority communities; it is quite sufficient that some such officers exist. It is illegal for public servants, including police officers, to be prejudicial or discriminatory in their actions. But in police work racist attitudes do more than violate the law and ideals of justice; they run counter to considerations of common sense and expediency. Considering what the police must try to accomplish, sending a racist out on the beat is not unlike letting a disease carrier do public health work.

The elimination of every vestige of racism and other forms of bigotry is only the first step in putting the relations between the police and the urban poor in good order. Beyond that must come the realization that the poor need competent police services to a far greater extent than people in the rest of society. People living in poverty are vastly more likely to be victims of common crime than are others, and they are considerably more likely to need help. The police mandate must be viewed in light of these considerations. It is, indeed, capable of being a provisional solution to some of the consequences of injustice and inequality in society.

POLICE WORK AS A VOCATION

It is well established that policing is *not* a simple ministerial function that can be performed with virtually no training by anyone with an above-average physical constitution and more or less average intelligence. But it is not yet clear what kind of occupation it *is*. Educational requirements and training standards have been raised considerably, and performance expectations have risen accordingly. But this change has not been guided by clearly formulated ideas of purpose and direction. Such unplanned outreach is not necessarily bad (in any case it is inevitable in periods of rapid change), but it produces stress in coordinating the demands of police work with personal and career aspirations of officers. The character and value of policing as a person's lifework will be influenced significantly by the way these tensions are dealt with now.

However beneficial the recent years of change may have been, they have created more uncertainty than police personnel should have to endure. Under these circumstances it is only natural that police officers should organize to protect their interests. Recent increases in police unionization demonstrate this tendency. Though one cannot generalize, it is probably fair to say that police unions are opposed to change. Further, it is not difficult to understand the reason for this opposition. Change or reform is, after all, something that comes down from the top, and it is the business of unions to negotiate the price of compliance. It is still not customary in police departments for the rank and file to participate in decisions regarding changes in organization and practice. Even where honest efforts are made to establish open consultation, the absence of experience with participatory management prevents the process from being effective. So it probably is not fair to think that police union representatives are simply stubborn in refusing to accept every proposed change enthusiastically. Instead, it seems more reasonable to conclude that efforts to make policing more socially responsible require that this be done in a socially responsible manner from within as well. There is a certain irony in the fact that line personnel in police departments have as much reason to be skeptical of police management as members of minority communities have to be skeptical of the police generally.

Given that understanding policing as an occupation must begin with a fair and practical recognition of where the occupation is now, what is the ideal for a person whose lifework is police service? Following are some observations about the nature of police work, appropriate preparation for it, and the organizational context conducive to optimum work.

First, policing is a complex occupation addressing serious problems. It calls for knowledge and skill. More important, however, its practitioners are entrusted with the very considerable power to use force when necessary. In a culture in which force seldom has the sanction of legitimacy, this trust has special significance.

Second, policing is not technical in the sense in which engineering is. Instead, it makes great demands on experience and judgment. Experience is accumulated knowledge on which is based the understanding of practical necessities and possibilities. This understanding guides judgment.

Third, in their day-to-day work police officers often deal with matters to which other people respond with fear, anger, or loathing. One could say that police work consists of proceeding methodically where an impulsive reaction would be the norm.

Fourth, the preponderance of police work is done by individual officers or pairs of officers. Thus, police officers depend primarily on their own knowledge, skill and judgment, and they must be prepared to finish what they start by themselves.

Fifth, more than almost any other occupation, policing offers opportunities for sloth, abuse, and corruption. This risk applies to individuals and also to the institution as a whole. The police can be—and often have been—used as an instrument of oppression.

This list is incomplete, but it is enough to make a person wonder how anyone could be adequately prepared for so demanding an occupation. Detailed discussion of preparation for policing is beyond the scope of this chapter, but two points can be made. First, it makes no sense to recruit police officers on the basis of an antiquated conception of what the work entails. Having learned that officers are required to make serious decisions, it seems absurd to accept candidates who have demonstrated only that they are capable of following simple commands. The quality of officers is being addressed by raising educational requirements and rewarding officers who increase their educational qualifications. But this is at best a stop-gap measure that often creates as many problems as it solves.[12] In the long run it will be necessary to convince the most talented and aspiring young people that policing offers a satisfying career.

Second, even though the preparation of police officers ought to involve an adequate general educational background, and even though other helping professions can provide auxiliary instruction, the invention and administration of the police training curriculum will have to come from the police themselves.

In light of all this, it hardly seems appropriate for policing to remain organized in its present form. It is scarcely imaginable that future police officers, fully aware of the nature of their mandate, would accept positions in a quasi-military hierarchy of command, the only conceivable purpose of which could be to make their work more difficult. Saying this strikes some people as suggesting the abandonment of organizational discipline. What actually is at issue, however, is the invention of an appropriate discipline that would function to control the risk of abuse and to enhance the effectiveness of the service.

NOTES

This essay previously appeared in *Local Government Police Management,* 2d rev. ed., ed. Bernard L. Garmire, Municipal Management Series (Washington, D.C.: International City Management Association, 1982), 1–12.

1. For a review of recent change in the field of policing, see Ruben G. Rumbaut and Egon Bittner, "Changing Conception of the Police Role: A Sociological View," in *Crime and Justice: An Annual Review of Research,* vol. 1, ed. Norval Morris and Michael Tonry (Chicago: University of Chicago Press, 1979), 239–88. For an argument demonstrating that the time has come to rethink the direction of reform, see Herman Goldstein, "Improving Policing: A Problem-Oriented Approach," *Crime and Delinquency* (April 1979): 236–58.

2. David H. Bayley, "Police Function, Structure, and Control in Western Europe and North America: Comparative and Historical Studies," in *Crime and Justice,* 109–43.

3. The richest collection of information about, and the most care-

ful analysis of, discretionary law enforcement is contained in Wayne R. LaFave, *Arrest: The Decision to Take a Suspect into Custody* (Boston: Little, Brown & Company, 1965).

4. The whole question of discretion in invoking the law was first analyzed with exemplary precision by Joseph Goldstein, "Police Discretion Not to Invoke the Criminal Process: Low Visibility Decisions in the Administration of Justice." *Yale Law Journal* 69 (1960): 543–49. A veritable flood of literature followed.

5. Jan M. Chaiken, Peter W. Greenwood, and Joan Petersilia, "The Criminal Investigation Process: A Summary Report," *Police Analysis* 3 (Spring 1977): 187–217.

6. I have tried to summarize and interpret the evidence concerning this matter in Egon Bittner, "Florence Nightingale in Pursuit of Willie Sutton: A Theory of the Police," in *The Potential for Reform of Criminal Justice,* ed. Herbert Jacob (Beverly Hills, Calif.: Sage Publications, 1974), 17–44.

7. One of the earliest statements about this came from an English scholar who observed police practices in the United States. See Michael Banton, *The Policeman in the Community* (New York: Basic Books, 1964).

8. This impartiality has an analogue in the formal properties of law in the Western tradition: see Isaac D. Balbus, "Commodity Form and Legal Form: An Essay on the 'Relative Autonomy' of Law," *Law and Society Review* 11 (Winter 1977): 571–88.

9. Allan Silver, "The Demand for Order in Civil Society: A Review of Some Themes in the History of Urban Crime, Police, and Riot," in *The Police: Six Sociological Essays,* ed. David J. Bordua (New York: John Wiley & Sons, 1967) 1–24; Robert D. Storch, "The Policeman as Domestic Missionary: Urban Discipline and Popular Culture in Northern England, 1850–1880," *Journal of Social History* 9 (1976): 481–509.

10. Bruce Johnson, "Taking Care of Labor: The Police in American Politics," *Theory and Society* 3 (1976): 89–117.

11. This whole troublesome topic is treated with remarkable fairness in Charles E. Silberman, *Criminal Violence, Criminal Justice* (New York: Random House, 1978).

12. Lawrence W. Sherman and the National Advisory Commission on Higher Education for Police Officers, *The Quality of Police Education* (San Francisco: Jossey-Bass Publishers, 1978).

7 | *The Impact of Police–Community Relations on the Police System*

A REASONABLE ESTIMATE of prevailing attitudes is that the concept of police–community relations has gained a secure level of acceptance in the law enforcement establishment and in urban government. By "acceptance" we mean that proposals to establish and maintain such programs tend to have a fair chance of success. Nor are there any organized factions publicly opposing police efforts to open and cultivate channels of communication with the public generally, and with the civic groups and social movements particularly. Whether those who were aligned against such attempts are now merely silent for the time being, or whether they have changed their views, is an open question. But there is no doubt that the activities included under the heading of police–community relations have achieved respectability, and that a large and growing number of police officials in positions of responsibility have come to view them as indispensable for effective law enforcement and peacekeeping.

The acceptance of these views is a sign of progress, a remarkable achievement. In less than two decades the most insular of all institutions in American society has become committed, at least in principle, to a program of ongoing exchanges about its mandate and practices. Secrecy and institutional separation have ceased to be a defensible position, although they have not completely disappeared.

It is important to begin the assessment of the current status and the prospects of police–community relations programs with this realization in order to place the review of actual practices in proper perspective. It is, of course, much easier to agree with the reasonableness and justice of a proposal than to implement it and live with the consequences of its implementation. Above all, when the task is to decide what must and can be done, it is important to measure aspirations against resistance and inertia. Thus, for example, despite the acceptance of the principle of police–community relations, no actually functioning police–community relations programs are fully deserving of the name. The very best among them have barely succeeded in laying the foundations for their own existence. Yet it should not be concluded that the entire attempt is nothing more than an exhibition of institutional hypocrisy. It would be more productive to begin with the hypothesis that newly functioning programs are somewhat in the middle of being accepted in principle and putting into operation the kind of activities the total acceptance would lead one to expect.

Therefore, it follows that we must look at the difficulties and risks that surround a new community relations program. We must also examine the far-reaching consequences of the ways in which these difficulties and risks are met. From this perspective, it becomes clear that the advocates of the police–community relations program face a real dilemma: They have to ask for recognition with appropriate modesty, and with a "live-and-let-live" attitude to prevent themselves from being rebuffed at the outset; yet they also must reckon with the fact that what is granted to them now will later be cited as the fairly negotiated limitations on the scope of their undertaking. The difficulty of this situation is compounded because claims, acceptances, and negotiations tend to be provisional and vague, and accommodations are reached in an informal process of give-and-take that leaves open the question of whether positions once given in to can be retracted or not. Thus, many programs tend to take shape because of circumstance, occasion, or passing expediency, but are later often spoken of as if they had been the product of planning and deliberate intentions.

Moreover, and perhaps more importantly, new programs face the problem of having to be advanced in the face of tight finances, against the claims of other existing programs that are oriented toward meeting long-established obligations. Thus, for example, in many police departments it is often said that a time when there is a need for increased resource allocation to crime control, traffic, training, and the like, the new effort, which even enthusiasts admit is of uncertain promise, constitutes a difficult-to-defend drain on the budget. Such arguments create pressures upon the advocates of the program to produce quick evidence that the program is good. The first line of defense in this regard is to show a lot of activity; at the very least this demonstrates that the personnel assigned to the police–community relations unit are not idle. In addition, it indicates that they are busily engaged in work that needs to be done. This is, of course, a quite common practice in all bureaucratically organized settings. Its existence in this case generally would not be of great interest, except that such defense tactics, undertaken initially to silence inside critics, can become permanent features of programs. Thus, problems that are attacked initially merely because they are easily available targets of opportunity become *preferred* targets. Dealing with them becomes routinized, and interest in them prevents the pursuit of more hazardous, but probably more important, ventures. A good example of this tendency is found in the widespread practice of many of the police–community relations programs that establish and maintain contacts with civic groups who are known to be receptive to police influence. Another example is the even more frequent practice of producing ceremonial occasions of contact between the police and citizens, which typically use public relations techniques and salesmanship.

Although the foregoing remarks contain examples of simple organizational analysis that might be helpful in assessing police–community relations programs, what has been said could apply to any program, whatever its orientation. That is, any undertaking will have to be initiated with consideration of its practicality. The project may, however, suffer from having set its sights too low at the outset. Thus, being exposed to the hard taskmaster of success, it is consequently channeled into easy accomplishments. But police–community relations programs face certain difficulties that appear to be uniquely particular to them. Nothing has been said about this yet. Therefore, in the following sections we will discuss some of these difficulties and attempt to show how they can be resolved. First, we will look at how police–community relations programs have developed in an asymetrical form. To do this, the following discussions will totally disregard simple one-way public relations efforts that do not even pretend to be reciprocal; they are not worthy of consideration as genuine forms of police–community relations. Instead, we will concentrate on those activities in which authentic exchanges take place. Next, we will consider the form that an exchange between the police and the community might take if the police establishment as a whole were to participate in it, instead of merely sending out envoys to certain limited constituencies. It will become apparent that the serious consideration of drawing the entire police department into police–community relations will add new dimensions to the idea—both in terms of who participates in these relations, and in terms of the substance around which these relations are organized. Finally, we will discuss why the concept of police–community relations has had consequences that were not initially envisioned: the police–community relations concept has gone beyond its initial objectives. Perhaps this should not come as a surprise, since communication produces change.

Before proceeding to a discussion of these points, we should clarify that everything said here is offered primarily as an argument; that is, it is offered for consideration. It is provisional simply because it deals with a continually changing condition; more importantly, it is provisional because, in the final analysis, the time will have to come when police will have to speak for themselves, not from prepared statements in textbooks.

BACKGROUND OF POLICE–COMMUNITY RELATIONS PROGRAM

Many of the aspects of police–community relations programs can only be properly explained by considering the circumstances that gave rise to them. As with all things, we are not compelled to accept what the past has handed down to us,

but we can neither accept it nor reject it without first understanding the substance of the heritage.

Contrary to what is generally assumed, the idea of police–
community relations is not altogether the brainchild of the
second half of the twentieth century. The Metropolitan Police
Act for the City of London, of July 19th, 1829, and the procedural instructions subsequently attached to it, made it quite
clear that the new police department was a civil force seeking to
attain the objectives of peace, order, and crime control in cooperation with the people. No aspect of police work was quite as
strongly stressed in these documents as the duty of every member of the force to protect the rights, service the needs, and earn
the trust of the population he policed.[1] These principles were
specifically imported from England into American police departments. This is clear from a review of the events preceding
the establishment of the municipal police in New York in 1844,
upon which most other departments were modeled.[2] The significance of this point can not be overstated. The establishment
of the police was strenuously opposed in England and in the
United States because of fears that it would become an organ of
executive government, indifferent to public influence, and functioning against the people. The opposition was finally silenced
by assurances that the new institution would function as the people's police.

It is an amazing testimonial to our short memory that we
generally forget that World War II, and the so-called Cold War,
were struggles against what were known as "police states." At
the time, in many European countries and in the United States,
the police worked hard to disassociate themselves from these
tainted practices. Thus, in the 1950s, in many European countries, as well as in the United States, police departments established public relations campaigns to portray themselves as open
institutions, to gain public understanding, and to actively seek
public support of a nonpolitical character.[3] Since these efforts
were established at a time when political propaganda and
commercial advertising became professionalized and used
highly technical methods of salesmanship, it should come as no
surprise that these arts played a decisive role in "selling the
police to the people." Although these tactics now seem mis-

guided and misleading, it appeared at the time, even to people of genuinely good will, that it was more important to "keep the product on the market" than to improve its quality. Nevertheless, some of the most effective propagandists of the police at the time, such as the late Chief William Parker of Los Angeles, were also engaged in vigorous efforts to purge the departments of corruption, sloth, and indolence.

While the specter of the police state has been kept alive by Hollywood, the majority of Americans have never experienced the use of police force as in Stalin's Russia or Hitler's Germany. Instead of playing a part in national partisan politics during the first century of their existence, the police forces in the United States were simply a corrupt pawn of corrupt urban government. Thus, the reformers of the 1950s felt that it was necessary to overcome the attitudes of contempt that middle-class citizens held toward police. This was done by sending speakers to high schools, to businessmen's luncheons, to meetings of civil organizations, to ladies' clubs, and so on. These speakers argued that the police are the "thin blue line," the last bulwark of defense against the dark forces of crime and disorder. Though we can see how selectively these police–community contacts were chosen, in the 1950s they did constitute a movement away from the exclusive dominance of police departments by city hall bosses.

There is little doubt that the American police moved into the 1960s with a solid sense of promise. They had moved toward freeing themselves from machine politics; and they had succeeded to a notable degree in rebuilding the image of the policeman, even if only in the minds of urban and suburban middle classes. But in the turmoil of the 1960s all this turned out to be of little use. As far as the police were concerned, whole segments of society, who, in the past, never had a voice in public affairs and whose fate was traditionally decided "by their betters," rose "out of the blue" in what could only be described as a wholesale revolt. Blacks, young people, the poor, and recent immigrants explosively announced their claims to new freedoms. Most of all, they demanded freedom from oppression and from want. And, although their quarrel was with society as a whole, or with the "system" as it came to be known, the confrontation took place between them and the police. In most cities the first impulse of the police was to resort to a show of force, and to the use of force, to control the varieties of the liberation movements. But the equipment of the police did not entirely consist of tear gas, bullets, and chemical mace. Some departments also had ongoing public relations programs.

It seemed proper to put these public relations programs to deal with the unforeseen troubles. Thus, it was in the heat of struggle, parallel with efforts to gain control over urban disorders by sheer armed force, that public relations became tortuously adapted to new tasks. Now, however, these programs were directed toward people who were hostile to the police.

A few additional remarks should be made about the transition from the earlier public relations approach to the new programs. An example of the process might help make it clearer. In the mid-1950s, the Metropolitan Police Department of St. Louis, Missouri, established a public relations division that became known as one of the best functioning programs of its kind in the country.[4] The division contained a speakers' bureau, published a newsletter, organized citizens' councils, and maintained school contacts, all of which were considered to be effective in accordance with their aims. There were also police and community relations committees in housing projects, which, in the department's own estimate, did not function well even as late as 1966. Nevertheless, the undertaking as a whole had an enviable reputation. In 1962, Chief Thomas Cahill of San Francisco visited St. Louis to help obtain answers to his own problems. Chief Cahill realized that it was important to use other resources, not just force, to deal with outbreaks of discontent. His department was faced with student protests against hearings being conducted by the House Un-American Activities Committee in the San Francisco City Hall. Chief Cahill took the new director of his community relations program, Lieutenant Dante Andreotti, to St. Louis to study their methods. While Cahill and Andreotti went to St. Louis to learn because they had a problem on their hands, their problem, however, was quite different from the situation that had motivated the St. Louis department. The St. Louis program was formulated primarily to address the "solid citizens." No one considered the program seriously impaired by the fact that the project that was directed toward working with the disadvantaged and the aggrieved did not function.

In the ensuing years, Lieutenant Andreotti developed a program in San Francisco which was vastly different from the St. Louis program. The direction of work that was permitted to lie fallow in St. Louis became the central interest of the San Francisco community relations unit. While Andreotti commanded the unit, "community relations" meant working primarily with the disadvantaged and the aggrieved segments of the population. The unit's officers were attached to organizations such as Youth Opportunity Center, which served ghetto youngsters, and the Office of Economic Opportunity. They also exerted themselves in trying to meet with, talk and listen to, and help people living in the tenderloin, the skid row, and the ghetto. The activities of the San Francisco unit are illustrated by the following example.

A robbery and beating of a white grocery store operator in a minority group neighborhood resulted in community-wide concern and tension. As a result of the efforts of the police and the community relations unit, together with minority group leaders, a group of youngsters (many of whom had juvenile records) were organized into a picket line which marched back and forth in front of the store carrying signs condemning violence and stating that they were ashamed of what had happened. Although the boys picketing were not involved in the robbery or the beating, they offered verbal apologies to the family of the victim for the act done by members of their race. The publicity given this parade by the various media communications resulted in an almost immediate lessening of tensions.[5]

This incident should not be taken as indicating the scope of the unit's program nor even its focal concerns. The routine work of the officers assigned to the unit concentrated much more on everyday kinds of predicaments, such as protecting persons who were not resourceful on their own, or helping persons with police records find employment or lodgings. What the officers did was to act upon the realization that life in the city has many conditions, circumstances, and troubled people, and when troubled people are left to themselves, they are likely to cause, or get into, great calamities of various sorts. The officers worked on the assumptions that ex-cons without jobs are likely to commit crimes again; intergroup tension may lead to violent confrontations; children without recreational facilities tend to get into mischief, and so on. According to this assumption, when such potential is not checked, it leads to consequences that will sooner or later have to be handled by detectives, riot squads, or juvenile officers, depending on the specific situation.

In all fairness, it must be admitted that the men in the San Francisco community relations unit were not the first police officers ever to help a former criminal find a job, nor were they the first to succeed in preventing public disorder. The innovation must be found in two additional aspects of their work: first, they did not simply go out to solve some problem; rather, they always dealt with problems in conjunction with other community resources. In the example cited earlier, they worked together with minority group leaders. The main point is that the cooperation was not simply a convenient expedient. Rather, it involved an established and ongoing, mutually cooperative arrangement between members of the police and members of the community. Second, the men in the unit felt that providing services to citizens was their primary job. In the past such services were rendered on rare occasions and only after the officers took care of more demanding crime control problems.

In conclusion, the establishment of the community relations unit in San Francisco meant that manpower resources were specifically assigned to the task of working cooperatively with the people. More important, the chief of the department referred to the existence of the unit with pride. He claimed credit for creating it, and he gave weight to its importance by having its commanding officer report directly to the office of the chief, rather than through the chain of command. Nevertheless, some commanding officers and several line officers did not like the unit. Yet, even though the unit did not have total acceptance within the department, it gained momentum. It soon was regarded locally and nationally as conspicuously successful.

Although others considered the unit to be a success, its commander, Lieutenant Andreotti, recognized the problems that still had to be faced. Speaking at a law enforcement conference in 1968, he said:

It is my belief that there isn't a successful police–community relations program anywhere in the country today, in terms of commitment by all members of the law enforcement agency. There have been successful police–community relations units, but practically all of them have been frustrated in their efforts to get the rank and file involved to the point of a genuine, personal interest and commitment.[6]

Since this remark comes from a man who has been one of this country's leaders in police–community relations, it deserves to be seriously considered. Andreotti does not find that those who work in the field have fallen short of the mark. Rather, he feels that they are not receiving the necessary support from their own agencies. Therefore, it is safe to assume that, even under the best circumstances, community relations programs suffer both from neglect and from being given low priority by the police department. At worst, these programs are resisted and condemned by personnel of all ranks.

The absence of commitment by all members of the police department indicates that the department believes that social problems are not "proper" police business. When long-standing tensions in the community result in violence, the police must address these problems directly rather than attempting to deal with the underlying causes. According to this view of the police role, the division of labor among the several agencies of municipal government assigns to the police the duty of preventing people from violating the law and to bring them to the bar of justice when they do. The responsibility for helping people to lead decent lives is assigned to other agencies; their personnel are specially trained and they have chosen social service work as their vocation.

Conversely, commitment to the principles of police–community relations by all members of the department means that the department considers it foolish to define the police role within narrow limits. Although an individual police officer may occasionally be justified in sticking to a narrow conception of his duties and thereby avoid dealing with a problem he might possibly solve, the problem will fall back into the lap of the police. To say that only social workers should deal with these problems is similar to arguing that a champion swimmer should not pull a drowning person from the water unless he has a Red Cross Life Saving Certificate. Commitment to the principles of police–community relations means acting on the assumption that the police are a service organization dedicated to keeping the peace, to the defense of the rights of the people, and to the enforcement of laws. In all these fields they are not merely an independent instrument of government; rather, they must work with individuals, community groups, and community institutions to achieve the desired objectives.

It was this latter attitude that governed the intervention of the San Francisco community relations unit in the incident mentioned earlier. This incident is a good example of commitment to the principles of police–community relations on the level of departmental organization. It is important to emphasize that the case is used only for the purposes of illustration. Because a full record of the case is not available, many of the factors will be introduced as unproven assumptions. However, it does not matter whether these assumptions were true in this instance. What matters is that the assumptions we shall make about the case are generally true.

Even the most uninitiated reader of the account of the case must have noticed that it is incomplete; details are lacking in one crucial aspect. What about the principals in the case, the victim and the assailants? It could be said that one does not expect to hear much about victims in such cases no matter how they are handled. What, then, of the assailant? It must be assumed that the assailant would have become the concern of the departmental unit dealing with this type of crime, and that procedures would have been set into motion leading to his apprehension and trial. It is fair to say that at this point the involvement of the community relations unit with the case stopped. That is, from this point on the community leaders would be told to stay out of it and let the experts take over. The community relations unit men would understand that the case had been taken away from them and that they should move on to the next case.

All this seems in good order and as it should be. One does not expect citizens to be involved in catching crooks; in fact, when they insist on becoming involved, they are more likely to cause harm than to do good. No doubt this is the view of policemen. But, perhaps more importantly, it is also the view of most judges, public prosecutors, city councilmen, and citizens. Indeed, as long as one thinks in terms of isolated offenses, it is difficult to reason otherwise. Thus, even those who are in favor of genuine police–community relations are forced to agree that the work must be assigned to special units which work independently while the rest of policing takes its ordinary course. In other words, progressive departments establish internal units to deal with the community, but these units must follow the department's conditions. In still different terms, it appears that accepting the principles of police–community relations in its present exclusively outward-oriented direction (somewhat in the way nations send envoys to other nations) does not mean that two-way police–community relations are the norm (or, to continue the analogy, that the other nations send their envoys).

Before we explore this onesidedness, it should be pointed out that this situation is not unique. The police are not alone in thinking that they can communicate adequately with the people by means of external ambassadors. Indeed, they have done better with this approach than other institutions. The educational system, for example, keeps parents at arms length while pretending to allow for involvement by letting assistant principals of schools deal with the PTA. Similarly, institutions that deliver medical services often do not even pretend to communicate with the people they serve. In each of these cases, it is argued that lay people could not possibly contribute to solving the case of a slow-learning child or a diabetic patient, just as it is said that lay people could not be helpful in solving a robbery.

All communities have educational needs, health needs, and law enforcement needs. It is neither proper nor efficient for the specialists alone to define the nature of these needs or the way in which they will be met. The specialist brings competence and skills to bear on meeting these needs, but he must communicate with lay citizens to determine what their needs are.

The establishment of police–community relations units is a first, long step in recognition of the usefulness of bringing needs and special resources together in a harmonious relationship. Nevertheless, it is just that—a first step. The establishment of community–police relations, in a much broader sense, is a logical next step. An example might help in making clear what this involves. It is commonly accepted that the black ghettos of our cities produce a disproportionately large number of people who engage in criminal activities and that the people living in the black ghettos are exposed to a far greater risk of being criminally victimized than other citizens. Finally, it is no secret that people living in the ghettos distrust the police and are often reluctant to help officers in their efforts to control crime. What would be more sensible than for the police to consider these three facts, together with their present ways of dealing with black suspects and black victims, as systematically related? Joint consideration of the larger problem suggests that a successful attack on the problem can come only from the establishment of a program of trusting and fully cooperative relations between the black community and the police.

The reversal of terms from police–community relations to community–police relations was not done simply to coin a new term. It could not matter less what the arrangement is called! What matters is that the full effectiveness of the program cannot be attained by merely having a special unit to implement it. At best such units can only succeed in doing an occasional good deed and putting out an occasional fire, while leaving the rest of the police department's work unaffected by even these accomplishments.

INTERNALIZING POLICE–COMMUNITY RELATIONS WORK

We have come a long way from the public relations programs that were popular in the post–World War II years through the unit-based police–community relations programs of the 1960s. We have learned that if the principles embodied in these programs are to be carried out fully, they cannot be assigned to special units. They must be incorporated into, and become an integral part of, every aspect of police work. Nevertheless, it would be totally irresponsible to leave it at that. Even if the example of crime in the black ghetto were to be accepted as the truth, an example like this should never be offered as proof of anything. After all, it is one thing to let a few police officers work in community relations, but if all police officers are required to be community relations officers as well, will anybody ever get around to catching crooks, stopping fights in bars, and attending to the endless variety of other emergencies?

Perhaps it would be easiest to explain what incorporating police–community relations into police work generally means by discussing what it does not mean. First, it does not mean requiring entire departments to do what their police–community relations units are doing now. In fact, the only reason that these units are now free to concentrate exclusively on their present activities is because they are special units, counting on other units to do the rest of the work.

Second, it would be totally wrong to think that the adoption of police–community relations principles into police work might somehow weaken commitment to criminal law enforcement. Contrary to what is often said, viewing crime as a social problem does not imply that the criminal should be let go, or let off easily. In fact, it is not unreasonable to assume that the police might become more strongly dedicated to crime control than they are now, especially the control of some crimes they presently fail to consider. That is, they may come to act upon the moral contained in the ancient ditty:

> The law locks up both man and woman
> Who steal the goose from off the common
> But lets the greater felon loose
> Who steals the common from the goose.

Third, although police–community relations programs have in the past primarily been supported by more liberals than conservatives, it would be a grave mistake to tie the fate of the program to partisan politics. Taken by itself, police–community relations involve a technique, a method of doing police work. But this method also implies a greater openness to all community situations. Therefore, it calls for extensive and explicit reckoning with the distribution of political forces and with the often controversial play among them. This becomes evident at two levels. On the one hand, the police, as an institution of city government, will need to gain public support and the support of city hall for its own modernization. Conversely, police officers need to mobilize support for specific police–community relations peacekeeping and law enforcement programs.

Fourth, it cannot be denied that opening police work to inputs from all segments of the community contains the risk of putting it in an impossible situation, requiring it to bend to different influences, while being driven into inactivity and ineffectiveness in this storm of conflicting demands. But this risk can be easily contained if it is kept in mind that being responsive to community needs and demands does not involve bargaining away the police mandate. In fact, because openness is a two-way street, the risk will become an opportunity for citizens to understand and respect the police mandate in society.

Fifth and finally, fears have been expressed that police–community relations programs turn policemen into social workers. These fears have gained some acceptance from observations of the activities of members of functioning special units. But these units should not be taken as models. These special programs allow the police officer to become a more effective public servant while retaining his full range of duties and responsibilities.

So much, then, for what is not true, or, in some instances, should not be permitted to be true. What does it mean to incorporate principles of police–community relations into police work generally, rather than assigning them to special units?

Above all, it means reviving the basic idea on which modern, urban police departments were founded; specifically, that these departments be the "people's police" rather than merely an arm of executive government. It could be said, of course, that executive government also belongs to the people. But executives tend to develop certain internal needs that are not all for the public good. For example, elected officials have a well-known tendency to want to remain in office; nothing strengthens their hand in this respect quite as much as the ready and unquestioned availability of the police. If being a "people's police" means anything, it means that the needs for the police service cannot be decided only from above. Determining the needs of the people and ways of meeting these needs must be continuously monitored in ongoing consultations between the people and the police. However, executive city government is a community structure too, probably the most important one the police must deal with. Police–community relations does not mean that the police should fight the power, the authority, and the needs of city hall.

Next, the acceptance of police–community relations means putting the work of policing on a reasoned basis. This is a far more complex and difficult matter than it is usually thought to be. Many people want to believe that the structure of police work is completely determined by what is written in the penal codes, in municipal ordinances, and by the evident situational needs present in the vast variety of emergencies police officers deal with. According to this view, the police officer simply moves from arresting a rapist, to taking a suicidal person to the county hospital, to quelling a campus disorder, to administering first aid to an automobile accident victim, to intervening in a domestic dispute, to investigating a reported burglary, and so on. In each case he does what needs to be done, and he never looks beyond the level of the clearly present situational necessity. But every police officer knows that these are not random events. He knows that each results from a complex network of problems. But under traditional constraint, he is required to act as if it was beyond his intellectual capacity to recognize such interests. Instead, he is supposed to assume the "I-just-work-here" attitude of someone who merely does what he is told to do. It should be mentioned, however, that the most skillful and most experienced police officers do go beyond the limitations of traditional constraint and handle complex matters in complex ways.[7] But this practice is not officially recognized and certainly not officially encouraged. A reasoned approach to police work requires that these practices be examined, debated, and assessed according to their merits.

Finally, the police–community relations approach calls for a wide-spread understanding, both in the community and among police, that the police are entitled to and are required to take an interest in human life before they are called to pick up its shattered pieces. This, too, sounds like a stilted formula. But if we disregard the sentimentality in this statement, it means very little more than what effective police officers already do in their dealings with people. These men already do this generally as a personal expression of humanity, but it should be considered part of their work. Nevertheless, it would be foolish to expect that all police officers would be idealists, just as it would be foolish to expect that all teachers would take a genuinely sympathetic interest in children. But teachers are not free to flaunt their contempt for people, not even for people who are contemptible. Thus, hypocrisy is put into the service of virtue. But among police it is often assumed that it is proper to maintain an attitude of cynicism toward human life. This attitude must be overcome, not only in the interest of virtue, but also in the interest of effectiveness. Taking an interest in human life, especially those aspects of life that are in need of interest—such as poverty, discrimination, racism, and exploitation—does not mean undertaking to solve them. It only means joining the struggle to solve them.

CONCLUSIONS

The police–community relations program of today took a form that was appropriate to the circumstances of their origin. First, they began to build on the foundations of the already existing public relations programs, adopting their exclusively outward orientation. This meant working with various segments of the community outside the department in ways that did not produce any substantial changes in the operation of the rest of the police system. Second, in accordance with the beliefs of the 1960s, the work concentrated on cultivating relations with the segments of the community that were most neglected by the earlier public relations approach. New partners to the exchange called for new forms of exchange. It is obvious that responsiveness to a civil rights organization is a much different matter than responsiveness to the chamber of commerce.

Third, in keeping with the overall tendencies of our age, the task came to be viewed as a technical specialty. The drift toward specialization was further strengthened by the almost irresistible tendency of bureaucracies to compartmentalize tasks in special units. Fourth, the 1960s were a time in which the presence of injustice, discrimination, and poverty aroused the conscience of America. Under these circumstances it seemed more important to get going in whatever way possible, rather than to begin with careful analysis and planning.

But starting with what was at hand, and focusing on those problems that were most obviously in need of being attended to, was not just the beginning. The establishment of the original and timely police–community relations programs eventually revealed things about the police that were not recognized at the time. Above all, it brought into full recognition the enormous isolation of the police in society. It became clear that policemen were strangers not only in the ghettos of our cities, but that they were also strangers in the hospitals, in the universities, in the union halls, in the various agencies of government and, most important, in the institutions of the criminal justice system.

Thus, having police–community relations officers working with tenants' councils in public housing, with representatives of civil rights movements, and with activists in the war on poverty was merely the beginning of a far more thoroughgoing reconstruction of the relations of the police to the community. Two things became clear as the result of the work of the special units. First, holding the fort of isolation was an exercise in stubbornness, keeping the police stationary in a rapidly changing society. Second, the maintenance of ongoing dialogues with all members of society could not be achieved without involving all members of the police system. The methods of some officers had to be built into the methods of all officers. The need for this is most evident in the relations of the police with other segments of the criminal justice system.

Though it is quite commonly assumed that the police are a part of the criminal justice system, it is more correct to say that they function apart from it.[8] While it may appear to the uninformed observer that policemen, prosecutors, judges, and corrections officers are united in the struggle against crime, they are, in fact, only very poorly coordinated. The police, especially, engage in a sort of take-it-or-leave-it relationship with the rest of the system. No better evidence for this fact exists than the recent history of the so-called exclusionary rules. These rules provide that when a criminal complaint is based on illegally obtained evidence, judges are obliged to dismiss it, in accordance with a series of Supreme Court decisions. These decisions were handed down to teach the police a lesson in the principles of legality.[9] But this form of teaching has led to nothing but frustration.

The problem of the exclusionary rules is a matter of delicacy, involving the independence of the judiciary in our system of government. Yet the frequently prevailing situation of the police and the judiciary working at cross-purposes is plainly in need of attention. But it must not be thought that the problem will be properly attacked by bringing police chiefs and presiding judges together into administrative conferences. The formal agreements that result from such conferences rarely affect actual practices, and virtually never affect underlying attitudes. The only hope seems to lie in the establishment of a mutual understanding, an understanding not only about the exclusionary rules but about many other matters as well.

In the complex network of relations between the police and the criminal justice system, the case involving the judges is by far the most difficult one. Police relations with probation and parole officers are more easily approached. In fact, policemen and probation officers assigned to juvenile law enforcement tend to work closely together. But this kind of cooperation is not the norm for the rest of the police department and probation. Some of the difficulties arise from the fact that in recent years probation practices have been heavily influenced by teachings drawn from casework practice—at this point the traditional aloofness between police work and social work comes into play.

When one says that the police must be open toward psychiatrists, judges, educators, civil rights activists, social workers, poverty warriors, and probation officers, and that they must somehow come to understand their concerns and work with them, this does not mean that policemen must adopt their attitudes, assume their methods, and ultimately do their work. Far from becoming like the groups, professions, and agencies with which police–community relations units function, the police will, in these interactions, find a more distinct and more clearly defined role for themselves. In the context of open relations, a clearer definition of the police role will be achieved.

NOTES

This essay previously appeared in *Community Relations and the Administration of Justice,* ed. David P. Geary (New York: John Wiley & Sons, 1975).

1. T. A. Critchley, *A History of Police in England and Wales 1900–1966* (London: Constable, 1967).

2. C. Astor, *The New York Cops: An Informal History* (New York: Scribners, 1971).

3. G. E. Berkley, *The Democratic Policeman* (Boston: Beacon Press, 1969).

4. *A National Survey of Police and Community Relations,* School of Police Administration and Public Safety, Michigan State University (Washington, D.C.: U.S. Government Printing Office, 1967).

5. Ibid., 49.

6. D. A. Andreotti, "Present Problems in Police Community Relations," in *Confrontation: Violence and the Police,* C. R. Chormache and M. Hormachea, eds., (Boston: Holbrook, 1971), 120.

7. E. Bittner, "The Police on Skid Row: A Study of Peace Keeping," *American Sociological Review* 32 (1967), 699–715.

8. E. Bittner, *The Functions of the Police in Modern Society* (Washington, D.C.: U.S. Government Printing Office, 1970).

9. F. P. Graham, *The Self-Inflicted Wound* (New York: Macmillan Co., 1970).

8 | *Police Research and Police Work*

DURING THE JUST PAST DECADE the police has been the subject of more scholarly research than during the entire one hundred fifty years of its prior existence as an institution of modern government. What caused the veritable explosion of interest in the police? Why did the studies take the form they took? Above all, what did the strenuous effort accomplish and what lessons can be drawn from it?

In what follows I shall try to suggest some possible answers to these questions. Before proceeding with this task, however, I should like to mention that I have focused on research not because it is my bailiwick and I had better stick to my knitting, but rather because I am convinced that police research is the business of police, at least to the extent to which medical research is the business of physicians and educational research is the business of teachers. In other words, I propose to address, with the candor of someone who is himself an old hand at it, matters you will have to get into, like it or not. I think that in the long run it simply will not do for me to tell you what policing is all about. In place of it, you will have to do your own social science and draw your own conclusions from it. It is with this future objective in view that I offer a tentative sketch of an assessment of the most recent development in police research.

I

It is always somewhat hazardous to speak of events of a just passed decade. Things have not yet stood still long enough, so to speak, to tell definitely what they were and what they amounted to. With this reservation in mind, I suggest that the flurry of research on the police in the 1960s was mainly the function of two relatively independent factors.

In the first place, police work gained in the 1960s a degree of public visibility it never enjoyed—or suffered, as the case may be—before. The circumstances under which the police moved into the spotlight involve a rich variety of trends of social change. Two of these trends can be singled out as having been of decisive importance, namely, the civil rights movement and the so-called war on poverty. Leaving aside the question of whether the picture of the police that came to view in its exposure to these trends was accurate or not, I merely wish to draw attention to what actually took place. After almost a quarter century of wholly unprecedented internal tranquility in the United States—in the period between the mid-thirties and the outset of the Kennedy years—political strife took once again to the streets and for the first time to the college campuses in the sixties. Moreover, while past protest and demonstration were carried out predominantly by people "from the wrong side of the tracks," they now appeared to recruit their participants in large numbers from among people of well-to-do backgrounds. These people, found especially on college campuses, who up to then had been oblivious to the existence of the police and ignorant of its activities, suddenly found themselves confronting police control measures that were often harsh and sometimes excessively harsh. At the same time, and in obvious connection with this experience, people from another segment of society, people who had always been under close police surveillance and control, without ever having had anything to say about it, somehow managed to speak out and be heard during this period. I have reference, of course, to a variety of minority groups who were traditionally without political power, without representation in the forum of public opinion, and whose attitudes toward all forms of public authority are quite understandably permeated with sustained and virulent resentment. Against this background the police became one of the most embattled topics of public debate. And in this thicket of accusation and defense the need for information and clarity became obvious and was picked up by social scientists.

While the circumstances of heightened visibility of the police were the more significant cause of the rise of interest in police research, there was another cause that probably mattered more in terms of practical expediency. The 1960s were the fat years of American social science research. To begin with, social science came of age in the United States during World War II and proliferated enormously in the years that followed it. So that when the Sputnik crisis came and vast amounts of money were funneled into research, social scientists were ready to take and use every dollar that came their way. And under these circumstances it was all but inevitable that as social scientists began to step on each other's toes in hospitals, schools, welfare agencies, industrial plants, the news media and so on, some would take a deep breath and plunge into the police. To be sure, some of the early police research, and some of the very best of it to this day, was done without support or with merely marginal support. But the growth of police research as a whole cannot be properly understood without taking into account the rise of funded research and of the actual availability of funds, especially not since the time some police departments themselves found out on which side the bread was buttered and joined the game of grantsmanship.

In sum, police research came about accidentally, in the sense that the timing of its outset was not determined by needs and developments within the police establishment itself, but by an external course of events that happened to place the police in a singularly unfavorable light. And projects of police research were externally formulated, in the sense that the police did not participate in the determination of their directions and conceptualizations.

II

The observations that the police were caught unaware, so to speak, by social research and had no voice in shaping it, gains in significance when it is considered that police work is the only vocation to whom this happened. Of all the occupations dealing with people, the police alone have not, at any time during this century, raised serious questions about the nature of their mandate, have never moved in any sustained manner in the direction of self-scrutiny and self-criticism, and did not attempt to build into their operations a stable program of study and research. That is, the police alone have never developed a program of research and study of their own. All the other occupations—physicians, clergymen, teachers, lawyers, nurses, social workers, salespeople, even the military— have, at some time in this century, once or repeatedly, to a greater or lesser extent, with more or less effect, taken a hard look at themselves, asked fundamental questions, purged their ranks and practices, updated their role in society, and generally sought to reason things out among themselves.

A brief example of this kind of critical rethinking and critical reorganization might help explain what I mean. About the time of the turn of the century a substantial proportion of the men who called themselves doctors and practiced medicine in this country were ignorant and unskilled. Moreover, these men not only pretended practicing medicine themselves, they were also free to set up medical schools and grant medical degrees to others who followed in their footsteps. Finally, even the graduates of reputable medical schools were far less educated and far less trained than was possible at the then existing state of knowledge. In short, the state of medical practice was a scandal. It would lead far afield to go into the details of the self-critique and reform undertaken by the responsible part of the medical profession under the aegis of an extensive study known as the Flexner Report. Suffice it to say that physicians did not hesitate to employ means that had the effect to reduce their numbers from 164/100,000 in 1910 to 125/100,000 in 1930, a reduction of twenty-five percent of the effective supply of medical care at a time when the need for it increased several times over!

I have simplified the story, of course, and I do not mean to suggest that reduction in numbers is the only road to reform. I only wish to place emphasis on the fact that physicians—a group at least as jealously protective of their own as the police— did not move into the twentieth century without the pains of self-scrutiny. And the same must be said, more or less, for the rest of the occupations I mentioned. Thus, when the floodgates of social research broke in the 1950s, the members of these vocations were ready to take part in the studies of their respective endeavors, and ready to absorb findings for further improvement. As opposed to this, the police admitted social scientists grudgingly at best, and had little interest in their doings so long as they caused no problems with city hall.

I must now take care of an argument that almost invariably comes up at this point. People generally, and especially policemen, tend to say it is foolish to liken cops to doctors. The implication is that policemen are so vastly inferior to doctors that it just does not make any sense to expect that they might come up with something like a Flexner Report. I happen to think that this puts things the wrong way. The police did not fail to produce their Flexner Report because they are inferior to physicians; they are inferior to physicians because they did not produce such a report or something like it! But things like this do not just happen and I should like to try to explain why the police assumed a stationary character in the twentieth century, and why they developed no studies or researches of their own.

One of the most widely popularized observations about the police, an observation that is mentioned at every opportune and inopportune occasion, is that the police are suspicious to the point of paranoia. As the saying goes, you ask a policeman the time of the day and he thinks you are up to something. With respect to the matter under discussion, that suspiciousness manifests itself in a strong aversion of the police against having their affairs looked into by outsiders and against acknowledging the existence of any internal problems whatever. The aversion is presumably connected with the belief said to be widespread among policemen that the only reason anyone could have for studying the police is to get the goods on them, and to do them in. I think there is probably a good deal of truth in all this and—which is far less often mentioned—there are also some good reasons for it being so. I do not mean reasons that justify, only reasons that explain. As is well known, the police in the United States have been, from the middle of the nineteenth to the middle of the twentieth century, the football of urban politics, and they are still the football of urban politics in some places despite the fact that they have been placed on a civil service basis virtually everywhere. A central part of this situation was the periodic "shake-up" in the departments. Thus, every sensible policeman had a realistic basis of thinking that when someone was taking a look at his doings, it probably had something to do with some politician's brother-in-law having an eye on his job, or some such cabal. Though this condition is no longer as pervasive as it used to be half a century ago, it is a rare department even today in which suspicions connected with the exercise of political influence are totally absent. Let me add that this kind of paranoia is oppressively present in all kinds of bureaucracies and has every where at least *some* foundation in fact. But it is nowhere quite as debilitating as in the police and, of course, nowhere are the fears of managed embarrassment as justified by experience as in the police. Justified or not, however, the suspiciousness kept the police from following the kind of path of development other professions followed.

The other barrier against autonomous police development of study and research has to do with something that needs to be said bluntly. No one, but absolutely no one in the whole world, has a lower opinion of the value, importance, and complexity of every day routine police work than policemen, especially in command positions. And no one is as contemptuous of the qualities and capacities of the rank-and-file of police personnel as policemen, again especially in command positions. To be sure, they all insist that policemen have many endearing traits; they are said to be loyal, courageous, honest, altruistic, occasionally even shrewd in a down-to-earth manner; and to be sure, they are all for the police. But if the truth be told, they are for a police comprised of men involved in a low-grade occupation, whose job it is to do what they are told, and whose lookout it is to stay out of trouble with their superiors. Naturally, I am not referring to the characterizations police brass use when they talk *about* their men to the public; instead, I am referring to the characterizations police brass have in mind when they talk *to* their men.

To some extent this tragically distorted and demeaning image is rooted in public prejudice which, as I once suggested, tends to see something of the dragon in the dragon-slayer. Public prejudice is, however, far less extensive and far less important than is sometimes thought. Much more significant for the continued survival of the image of the hapless flatfooted cop, in my view, is the internal organization of work and accountability prevailing in the urban police department of America. To put it in positive terms, the existing authority structure, division of labor, and patterns of reward distribution cannot but deaden every vestige of aspiration, every spark of initiative, and every bit of a sense of purpose in even the most dedicated men, while at the same time exerting pressure for them to move either in the direction of the kind of crimebusting entrepreneurship exaggerated in some recent films like *The French Connection,* or in the direction of personal careerist advancement on the bureaucratic ladder. While gifted and well-meaning men are sometimes found along these paths, they can scarcely be expected to be dedicated to the reform of the police since their individual successes are buoyed by the inadequacies of the institution of which they are a part.

In sum, the combined effect of the policeman's not unfounded suspicion that every kind of scrutiny of his activity or background is a prelude to indictment and ruin on the one hand, and on the other, his resigned belief that he is involved in a low-grade occupation which neither entitles him nor equips him to determine its structure or course, precluded police initiative in the study of itself and delayed by at least a decade the involvement of the police in research projects of external origin.

III

I think it is very important to keep in mind these rather inauspicious beginnings of modern research on the police when one tries to assess its merits and divine its lessons. In fact, the first important lesson police research teaches, albeit a lesson that is difficult to put in so many words, is literally contained in the experience of the early, uncertain efforts to bridge the gap between police official and social scientist. It is not farfetched to say that the ambiguities, and the difficulties, and the distrust that permeated these early contacts helped more than any other factor to bring into prominence questions about the role of police in society. In other words, in these conversations it became apparent—though not necessarily always admitted—that no one could say with final authority what police work was supposed to accomplish. I doubt very much whether the fundamental question about the police role would have received that kind of explicit attention had police research begun as an inside development. After all, what we refer to as the police role is nothing else than all that which every policeman knows about his job without paying attention to it, all that which he sees without noticing, and all that which he takes for granted as the basis for thinking about problems and not in need to be thought of itself. In fact, only outsiders could be counted on to fasten their interest on efforts to achieve an explicit formulation of the totality of benefits the presence of a policeman on the street makes available to society.

This is not the proper place and time to review the answers that have been and still are being proposed concerning the police role. Instead, I should like to focus on one big discovery, a discovery so big that in my view it overshadows all the others. And I shall briefly mention the lesson which I believe must be drawn from this discovery.

The discovery has three related parts. First, there is general agreement that the vastly preponderant majority of police manpower, time and resources, is and must be, allocated to activities that have either nothing, or only very little, to do with law enforcement in the strict sense of the term. Second, these activities, commonly referred to as peacekeeping, entail the methodical handling of an enormously wide-ranging variety of often highly complex and almost invariably very serious human problems. Third, policemen typically receive no instruction, no guidance, and, above all, no recognition for doing this work.

I think it would be difficult to find a more remarkable situation in the entire field of public affairs. Here is a corps of officials, functionaries, professionals, call them what you will, charged with what is obviously an extraordinary difficult and varied job, involving immense responsibilities, the immenseness of which can be readily brought to mind by considering how much can depend on a policeman's decision and how easily his mistakes can cause loss, injury, disaster, and ruin. Here is a corps of officials dealing with problems that are almost always of critical importance to the people who are the targets of the service. Here is a corps of officials who must deal with such problems under the most difficult circumstances, namely, wherever they happen to occur and generally out in the open, and who in dealing with these problems, have very little else going for them than personal luck, skill, and judgment. And finally, here is a corps of officials about whom it is commonly assumed—and with very good reason, I might add—that they must not be opposed in carrying out their decision, a power that is totally and uniquely theirs.

Into this corps of officials we recruit people—apparently on the basis of a belief that virtually anyone can be expected to do this kind of work—of more or less average intelligence, of distinctly below-average aspiration, and of absolutely no prior preparation for the work, except for such preparation as is contained in the widespread assumption that to be a policeman one must be endowed with what are thought to be 'manly virtues.' And we give these recruits to understand that we do not consider it to be a matter of great moment whether their work is done well or poorly since the recruits learn very early that in the police, it is as unlikely that a job well done will be rewarded as that a job botched will lead to chastisement.

Now, I do not mean to overdraw the picture; I know that a large proportion of things patrolmen do—and my remarks pertain especially to them—is fairly ordinary and relatively few tasks present highly taxing demands on skill, understanding and judgment. In fact, I think it is a fair assumption that in police work the ratio of routine to the exceptionally difficult is probably more or less the same as in teaching, medicine, plumbing, or any other line of work. But even with this qualification in mind, it seems to be plain to see that the main lesson contained in these observations goes far beyond saying that the quality of our police must be upgraded by inducing policemen to take some courses in colleges. If what I have suggested about the complexity, seriousness, and importance of police work is even only approximately correct—and I cannot see how anyone can gainsay that—then nothing short of the total transformation of the concept of the job and of the man who does it is called for.

This brings me to the central point of my remarks. The truth of the matter is that all of us outsiders who talk about the police have had not more than a glimpse of it, and all of us know that what we say is highly provisional. As far as the police are concerned, the main value of our work is that there is just enough in it to get something going. The "something going" has reference to the task of bringing the police of this country into the second half of the twentieth century. Following the example of all the other services and professions, this requires the building up within and around the police of a whole range of activities that are associated with scholarship, study, and research. Even though there is always room for outside technical advice in any endeavor of this kind, the bulk of its burden must be borne by the police themselves. From nowhere but from the ranks of the police will come the people who will undertake to discover, describe, systematize, codify, innovate, teach, and so on, the body of knowledge and skill that goes into doing a good job of policing.

Let me put it this way. As I see it, the main lesson to be drawn from police research of the 1960s is that police work is an occupation that deserves and needs a hefty infusion of dispassionate and critical reason of the kind that can only be obtained by building into its every day function the practices of study and research. Of course, I am not suggesting that every policeman must be a scholar but only that he must have awareness that his craft is rooted in efforts involving the rational pursuit of truth. I don't think one can have this condition while recruiting from among those who choose to be policemen because they believe that they are not suited for a better job. It means recruiting competitively for the most gifted, the most aspiring, and the most dedicated of our young people. Naturally, I do not mean recruiting types who should become clergymen, teachers, or physicians. Instead, I mean recruiting in ways that seek out rather than turn away persons of talent, enterprise, and accomplishment. It is rather obvious where such people must be sought, namely, among the top graduates of our best colleges. I don't intend to imply in any way that I think college prepares for police work, nor that all good people go to college. I am merely suggesting how one would have to play the percentages. Naturally, one still has the problem of ensuring that the cream of the crop will want to join police work. Without attempting to settle this difficult problem with a short answer, it seems to me that it would mean taking a long step in this direction if it were possible to make clear to them, and to the world generally, that the vocation deserves the best effort of the best among us.

In sum, I argue that police research has demonstrated that police work, far from being the kind of low-grade occupation it is thought to be, in fact involves the exercise of judgment and skill in handling problems of great complexity and importance. But in order for police to become fully equal to the tasks of our times, they must install study and research into their mandate. Only in this way can the police hope to advance and retain control of the direction of their efforts.

NOTE

This essay previously appeared in *The Police Yearbook, 1973* (Gaithersburg, Md.: International Association of Chiefs of Police, 1973). It is based on remarks presented at the Annual Conference of the International Association of Chiefs of Police in Salt Lake City, Utah, October, 1972.

9 | *Policing Juveniles*

The Social Context
of Common Practice

WHEN ONE ASKS on what terms police service is made available in society, two significantly distinct answers are possible. The police mandate may be said to derive wholly from codes, statutes, ordinances, or case law. These authorizing norms are taken as determining the scope of substantive responsibility and of proper procedure, and thus also as furnishing all relevant categories for the description, analysis, and critique of observed activities. Or the police mandate may be considered to consist of a readiness to respond to a vast array of recognized service needs. Although it is possible to anticipate the types and volume of such needs and to prepare to deal with them, categories of problems and procedures remain permanently open, and their description, analysis, and critique must emerge from observations of police work.

Neither of the two answers ought to be taken as doing full justice to the question. They are both relatively plausible starting points for further inquiry. Choosing the first option means that inquiry will focus on problems of authorization, and observed facts will be seen and assessed in relationship to it. The second option will give priority to the description and analysis of pressures that arise from exigencies and of practices oriented to them, and matters connected with authorization will be treated as part of the factual circumstances.

In the following I will deal with the policing of juveniles as a need-responsive practice, following the second of the two study options. In particular, I shall attempt to review, and to assess the consequences of, two sets of considerations that frame the ways in which policemen recognize and cope with juvenile problems. Both sets of considerations—one concerning the status of youth in modern society and the other concerning certain routines of police practice generally—tend to be subsumed under ceteris paribus clauses in most modern police studies. I must add that in talking about needs I shall refer solely to actually perceived needs. While questions concerning the desirability of these perceptions are obviously implicit in the discussion, I do not undertake to advance explicit answers to them. I shall weigh *what is* against *what ought to be* only by employing criteria that are internal to the problems under consideration.

THE STATUS OF YOUTH

From Middle Ages to Modern Times

The historical understanding of our times centers heavily on three trends originating in the period between the Renaissance and the Reformation, which constitutes the break between the Middle Ages and the following Modern Age. The first subsumes the complex of events connected with the formation of the nation states. The second consists of the rise of the commercial-industrial system that goes under the name of capitalism. The third encompasses the growth of secular culture with special emphasis on the development of science. There is also a fourth trend with a claim to equivalent social significance. It concerns the evolution of the concept of the family and of the idea of childhood from the seventeenth century on.

Of course, neither childhood nor family were wholly discovered in the seventeenth century. But since that time both have been undergoing profound transformations, which have culminated only in our times. Approximately four hundred years ago, "the family began to hold society at a distance, to push it back beyond a steadily extending zone of private life" (Ariès 1962, 398). The withdrawal of the family from the hustle and bustle of wide open sociability became possible with the development of a relatively closed urban, family household. In this newly constituted home, "the child . . . had won a place beside his parents to which he could not lay claim at a time when it was customary to entrust him to strangers. This return of the children to the home was a great event: It gave the seventeenth-century family the principal characteristic, which distinguished it from the medieval family. The child became an indispensable element of everyday life, and his parents worried about his education, his career, his future" (Ariès, 1962, 403).

It would lead too far afield to go into the details of this momentous revolution, but it seems clear that the encapsulation of child raising in isolated families would have far-reaching consequences for opportunities for interaction among various age groups, and that this would have further impact on the age-grading system and on age-related status in society.

In the European Middle Ages, the "ages of man" were still recognized, but available evidence indicates that these distinctions were maintained and the transitions between them were celebrated only with regard to certain special considerations. Life in its more mundane aspects was a matter for all the people to partake in without regard to age, virtually from the time a person had left the physical dependency associated with early childhood. Children of a rather tender age, in terms of our values, had uninhibited access to participation in adult work and fun, and their manners and morals were not subject to special adult solicitude. In contrast, among ourselves the lives of young people are structured, often well past adolescence, by the prominence given to dealings with either their parents or with close age-mates. Coupled with these prolonged childhood relationships is the strict segregation of young people from adult work and fun while interactions between young people and adults are generally regulated on both sides by a special code of decency and decorum. Where everyday life in the Middle Ages consisted of indiscriminate intermingling of persons densely distributed on an unbroken age continuum, being a young person in the Modern Age, up to the age of eighteen or even later, appears to call for a radically separated form of human existence.

It is important to note that the segregation of family life

from general sociability, and of young people from adults, is strongly class-related. At its outset the trend was reflected only in the lives of a narrow elite. During the Industrial Revolution it permeated the propertied middle classes. The people who made up the peasantry and the urban proletariat of the nineteenth century were still untouched by it and their children were drawn into the vortex of adult misery and pleasure in ways that scandalize contemporary consciousness. Moreover, the classbound culture of the urban ghettos and of certain "backward" parts of the United States does not yet reflect the degree of protectiveness toward the privacy of the family and of the sheltering of youth that has become the dominant social norm of our time. These ideals determine the orientation of the political, educational, and economic institutions toward young people. And the norm hangs over the heads of people who have not spontaneously adopted it, or who have not succeeded in accommodating to it because of the intractable realities of their existence. Compliance with the norm does depend upon the attainment of a certain level of material well-being.

This brief allusion to cultural history would not be complete without mention of circumstances peculiar to the American past. The conditions in the United States were auspicious for the ascendance of a strong and independent nuclear family unit because of the immigrant origin of its people and because the trend was not impeded by the survival of medieval institutional culture and polity. As Tocqueville said, "Whereas the European tries to escape his sorrow at home by troubling society, the American derives from his home that love of order which he carries over into affairs of state" (Tocqueville 1969, 291–92). But the expectation that the family would be able to take care of its own weakened around the turn of the last century with the influx of large numbers of immigrants from non-English-speaking parts of Europe. In response, the child-saving movement came into existence to aid in the Americanization and embourgeoisiement of their offspring. Though this movement issued from philanthropic and charitable impulses, it involved the use of those coercive measures that are now associated with the administration of juvenile justice (Platt 1969).

The American picture thus consists of the interpenetration of (1) the general evolution of the ideals of the family and childhood which have come to be embodied in the standards of middle-class culture (Parsons, 1942, 1943), and (2) a well-established set of mechanisms for externally and forcefully imposing these standards on those segments of society that do not measure up to them (cf. Rainwater and Yancy 1967). In this way American expectations have been tempered by realism. The common attitude seems to have been that the place of children was the parental home and the duty of parents was to turn them into useful citizens, but that in the case of many people, especially people who spoke in foreign tongues or were dark-skinned, something had to be done about their children by their betters. Therefore, although the juvenile problem today is not limited to dealings with these populations, the methods of coping with it are tainted by this background.

The Seamless Dome of Control

There is probably nothing quite so revealing of American attitudes toward children as the nervous amusement caused by W. C. Fields's unabashed assertion of distaste for them. Underlying the response is a deep unease about the immense responsibility each set of parents separately bears for the raising of their offspring. Our feelings about children are confused by an ambivalence that recognizes in them both a source of great joy and a heavy burden, by a doubt whether children betoken a bright future or decadence for our civilization, and by fear of being overtaken by them and sent into premature and undeserved retirement. Unable to face the problem of youth, Americans have mounted an attack of mind-boggling complexity to cope with it. Not only are more parents than ever before well-instructed and considerate in their dealings with offspring, but their strenuous efforts are augmented by the services of an army of professionals, including pediatricians, teachers, child psychologists, recreation specialists, clergymen, authors of children's books, athletic coaches, and many others. While all this makes the burdens of parenthood somewhat easier to bear, the common view is that it is arranged entirely for the benefit of children, with all its costs charged to adults. But it is not too difficult to recalculate the credits and debits of this arrangement by taking a close look at what is being asked of children in return for all the benefits bestowed upon them. They are expected to be good. Let us take a look at what this expectation means in practice. For clarity's sake, I will overdraw certain features of the demands made of young people. Furthermore, I must stress that I shall be talking about the demand-in-effect without necessarily implying that adults mean it that way.

Perhaps the most important and least appreciated norm governing the lives of young people is that they are in every aspect of their presence, demeanor, and appearance *accountable*. Unlike adults, who can hold each other to account only on the basis of certain special entitlements and only to a limited extent, young people must answer fully to their parents. Adults are, mercifully, not methodical in applying the norm. They invoke it most often in the breach but regularly enough to remind young people about its availability, a fact to which young people refer to as "the hassle." Even psychologically sophisticated parents who recognize the child's need for privacy retain the right to limit its scope, determine its occasions, and revoke it peremptorily.

The condition of "watched freedom" for the child binds children and parent alike. Parents are not merely entitled to know everything, they are obliged to find out. The presumption of total parental control colors the meaning of a young person's presence everywhere in society. The question, "Do your parents know where you are?" is never wholly impertinent. Both the assumption of functioning parental control and the suspicion that it may have lasped create a peculiar asymmetry in the dealings between young people and adults. It is difficult to overestimate the advantage any adult has over a young person, an advantage that is often buttressed by the claim that the interest advanced by the adult is social, rather than merely personal. For example, people who put up with a great deal of adult outside interference in their work or any other activity are characteristically free to say, "Beat it, kid!" Because young people are socially incomplete persons, it is possible to deal with them as tractable nuisances. Policing juveniles is not a task created by or for the police; it merely devolves upon the police when juveniles are, or are thought to be, beyond the reach of primary supervisory control.

The seamless dome of control over youth is supported by the adult conceit according to which everything in the life of a young person is in some sense only propaedeutic and devoid of any inherently valuable significance. Since young people cannot be counted on to have a proper appreciation of whatever they are being prepared for, they cannot be trusted to know what to do. This is not, however, a simple matter of lack of foresight or knowledge. It must be remembered that children do not grow up amid those circumstances of human existence over which they will later be expected to exercise mastery. Rather, they are confined to a world apart, one specially constructed for them from nursery to college, whose pedagogic design they are specifically held incompetent to participate in. It is true that the design includes opportunities for choice within it, and young people have succeeded in constructing within the reservation a form of human existence all of their own. Outside observers call it youth culture.

It is generally agreed that this culture regulates certain of the activities young people engage in, certain understandings they have among themselves, and certain modes of expression that have developed spontaneously in their midst and distinguish them from the rest of society (Berger 1971). The most interesting part of the youth culture concept is that it has—compared with similar uses of the term "culture," as in "culture of poverty"—an extraordinarily narrowly defined scope of relevance. In fact, it might be considered more correctly as a distinct form of esthetic appreciation of leisure. As far as adults are concerned, in any case, it carries a charge somewhat akin to that formerly associated with the "culture of slaves"—it is capable of getting out of hand if not watched and of conflicting with the interest of the ruling class, but within its proper bounds it touches only the nonserious aspects of life.

Now, it is a serious matter that young people do what they are told, particularly that they go to school and study faithfully. Even so, it is clear that nothing young people do has the seriousness, necessity, or importance attached to practicing medicine, fighting wars, or making money. Accordingly, any adult interest enjoys a claim of precedence over any youth interest that is nontraversable. That many adults are quite generous and tolerant and that many more seek to avoid confrontations creates more uncertainty than freedom. And so young people find it expedient to resort to guile, concealment, and extortion to get their way, acting on the well-founded assumption that adults do not understand anyway. At the very least, young people face the hazard that any claim of interest they may advance will be assessed by standards extraneous to their own lives. That is, the judgments will reflect either pedagogic considerations and adult conceptions of wholesomeness or the constraints and conveniences of the adult order of society.

The seemingly nonserious nature of the concerns of young age is romantically aggrandized by attributions to youth of innocence and freedom from adult responsibility. The notion of childhood innocence has a long history, dating back to the Sermon on the Mount and continuing into modern advertising. But innocence has its correlate in irresponsibility, and there also exists a long tradition representing the dangerous and amoral character of the child, extending from the myth of Oedipus to Golding's fable, *Lord of the Flies*. Freedom from adult cares, on the other hand, is darkened by the expectation that in return children will at all times live up gratefully to an extraordinarily high standard of decorum. Thus risks are controlled and the trade-off is brought into a just balance, all at once, by requiring young people to be unconditionally nice and surrounding young people with walls of censoriousness. Of course, not only children are supposed to be well mannered, but their manners draw a vastly greater amount of attention than the manners of adults. An adult can be considered a diamond in the rough, or a coarseness of demeanor may be mitigated by the seriousness or pressure of the business at hand. The general unavailability to young people of such dispensations is evident in the dismissal, during the so-called youth revolt of the sixties, of many of their arguments solely on grounds of the offensive manner of presentation. Without ignoring the harm caused by campus revolutionaries, commentators have noted that most of the outrage and many of the reprisals were brought forth mainly by symbolic indecencies. Hence the paradoxical situation: young people can get away with anything, but their breaches of etiquette are wholly unforgivable (Slater 1970, chap. 3).

Because their concerns are not accepted as mattering in the way such concerns matter in the adult world, young people find their transactions with adults permeated with formalism, ritual, and drama rather than with substance—all of which abets evasion, deceit, or provocation. Adult emphasis on etiquette does not stand alone. There is an academicism that pervades formal education, which accepts, say, a young person's espousal of communism as merely preparatory to becoming a good capitalist. By not taking what young people say or do as real coin, adults feel relieved of the obligation to pay attention to it and thereby push the social existence of young persons to the edge of nonexistence. How well this confinement is sealed off! We do not even become aware that young people might want to break out of it. When they do, we are stung by the insult of their intention, and even then the most enlightened adults tend to view the assault as a mere phase in their development (Feuer 1969).

The principal way of judging how well young people are growing up is how well they do in school. But even the rigors of education in our society are interlarded with substantial amounts of recreational activity. Now it may seem difficult to conceive that fun could be visited by troubles. But this is a singularly shortsighted view, however, which could gain acceptance only in a wholly secularized society in which the value of any human activity is determined by its relationship to the paramount interest in "making a living." The inadequacy of the usual negative definition of recreation—merely time away from the stresses of making a living—is easily realized by considering the threat of tragedy lurking in virtually every form of fun. To understand the structured potential for conversion of fun into trouble, to understand the nonadventitious nature of the frequent outbreaks of serious disturbance and violence in connection with dances or athletic events, we must understand play and games as independently serious activities.

In archaic, tribal, and peasant societies all occasions of recreation stood under sacred auspices. Fairs and holidays had the patronage of deities and saints, and were, like everything done in connection with the supernatural, highly structured even when they included orgiastic excesses. As long as the doings were kept within the set limits, they were seen as boding well for those who participated in them; they "recreated" the unity and harmony between man and the powers in the cosmos. Breaches of order, time, and place, on the other hand, caused forebodings of evil. In secular society, the whole penumbra of the supernatural fell away and recreation acquired the primarily psychological significance of character building and tension release (Huizinga 1950; Caillois 1961). Even in its secular form, recreation activity incorporates canons of morality, fair play, and esthetic appreciation. That is why it is considered wholesome. Yet, while proprieties of order, time, and place remain recognizably significant, the absence of ritual sanctions weakens their force. Thus, the momentum of having fun tends to overshoot the boundaries set for it, turning recreation into scandal. Since this is quite common, there are special dispensations for it, as implied in the expressions, "boys will be boys" or "feeling one's oats." There is, however, no assurance that a breach of limits will receive the benefit of dispensation, especially if it conflicts with adult convenience or is seen as having causes beyond the case at hand, such as, for example, "typical" lower-class licentiousness which portends even greater scandal. Things do not need to go that far for reaction to set in, however. Because the boundaries of recreation are ill-defined, there is a tendency to overcontrol it. The absence of patent evidence of strict control worries adults even while fun is still well within accepted limits. It is only a short step from worry to seeing any aggregation of young people having fun as betokening trouble.

Before moving on, I should like to repeat the warning I gave at the beginning of this chapter. It has not been my desire to render a well-rounded picture. Instead, I attempted to present a tendentious sketch of the unintended but inevitable consequences of certain good intentions. Above all, it is important to emphasize that the status of young people is not simply a function of adult pigheadedness. The condition is part of a general social, economic, and political order that entraps the parent no less than the children. Moreover, I have discussed those aspects of the problem which are, in my view, generally neglected but crucially relevant to consideration of police-juvenile relations. These aspects constitute background conditions to which the police are responsive when they deal with young people.

POLICE WORK WITH JUVENILES

For several reasons, we must begin the discussion of policing juveniles with some observations concerning crime and crime control. In the first place, the public and the police share a common conception, that the control of crime is at the center of police work. Regardless of the substantive merit of this presumption, it colors the perceptions and procedures of police officers. Second, a large and increasing proportion of all serious crime reportedly is committed by young people. The demographic distribution of crime suggests that criminality reaches its peak early in life and declines progressively in older age (President's Commission on Law Enforcement and Administration of Justice, 1967). This finding can be disputed, to be sure, because it rests in the statistics of cleared crimes and may merely indicate that young people are less adept at, or less interested in, evading arrest than are their older counterparts. But discounting rates still leaves the absolute numbers intact, and there is no getting around the fact that alarmingly large numbers of young people steal and commit assaults of all degrees of seriousness.

The seriousness of the crime problem notwithstanding, and with all due regard for police concern for it, it is important to note that crime control and policing are not coextensive activities. It has been widely acknowledged that the preponderant part of police work has nothing to do with crime control (Niederhoffer 1967), and that this is especially true of police work involving juveniles (Goldman 1963; Rubinstein 1973). Accordingly, to keep things in their proper place and to assess their actual practical significance, the matter of policing juveniles must be considered in the context of routine police practice, only part of which is concerned with crime control.

One further presumption deserves to be mentioned at the outset. In keeping with the general cultural view of the young as a separate species, the police allow that working with juveniles constitutes a special police activity. Modern departments have, resources permitting, juvenile officers who are presumed to draw on special skills and resources in their work (Kenney and Pursuit 1970). While the institution of this specialty is a very important innovation in police work and has impact on the lives of some young people who run afoul of the law or otherwise come to the attention of the police, it must be remembered that virtually all contacts between young people and the police initially involve members of the uniformed patrol, and most never progress to the point of involving a juvenile officer (Reiss 1971). Aside from dealing with far more cases, patrolmen also deal with a considerably wider range of cases than do juvenile officers. Still more important, the work of the patrol is fully exposed, which makes it difficult for patrolmen not to see what they are supposed to see and not to do what they are supposed to do. In contrast, the juvenile officers' less public situation somewhat protects them from both external popular pressure and internal police constraint; they therefore have much greater control over what they elect to see and do. Hence, the following several characterizations of police work with juveniles refer principally to members of the uniformed patrol, but what will be said applies, mutatis mutandis, to the police as a whole.

The Low Status of Juvenile Work

However broad, varied, and ambiguous a conception of the police mandate patrolmen may have, they assign a low priority to working with troublesome juveniles. Their experience teaches them that the majority of cases in which they are called upon to act are trivial, that most of these cases allow no good solutions, and that even a successful treatment of a case is not considered an accomplishment of note in the hierarchy of police values. The risk of frustration and the absence of credit lead patrolmen to shun assignments involving young people, to get involved as little as possible when they cannot be avoided. Consequently, skill in the handling of juvenile problems is less well developed than skill in other areas of police work, such as the handling of mentally ill persons (Bittner 1967a).

In no other aspect of police work is the inherent irony so poignantly apparent as in the patrolmen's aversion to work with juveniles and its unavoidability. Always pursuing the elusive "big pinch," forever hoping to solve important crimes for which they lack both skill and means, patrolmen unhappily accept its necessity. This circumstance is fundamental for understanding the policing of juveniles.

The crucial reasons that the police are disinclined to work with juveniles are, first, the internal police organization and, second, the personal career interest of patrolmen. No points are gained by careful and considerate handling of a juvenile problem, and there is some risk that attention given to it will be judged excessive in relation to problems deemed more important. Moreover, juvenile problems are more likely than other kinds of police problems to have untoward consequences, about which grievances will be posted with patrolmen's superiors, thus spoiling their performance records. Against this background, patrolmen feel compelled to minimize their involvement and structure it to avoid troubles. And they will have to be guided by these considerations even if they must employ solutions they know to be less than commensurate with the problem at hand. Minimizing involvement includes, indeed favors, resorting to strongly coercive measures without first assaying the feasibility of alternatives, except in cases where violence or arrest might produce protests from politically powerful parents.

The Function of the Police

Three expectations define the specific function of the police in modern society more than anything else. First, it is expected that they will do something about any problem they are called upon to deal with; second, it is expected that they will attack problems wherever and whenever they occur; and, third, it is expected that they will prevail in whatever they undertake and that they will not retreat in the face of opposition. This does not mean that the police cannot occasionally refuse to deal with some matters or that they cannot advance good reasons for such refusals. Nor does it mean that policemen can never refer some problems presented to them to be dealt with by someone else at some other place and time. Nor, finally, does it mean that policemen can never be brought to desist from carrying out their decisions by pleading or suasion. It does mean that when people call the cops they do so with the above expectations, that when policemen are mobilized to act they reckon with these expectations, and that these expectations are uppermost in the minds of the persons against whom policemen proceed.

Police power to impose solutions in the natural habitats where problems emerge is restricted, of course, by the supposition that solutions are provisional and subject to review. Nevertheless, many provisional solutions have lasting consequences, and the police emphasis on prevailing often impedes other avenues of recourse. Further, to make it possible for policemen to prevail in a wide range of circumstances, they are uniquely authorized to use physical force in an amount measured not to exceed the requirement of the situation, but they are given no guidelines to what the proper measure of force might be and are largely without effective external control in this regard (Bittner 1970).

The requirement of active and immediate intervention does not appear to present any special problem in situations involving individual juveniles. Even in relatively serious cases, patrolmen tend to avail themselves of the option of returning a young person to parental control because they consider it the right solution, and because it happens to be the easiest thing to do. Where detention is required, the detained youngster is, where possible, taken to a special facility. But in the majority of juvenile cases, patrolmen do not confront individuals. In matters ranging from riotous and destructive conduct, to noisy and boisterous behavior, to groups of youngsters hanging around some street corner, patrolmen must deal with aggregations of young people in which individual culpability cannot be easily determined. Where alleged deeds cannot be associated with doers and the business at hand cannot be readily defined by what has happened, patrolmen's attention tends to focus on what is taking place during the intervention. The decision of what has to be done takes shape in relationship to how the young people act toward the intervening patrolmen. Within a considerable range, police judgment of substantive misconduct will be mitigated by expressions of diffidence on the part of young people and aggravated by their arrogance (Cicourel 1968; Piliavin and Briar 1964; Sullivan and Siegel 1972).

Three factors complicate this situation. First, though it is true that policemen tend to be sensitive concerning respect, they are not interested in the show of good manners for their own sake, but see in rudeness the portents of more serious opposition. They apparently believe that anyone who would risk being rebellious and unruly in their presence can be counted on to go even further if left alone. Second, the expectation of doing something is joined with the desire to gain tactical advantage over resistance even before it is manifest. Thus, patrolmen tend to take an approach they consider aggressive but which others may call "overreacting." Third, the signs of contrariness detected by patrolmen are often exceedingly subtle. For example, policemen are accustomed to people not returning their gaze and they sometimes take being stared at as a sign of provocation (Rubinstein 1973).

Almost all juvenile disturbances occur in public places. Thus the duty to deal with them at the time and in the place of their occurrence combines with policemen's concern for maintaining dominion over the public space (Rubinstein 1973). Since, in a manner of speaking, patrolmen host the presence of young people on the streets, in the parks, and elsewhere in the city, they not only act whenever and wherever incidents happen, they actually decide at what times and places the presence and manner of youngsters jeopardize their ability to control ongoings in public places.

I have already mentioned that the duty to prevail must be understood in connection with the expectation of doing something. It deserves mention that prevailing and overcoming the resistance of youth are subject to peculiar distortions. In many instances policemen must proceed on no more than an allegation of misconduct. Since they assume that if the allegations were true the young people would not admit it, they cannot credit denials. In accepting the allegation as their working hypothesis, they can only make errors of judgment that weigh against young people. The likelihood of such errors is enhanced by the often nondescript character of citizens' complaints and the possibility that the youngsters who become the target of police intervention are not the ones whose misconduct occasioned the complaint. Even when witnesses are present the onus of the accusation is frequently placed on "the whole bunch of them." It is not surprising, therefore, that young people feel that policemen accuse them of doing things they have not done and force them to submit to arbitrary restrictions and commands (Bouma 1969).

In the light of the foregoing it does seem somewhat off-base to complain that police dealings with youngsters do not conform to the latest insights of child care. In fact, what is commonly expected of the police leaves them with little choice but to make certain that young people cannot have their way in the city, and this is what many encounters with young people are reduced to, whatever the occasion. Moreover, in placing great emphasis on manners, in considering the use of public space to be an occasional privilege rather than a right, and in invoking ambiguous rules about proprieties of time and place to limit juvenile fun arbitrarily, the police are simply doing society's dirty work. Police activity alone clearly does not explain how it is so amazingly easy for an innocent young person to get into trouble, quite aside from (and without disregarding) the many instances in which the trouble is far from innocent. It is probably right, however, to say that standard police procedure contains no safeguards against unwise and improvident action and that the expectation of having to prevail induces the police to employ measures that might be appropriate in some circumstances to cases where they are not.

"Proactive Intervention" in the Field

Several factors shape the policing of juveniles beyond specific incidents of encounter. Because behavior in the public spaces of the city tends to be structured around exigencies of adult life, and because the police jealously guard their right to control public spaces, the mere conspicuous presence of young people can cause concern. They are, as it were, off the reservation and, lacking justification for being abroad, they are subject to preventive regulation. Moreover, juvenile trouble is patterned, partly because of large numbers of youths in certain neighborhoods and partly because school and other facilities cause regular aggregations. Hence, incidents can be anticipated and are watched for with a wary eye. Finally, because young people are unable or unwilling to respond to contradictory expectations—for example, that they accept as normal the filth in the neighborhoods in which they live but refrain from littering in certain other places—the police face the perennial disciplinary task of holding young people to arbitrarily high standards of conduct. Much more could be said to show that for the police the juvenile problem exists long before it takes the shape of an incident. Indeed, it is not too much to say that as far as a working patrolman is concerned kids do not so much make trouble, they are trouble.

The strength of this assumption varies, but it applies in full force to young people from race- or class-disadvantaged segments of the society. These youngsters are made to feel the whole burden of race and class inequality, and in turn they express the pain of this burden in ways that violate the usual boundaries imposed on such expressions. It is superficial to say that policing imposes unwanted and unwonted middle-class standards upon them. It would be more to the point to argue that the struggle between the police and race- and class-disadvantaged youngsters, into whose family life the "new" ideals of family and childhood have not descended, is one of the few overt manifestations of class struggle in our society. Their elders may have settled for what society has in store for them and the "lower-class ways" are part of this lot. But the life of young people is not supposed to reflect the divisions of society because young age is lived in a domain in which the relevance of the factors determining these divisions is suspended. However laudable and absorbing the aspiration might seem to others, the police are attuned to the dark threats emanating from the "dangerous classes" (Silver 1967), which they find contained in the nuisances and harm created by the offspring of people from the lower depths of society.

To forestall lurking danger, to gain advantage over what might happen, patrolmen engage in what is euphemistically called proactive intervention. They consider it especially necessary to engage in this practice in blighted areas of the city simply because the young people there are very often found in places where they are not supposed to be—other places being in short supply. Moreover, they act in this way because there has grown up a stabilized relationship of conflict, or at least contest, between the police and kids who feel that they have nothing to lose in giving the police a hard time because they would not be left alone under any circumstances (Werthman 1967). Some of the efforts of young people to bedevil police attempts at preventive surveillance are undertaken in the spirit of fun and adventure. But often the resentment at being hassled is bitter enough to produce the more serious reactions associated with overly strict controls of all kinds (Taylor and Walton 1971). Thus the proactive approach, far from preventing troubles, is a source of them. Aside from occasionally leading to ugly flareups, the patrolmen's gratuitous poking around in their affairs causes many young people to grow up accepting hostility between cops and kids as a natural fact of life (Brown 1965). Believing that cops always accuse and insult people for no good reason, they search anything a policeman says for the accusation or insult supposedly contained in it. The result comes to be a pervasive atmosphere of distrust on both sides, and a freewheeling search for opportunities to get at each other.

Transfer of Cases to Juvenile Authorities

Though the bulk of police work ends where it begins, in the field with only the patrolmen involved, certain cases do move on to the care of juvenile police officers, juvenile probation officers, and the juvenile court. Many of these cases involve child neglect rather than misconduct. Though such activities are not celebrated as achievements, in these cases, as in most instances where policemen deal with people plainly in need of help, they take care of neglected children with conspicuous consideration and often do much more than is generally expected of public officials. Though such consideration certainly does not characterize every patrolman, the humane and resolute attitude toward the helpless is, broadly speaking, more often found among the police than in any other official agency of society, including the schools, public health, and probably also the religious institutions (Bittner 1967*b;* Cumming, Cumming, and Edell 1965).

The rest of the cases involve formally labeled delinquency. The concept of juvenile delinquency refers to the fact that the state is empowered to proceed coercively against young people (in some states on grounds that would not be sufficient to justify such process vis-à-vis adults) and to remove from the criminal process young people who are alleged to have violated provisions of the penal code. Juvenile delinquency shares one formal feature with adult criminality, namely, that persons to whom the designations are applied are removed from the context in which they have done what they are said to have done into a separate institutional context where the facts are reviewed and judged (Bohannan 1965). Though this process differs in the two instances, in both it is based on specially formulated accounts of facts. This would be too obvious to mention were it not for the circumstance that police decisions concerning both crime and delinquency are based partly on considerations that do not enter into the subsequently reviewed and judged accounts. What these police-specific considerations are is a huge and poorly investigated topic which I must treat here in the briefest possible manner (LaFave 1965).

Though it is of course true that policemen receive accounts of events and treat them with due regard for their schematized significance (that is, knowing that they are never told the whole story), the determination they make about a case also always draws on aspects of context that elude formulation. It is possible to argue proof of the connection between the presence of a young person and of a broken window, but the full force of the directly intuited conclusion cannot be revived in the way it presented itself and appeared to matter in the realities of the occasion. In other words, what informed persons can plainly see they cannot always tell in ways that will make the matter "visible" to others. It is a peculiarity of police work that policemen are not supposed to act on considerations they cannot place into evidence but they are not supposed to disregard them, either.

Whatever formal significance may be attributed to the concepts of crime and delinquency, their actionable sense is always colored by the work situation of those who invoke them. The work situation of the judges and law professors who define the meaning of these concepts is not the work situation of policemen. While it is easy to overstress this point, it is important to remember that to understand how and why policemen charge people with delinquency, one must see the decision to charge in the context of police work rather than court work. While policemen are informed about the subsequent fate of the charges they file and take this information into account, they may treat it as merely one fact in a matrix of facts on which their decisions are predicated. One way of explaining this is to say that the matter mentioned in the charge might have been no more than the proverbial last straw. The decision to arrest someone may have had more to do with routines of police work rather than with accountable merits of the case. Now, I do not mean to argue that the substantive reasons advanced in the charge always lack merit in such cases (although this is often enough true in fact), only that the decision was not actually based on these merits. For example, a fellow may have broken the window and his past may have been suffused with all sorts of trouble making, but the decision to refer him to the juvenile court on that particular occasion may have been wholly dependent on a combination of factors located in *that* particular situation and on the constraints of expectations to which the policeman was responsive, namely the expectations to do something and to prevail in doing it.

Because the policeman deals with matters in vivo while those to whom he refers them deal with them in vitro, and because the practicalities of his work situation influence what he does, there is a communication gap between him and officials of the administration of justice that is possibly unbridgeable. The police are distressed by what they consider excessive permissiveness on the part of juvenile court judges and believe that the judges do not sufficiently appreciate the seriousness of juvenile delinquency. Convinced that they arrest young people only when it is utterly unavoidable, policemen feel betrayed when sanctions are not applied and the arrested youngster is set free even before they return to their beats. They conclude that the courts, more than anything else, must be blamed for the proliferation of lawlessness and for the scorn heaped upon the police for attempting to control it. Whether these views are justified matters little; the bitterness they reflect interferes with the development of a fully reasoned approach to the policing of juveniles in concert with other public agencies (Ferster and Courtless 1969).

CONCLUSION

This chapter was written to draw attention to some facts not generally known or sufficiently appreciated. In a way, its task is accomplished by furnishing grist for the mill. Still, some concluding remarks are in order.

Over a quarter of a century ago there appeared a book on the changing American character that enjoyed some popularity before it became a classic (Riesman, Glazer, and Denney 1950). Its principal thesis was that in our society the ideals and aspirations connected with work, industry, and production have begun to yield precedence to ideals and aspirations connected with leisure, life style, and consumption. Official homiletics still place work before pleasure, but the work of large and increasing numbers of people no longer possesses compelling necessity, seriousness, and importance (Mills 1953; Goodman 1962), while others, especially persons in executive and professional occupations, import added interest into their work through the search for psycho-social adjustment and personal gratification. Coincident with this change, people have ceased to rely on the resources of inner strength of character and the material evidence of achievement to feel justified, and have begun to search instead for approbation and validation from others.

This early pall of doubt about the value of work acquired

new life in recent debates on the future of work (Bureau of Labor Statistics, U.S. Department of Labor 1966). The question now is whether there will be enough work in the future to justify the common assumption that gainful employment of some sort is indispensable to normal human life, and whether, accordingly, work can remain the paramount calling of man. While the debates concerning work are exciting and fruitful, they gave short shrift to one question, perhaps because raising it is considered premature. The question is, How is society without work possible? I do not mean, of course, work as a source of wherewithals, but work as a foundation of order. There have been societies founded on other principles—indeed, it seems that virtually all other societies were founded on other principles—but with us what a person does for a living determines who he is, what he can do, what he is entitled to, with whom he lives and interacts, where he lives, and how he dies. By extension, the occupational system and the social organization of work determine the proper place and weight of all things—such as, whether we wage war, how we distribute wealth, and how we locate our holidays—more than any other factors. With us the division of labor in society is the most general framework for the distribution and maintenance of trust among ourselves (Durkheim 1933). Moreover, it is integral to this order that it contain allocative mechanisms by which those "minorities" of persons who do not work are somehow incorporated into society.

The purpose of this digression is to lay the foundation for a brief animadversion concerning these mechanisms. Our economic system is based on formally free labor, as opposed to systems where the duty to work is politically enforced, as in slavery, villeinage, or serfdom (Polanyi 1957). In return for working, people earn wages and leisure, which they are free to spend as they choose. If for the moment we ignore people of independent means, this means that only people who work earn their freedom to do as they please and be left alone, while people who do not earn income and leisure cannot do as they please and should not be left alone. Their lives are subject to being policed in ways the lives of working people are not. When work is the basis of order and freedom, people who do not work cannot be expected to lead orderly lives and be trusted with freedom.

But young people do not have that option. I suggested earlier that being young means living under continuous supervisory control and having to live up to higher standards of decency and decorum than are required of one's supervisors. Normally, parents and teachers are in charge of young people, but those youths who elude their erratic mastery fall into the laps of the police. And thus the police become the final cutting edge of the society that has liberated young people from the necessity to work gainfully without giving them freedom, and without even considering that it is one thing to say that one must earn what one gets but quite another that what one cannot earn one must do without. Even though the policing of juveniles is rooted in the condition of young age as an unfree status in our society, and not in the existence of policemen, the police do play an important part in the lives of the young.

During the past decade the modern police have received a far greater amount of attention than during the entire century and a half of their previous existence, dating from the institution of the Metropolitan Police for the City of London. As a result of this recent study, it has become clear that police work is not a low-grade occupation in which men do what they are told and may be said to attend to their task well enough as long as they stay honest. Many people now say that police work is a complex, serious, and important public service, perhaps even deserving the dignity of being called a profession. But I believe that such sentiments do not begin to do the case justice. The matter is quite simple: policemen have truly awesome powers and what they do can have irreversible effects on the most vital interests of the people with whom they deal. I would even say that anyone who feels fully adequate for the job is thereby disqualified from it. There exist, after all, virtually no norms of judgment and procedure, no body of technical knowledge, and no standards by which to judge performance, that policemen can refer to in their work. Judges hear motions and pleadings before deciding what to do, physicians discuss their recommendations with their patients, and both may postpone resolution of the problem they confront until they are ready to take steps. But policemen must do what needs to be done alone and may not desist in the face of either argument or opposing force, regardless how critical a problem they face. It seems paradoxical, to say the least, that we do not insist on recruiting policemen from the most gifted, the most aspiring, and the most equipoised among us.

All this may seem to be an outrageous exaggeration to those who know the police as they are. It is one thing to say that policemen ought to be better educated, but it is quite unrealistic to suggest that we recruit from among the cream of youth. Surely those who could be physicians would not want to go into an occupation in which they may have to direct traffic, transport prisoners, type their own reports, work under the control of a sergeant, and so on. But suppose being a physician required doing the work that nurses, secretaries, and orderlies do, and following the orders of hospital administrators, in addition to saving lives? Would the choice still be clear-cut? Somehow, in appraising police work, "realism" drives us to judge policing at the level of its most menial aspects and, in consequence, to entrust it to people who are deemed competent to operate at that level. We then hope that the more serious and important tasks will somehow get done with the least possible amount of trouble.

NOTE

This essay previously appeared in *Pursuing Justice for the Child*, ed. M. K. Rosenheim (Chicago, Ill.: University of Chicago Press, 1976), 69–93.

REFERENCES

Ariès, P. *Centuries of Childhood: A Social History of Family Life.* New York: Alfred A. Knopf, 1962.

Bell, D. "The Bogey of Automation." *New York Review of Books*, 26 August 1965, 23–25.

Berger, B. M. *Looking for America: Essays on Youth, Suburbia, and Other American Obsessions.* Englewood Cliffs, N.J.: Prentice-Hall, 1971.

Bittner, E. "Police Discretion in Emergency Apprehensions of Mentally Ill Persons." *Social Problems* 14 (1967*a*): 278–92.

———. "The Police on Skid-Row: A Study of Peace Keeping." *American Sociological Review* 32 (1967*b*): 699–715.

———. *The Function of the Police in Modern Society.* Washington, D.C.: U.S. Government Printing Office, 1970.

Bohannan, P. "The Differing Realms of the Law." In *The Ethnography of Law,* ed. Laura Nader. Special Publication of *American Anthropologist* 67, no. 6. pt. 2 (1965): 33–42.

Bouma, D. H. *Kids and Cops: A Study in Mutual Hostility.* Grand Rapids, Mich.: Eerdmans, 1969.

Brown, C. *Manchild in the Promised Land.* New York: Macmillan Co., 1965.

Bureau of Labor Statistics, U.S. Department of Labor. *America's Industrial and Occupational Manpower Requirements. 1964–1975.* 6 vols. Prepared for the National Commission on Technology, Automation, and Economic Progress. Washington, D.C.: U.S. Government Printing Office, 1966.

Caillois, R. 1961. *Man, Play, and Games.* Glencoe, Ill.: Free Press, 1961.

Cicourel, A. V. *The Social Organization of Juvenile Justice.* New York: John Wiley & Sons, 1968.

Cumming, E., I. Cumming, and L. Edell. "Policeman as Philosopher, Guide, and Friend." *Social Problems* 12 (1965): 276–86.

Durkheim, E. *The Division of Labor in Society.* New York: Macmillan Co., 1933.

Ferster, E. Z., and T. F. Courtless. "The Beginning of Juvenile Justice, Police Practices, and the Juvenile Offender." *Vanderbilt Law Review* 22 (1969): 567–608.

Feuer, L. A. *The Conflict of Generations.* New York: Basic Books, 1969.

Goldman, N. *The Differential Selection of Juvenile Offenders for Court Appearance.* New York: National Council on Crime and Delinquency, 1963.

Goodman, P. *Growing up Absurd.* New York: Vintage, 1962.

Huizinga, J. *Homo Ludens: A Study of the Play Element in Culture.* New York: Roy, 1950.

Kenney, J. P., and D. G. Pursuit. *Police Work with Juveniles and the Administration of Juvenile Justice.* Springfield, Ill.: Charles C. Thomas Publisher, 1970.

LaFave, W. *Arrest: The Decision to Take a Suspect into Custody.* Boston: Little, Brown & Co., 1965.

Mills, C. W. *White Collar Worker: The American Middle Classes.* New York: Oxford University Press, 1953.

Niederhoffer, A. *Behind the Shield: The Police in Urban Society.* Garden City, N.Y.: Anchor Books, 1967.

Parsons, T. "Age and Sex in the Social Structure of the United States." *American Sociological Review* 7 (1942): 606–16.

———. "The Kinship System of the Contemporary United States." *American Anthropologist* 45 (1943): 22–38.

Piliavin, I., and S. Briar. "Police Encounters with Juveniles." *American Journal of Sociology* 70 (1964): 206–14.

Platt, A. M. *The Child Savers: The Invention of Delinquency.* Chicago: University of Chicago Press, 1969.

Polanyi, K. *The Great Transformation.* Boston: Beacon Press, 1957.

President's Commission on Law Enforcement and Administration of Justice. *Task Force Report: Crime and Its Impact: An Assessment.* Washington, D.C.: U.S. Government Printing Office, 1967.

Rainwater, L., and W. Yancy. *The Moynihan Report and the Politics of Controversy.* Cambridge, Mass.: MIT Press, 1967.

Reiss, A. J. *The Police and the Public.* New Haven: Yale University Press, 1971.

Riesman, D.; N. Glazer, and R. Denney. *The Lonely Crowd: A Study of the Changing American Character.* New Haven: Yale University Press, 1950.

Rubinstein, J. *City Police.* New York: Farrar, Strauss & Giroux, 1973.

Silver, A. "Demand for Order in Civil Society: A Review of Some Themes in the History of Urban Crime, Police, and Riot." In *The Police: Six Sociological Essays,* ed. D. J. Bourdua, 1–24. New York: John Wiley & Sons, 1967.

Slater, P. *The Pursuit of Loneliness: American Culture at the Breaking Point.* Boston: Beacon Press, 1970.

Sullivan, D. and L. J. Siegel. "How Police Use Information to Make Decisions: An Application of Decision Games." *Crime and Delinquency* 18 (1972): 253–63.

Taylor, L. and P. Walton. "Industrial Sabotage: Motives and Meaning." In *Images of Deviance,* ed. S. Cohen, 219–45. Hammondworth, England: Penguin, 1971.

Tocqueville, A. de. *Democracy in America.* Garden City, N.Y.: Anchor Books, 1969.

Werthman, C. B. "The Function of Social Definitions in the Development of Delinquent Careers." In *Task Force Report: Juvenile Delinquency and Youth Crime.* President's Commission on Law Enforcement and Administration of Justice, 155–70. Washington, D.C.: U.S. Government Printing Office, 1967.

10 | *Legality and Workmanship*

Introduction to Control
in the Police Organization

THE ORGANIZATION AND CONTROL of police work is
said to be in very sad shape. We have heard this said for a long
time, we hear it often, and we hear it in various contexts; one
wonders if there are any experts left who have not yet joined
this chorus of condemnation. This unanimity is not matched
by a unanimity of opinion on what, precisely, is the matter with
the prevailing state of affairs. Nor is there very much agreement on what, specifically, ought to be done about it. Of course,
the absence of consensus has not kept resourceful people from
mounting projects of every conceivable kind to change the ways
policing is done. Borne by a sense of urgency, most of these
projects did not produce the expected results. Thus, the complaints survive the efforts to meet them.

George Kelling, in "On the Accomplishments of the Police,"
eloquently expresses the feeling of many people who participated in police affairs during the past fifteen years, namely,
that nothing has changed, that things are done today as they
were done two decades ago, and that the oldest prejudices
about the way policing ought to be done not only survive but
now appear strengthened by, no less than, scientific evidence.
But how much lasting change can one expect to take place in
any fifteen years? And how much of the frustrating perception
of sameness arises out of the sheer proximity of the observer
to the observed? One thing seems fairly clear: two decades ago
the topics of this volume of studies could not even have been
formulated. How naive the recommendations of the President's

Commission on Law Enforcement and Administration of Justice of 1967 seem now! Some of the specifics, to be sure, are as germane today as they were then. But no one thinks any longer that to argue the cogency of going back to an increased use of foot patrols, is enough to bring it about. Thus, one might say that while it is true that the considered or attempted changes have not yet taken a firm hold, the introduction of change has become a realistic and respectable project for all concerned.

It is tempting to think that the time may have come to try to formulate some detailed and systematic conception of all the elements of the control of policing. Building on what has become known about the nature and scope of police work, one could begin to develop a fully integrated method of internal coordination and the appropriate structures of supervisory monitoring. The authors of the essays in the volume edited by M. Punch have not undertaken anything of this sort, even by implications. Instead, they elaborate on various specific aspects of potentially stable, practically feasible, and rationally purposeful forms of police organization and control. In some of the essays the focus is on matters that impede stability, feasibility, and rationality; in others, it is on structures that do or could enhance them. In either case, the studies are grist for the mills of some hardheaded managerial thinking and planning of the sort the editor of the volume urges. Such thinking, it must be emphasized, is guided by the permanent consideration of the actual realities of police work, on the one hand, and by a willingness to draw on the resources of comparative organizational analysis, on the other. But while the work offered here is always specific, concrete, and practical, its reading suggests a possible conceptual systematization of control in policing, a tentative version of which might possibly involve the following.

Police work, like many other activities that comprise the execution of a public trust and that do not have an easily identifiable and tangible output, is troubled by two relatively distinct adequacy problems, which call for two correspondingly distinct control mechanisms. The first, which might be called the problem of *legality*, concerns compliance with explicitly formulated schemes of regulation. While there is no general principle for excluding anything from explicit regulation, experience indicates that some aspects of police work lend themselves more readily to such regulations than others, while some may be wholly incapable of being explicitly regulated. The second problem, which might be called the problem of *workmanship,* involves the maintenance of minimally acceptable levels of knowledgeable, skilled, and judicious performance. The criterion of workmanship, in the sense intended here, always allows—indeed, calls for—reference to standards of excellence that cannot be fully formulated in advance of the occasions of use. Nevertheless, in every known sphere of vocational competence people assess work critically by the use of such standards. To be sure, elements of routine do enter workmanship, and they can be made more or less explicit; but at its core workmanship consists of the ability to call upon resources of knowledge, skill, and judgment to meet and master the unexpected within one's sphere of competence.

One should consider, with some justification, that the criterion of legality specifies the level of adequacy people are entitled to expect because the body of governing regulations contains what has been spelled out, in so many words, as the terms on which the public employs its public servants, which are also the terms on which the servants agreed to serve. The criterion of workmanship would, then, specify a level of adequacy one might possibly hope for, but solely as a product of the servants' dedication and loyalty, so to speak, over and above what was paid for. But this is true only for functions that can be limited, in all their essential aspects, to following instructions. While such functions no doubt exist, policing is most assuredly not one of them. Not only are many aspects of police work not explicitly regulated, but it is clear that competent officers are, at times, expected to act contrary to formulated regulation on the basis of what is colloquially referred to as "knowing better," and what, in the terms proposed here would be regarded as considerations of workmanship. Thus, while it is true that the criterion of workmanship represents a higher vocational aspiration than the criterion of legality, the real significance of the distinction proposed here is missed if the two criteria are treated as merely two points on the same continuum of relative adequacy of performance.

The control mechanisms that correspond to the legal and workmanship criteria of adequacy are, respectively, *regulatory supervision* and *accountability*. The former constrains action in advance or at the time of occurrence. The constraint is produced by the presence and activity of personnel specifically deputized to examine compliance with rules of procedure, schedules of performance, tables of organization, schemes for the allocation of facilities and resources, and invoke and apply sanctions that are also specified explicitly. The latter consists of a state in which accountable persons must accept the scrutiny and critique of authorized others, largely with regard to actions that have already taken place. Two kinds of persons are authorized to conduct audits of workmanship. The first derives the entitlement to judge from working under the rule of the very same criterion of workmanship they apply; that is, police officers are accountable to police officers. The second kind of person derives the entitlement to judge from being the one on whose behalf the work is done, that is, the community or its representatives. Since the police, like all organs of government, are comprehensively responsible to the community, the point made here is that the police are accountable to the community for meeting even those standards of adequate workmanship that cannot be formulated in advance, and explicitly.

In a formal sense, regulatory supervision and accountability stand to one another in a reciprocal relation. The more complete and the more effective regulatory supervision is or can be made to be, the less room there is for accountability; in fact, the less need there is for accountability. Under conditions of complete control through regulatory supervision, that which is not supposed to happen cannot happen, and that which is supposed to happen cannot not happen. This state, of course, describes faultless stagnation and the reduction of the so controlled activity to mechanical repetition of fixed routines. Under ordinary conditions adequacy control involves various combinations of the two mechanisms. In connection with this it must be mentioned that neither regulatory supervision nor accountability can ever be maintained by the mere measuring of performance against norms of conduct. This is quite obvious for the mechanism of accountability, but it is also true for regulatory supervision. That is, even the auditing of compliance with criteria of legality of conduct, insofar as it is itself a form of policing, contains its own standards of workmanship. Indeed, it can be shown that strictly nondeviating enforcement of legality inevitably leads to the same kinds of mischief as the strictly nondeviating compliance with any norm of conduct. It is, after all, well known that such strict compliance is an extraordinarily effective form of sabotage.

When one considers the present, much lamented state of control of police work with the aid of the proposed conceptualizations, one is struck by the apparently prevailing tendency to administer control relative to adequacy problems of legality at the expense of any interest at all in adequacy problems of workmanship. That is, in police departments, control, insofar as it is exercised at all, is exercised in the form of regulatory supervision. Accountability, in the sense proposed here, tends to lack legitimacy; the prevailing inclination is to treat the auditing of skill and judgment as "Monday morning quarterbacking."

The prevalence of regulatory supervision, that is, control that merely measures performance against formulated norms of conduct, can only produce judgment that the assessed person did nothing wrong. Insofar as this is the case, an incompetent, ineffective, and injudicious officer could remain in good standing in his department provided it cannot be shown by any accepted method of proof that he has violated some expressly formulated norm of conduct. This comes very close to saying that an officer who shows up for work, does what he is told to do and no more, and stays out of trouble meets the criterion of adequacy demanded of him. Of course, this could not be the case and indeed is not the case, but not thanks to the existence of any stable forms of adequacy control that would ensure it. That is, expectations of workmanship are not entirely extinguished, but neither are they encouraged, or even permitted, to emerge as independently significant criteria of adequacy control.

The overwhelming preference for regulatory supervision in

policing does not reflect simple managerial incompetence that could be remedied through executive training or some simple reorganization of control procedures; instead, it is a natural and unavoidable consequence of some deeply ingrained assumptions about the nature of police work that are shared by the overwhelming majority of people inside and outside the police establishment. The assumption is that police work, especially the work of the uniformed patrol, is a low-grade occupation and that not much can be expected of the persons engaged in it.

No amount of ceremonial oratory about the virtues, valor, and dedication of "our men in blue" can negate, conceal, or even diminish the significance of what is plainly visible in the practices of police departments. Even though it is known that officers often confront problems of great complexity, importance, and seriousness, the occupation of policing is typified around the simpler and more menial tasks that are also associated with it.

Teachers are taught how to educate, clerics how to minister to spiritual needs, social workers how to assist troubled people. All of them are expected to use the learned principles, to exercise judgment in putting them to use, and to gain further skills through practice. Police officers, however, are trained to follow instructions, and this is done even though it is known that they will be required to do things for which no instructions exist. But these uninstructed activities are held in such contempt that no preparation for engaging in them is thought necessary. The argument that no one knows how to prepare officers for activities for which no regulations exist is specious, for no one actually knows how to prepare people for teaching, the ministry, or social work either, except in such aspects of it as could be quite easily developed for policing, too. Teachers, clerics, and social workers are prepared for what are regarded as complex, important and serious tasks, making high demands on their knowledge, skill, and judgment. The opposite assumption is commonly made about persons who go into policing.

Consider what happens when a police officer, by using his firearm, kills or injures someone. Almost invariably inquests are held to determine if the involved officer is criminally or civilly liable for the act. If it is established that he is not liable, the question of the competence of the officer is regarded as established. Only very rarely, and then usually only in connection with special programs, are such actions reviewed for the purpose of determining if recourse to deadly force was unavoidable and necessary on terms of technical standards of workmanship. What is true of deadly force, an especially stressful and difficult problem, is also true of the use of physical force generally. Inquiries undertaken as the result of complaints about allegedly undue use of force are usually directed to determining if the accused officer transgressed against some rule, and ordinarily questions are not asked if he acted skillfully and judiciously prior to the moment when recourse to force became unavoidable. One cannot praise and reward something if one cannot condemn the opposite of it. To do this, however, it is first necessary to move away from the notion that policing consists of sending whoever happens to be available to do whatever they can as quickly as possible about a problem the police are usually summoned to deal with, and it is necessary to move in the direction of recognizing that dealing with an insolent and unruly youngster, resolving a potentially deadly household dispute, talking a kidnapper into giving up his hostage, arresting a mugger, etc., are in their own way as demanding activities as teaching a ninth grader algebra, dealing with a religious penitent, or helping a distraught widow. Each of these activities involves the use of knowledge, skill, and judgment; in short, they involve workmanship. Their performance cannot be determined by simple norm, but their greater or lesser adequacy can nevertheless be analyzed and judged from case to case. To put it quite bluntly, it is not likely that police work generally, and the work of individual officers, will be appreciated at its actual value—that is, as a service capable of being complex, important, and serious—until we begin to give a damn whether it is done well.

Admittedly, the criterion of workmanship and the state of accountability with respect to it are not entirely absent in the police. Ironically, they matter the most in connection with promotions to supervisory positions. That is, the adequacy of one's knowledge, skill, and judgment—that is, the adequacy of workmanship—is taken seriously when one's removal from actual police work is under consideration. Here, if it can be shown that one's workmanship in policing is not adequately high, one is returned to doing it, but if it can be shown that it is, then one is given other assignments. This does not mean, of course, that standards of workmanship are not respected at all in police work. In fact, there is little doubt that individual officers possess and exercise a high level of skill and that they respect evidence of skill in the work of fellow officers. What is lacking is a deliberate, systematically organized effort to develop and transmit workmanship, a resolute insistence that workmanship is a standard occupational expectation, and the willingness to examine performances of officers for workmanship with the understanding that minimal levels of it are a condition of employment.

It is quite clear that criteria of workmanship and procedures for examining it must be developed from within policing. The purely technical aspects of workmanship in policing can only acquire formulation and development from the practitioners of the craft themselves. But, as is well known, policing cannot be reduced to the mere exercise of a technical craft; it is, in the first place, a public trust. Therefore, the audit of workmanship must ultimately be public. The central point here is that the police are publicly accountable not merely to the extent of not being wrong but, beyond that, for being right. Naturally, the public is entitled to assurances that officers will not transgress against any explicit regulations in doing their work, but it is also entitled to assurances that they will act with the degree of prudence, foresight, and technical acumen that distinguishes them from laypersons.

One note of caution deserves mention. Public accountability for workmanship is important because in the case of the police, a high level of technical efficiency has obvious political implications. While it matters that an officer act in an informed and skilled manner in achieving desired ends, neither the choice of the information nor of the skill are matters of moral and political indifference.

It is of some interest to note that of the two adequacy problems we have identified, the one connected with the criterion of workmanship deserves closer public scrutiny than the one connected with the criterion of legality. It is of interest because even while we seek to create better police services, we must be mindful of the fact that the police organization can be the more dangerous the better it is. It is in some ways sad and reassuring that we are a long way from having to fear the kind of police we would like to have. In North America and in western Europe the stirrings of the past two decades have brought about the realization of the need for change in policing, and they have set some change into motion. While research on the topic clearly indicates how much remains to be done, outsiders might be surprised by the richness of topics of inquiry in what at first glance must seem to be a rather narrow area of concern.

NOTE

This essay previously appeared in *Control in the Police Organization,* ed. M. Punch (Cambridge, Mass.: MIT Press, 1983), 1–11.

11 | *The Rise and Fall of the Thin Blue Line*

"THERE IS NO DENYING," wrote James Bryce in 1888, "that the government of cities is the one most conspicuous failure of the United States." The condemnation is not wholly undeserved, but it is vastly overstated. Surely, city government did not deserve being singled out as the *one* most conspicuous failure. The federal and state governments were scarcely in much better shape at the time; in any event, they must bear part of the blame for the state of the cities. More important, however, what the opprobrium aims at is not so much failure as it is scandal. The city governments that somehow managed to superintend the absorption of a half million immigrants annually into an already overcrowded space, and that somehow managed to coordinate the creation and proliferation of urban amenities on a vast scale, could not be indicted simply for failure. What rankled Bryce, and those Americans who shared his views, was the political entrepreneurship of ethnic parvenus who had seized firm hold of the administration of urban services in the United States in the last quarter of the nineteenth century. These leaders of urban tribal politics, the ward bosses, lacked the hereditary breeding and entitlements regarded as prerequisite for positions of civic prominence. Worse yet, these notorious bosses distributed paid employment in public service in return for personal loyalty, which enabled them "to turn out the vote" at the high holidays on the liturgical calendar of democratic politics. And worst of all, these notorious bosses collected heavy tribute from merchants of veniality for the license to operate in open but orderly transgression against the law. To be sure, the philanthropic wing of the Progressive movement was also dismayed by the fact that the tired, poor, and huddled masses remained tired, poor, and huddled after they passed through the gates of Ellis Island. But it is unimaginable that any thoughtful person could have been convinced that the abject misery of the urban proletariat was significantly determined by urban politics as such. That misery was, of course, the central fact of city life of the time, but no one thought that government had any responsibilities in this regard and, therefore, it could hardly be said that it failed.

Still, the graft-ridden urban politics of the two decades before and the two decades after the turn of the twentieth century are commonly regarded as the epitome of corruption in the public sphere, and are the most eagerly confessed national sin, of Americans. Only in the most recent past have American historians begun to teach us that the conventional black-and-white portrayals of these years do not contain the whole truth of the matter. But the new understanding does not make national heroes out of Boss Tweed and his cohorts. Instead, it simply stands apart from, instead of being a part of, the moral crusades and of the rhetoric of indignation directed against them. The moral and political judgment contained in older tirades may well be vindicated, but now on grounds of reasoned scrutiny rather than felt passion.

Of all the institutions of city government in late nineteenth-century America, none was as unanimously denounced as the urban police. According to every available account, they were, in every aspect of their existence, an unmixed, unmitigated, and unpardonable scandal. Robert Fogelson's book on the history of police reform in the United States—somewhat misleadingly entitled *Big-City Police*— begins at "the turn of the century, [when] many Americans were no longer willing to put up with the customary policies and practices of the big-city police" (10). Fogelson is generous to the point of redundancy in describing the policies and practices of the police Americans decided to repudiate. Indeed, he leaves no doubt that even if only a fraction of the alleged facts of misconduct was true, it would have been sufficient to put an end to the whole misbegotten enterprise. But it should be borne in mind that the facts brought before us are drawn almost entirely from the records of hearings, inquiries, inquisitions, and surveys mounted for the purpose of exposing police misdeeds and from journalistic exposés of obviously muckraking intent. The testimony comes from witnesses who had to be "coaxed, prodded, and sometimes bullied" to tell their shocking tales of police brutality, corruption, and sloth. This should come as no surprise; testifying against the police has always been, and will forever remain, a hazardous business. It is quite possible that the accusations and the evidence adduced to support them are not only true but, in fact, the whole truth; but note must be taken of the absence of any brief for the defense. In fairness to Fogelson it should be said that no defense of the nineteenth-century urban police exists in the literature, nor does the literature contain any hints of where one might find one or of how one would go about putting one together. The absence of a defense is not troublesome just because it leaves a lingering doubt about the validity of the judgment. More important, the merely accusatory character of the account raises questions about the descriptive adequacy of what we are told. It may well be entirely correct to say that the policemen of the turn of the century were, as a rule, corrupt and brutal minions of city bosses. But this does not tell us very much about the routine activities of policemen during ordinary tours of duty, and about other functions of the institution as a whole. Of course, one can argue that the service the police performed for the machine was the raison d'être of the institution and that every other good or harm policemen caused was merely an incidental by-product of their existence. But this argument would surely presume what it purports to explain.

As I understand it, Fogelson sees the conditions that became the target of Progressive reform in the following terms. During the nineteenth century the urban patriciate—which controlled the churches, the city-wide civic associations, the institutions of finance, commerce, industry, and higher education—permitted the control of the rapidly growing city services to slip into the hands of bosses of decentralized ward organizations. The political machine that integrated these elements was the real government of the city of which city hall was merely an outward expression. In the manner of traditional rulers, the bosses did not keep their private and the public fiscs separate, and their revenue consisted of nonlegal taxes, tolls, and fines collectively known as graft. The rule was based largely on the support of communities of recent and propertyless immigrants, and it was mobilized by serving the needs of the people in ways that marked the service as personal favors. The most important favor a ward boss had to confer was a job on the city payroll, especially if it contained the promise of upward social mobility. Of those jobs, jobs on the police force were the most cherished. The policeman knew that he owed his job to the boss and he knew also that he could keep it only exactly as long as he did what he was told. In fact, the policing he felt entrusted with was policing according to the rule of the ward boss. From the point of view of the bosses, in turn, it was a matter of premier importance that they have a police force that could be trusted to keep the cutting edge of their rule sharp and close to the vital interests of the ruled.

The reformers, of whom the Reverend Charles Henry Parkhurst of New York was a leading example, liked no part of this arrangement, but what offended them most deeply—if what they said can be trusted—was that the police let whoring, boozing, and gambling go unchecked in the city. Fogelson makes a good deal of the fact that the reformers sought to impose middle class standards of conduct on people of lower class origins. The idea that the poor are somehow more favorably disposed to sin and mischief than the well-to-do, and that it is unjust to deny them access to it, no longer seems as plausible as it used to, if only because we have learned that when the veil of privacy is lifted, the well-to-do match the poor in any contest involving the breaking of sumptuary laws. Hence, if the matter of life-style is to be brought up at all it ought to be stated as involving the hypocritical imposition of constraints upon the lower classes which the upper classes themselves consistently failed to respect. Fogelson knows and makes quite clear that the moral crusades were above all symbolic expressions of a power struggle between the interests of the teeming masses of recent immigrants who fought to realize *their* dream of liberty and well-being and an older society that regarded the country as belonging to them. The older society was, however, anything but united, and the only line along which its varied parts could form a common front vis-à-vis the Irish, Italian, and Slavic *Völkerwanderung* was the vulgarization of the Protestant ethic that expressed itself in the militant prudery of temperance movements of all sorts.

The politicization of sex, alcohol, and gambling lent importance to the urban police in the United States it would probably not have gained otherwise. Surrounded by a thicket of legal prohibitions and regulations, alcohol, and other sources of illicit pleasure, became a way to wealth and power, and in the regulations of these opportunities the police played a decisive role. The opponents of the nefarious rule of the urban machines knew that they had to break the triangle involving the ward bosses, the police precinct captains, and the purveyors of vice. Police reform set into motion in the last decade of the nineteenth century by the Lexow Committee in New York, and similar bodies elsewhere, was an element of this strategy.

It is the very great merit of Fogelson's account of changes of police organization and practice in the past eighty-five years in the cities of the United States that it makes us see them in relationship to the political struggles from which they issued and that it shows that though changes were always advocated as simple improvements in service, not all segments of American society were affected in the same way by them. "These changes," writes Fogelson, "had an impact on more than just the quality of law enforcement and criminal justice in urban America. For the big-city police have always done more than just enforce the law, keep the peace, and serve the public. They have also decided, or at least helped to decide, which laws to enforce, whose peace to keep, and which public to serve" (12).

Police reform, as depicted in *Big-City Police*, was set into motion in the 1890s, progressed in two distinct phases of approximately equal length, and came to a standstill at about 1970. The first phase was the product of campaigns fielded by commercial, civic, and religious groups, which generally represented the outlook and the interests of upper- and middle-class people of native stock. Fogelson is very impressed by these reformers, characterizing their "diagnosis [as] an impressive political achievement," and referring to their "prescription [as] a formidable ideological accomplishment" (53, 61). Well, perhaps their grasp of the situation was shrewd and their plan of action clever. But the ends they intended were reached in ways they could not have anticipated, through developments they did not control, and with results they would have found surprising, to say the least. When judged in terms of their own formulated intentions and plans, the reformers rate barely a passing mark. Their idea of wresting the control of the police from ward bosses by eliminating precinct autonomy and by urging a centralized administration according to a military conception of operation was naive. Indeed, one gains the impression that the choice of the military model of operation by the reformers was based less on analysis than on a figure of speech. If the police were engaged in a "war against crime" then, by all means, let them be soldiers! Moreover, the reformers speculated that since the American military establishment was not responsive to political influences, militarizing the police would achieve the same effect, disregarding the easily observable fact that there is nothing inherently apolitical about the military. To be sure, some measure of centralization was achieved through the creation of specialized squads which operated from headquarters and whose existence strengthened the power of chiefs. But these new forms were superimposed upon the inherited distribution of police work in precincts over which the central administration often had little control even as late as in the 1930s. Moreover, as an unbroken series of investigations of police in all major cities revealed (of which the Wickersham Commission investigation during the Hoover administration is the best known example), the overall quality of the urban police service in the United States was not significantly better in 1930 than in 1890. And even after the political machines had lost some of their clout and dominance over the police, the personnel of most departments continued to be drawn primarily from those ethnic groups whom the machines in the past both represented and exploited. These men felt unfairly attacked by the reformers and opposed virtually every change—now, however, on their own behalf, and over time as one of the most formidable public service pressure groups.

Fogelson believes that the main impact of the first phase of reform is not to be sought in practical accomplishment but in the formulation of three basic "assumptions" about policing, which became the articles of faith of subsequent reform efforts. These assumptions were: first, that the purpose of urban government should be to supply the best possible service for the lowest possible cost; second, that the control over urban services should be vested in central administrative offices; and third, that the police should be committed unreservedly to wiping out vice in urban America. Strange as it may seem, Fogelson presents a good deal of evidence showing that it was not until well after World War I that these values were openly, albeit often hypocritically, espoused by police officials. Thus it would appear, though Fogelson does not advance this view, that the main difference between the first and the second phase of reform was in the identity of the reformers rather than in direction or doctrine. The first generation consisted of civic leaders from outside the police, the second consisted almost entirely of members of the law enforcement community. Fogelson argues, however, that the difference was more than merely a matter of affiliation. He believes that the second generation of reformers attempted to align the police in accordance with a professional model of practice, in place of the military model advocated by their predecessors. By this he means that the reform-oriented police officials concentrated on "three distinct yet closely related recommendations, which incorporated and extended the Progressive prescription for police reform" (159). They struggled toward greater organizational centralization and streamlining, they fought for improvements in staffing quality, and they urged the elimination of all responsibilities that were not demonstrably connected with policing, which they regarded as centering around crime control.

It can be shown, however, that the so-called professional model, as it was advocated in the 1950s by officials like William Parker of Los Angeles, Stanley Schrotel of Cincinnati, Herbert Jenkins of Atlanta, and Thomas Cahill of San Francisco, was probably not intended in any carefully considered sense. Indeed, it is most likely that what these men had in mind when speaking about the professional police officer was someone akin to the professional soldier, that is, someone who was serious about a certain activity rather than being an amateur or merely someone's flunky. Being a professional in this sense of the term also meant a strong personal commitment to the vocation, it meant personal honesty and political neutrality, and it also meant the command of certain information and skill. But the police reformers would not have accepted the view that the patrolman on the beat was invested with freedom of discretion in matters of importance. Quite the contrary, what they sought to achieve, above everything else, was a tight organizational structure that was run with the aid of an enormously detailed body of internal regulation. Their subordinates were supposed to do what the rules said, and even when they were called upon to use judgment, it was mainly to stay out of trouble. The claim to autonomy that professionalization implied was made primarily for the institution of policing, and only secondarily, and then only in a severely limited sense, for its functionaries. Certainly, those reformers emphasized training, and they stressed the need for that type of literacy and general competence civil service exams are good in identifying. But what is referred to as training involves mainly the teaching and learning of regulations, and the civil service exams test for knowledge and aptitudes that bear no discernible relationship to police work. Admittedly the picture is not quite so simple and uniform. O. W. Wilson, the leading police official of the period, probably had a more complex conception of the craft of policing than most of his contemporaries, but even he too placed extraordinarily heavy stress on strong organization.

In my view Fogelson misjudges the second generation of reformers when he portrays them as thinking of the work of the patrolman as being serious, important, and complex enough to deserve the prestigious designation of a profession, because he extends their period of influence to the present. The men I have identified above dominated the police establishment in the United States until about the middle 1960s. They deserve the credit for purging the urban police of the worst excesses of corruption, for freeing the police from dependence on partisan petty politics, for creating the model of the policeman who bravely and obediently followed orders, and for producing a governmental organization that functioned in a more or less modern fashion. Whether they have increased the crime control capacity of the police is quite uncertain. Our crime statistics then and now are so imprecise as to make the answer to this question anybody's guess. But in every other respect they seemed to have fulfilled the aspiration of the Progressive reformers of the turn of the century reasonably well. And therein is contained a peculiar irony, a situation which Fogelson illuminates deftly. The ward bosses have disappeared; but the sons and the grandsons of the men the bosses installed in the police still dominate it. They dominate the police not thanks to political pressure, but despite it. They no longer defend the line that men deserve to be appointed to the police because they are Irish but rather that the Irish deserve appointments because they "make the best cops in the world," to paraphrase a former police chief from Kansas City. That is, the criteria are objective, they happen to work out in such a way that the most heavily policed segments of the population of our cities, the people of color, are dramatically underrepresented in the police. The Yankee aimed at the Irishman, but the black man caught the blow.

Fogelson believes this description fits the situation as it exists today, and that reform has come to a standstill. He may be right in thinking that progress has come to an end. But I believe he is wrong in letting the period that began during the depression run into the present. The era identified with the names of Wilson, Parker, Schrotel, and so forth, came to an end a dozen or so years ago. In fact, it overdramatizes things only very slightly to say that this period came to an end at the hundredth anniversary of the ratification of the Thirteenth Amendment to the U.S. Constitution, in the heat of the Watts uprising. Fogelson knows about the developments of the past ten years but he downplays their significance, and in drawing no distinction between the ideas and work of men like Patrick Murphy, Clarence Kelly, Charles Gain, and the just-mentioned chiefs of the preceding period, he denies recognition to the inroads that have been made, or have been accepted, by the former in the legacy left by the latter. This is a great pity, because it mars the conclusion of a book of distinction which up to its conclusion is precise in characterization and unfailing in interpretation.

I cannot conclude without mentioning that the book is not an account of the history of the big-city police—as the title is apt to suggest. It is a book about what was wrong with that police and what was done to correct it. Within its own sphere, however, the work is both pathbreaking and definitive (save for the exception I just noted).

NOTE

This review of Robert M. Fogelson's *Big-City Police* (Harvard University Press, 1977) previously appeared in *Reviews in American History* 6, no. 3 (September 1978): 421–28.

12 | *The Broken Badge*

Reuss-Ianni and the Culture of Policing

ELIZABETH REUSS-IANNI advances the thesis that there has come into being in the American police, during the past fifteen years or so, a troublesome and pervasive schism between the line personnel and administrative staff, or between street cops and management cops, as she refers to them. The book she has written about this is an important and interesting addition to the police literature, even though the existence of the schism has been in various ways intuited, assumed, or suspected by many students of the police. The information on which the book is based was collected by Reuss-Ianni and Francis Ianni during an eighteen-month period of intensive field work in the late 1970s, in two precincts of the New York Police Department. The fact that all the field work was done by two researchers whose superb qualifications are firmly established compensates for what will more than likely be singled out as methodological shortcomings of the project. Because these apparent shortcomings could trouble many readers, it might be useful to discuss them in advance of everything else and assign them the significance to which they are entitled in the evaluation of the overall merits of the work.

It does not take a very fastidious critic to note that in this book the posited existence of the schism is documented primarily by observations focused on a single precinct in what most people would agree is the most troubled part (South Bronx) of a city that is quite unusual itself. Information obtained in a second precinct (Manhattan) involved far less intensive scrutiny; though the evidence from the second precinct generally supports the conclusion formed during the study of the first, the latter case is not quite as persuasive as the former. A friendly critic might be justified in saying that the evidence is sufficient to support the claim that the New York Police Department has an organizational problem of an urgent and serious nature, a problem that might possibly also exist elsewhere. An unfriendly critic could be excused for suggesting that the materials in the book document the existence of a small group of disgruntled cops (somewhere on the order of 1 percent of the total force), who have drawn one of the least desirable assignments in the city, probably because they are regarded as not deserving a better one. Moreover, both critics would probably say that the schism posited is described merely as it appears from one side, namely, the position of the street cops. Apart from occasional and passing allusions, the picture (if there is a picture) seen from the perspective of management cops is left largely unstated.

Certainly people who think of social research in simple terms, terms similar to those which inform the judgment of people who think of art as involving painting by numbers, might find these methodological problems insurmountable, and they might be puzzled why Reuss-Ianni, who not only was aware of them but even made a point of drawing readers' attention to them, did not do anything about them. Two appendixes contain remarks dealing with the methodological outlook and research procedures employed in the study. In my judgment this discussion is not quite as clear as it could have been, although it will no doubt satisfy those readers who are already committed to the superiority of the ethnographic approach. What should have been said, in my judgment, is that the study is not empirical in the ordinary sense of the term, even though it quite plainly involved careful observation. Instead, data collection and interpretive reasoning are intertwined, in a manner reminiscent of what Glaser and Strauss[1] referred to as the discovery of grounded theory. In such studies, interpretation always plays a more important— certainly a more prominent—role than in studies in which precisely formulated hypotheses are strictly tested in a technically fixed procedure. In this kind of research the phenomenon whose existence is asserted is described with as much detailed specificity as possible. But, though the characterizations refer only to conditions at a particular site, there is the assumption that the findings are of more than local interest. Thus, the descriptions of what is found in one precinct in the South Bronx, and the commentary about them, become grist for the mills of thought, possibly about an organizational problem that is pervasive even though it may appear in various guises in different sites. Indeed, Reuss-Ianni's account discourages thoughtful students from assuming that the same phenomenon could be found in the same form in a different setting and leads them to expect that it would exist elsewhere in forms attuned to the particularities of its setting.

What are the "essential" features of the schism between street cops and management cops? Reuss-Ianni stresses that the break is between two "cultures." Thus, while the rift has organizational aspects, and certainly has organizational implications of the greatest gravity, its primary manifestations are found in conflicting belief systems, in the opposition of value commitment, and in an intraorganizational ideological struggle between two factions whose interests are contradictory. The split is manifest in tangible ways—principally in the form of communication difficulties and organizational breakdowns—but even they matter more through the significance attributed to them by staff than through their own direct impact. Thus, for example, the lack of coordination that was so prominent in the police response during the citywide electrical blackout in July 1977 was seen by the street cops less as an instance of merely inadequate planning than as evidence that management had an agenda of its own that conflicted with what the street cops considered necessary action. In fact, the street cops viewed with suspicion help from parts of the system not directly affected by looting, fearful that those outsiders would report actions that did not comply with consideration of legality but that were viewed as standard and effective procedure.

Reuss-Ianni's own characterization of the schism emerges in the context of four critical incidents that took place during the period of her field work. The reader who is one step removed from those realities could perceive the schism somewhat more abstractly as consisting of the following elements.

1. There is a widespread belief among street cops in a past, golden age of policing during which the department was one

happy family, united in a common cause, permeated by unquestioned trust and unbreakable loyalty, from top to bottom. This state is said to have deteriorated progressively from
the middle 1960s on to its present nadir. The nostalgia is, of
course, misplaced. In American police departments heavy stress
was always placed in maintaining separation between the ranks,
and the hierarchy was always harshly punitive in matters of internal discipline. Trust, insofar as it existed, existed where it
exists now, predominantly among immediate coworkers. But the
institution was hermetically sealed and nonresponsive to outside
influence, with the result that officers had nothing to fear from
"civilians." That is, one thing a street cop could always trust the
management cops to do was to protect him against accusations
of malfeasance, although even that was probably not nearly as
safe an assumption as it is now said to have been. Present management is probably less repressive than its predecessors, and it
is probably more open to communication across ranks than it
was earlier. But it has opened somewhat to outside pressure and
is far more responsive to the demands of those segments of the
community who in the past received no recognition at all. This
is perceived as a breach of a romanticized ideal of internal coherence.

2. The relatively greater openness and responsiveness of
present police forces came into being during the struggles for
greater social, political, and economic equality that moved the
nation in the 1960s and 1970s, and to some extent in response
to the cycle of reforms initiated by the recommendations of the
President's Commission on Law Enforcement and Administration of Justice of 1967 and carried out with the support of the
Law Enforcement Assistance Administration. In New York City
the Knapp Commission is reserved a place of honor in this
complex of factors of change, even though its inquiries and
recommendations were narrowly focused on local problems of
corruption. As seen by the street cops, any indication of outside influence is evidence that management cops have sold out.
Since much of the outside pressure often comes from segments
of society the police have traditionally controlled pretty much
as they saw fit, responding to that group is perceived as embold-
ening the troublemakers and thereby making the job of po-

licing more difficult and more dangerous. Moreover, by aggressively recruiting—as perceived by street cops—among
traditionally excluded minority populations, management has
turned their backs on their own, making life in the ranks
unpredictable among peers as well as in the hierarchy.

3. In the view of street cops, management has not just caved
in to pressure; management cops found that in yielding to
outside influence they could advance their own careers. Thus,
there comes into view a form of internal class conflict. Management cops have something to gain from acting in ways opposed
to the interest of street cops, especially by throwing to the
wolves street cops who try to do their job as they understand it,
which involves cutting legal corners. This kind of breach of
trust is illustrated by Reuss-Ianni with a case of a patrolman
who was indicted and convicted for killing a suspect in police
custody. Even though most of the street cops who commented
about this case were prepared to condemn the action of the
convicted patrolman, they resented having him sacrificed to
public opinion and they felt that those among them who
testified against their comrade at his trial were coerced to do so
by the bosses. The pervasiveness of this sentiment suggests that
what is at issue here has less to do with either the desire to
cover malfeasance (as accusers hold) or sentiments of fraternal
loyalty (as defenders believe) than with the kind of intolerance
for lay control encountered in other lines of work, for example,
medicine, education, and law.

4. One of the most conspicuous effects of the recent cycle of
police reform is the emergence of a pronounced stylistic difference between management cops and street cops. This is no
doubt in large measure the function of a heavy influx of
"civilians" into management. Thus, what is cooked up in headquarters is not only a departure from all established principles
of policing, it also looks strange and often is incomprehensible.
Reuss-Ianni cites a no doubt apocryphal story of distortion, a
directive experienced on its way down the ranks that nicely
illustrates how, in the end, the street cop cannot escape the
impression that the "civilians cannot get anything straight."
Quite apart from the fact that the street cop is put off by what
looks to him like bureaucratic busy-work, the intrusion of

"civilians" constitutes a unilateral alteration of conditions of employment. In the past, many of the interstitial positions in the police organization now occupied by "civilians" were filled by street cops who for various reasons could no longer work the streets. In addition to being able to look forward to such shelters, street cops also could rely on these former comrades to protect the interests of the troops in the field. Obviously, there is no reason to assume that "civilians" are motivated by such concerns.

In sum, Reuss-Ianni shows that street cops believe that there has come into existence a ponderous and alien managerial structure within the police department that denies them the support they require to meet their responsibilities and that often acts in ways that make policing a less effective and more dangerous activity than it was in the past and needs to be at present. Most important, she shows how perception affects a variety of critical incidents, giving readers a documented view of a complex phenomenon rather than a schematic concept of organizational theory. This fact, more than any other, makes the book a distinguished contribution to the literature of police organization.

Reuss-Ianni has very little to say about the perception of the schism from the other side, that is, from the perspective of the management cops. The reason for this omission was not lack of interest but lack of access to information. What management thinks about the rebellion among the troops is, however, fairly well known, even though one would wish for a description of it as rich in factual detail as we now have of the street cops' views. Management sees disaffection among members of the line personnel mainly as an expression of resistance against reform and innovation in the interest of protecting employee interests, some of which were won in collective bargaining and some of which consist of tacitly accepted adjustments between employee convenience and organizational exigency. Management, that is, appears to have absorbed into its own working the effects of recent police reform drives, especially those involving administrative technique, and it seems stymied in its efforts to transmit the change to the ranks. It would be supremely ironic, of course, if the great reform efforts of the past fifteen years had as their principal effect the administrative streamlining of management, the establishment of some cooperation between police management and outside social and political structures, while leaving those who do the actual policing largely unaffected in their outlook and practices except for causing a state of pervasive estrangement between them and their superiors. Reuss-Ianni makes as strong a case in support of this conjecture as possible. It would be premature, however, to conclude that this diagnostic work is finished. Indeed, it would be just as indefensible to accept the case she makes as it would be utterly foolhardy to disregard the arguments and evidence she marshals. Evidence indicating the estrangement of street cops from management, and practical implications flowing from it, are widespread, albeit in various degree and in manifold forms. Reuss-Ianni has found an instance in which these sentiments appear in their least alloyed and most virulent form. No thoughtful police officials can take comfort in the fact that in their organization things are not nearly as bad; this book has given specificity and substance to what ought to be one of their worries.

In Reuss-Ianni's case street cop culture appears to be decisively colored by resentment against management, but this is by no means all that is said about it. In fact, she attempts to epitomize the other aspects of the outlook of street cops in an inventory of maxims of conduct. Apart from some minor differences here and there, most students of the police would accept these characterizations as valid. She stresses the fact, as have other authors before her, that these are elements of an occupational culture; that is, these are principles, criteria of judgment, attitudes, sanctioned practices, and understandings that arise in connection with, and matter for, a specific way of making a living. All this granted, the most remarkable aspect of this widely shared understanding of street cop culture is that it is completely lacking in any reference to what might be considered occupational technique or method, in the broadest sense of these terms. I do not mean that there is no detailed description of this or that procedure; one would not expect that in an outline of an occupational culture. Instead, I mean that what is said about policing as a vocation makes it look much more like an adventure than work. To be sure, there is talk about the value of experience in policing, there is recognition of something that might be called the tricks of the trade, and there is emphatic insistence that street cops are expert at something outsiders simply do not grasp. But regard for values that are specifically associated with work, industry, efficiency, the planned approach to tasks, the carefully calculated matching of means and ends, or just workmanship in the ordinary sense of the term are conspicuously absent.

In a world choking in a flood of technical regulation of almost every conceivable activity, much of which involves the fake appearance of technique, it is refreshing to find an occupation that resolutely adheres to maintaining an inherited, intuitive sense of expertise. And, of course, there is expertise in police work. People who had the opportunity of observing the police in action are likely to have seen street cops dealing with complex and serious problems with the kind of know-how that indicates craftsmanship. But, as almost all such observers have also noted, these aptitudes and accomplishments are not highly valued among officers, and they utterly pale in significance when put next to the huff and puff of a chase that nets a petty offender. The usual explanation for this is that street cops see law enforcement as "real" police work, while peace-keeping involves them in doing social work that they should not be required to do. There is a good deal of truth in this. But I believe it worth considering that this effect is augmented by another factor. The preference for the kind of law enforcement street cops get to do also expresses a preference for rushing headlong into activities that produce exhilaration over those concerned with practical accomplishments of a comparatively mundane nature.

Insofar as there is truth in this conjecture, it is clearly a bar against the introduction of reform by regulation of the sort attempted by management cops. For people who have chosen policing as their career—on the assumption that it consists of struggles against the forces of evil and with the understanding that they will be free to do in every specific encounter what in their own judgment circumstances call for—must view every regulatory restriction and every attempt at scrutiny as a fundamental change in the conditions of their employment. I believe this is what street cops have in mind when they say that outsiders just don't know what policing is all about. And when they say theirs is the only way policing can be done effectively, they mean that when one of them knocks on the door of a dwelling, having been sent there by the dispatcher to attend to some problem, he is in for an adventure from which he may not retreat, which may involve violence, and in which he should not be second guessed for taking "a five-foot jump over a four-foot ditch." In other words, so long as policing is the kind of occupation in which officers face the possibility of physical combat, they ought not be restricted in their individual efforts to gain advantage over actual and potential opponents.

The street cops who appear on the pages of this book believe that management cops are engaged in a methodical withdrawal of precisely those conditions of discretionary freedom that tended to increase the safety and effectiveness of officers. "With all the restrictions they place on us, it's worth your career to use your gun or to put a little muscle on a guy who would just as soon blow you away," one of them is quoted as saying (98). It is difficult to imagine a better illustration for the point I am trying to make. But what is at issue, as street cops see it, is not only the safety and effectiveness of the individual officer but the integrity of policing itself. For as Reuss-Ianni paraphrases an expression of the view elsewhere (67), "unless everyone in the system insures that every potential cop killer knows that he will be dealt with summarily by the police, no officer is safe."

All this makes a good deal of sense so long as one adheres to the view that policing is essentially a sequence of adventurous encounters with evil by individual officers or pairs of officers, who are for the most part left to depend on their own strength, courage, and wit in critical situations, interrupted by stretches of banality and boredom. But this is certainly not the only tenable view. The idea that policing is not, or at least not primarily, a quasi-military adventure has already taken hold in the minds of many police officials and has led to the introduction of demands for a higher level of social and psychological sophistication on the part of officers than has been expected in the past. There has also been some enhancement of the awareness that peacekeeping is an important and serious police responsibility. In all this, however, there has been very little suggesting that a police officer ought to approach his responsibilities in the way a carpenter attacks a building problem, a dentist deals with an infected tooth, or an accountant approaches an audit, that is, as something for which knowledge, skill, and method are important. Admittedly, there exist no established knowledge, skill, and method that could come into play in most police tasks; but there existed no such knowledge for building, dentistry, and accounting before it was developed. If the task of creating craftsmanship were undertaken seriously, then one would expect an officer saying "it is worth your career to use your gun," to have meant it in the very same sense in which a surgeon might say "it is worth your career if you use your scalpel." That is, in both instances it actually would be and should be worth their careers!

It must be said that Reuss-Ianni has not proposed the conclusion suggested in the foregoing remarks. Her task was to propose that a careful look at policing in New York City reveals that in the recent cycle of police reform management has become uncoupled from the line personnel. Line personnel regard themselves as unprotected, endangered, and ineffective because of what has taken place within management. Even if the account she has presented is overdrawn and somewhat one-sided, and quite apart from the questions of fault and responsibility, this is a matter of utmost seriousness and urgency. All concerned with policing owe her a debt of gratitude for bringing into focus, and for defining—even if only provisionally—a problem that was neglected.

NOTES

This review of Elizabeth Reuss-Ianni's *The Two Cultures of Policing: Street Cops and Management Cops* (Transaction Books, 1983) previously appeared in *American Bar Foundation Research Journal* 1984, no. 1 (Winter): 206–13.

1. Barney G. Glaser, and Anselm L. Strauss, *The Discovery of Grounded Theory* (Chicago: Aldine Publishing Co., 1967).

13 | *Applied Research in Criminal Justice and Ethical Considerations*

I INTEND TO DISCUSS three topics: first I have in mind to say something about applied research generally; next I propose to speak to an item of great concern to me, namely, ethical questions in applied research; and finally, I shall make a few comments about certain issues that have received attention in task force discussions here.

I knew, of course, that this Criminal Justice Research Conference would be dedicated to the discussion of applied research in the field of criminal justice. I did not think people would necessarily be overly strict about the topic, but I expected that several areas of applied research would be the focus of interest even though these interests might not set limits on what one could discuss. Thus I was somewhat surprised to find what I perceived to be an uneasiness in discussing applied research. Naturally, I did not have the opportunity to diagnose the situation reliably, but I sensed over and over that people were talking about applied research as sort of the "poor relations" of pure research, and about people doing applied research as the "poor relations" of academic scholars. Since I am myself in the latter category, I think I am in a good position to try to dispel that notion.

There are at least two good reasons why applied research need not be defensive about its enterprise. One has to do with its past and the other with its present.

Let me begin by observing that the distinction between pure and applied research and the unfortunate contempt—in some parts—for the latter, reflects merely a modern attitude. If I am not mistaken, it came into prominence during my lifetime, certainly not before the generation of my teachers. To be sure, there is an illustrious precedent for it in the case of Plato who, according to Plutarch, inveighed against those who employed the devices of vulgar handicraft and sought the attainment of practical ends in their studies. This suggests that the distinction was salient only at what might be called the beginning of scientific scholarship and now. As far as modern science is concerned, during the time from, let us say, Galileo to Hermann von Helmholtz, scholars were unconcerned with the whole matter. They did their research and conducted their studies in a highly principled manner and cared little whether a certain aspect of what they studied stood in any direct and demonstrable relationship to the world of everyday life and practical affairs. To put it differently, life and study was to them much more of one cloth than it seems to us. What is true in the so-called natural sciences is also true for scholars who busied themselves with what we would today call the social sciences, that is, for all those greats between Machiavelli and Auguste Comte.

Not only was there no distinction made between applied and pure science during the four centuries of their most rapid advance, but some of the most celebrated advances resulted from what we would today consider to be applied projects of research. By far the most spectacular example of this is the work of Copernicus. We do not know whether the great astronomer felt the thirst for knowledge for knowledge's sake. We do know, however, that he spent his life studying the movements of the celestial bodies to help the Roman Catholic Church reform its liturgical calendar. At the time, dates were getting out of hand and as time was slipping, some people saw a real danger that Christmas might have to be celebrated on Easter. This in particular was a very serious source of practical concern for the prelates of the Church.

Another, and more recent example along these lines has to do with medicine. The discoveries that led to the conquest of the so-called infectious diseases were not made by the faculties of the schools of medicine at university centers, but rather in the laboratories of public health physicians who had the noble, but quite practical, task of keeping people from getting sick and making them well when they did get sick.

The second reason why applied research, especially in the field of criminal justice, need not be defensive pays tribute to realities of modern life. There exists an exalted ideal of research that is written about in certain textbooks of scientific methods, and there are some research endeavors that are in assiduous compliance with it. I do not mean to disparage any of it; I only want to put it aside for the moment, because there is another meaning of research that has far greater currency. What I mean is that scientific research practiced with somewhat attenuated rigor has subsumed the exercises of critical reason, of rational scrutiny, of information gathering and storage, and of considered decision making of all kinds.

In other words, it seems to be perfectly sensible to say that when one wants to conduct one's affairs in a sensible manner, he or she must do research, or, better yet, that doing research civilizes the enterprise within which it takes place. As far as I can see, this is a very decent objective and in no way a lesser one than the objectives of so-called pure research.

Now to my second topic. Applied researchers are, of course, very much aware of the consequential nature of their activity. Their research is, after all, deliberately oriented to desired consequences. But I am not certain whether applied researchers are as discriminating—that is, whether they are as unceasingly discriminating—on the question of good and bad consequences as I think they should be. This is a difficult matter; research is a highly technical business, and it is all too easy to become so absorbed in the technical aspects of it that one overlooks its potential for good and for harm. This is especially likely to happen in an area of research like criminal justice, precisely because in it the most serious moral problems are encountered at every step. Under these circumstances, it becomes quite understandable that many will settle for, as the saying goes, "meaning no harm" and pleading for an acquittal on counts of further moral responsibility. But, I propose, we must not expect too much from "meaning no harm" and we certainly cannot expect that meaning no harm is an adequate method of ethical control.

In what follows, I propose some more objective reasons for interest in ethical questions in applied research concerning criminal justice administration. What I mean, of course, is that these things deserve attention not because of my preference, nor because of anyone else's—whatever it might be—but because ethical concerns inhere in all aspects of the criminal justice system in an objective sense.

Consider this: faced with someone who transgresses, one experiences feelings of indignation and anger. These feelings shape the impulse to strike back. Moreover, there is among us all the power to strike back, an awesome power that is readily at hand as collective actions go. The impulse to strike back is not very discerning, and the power to strike back is not very well controlled. So we might find ourselves sometimes enraged by blasphemy and rush over and cut out the blasphemer's tongue. With the rage spent we might then be overcome with remorse, or, in any case, we might decide on reflection that we should not be cutting out the tongues of blasphemers. And having decided this, we might want to set forth some rule governing our behavior. Perhaps we might decide that blasphemers must pay a fine or serve a term in jail.

Notice what is happening. Our knowledge that blasphemy is evil does not derive from knowing that it is punishable by fine or imprisonment, nor does this kind of information come from reading penal codes. This knowledge presents itself in the impulse to strike back; its root is in a widely prevailing moral sentiment, from whence it gets into the code in the first place. Admittedly, in a civilization such as ours, we do look into the codes to find out whether something will pass, but we should know that these parts of the codes are not native to them. What is native to the codes, or native to law in the broad sense, is the qualified rule specifying that blasphemy is evil *and* punishable in this manner and not otherwise. On reflection, it is quite clear that the provisions of criminal law have *two* inseparable objectives and that having these two inseparable objectives is, in a sense, fundamentally constitutive of their legality.

First, there is the intention that the law will control the incidence of transgression, that it will somehow deter it. By fining or imprisoning those who blaspheme, we make it an expensive freedom or license. Second, it is in the nature of the provisions of criminal law that the price is fixed and that nothing beyond the fixed price may be said to be receivable from the transgressor. Thus every law is meant to control and deter crime *and* every law is also a check on the operation of the retributive impulse. It is important to remember that the impulse is there, even before the law is there. The impulse emerges as law when people resolve to curb their retributive impulses toward transgressors in their midst. By restraining the retributive impulse, people refuse to descend to the moral level of the crime they seek to control. In prohibiting the maltreatment of criminals, the criminal law embodies the moral aspirations of the polity; going against them is thus no less a transgression than going against any of the other norms the criminal code contains.

At this point the scientific researcher enters and says, "Hey, you know what? My research shows that cutting out tongues prevents blasphemy a lot better than fines." If the law had only one purpose—to control crime—that would be a reasonable argument. But the law also has the purpose of controlling what may be done about crime, and, therefore, we are obliged to send our researcher back to his studies.

It is well known, that the institutions of the law are not doing a very good job of controlling crime; therefore, it is perfectly sensible that there be a two-and-a-half-day conference during which concerned officials talk about this situation. Even with this focus, it seems to me intolerable to overlook the fact that the law is not doing a better job in realizing the moral aspirations of the community. In the field of criminal justice, research about the disease without research about the corresponding remedial practice is a job half done. Thus research in criminal justice should take precedence over research in crime control.

I will provide two examples of what kinds of problems should have been addressed during a conference on research in criminal justice.

First, I think it ought to be considered an arresting and awesome mystery that the protagonist of *Man-Child in the Promised Land* (I refer to the jarring book by Claude Brown, of course) has, at the age of six, the fully formed idea in his mind that there is absolutely nothing he can do to stay out of trouble with the law. This happens in a world where we, the people, have his attention while he goes to the movies, watches television, listens to the radio, reads the papers; where we deal with him through our teachers in school, our ministers in the churches, our social workers in the welfare agencies, our policemen on the streets; in short, where we have him literally immersed in a sea of our influence and control. How can that be?

Another example concerns a man who is held in jail for a period of nine months on charges of aggravated assault and kidnapping, at which time his attorney suggests that if he would plead guilty he might be freed on time served. The attorney also suggests that if, on the other hand, he keeps insisting his innocence and demanding trial, then he would have to serve another three months before a trial could be scheduled. If this man were found innocent, it would have been shown that in our system an accused, innocent man may serve a year in jail, whereas a guilty man need only serve nine months.

I do not want to overdo the point. I only suggest that these matters I have just mentioned should receive more than a passing comment at a conference on research in criminal justice. There may be some who think I worry too much about formal correctness or the avoidance of mistakes in the criminal process; after all, they might say, with crime rampant on the streets, first things come first. I am not wholly opposed to this view; but under certain conditions, the victory over crime may not be worth the trouble. It seems to me that the uncompromisingly moral control of crime is not a luxury to be indulged when we can afford it and cut back when the going gets rough. Rather, an unimpeachably honest and restrained administration of justice, in the broadest sense of the term, is the lifeblood of the republic and absolutely indispensable for its survival.

Now to my third topic. I have no overall synthesis to offer of research in criminal justice but would like, instead, to touch on some points of task force discussions that seem to me to be especially worthy of attention.

There has developed within the field of applied social research in criminal justice, a special bailiwick encompassing the so-called evaluative studies. This endeavor grew proportionately with the growth of demonstration projects, that is, projects in which certain new procedures are tested under the aegis of special sponsorship and with the aid of special financing. Of course, the intended unbiased assessment is absolutely indispensable. Its rapid proliferation in the recent past has unfortunately given rise to peculiar pathologies, of which two are noteworthy. In the first, accountability to outside sponsors imposes special stringencies on operations that are not necessarily connected with real effectiveness. For example, outsiders tend to require more visible and more measurable evidence of effectiveness than might satisfy insiders. An all but inevitable consequence of this is a concentration on those aspects of the operation that exhibit such evidence. There is not too large a gap from the feeling that certain things must be done not because they are inherently meritorious, but because they happen to satisfy sponsors, to cynical mendacity. Closely connected with the vicissitudes of sponsor-oriented evaluation is the risk of the growth of certain vested interests around this type of research. Since much of this kind of work must be done within ramified bureaucracies, it is rather easy to imagine how the functions of evaluative research could become an entrenched structure. Yet, paradoxically, there is merit in the idea that the development of a new breed of researchers—whose forte would consist in the mastery of evaluative accounting techniques, in certain ways analogous to the skills of CPAs in the field of finance—should be encouraged. The dilemma is between the need for persons who will possess the skill and occupational commitments to evaluative research and the risk that these people will perpetuate the activity beyond any reasonable need for it.

A second area of internally related problems in applied research in criminal justice has to do with levels of generality, storage and retrieval, and implementation of findings. One of the most irritating difficulties of which researchers often complain is that the degree of applicability and usefulness of findings is inversely related to their generality. Part of this is because circumstances of application vary; but, in some measure, the difficulty can be traced to the practitioners' preference for the concrete over the more abstract. Combined with problems of relative generality of findings is the problem of making information available. Since much of applied research is not published, or not published soon enough, there exists a serious information storage and retrieval problem even within rather narrow fields of application. Nor is this a problem that can be easily solved by mechanical devices made available through advances in computer technology. As is well known, computerized data banks raise all sorts of hazards stemming from invasions of privacy and the abuse of power. This is because there is much less public control over information stored in data banks than there is over published findings. But even when relevant information is accessible, and is at a suitable level of generality, there still remains the problem of resistance to the implementation of recommendations derived from it. This is the age-old struggle between the forces of inherited lore and routinized practice, not to mention vested interest, versus the fruits of rational scrutiny.

The last topic that I will discuss here has to do with the connection between research conducted in an action setting—that is, in the context of the administration of criminal justice—and academic scholarship. You must first realize, that the preponderant majority of university scholars are disillusioned with and condemn much of what is going on under the umbrella of criminal process. I do not intend to defend this position now, as much of it reeks of the kind of snobbery that ill becomes an intellectual elite, but I draw it to your attention. As you know, there is a big chasm now between the agencies of the criminal justice system and the universities, but the chasm is not too big to be filled. On the whole, I think the people in the agencies are in a better position to take the first step, if only because access to the universities is more openly available than vice versa.

Let me conclude by adding an important proviso to this last comment. I do not think that the reconciliation between the applied researchers in the administration of criminal justice and academic scholars is desirable because the latter have a very important contribution to make on their own. In fact, I cannot think of anything that academic scholars could say or do to help make things better; they have neither the facts nor the methods to make much of a difference. The university is important for other reasons: first, because it is the source of unintimidated critique, and second, because it is the place where one can recruit gifted persons of high aspirations. I consider the need for unintimidated critique (free speech) too obvious a need in a free society to require further explanation. But I would like to say a word about the need for gifted persons with high aspirations. Whatever the mechanism might be in our times that distributes talent into the various parts of society, it is fair to say that it works in such a way that it is the exception rather than the rule for the best endowed to find their way into the administration of criminal justice. This is especially true for the police and the penal system. It is also true of the prosecution, the defense bar, and even the lower bench. There is a long and prejudicial history, but no good reasons, behind this relative failure to attract gifted students into the administration of criminal justice. But we have finally realized what important powers are in fact vested in correctional personnel, in police officers, and in magistrates. We can no longer fail to conclude that only persons of the very highest qualifications can be expected to meet the demands of these vocations adequately. It may take a long time to achieve the full realization of this insight, but the presence of applied research in the administration of criminal justice is the first step in this direction.

NOTE

This chapter is based on the summary address presented at the Criminal Justice Research Conference, March 15–17, 1972, sponsored by the California Council on Criminal Justice.

14 | *The Concept of Mental Abnormality in the Administration of Justice Outside the Courtroom*

No AREA OF PUBLIC POLICY has been more exposed to controversy in recent decades than that comprising the responses of the community to deviance. Opposing views are in heated confrontation and no particular sentiment is clearly dominant. While all institutions of social control are beset by uncertainties, uncertainty about the inherited law constitutes a critical case because of the paramount significance of the legal order in modern life.

The leading theme of all questions about the law as an instrument of social control, and the leading theme of its defense, is the problem of individual responsibility in the broadest sense. The traditional view of individual responsibility is that every person is the sovereign steward of his fate, free to opt for a life of his choice, and fully accountable for his option. This view furnishes the tacit foundation of democratic government, in which the use of coercive restraint is the exclusive monopoly of the legally constituted administration of justice. The unqualified primacy of legal control—that is, control by means of an abstract body of norms—and the traditional view of responsibility are inextricably related. Only when it is taken for granted that virtually everybody is capable of complying with the expectations of the law, and that virtually all contenders before the law are of basically equal competence, is the balance of justice guaranteed by the disinterested review of competing claims. Although impartiality and equality are never fully realized in practice, the system will remain compelling as long as its failings can be blamed on lawyers. Indeed, a high respect for the legal order is commonly accompanied by a jaundiced opinion about its officials (Commager 1950). In recent years, however, the onus of blame has shifted from the officials to the mandate itself. Freud, Pareto, Spengler, and countless other scholars of the "generation of 1890" (Hughes 1961) found fault with the concept of man implied in the traditional view of individual responsibility. According to their teachings, man is not capable of self-control in more than a marginal sense and most of his actions are beyond the scope of his comprehension and will. From this perspective, the inference is close at hand that the old norms do not fit the newly discovered measure of man.

To be assimilated into the law, the new teachings required a suitable expression. While criminologists of social science provenance have richly documented the causal influence of cultural and environmental factors upon criminality (Sutherland and Cressey 1966), their formulations do not lend themselves to the development of remedies within the scope of the means and authority of the administration of justice. The formulation that does seem to serve this purpose is the concept of mental abnormality.

The very circumstance that makes the concept of mental abnormality a suitable vehicle for change—its time-honored meaning and import in jurisprudence—also sets certain restrictions on its use. These restrictions do not have a uniformly binding force over the entire range of the processes of the administration of justice. Certain parts of the overall system are under more explicit and formalized control than others, and in the former the pace and direction of innovation are more likely to follow the course set by the past than in the latter. Yet it is reasonable to assume that the possibility of change in the various parts of the system would be interdependent. Thus, though the following remarks are devoted to the discussion of the role of the concept of mental abnormality in the administration of justice outside the courtroom, it is necessary to give some consideration to the status of the concept in the forensic sciences and to the debates that surround it.

THE FORENSIC MEANING OF MENTAL ABNORMALITY

Formal trial procedure requires that all decisions be based on explicit justifications in terms of established rules and precedents. In keeping with this style, the courtroom meaning of the dispensation on account of mental abnormality has changed remarkably little with time. Even though the ambience of applicability of the norm of dispensation has been loosened, to invoke it still constitutes an exception. The official interpretation of crime in our own day, as in the past, is that the criminal is generally culpable and that this presumption can be suspended only under special conditions spelled out in valid tests of insanity.

The evaluation of change in courtroom use of the norm of dispensation is, of course, relative. Hence it is not surprising that recent innovations have been attacked as excessive. Among the critics, Thomas Szasz has vigorously advanced what might be called a conspiratorial interpretation of the loosening of standards that, according to his views, opens the door to a repressive tyranny defying both law and science (Szasz 1965). Also prominent among the objections to forensic innovations is the view that they constitute a subterfuge allowing society and, by extension, the courts "to utilize psychiatry to provide a rationale for its wish to excuse certain offenders" (Halleck 1966, 397). While the specter of an uncontrolled tyranny is polemically more alarming, the allegation of possible spuriousness is potentially more damaging. It is, however, possible to avoid meeting this objection and to interpret it as merely pointing to a type of definitional transformation that is not unusual in the history of jurisprudence.

An example from the history of forensic uses of dispensations might help to clarify this point. Since times of great antiquity members of Holy Orders in England were exempt from criminal prosecution in the ordinary sense. The dispensation was known as Benefit of Clergy; it allowed judges not to impose the supreme penalty that was otherwise mandatory. In 1350, the norm was extended to a class of persons conveniently identified as "secular clerics," which encompassed everybody able to pass a rudimentary reading test. By 1547 all peers, and by 1622 most women, were able to invoke the Benefit of Clergy to mitigate the force of accusations against them. At the time the dispensation was formally abolished—in the first half of the nineteenth century, when the need for this dispensation waned because of drastic reductions in the number of capital crimes—its scope was so wide that offenses that were meant to be punished by death had to be officially defined as punishable without the Benefit of Clergy (Stephen 1883). This is clearly a case history of five hundred years of "subterfuge." The actual use of the dispensation constituted a departure from the technicality of institutional segregation of jurisdiction, between the Church and the Crown, that initially led to its formulation.

The point of the example is that when the administration of justice requires dispensations it uses the ones that are available. In accordance with demands issuing from changing sensibilities and circumstances, the initial intent is reinterpreted by analogy to allow use in new and unforeseen ways. At distant intervals the formulary is revised to bring the "law stuff" up to date with the "law jobs," in the pithy terminology of Llewellyn (1940). Thus it would seem to be the normal, though probably not the necessary, course in the development of jurisprudential meaning of dispensations, that the rule that initially protected only "real" clerics should have been widened to protect "secular" clerics, even as the M'Naghten rule is succeeded by the Durham rule, and so on. At any particular moment, however, there is probably always a great deal of ambiguity about the limits of applicability. Moreover, insofar as change is in the direction of loosening standards, it must be assumed that the same impulse that presses for innovation will also find that each successive liberalization sets too stringent limits.

Many thoughtful and informed observers see the presently acknowledged import of mental abnormality in the courtroom as anachronistically restricted. The advocates of reform maintain that existing standards still do not give best professional judgment the full weight to which it is entitled. What constitutes best professional judgment in psychiatry is debatable. But even if the complaints were admitted as valid, to the extent that they are valid they also reflect the same narrowness of perspective that was attributed to the conservative argument in the foregoing remarks. While changing law jobs leads periodically to reformulations of law stuff, this is not the only way by which the functioning of the law enforcement system is updated. Other mechanisms exist that allow the law to retain its seemingly anachronistic form, while ameliorating many of the consequences.

Another historical example may help to make the point. In 1866, the Royal Commission on Capital Punishment heard testimony on, among other things, the crime of child-killing. It came to light that many judges found pronouncing the death penalty repugnant in cases where the mother of the victim was the accused. To avoid this unpleasant duty judges often resorted to subterfuge. Failing this, they pronounced the death penalty knowing that the condemnation would be followed by automatic reprieve. Though there was no doubt about these facts, and although many judges decried this "solemn mockery," the law was invoked continually until at least 1927 (Davies 1937). Since the last known execution for this crime took place in 1849, and the law was not formally changed until many years after 1927, the reform apparently waited an entire century. But it would be absurd to claim that the real change occurred in our times. Child-killing was not punishable by death during the second half of the nineteenth and the first half of the twentieth century in England. Instead, the real penalty was death followed by automatic reprieve. This was the law in effect, and there was no more and no less certainty about it than there ever is about any law, written or unwritten.

As this example shows, the appraisal of the import of any legal norm, including the norms of dispensation, cannot rest on observations of judicial reason alone. Important as this phase of study is, it is incomplete without broadening the investigation to include the penal, accusatory, and investigatory phases of the criminal process. Viewed in isolation, the forensic method is ambiguous, concentration of attention on it is apt to lead to fruitless casuistry, while seemingly intractable problems find practical solutions outside it.

THE MEANING OF MENTAL ABNORMALITY IN PENOLOGY

The area of the administration of justice, outside the courtroom, in which mental abnormality receives most recognition is penology. This recognition is not usually expressed in any official legal-psychiatric formulations. Instead concern is manifested in broadly conceived treatment programs applicable to a wide range of offenders (Conrad 1965). But wherever such programs exist they tend to be strongly oriented to coping with psychopathology. The recognition of psychopathology in the penal treatment process does not ordinarily cause an institutionally sanctioned shift in the judicial disposition. Officially the offender expiates guilt by serving his sentence; in practice the significance of the sanction changes, to some extent, from punishment to therapy. To be sure, such treatment programs are still to a large extent in the state of advocacy rather than full-fledged realization; they are often beset by vexing problems, but rarely opposed in principle.

It might be objected that the introduction of the psychiatric perspective into penology does not necessarily transform those to whom it applies into mentally abnormal persons. But this objection raises a mere verbal issue. In the legal system mental abnormality is not of interest in the psychiatric sense. Instead it constitutes, howsoever recognized, the warrant for a particular course of action. Insofar as it can be shown that such a course of action is in practice implemented, that is, persons do receive the sort of treatment that is appropriate to the finding of psychopathology, it must be assumed that the presumption of mental abnormality functions, whether acknowledged or not. The institutional appurtenances of the transition in the meaning of the sanction are lacking, but there can be no doubt that the psychopathology which could not receive proper recognition in the courtroom is given a reprieve in the modern penal process. In other words, no one can fail to observe that in the sanctioning process, as distinct from the external form of the sanction, there has occurred a shift from the notion of culpability based on individual responsibility, to treatability in the therapeutic sense.

THE MEANING OF MENTAL ABNORMALITY IN PROSECUTION

The role of the concept of mental abnormality in the accusatory phase of the criminal process is partly visible in the courtroom. The visible part encompasses procedures relating to the involvement of the prosecution in decisions about the capacity of the accused to stand trial or, as it is sometimes called, "fitness to proceed" (Silving 1962). The traditional assumption is that raising the matter of mental abnormality, either as a defense or for the purpose of suspending proceedings, is the exclusive privilege of the defendant. More recently, it has become accepted to extend the privilege to the prosecution (Whitlock 1963; Reid 1960). This raises serious problems because, "in calling a man sick [prior to trial] we exempt ourselves from the requirement of defending our charges against his belief and behaviour" (Louch 1965, 500). This objection acquires urgent importance on consideration of countless cases in which the finding of incompetency to stand trial resulted in protracted confinement in mental hospitals, far beyond the length of the sentence that would have followed conviction. Nor can it be maintained that the length of such hospitalization is merely the function of the confined person's illness; according to available evidence, the standards of mental health that such persons must satisfy before they are discharged are much higher than those applied to other patients (Hess and Thomas 1963). The "fitness to proceed" norm offers the prosecution, in effect if not in intent, a powerful device for controlling certain persons by employing what has been called "praetorian psychiatry" (Wertham 1963, 404).

It is less well known that recognition of mental abnormality also plays a part in the decisions to initiate prosecution and in the formulation of charges. Here it is one of many considerations relevant in the prosecution's "exercise of a kind of unarticulated authority to mitigate the general provisions of the criminal law to prevent absurd applications" (Wechsler 1962, 105). A great deal of this unarticulated authority is exercised with the knowledge of judges and sometimes elicits comments that are reminiscent of the solemn mockery complaint of English judges of the nineteenth century. "One wonders why you find, for example, a judge . . . willing to do in chambers what he won't do in the open" (Bear 1962, 297). The answer to this query is rather simple. Leaving aside the judges who actually seek changes in the law, most find the present arrangement adequate not because they are oblivious of the role of psychopathology in crime but because they consider the in camera part of the criminal process an integral element of the administration of justice. Moreover, in de minimis infractions the system must rely on the discretion of prosecutors not to proceed, even without consultation.

The decision not to proceed against some offenders is for the most part based on exceedingly complex considerations, and the discernment of mental abnormality is a part of this complex (Newman 1966). For example, the decision may be reached when a trial would excessively damage someone's reputation and when it is thought that his tendency to transgress would be better controlled by psychiatric care than by punishment. In fact, law enforcement officials are increasingly prone to think that persons who would not ordinarily be expected to commit crimes must be sick if they do (Aubert and Messinger 1958). But as they are not so sick as to come under the admissible tests of sanity, they can be spared punishment only when they are dealt with without trial.

The desire to achieve control expediently is the most important consideration in assigning priority to mental abnormality over criminality in the accusatory phase. In some cases, persons who appear to suffer from a psychological deficit would, if prosecuted successfully, receive a short sentence or probation. But if the deficit is interpreted as an omen of greater mischief, then prosecutors may wish to avert this by hospitalizing the person in a mental institution. In other instances, the chance of obtaining a conviction of any kind is poor, but the accused person is perceived as patently deviant, and potentially dangerous if not subjected to some form of control. Often it is not even a matter of estimating the possibility of conviction. Rather, certain persons are viewed as constituting a serious risk, even though they cannot be clearly defined as criminal in the legal sense or sick in the psychiatric sense. But, as Judge Biggs (1965) stated, speaking for the courts, "we cannot exercise legal control or sanction over such [dangerous] persons."

This disability of the courts to formulate judgments on the basis of appraisal of character, while officialdom feels compelled to take some action, causes the transfer of the responsibility to the pretrial phase of the criminal process. Thus the courts are relieved from having to condemn some persons who, according to prevailing sensibilities, should be spared. At the same time others, whom the judges could not properly condemn, can be restrained or, at least, prosecution can be manipulated to approximate to this objective. Accordingly, the informal remedies, far from merely mitigating the full force of consequences of the principle of personal responsibility, also extend control to problems that cannot be legally controlled under its aegis. In addition to the structuring influence issuing from the reciprocal relationship of the trial and pretrial phases, that is, disposing of certain cases in the pretrial phase *because* courtroom procedure excludes certain desired solutions, a more direct type of influence must also function. The horizon of recognized relevance of the concept of mental abnormality in the forensic sciences probably determines the horizon of recognizable relevance in informal pretrial remedies. That is, as one is loosened, the other will be loosened accordingly. But even as the ambience of the dispensation in the courtroom passes on to the accusatory phase, so the practices installed there must exert influence on the procedures of criminal investigation that precede this phase.

THE MEANING OF MENTAL ABNORMALITY IN POLICE WORK

The discovery and investigation of crimes and the apprehension of offenders is the province of the police. In recent years it has become increasingly clear that this is not a mere ministerial function but that it involves the exercise of discretion (Goldstein 1960; LaFave 1965). That is, police officers do not invoke the law automatically, on adequate evidence, but selectively. The exercise of discretion is especially prominent in the enforcement of the law with respect to minor offenses. Moreover, this area of police work shades over into the area of keeping the peace, in which officers act, by and large, as terminal, all-purpose control agents. Keeping the peace encompasses a virtually unlimited variety of authoritative interventions ranging from dealing with minor breaches of the peace and disorderly conduct, through crowd control and traffic management, to giving first aid and supportive guidance (Banton 1964). One of the many routines belonging to peace-keeping involves dealing with persons who are perceived as mentally ill (Bittner 1967). In many jurisdictions, statutory authorization for police intervention in cases of mental illness (defining these as being of a civil rather than criminal nature) exists (Bleicher 1967). Recognition is not lacking, however, that encounters with the mentally ill cannot always be easily segregated into one or other domain of the law. Thus, for example, the Association of the Bar of the City of New York (1962), in recommending the revision of statutory law, proposed that officers be authorized to hospitalize instead of arresting, "the person [who] appears to be mentally ill and is conducting himself in a manner which in a sane person would be disorderly" (33). This recommendation does no more than seek official authorization for what has long been standard practice.

Observation of the routine work of the uniformed patrol in the United States indicates that officers deal quite often with mentally abnormal persons. In many cases the sole cause for police intervention is the sign of illness. In the majority of cases, however, the person who is viewed as sick is also the perpetrator of some offense. As a rule, police action in these encounters is not based on careful evaluation of the legal or psychiatric aspects of the case. Instead the main concern is the isolation of the offender who is perceived as mentally abnormal, and thus the checking of the risk of proliferation of trouble. When the offense is relatively minor, and when the signs of illness are compelling—especially if it is also known that the offender is or recently was under psychiatric care—some alternative to arrest will be used. These decisions are made in the field, generally without consultation, and rarely is a record kept of the action. What the particular course of remedial action will be is decisively influenced by the degree of perceived danger. Emergency referrals to hospitals are ordinarily not made merely on the ground that a person is ill, nor in order to condemn his delinquency vicariously. Rather, they are made when someone's continued presence in society is viewed as creating serious hazards to safety. In practice, this often comes down to saying that the person is apt to continue creating problems for the police.

It is, unfortunately, impossible to estimate the relative frequency with which police officers deal with offenders as ill rather than criminal. Practices undoubtedly vary greatly from jurisdiction to jurisdiction. In one large American city, where most of these observations about the police were made, approximately one offender in fifty is hospitalized rather than booked, and slightly more than 10 percent of the total intake of the closed psychiatric inpatient service of the public hospital comes from this source. This estimate is guardedly conservative. Under a somewhat more generous definition of a police referral the proportions could be doubled. For example, the count does not include alcoholics who, because of hospital policy, had to be taken first to the jail to sober up before they could be admitted, nor does it include persons who are taken by the police to medical aid stations distributed through the city. And, even if all these factors are allowed, the resulting estimate would not reflect fully the extent to which officers recognize mental abnormality as a consideration in their control of minor offenders.

By no means all persons judged by police officers to be mentally ill, who could be (though not necessarily would be) arrested if they were perceived to be sane, are hospitalized. It seems, though this estimate, too, must be viewed with caution, that about one-half of such encounters do not result in confinement in a hospital. Officers are quite reluctant to take people to the hospital, however, not because they fail to see reasons for it but because they find the referral procedures cumbersome, potentially compromising, and not in keeping with certain ideals of police activity. For these reasons, most of their encounters with mentally abnormal offenders lead to even more informal remedies. There are three overlapping procedures for the direct handling of situations involving minor infractions perpetrated by people perceived to be mentally ill. First, in cases where the offense can be construed as having resulted from a lapse of normally functioning controls, the mentally abnormal offender will be returned to his custodians, for example, his kin. Second, officers often engage in what must be thought of as psychiatric first aid. This is mainly a pacifying procedure in which highly agitated persons are segregated from the source of their irritation. Third, some patrolmen know certain mentally ill persons living in their district, know them to be constantly in and out of trouble, and establish with these persons a more or less regular pattern of running into them. Contrary to the procedure of psychiatric first aid, the last method has the aspect of continued care and seems to be confined to persons living in blighted neighborhoods. While it is quite obvious that the sick person is as much the beneficiary of service as he is the subject of control, it would be a serious mistake to neglect the latter aspect. The more proper view is that control functions through service. The transgression is made innocent by the background of illness, but the acceptance of remedies is not optional.

The police practices of informal intervention—that is, intervention that begins and ends in the field without involving any other part of the administration of justice—are not new. On the contrary, available evidence indicates that the modern uniformed police patrol used them from the date of its creation in 1829, exerting direct authority in lieu of invoking the law (Reith 1938). Though there exists no formal mandate under which the informal peacekeeping services are made available to society, they are clearly provided in response to public demand and have public sanction. Police intervention in cases involving danger are viewed as especially legitimate. But since the police are an element of the administration of justice, what they do must be considered to be a part of the system's function. That is, the discretionary freedom of the police officer allows him to handle an array of problems that properly belong to the enterprise known by the too-narrow designation of forensic psychiatry but have, so far, escaped its notice. The point deserving special emphasis is that the infusion of mental health principles into law enforcement provides an authorization or, at least, a rationale for the exercise of coercive power with respect to persons who are criminal only in a trivial sense, and who typically are seen as ill only when they are also ambiguously delinquent, but who are unambiguously perceived as dangerous. Under the present distribution of labor in legal proceedings, the handling of such cases in the accusatory phase would be more cumbersome than it is in the police phase, and they would swamp the courts if they were allowed to reach them.

CONCLUSIONS

The argument has been advanced that the import of the concept of mental abnormality in the contemporary administration of justice must be understood in the context of historical change. One of the organizing themes in the transformation of all social control is the idea of individual responsibility. While this idea was the cornerstone upon which the institutions of the modern polity were built it is no longer the naïve article of faith it once was. Obviously, it was not only the work of scholars that led to uncertainty. The changes in the ways deviance is now controlled and the scholarly work to which the advocates of change refer for polemic support are the concomitants of the growth of mass society and the increase in bureaucracy (Selznick 1963). From this perspective the concept of mental abnormality may be thought of as merely a vehicle of innovation. Analogy with the history of Benefit of Clergy supports the contention that a legal dispensation need not retain the specificity of its initial formulation. Yet, even while the scope of application of the dispensation widens in forensic science, it is always limited in certain ways. Thus, whatever the legal test of insanity might be, it will always frustrate in some cases the desire to mete out justice. Mercifully, not only for the offender but also for those who have to sit in judgment, this was never an unsurmountable problem in law enforcement. The drama of the trial is situated in a context, and problems that do not admit a solution that accords both with the formulary of inherited law and the voice of conscience or circumstance can be remedied in the contextual environment. Thus, those who have to be tried as sane can today gain some measure of reprieve from the circumstance that their mental abnormality will be recognized in practice in the penal process.

More important, however, than the amends resulting from the treatment of inmates as quasi patients is that the restrictions that bind judges can be effectively anticipated and neutralized

MENTAL ABNORMALITY IN THE ADMINISTRATION OF JUSTICE 399

in the accusatory and investigatory phases of the criminal process. That is, cases for which the valid formulary of the law provides solutions that seem unjust, impractical or insufficient are handled informally by prosecutors before going to trial, or without going to trial, and many are handled informally by the police without invoking the law at all. In these dispensatory mechanisms, the idea of psychopathology is certainly not the only consideration, it is probably not the most important consideration, but it is of growing importance. At the same time, the concept of mental abnormality does not function merely to diminish the importance of punishment as a method of control, it also leads toward the extension of control. While it renders impotent certain devices developed under the auspices of the idea of individual responsibility, it causes the development of other devices that follow the path of modern searches for certainty.

One might ask why this should be so, and the most obvious answer lies in the immense influence of psychiatric thought in modern life. But perhaps there is a deeper reason for it, of which the ascendancy of psychiatry itself is only an outward aspect. The hallmark of the epoch of history encompassing the past one hundred years is a succession of holocausts of violence in incongruous combination with an unprecedentedly sustained aspiration to install peace as a stable condition of social life. Yet, despite the proliferation of formal means for keeping the peace, we have found no good ways of coping with danger. We can no longer banish those whom we perceive as potentially dangerous into the status exile of vagrancy where they could be summarily controlled (Sherry 1960). But the specter of transgression is perennial and the spirit that seeks to avoid violence and archaic discrimination finds in the definitional exile of illness an immensely tempting principle of control. This does not make the doctor an arbiter of justice, nor does it necessarily summon him personally to the role of the guardian of the peace. But it does raise the question of how the decisions that issue from the teachings and practices of psychiatry will be assimilated into the scheme of public accountability known as the legal order.

NOTE

This essay previously appeared in *Ciba Foundation Symposium on the Mentally Abnormal Offender*, ed. A. V. S. de Reuck and R. Porter (London: J. & A. Churchill, 1968), 201–13.

This research was supported in part by grant 64-1-35 from the California Department of Mental Hygiene.

REFERENCES

Association of the Bar of the City of New York. *Mental Illness and Due Process*, Ithaca, N.Y.: Cornell University Press, 1962.

Aubert, V., and S. L. Messinger. *Inquiry* 1 (1958): 137–60.

Banton, M. *The Policeman in the Community*. New York: Basic Books, 1964.

Bear, L. A. In *Law, Medicine, Science, and Justice*, ed. L. A., Bear, 297. Springfield, Ill.: C. C. Thomas, 1962.

Biggs, J., Jr. *American Journal of Psychiatry* 122 (1965): 652–55.

Bittner, E. *Social Problems*, 14 (1967): 278–92.

Bleicher, B. K. *Cleveland-Marshall Law Review*, 16 (1967): 93–115.

Commager, H. S. *The American Mind*. New Haven: Yale University Press, 1950.

Conrad, J. P. *Crime and Its Correction*. Berkeley and Los Angeles: California University Press, 1965.

Davies, D. S. *Modern Law Review*, 1 (1937): 203–23, 269–87.

Goldstein, J. *Yale Law Journal*, 69 (1960): 543–94.

Halleck, S. L. *Wisconsin Law Review*, 51 (1966): 379–401.

Hess, J. H., and H. E. Thomas. *American Journal of Psychiatry*, 119 (1963): 713–20.

Hughes, H. S. *Consciousness and Society*. New York: Alfred A. Knopf, 1961.

LaFave, W. R. *Arrest: The Decision to Take a Suspect into Custody*. Boston: Little, Brown & Co., 1965.

Llewellyn, K. N. *Yale Law Journal*, 49 (1940): 1355–1400.

Louch, A. R. *The Monist*, 49 (1965): 485–503.

Newman, D. J. *Conviction: The Determination of Guilt or Innocence without Trial*. Boston: Little, Brown & Co., 1966.

Reid, J. P. *University of Miami Law Review*, 15 (1960): 14–58.

Reith, C. *The Police Idea: Its History and Evolution in England in the Eighteenth Century and After*. London: Oxford University Press, 1938.

Selznick, P. *Vanderbilt Law Review,* 17 (1963): 79–90.

Sherry, A. H. *California Law Review,* 48 (1960): 557–73.

Silving, H. *Journal of Criminal Law, Criminology, and Police Science,* 53 (1962): 129–63.

Stephen, J. F. *A History of the Criminal Law of England.* Vol. 1. London: Macmillan Co., 1883.

Sutherland, E., and D. Cressey. *Principles of Criminology.* 7th ed. New York: Lippincott, 1966.

Szasz, T. S. *Psychiatric Justice.* New York: Macmillan Co., 1965.

Wechsler, H. In *Proceedings XXXIX A Meeting of the American Law Institute,* 105. Philadelphia: American Law Institute, 1962.

Wertham, F. *American Journal of Psychotherapy,* 17 (1963): 404–16.

Whitlock, F. A. *Criminal Responsibility and Mental Illness.* London: Butterworth, 1963.

Index